THE FAT
AND SODIUM CONTROL
COOKBOOK

S. Turner

THE FAT AND SODIUM CONTROL COOKBOOK

A Handy and Authoritative Guide for Those on
Sodium-Restricted or Fat-Controlled Diets—Including
Suggestions for Controlling Carbohydrate, Cholesterol
and Saturated Fats

FOURTH EDITION, COMPLETELY REVISED

Alma Payne, M.A.
Dorothy Callahan, B.S., R.D.

with an introduction by Francis L. Chamberlain, M.D.,
M.Sc.D., Clinical Professor of Medicine, University of
California Medical School, Past President of the American
Heart Association and First President of the
Paul Dudley White Medical Society

LITTLE, BROWN AND COMPANY — BOSTON – TORONTO

FOURTH EDITION
Fifth Printing
T 08/75

LIBRARY OF CONGRESS CATALOGING IN PUBLICATION DATA

Payne, Alma Smith.
The fat and sodium control cookbook.

First ed. published in 1953 under title: The low
sodium cookbook; 2d ed. in 1960 under title: The low,
sodium, fat-controlled cookbook.
Bibliography: p.
Includes index.
1. Low-fat diet.   2. Salt-free diet.   I. Callahan,
Dorothy, joint author.   II. Title.
RM237.7.P38 1975   641.5′638   75–9902
ISBN 0–316–69542–4

MV

Designed by Susan Windheim

*Published simultaneously in Canada
by Little, Brown & Company (Canada) Limited*

PRINTED IN THE UNITED STATES OF AMERICA

We dedicate this book to the memory of Buff, who started it all — and to the countless other dieters, who inspired us to finish it.

CONTENTS

   The facts behind the headlines on saturated, unsaturated fats, and carbohydrates and how they
   may be controlled in the diet, with or without sodium restrictions. Some definitions of general
   terms and suggestions for carrying out diet orders.

   The whys and wherefores of the sodium-
   restricted diet. The definition of terms and a lot
   of other practical matters are covered here to help
   you in your planning and preparing of meals for
   the sodium-restricted dieter.

   Nothing fancy, to be sure, but getting you off to
   a quick start. This chapter tells you how to put
   your physician's instructions to work — how to
   plan special and family menus without too much
   extra effort — with suggestions for adapting family menus for the dieter.

plain or fancy, and yet keep within your restrictions.

This chapter lets you in on some secrets of fish cookery and exposes some of the sins committed in its name. It includes sauces, too. Of special importance to those concerned with high unsaturated fat.

Here is an array of allowables, and suggestions for presenting them at their best.

You can make a very simple salad, and a good one. You will find salads for every mood in this chapter — dressings, too, for the sodium- and fat-restricted diet.

Of course man wants his breads, restrictions or not, and may have same by use of substitutes from your kitchen shelf. Tips on home baking are here, with recipes for yeast and quick breads made with low sodium "substitutes."

Indeed they do have a place in your planning of sodium-restricted and saturated fat-restricted meals if they are good, nutritionally speaking.

For those of you who are running small institutional facilities requiring restricted diets, controlled in sodium, fat, carbohydrate, and calories, and have to operate on a limited budget without the use of convenience foods. Recipes and calculations per individual serving are included.

ACKNOWLEDGMENTS

FOR THEIR HELP AND ENCOURAGEMENT in the development and writing of this book, we wish to thank: Francis L. Chamberlain, M.D., M.Sc.D., Clinical Professor of Medicine, University of California Medical School; Dietary Staff and Diet Kitchen of the Massachusetts General Hospital; Sunkist Growers, and especially Barbara Robison, Manager, Consumer Services; Corn Products Company; René Bine, M.D., Associate Chief of Medicine, Mt. Zion Hospital, San Francisco, and former Chairman, Nutrition Committee, American Heart Association; William H. Thomas, M.D., Assistant Clinical Professor of Medicine, University of California Medical School; Harold I. Griffeath, M.D., Associate Clinical Professor of Medicine, University of California Medical School; Raleigh H. Lage, M.D., Assistant Clinical Professor of Medicine, University of California Medical School; Benjamin Lieberman, M.D., President, Alameda County Heart Association, 1959–1960; Maurice Sokolow, M.D., former Chairman of Committee on Low Sodium Diets, San Francisco Heart Association; John Luetscher, M.D., for allowing use of facilities of Stanford Medical School laboratories for some of the sodium analyses for the first edition; John W. Ferree, M.D., former Associate Medical Director, American Heart Association (first edition); Beth Heap, Nutrition Consultant, Heart Disease Control Program, Division of Special Health Services, Department of Health, Education and Welfare (first edition); Callie Mae Coons, Ph.D., Human Nutrition Research Division, Institute of Home Economics, United States Department of Agriculture (first edition); Natalie Ralston, Charlene Rose, and Nancy Sarkany for their editorial suggestions and for manuscript typing; Alameda County Heart Association, and particularly Gale Smith, R.D., for materials, reports, and product information; American Heart Association, for material and reports; California Heart Association, for various research data and invaluable assistance, particularly Francis MacKinnon, Associate Director; Central California Heart Association, especially the late Grace Fowler, Nutritionist, for material and reports; Council on Foods and Nutrition of the American Medical Association, for information on sodium-restricted products; Los Angeles Heart Association, for material and reports; San Francisco Heart Association, and particularly Evelyn Bergen, R.D., for material and reports; Agricultural Extension Service, University of California, for material and assistance, especially for the use of the circular *Frozen Desserts*, by Hilda Faust (first edition); California Prune Advisory Board, for materials; Dairy Industry Advisory Board, San Francisco, for sodium and fat information for dairy products; National Canners Association, for suggestions about use of wine in low sodium cookery and permission to use material regarding quick test of water for sodium content; Fisher Flouring Mills, for information and analysis of "Ala" and other products; Home Advisory Service, Wine Institute, San Francisco, and especially Marjorie Lumm, tested recipes for "A Primer of Quantity Recipes"; Terminology Committee of the Food and Nutrition Division, American Home Economics Association, for material from the *Handbook of Food Preparation*, especially the reproduction of the *Baking Chart and Oven Temperatures;* Smithwick Foundation, for the baking powder formula from the Smithwick Foundation recipe book; *Today's Health*, for permission to reprint (in Chapter 17) excerpts from "How to Travel with a Bad Heart," by Alma Smith Payne.

Authors and Journals, for permission to use material or tables from the following articles and booklets: Bills, et al., "Sodium and Potassium in Foods and Waters," *J.A.D.A.*, 25:304, April, 1949; Feeley, et al., "Cholesterol Content of Foods," *Journal of the American Dietetic Association*, 61:2, August, 1972; *Let's Cook Fish, A Complete Guide to Fish Cookery*, Fish Market Development Series No. 8, Department of Commerce, National Oceanic and Atmospheric Administration, National Marine Fisheries Service; Lucia, Salvatore P., and Hunt, Marjorie L., "Dietary Sodium and Potassium in California Wines," *Ameri-*

can *Journal of Digestive Diseases*, 2:26, January, 1957; Page, Irvine H., and Brown, Helen H., *Vegetable Oil Food Pattern and Recipes*, Cleveland Clinic Foundation, Research Division; Sokolow, et al., "Practical Aspects of the Low Sodium Diet," *California Medicine*, 74:1, January, 1951.

The nutrient values were calculated from the following sources: "Cholesterol Content of Foods," Feeley, et al., *Journal of the American Dietetic Association*, 61:2, August, 1972; *Composition of American Foods Materials*, by C. Chatfield and G. Adams; *Composition of Foods*, Agriculture Handbook No. 8, revised 1963, by Bernice K. Watt, Annabel L. Merrill, and others, United States Department of Agriculture; "The Fatty Acid Composition of Milk and Eggs" — Provisional Tables — by L. P. Posati, J. E. Kinsella, and B. K. Watt, Nutrient Data Research Center; *Food Values of Portions Commonly Used*, Eleventh Edition Revised by Charles Church and Helen Church; *The Nutritive Value of Cooked Meat*, by Ruth M. Leverton and George V. Odell; *Nutritive Value of Foods*, Home and Garden Bulletin No. 72, revised 1971, by Consumer and Food Economics Research Division, Agricultural Research Service, United States Department of Agriculture; Recommended Dietary Allowances, 8 ed., Food and Nutrition Board, National Academy of Sciences — National Research Council, Washington, D.C., 1974; "Sodium and Potassium in Foods and Waters," by Charles Bills and others, *J.A.D.A.*, 25:304, April, 1949; *Sodium Restricted Diets, the Rationale, Complications, and Practical Aspects of Their Use*, A Report of the Food and Nutrition Board, Publication 325, by C. S. Davision and others, Division of Biology and Agriculture, National Research Council; *Alcoholic Beverages in Clinical Medicine*, by Chauncy D. Leake, and Milton Silverman, Year Book Medical Publishers, Chicago (in press); *Nutritional Value of Fish in Reference to Atherosclerosis and Current Dietary Research*, by Charles Butler, Commercial Fisheries Review, July, 1958; "Vitamin, Mineral and Proximate Composition of Frozen Fruits, Juices, and Vegetables," by Marie Burger, L. W. Hein and others, *Agricultural and Food Chemistry*, 4:418, May, 1956; *Analyses*, by Nicolas Zenker, Cd. Sc. Ch., Université de Louvain, Belgium. *Analyses*, as supplied by commercial firms; *The Diet Heart Study Meat Guide*, prepared and published for Diet Heart participants by the National Diet Heart Study, 1964.

INTRODUCTION

By Francis L. Chamberlain, M.D., M.Sc.D., Clinical Professor of Medicine, University of California, San Francisco; Past President American Heart Association; President, Paul Dudley White Medical Society, 1972–1974.

Control of Blood Fats

Great research advances have been made in the past fifteen years helping us to understand and to treat abnormal blood fat levels more effectively.

Elevated cholesterol (and to a lesser extent triglyceride) blood levels increase the frequency and severity of atherosclerosis ("hardening of the arteries") in man and in experimental animals. A study by the National Heart and Lung Institute (1967) showed that coronary heart disease caused 54.1 percent of all fatalities in the United States. Stroke due to atherosclerosis of arteries to the brain was the second most prevalent cause of fatalities. Elevated blood cholesterol levels in man are widely recognized as one of the treatable cardinal risk factors ("building blocks") leading to atherosclerosis causing coronary disease and strokes. High blood cholesterol ranks about evenly with cigarette smoking, high blood pressure, and is even more important than diabetes and obesity. Nearly all victims of heart attack due to coronary artery atherosclerosis have abnormalities of one or more of these risk factors and most victims have at least two abnormal risk factors. The famed Framingham studies, which were undertaken to identify risk factors related to cardiovascular disease, reported heart attack incidence to increase strikingly with increasingly high cholesterol levels. For example, their twelve-year follow-up showed a man with a blood cholesterol level over 240 milligrams percent has more than three times the risk of a man with a level of 200 milligrams percent in a ten-year period.

Recent animal studies show that lowering blood cholesterol levels can make atherosclerosis regress and that it can even prevent heart disease.

Studies on mass populations in various parts of the world ("epidemiological") and considerable circumstantial evidence suggest atherosclerosis can be helped or prevented by the proper diet regimen. Long-range nationwide carefully controlled "double blind" experiments must await availability and spending of many millions of dollars of research money and more years for final proof. For the present, most authorities agree that abnormal blood cholesterol and triglyceride levels should be kept at normal levels for prevention and/or treatment of atherosclerosis. The American Heart Association published a statement to the American people in 1961 saying that we had sufficient scientific knowledge to incriminate the association of high blood cholesterol levels with atherosclerosis and that dietary attempts to reduce these levels were indicated. I was privileged to be a member of the study committee that made this first report. Since that time, the American Heart Association has made increasingly stronger statements to the American public (1965, 1968, and 1973) calling attention to the increasing scientific advances in this field, the safety of this approach and the desirability of extending prophylactic therapy even in the very young.[3] The 1973 report, in addition to praising the dietary control of blood cholesterol in man, concluded: "Present evidence also suggests that maintaining serum lipids at reduced levels will lower the incidence of heart attacks caused by atherosclerosis of the coronary arteries."

Success with most drugs for lowering high blood cholesterol has been spotty and rather disappointing and occasionally dangerous. It is generally agreed that "diet is the keystone in this treatment."

Studies in the last few years have shown the importance of testing blood triglycerides as well as blood cholesterol. If one or both of these is very high, further studies are often indicated to see if the lipid panel fits into one of six Levy and

Fredrickson classification types[1] since patients with very high lipid levels, especially if refractory to usual treatment, tend to respond better to a type-specific treatment. Triglyceride levels are only valid if the blood is collected after a *14*-hour fast (e.g., 7:00 P.M. to 9:00 A.M.).

The specific types can usually be determined for practical purposes simply by finding the blood cholesterol and triglyceride levels followed by an overnight "settling" test of blood serum in an ordinary icebox to see if a creamy layer appears at the top. Failing this, more elaborate tests (electrophoresis or centrifugation) can be done to determine the specific percentages of the varying types of lipids in the large protein transport molecules. Most people will have normal or only slightly elevated cholesterol or triglyceride levels which either fit no classification or they will have mild elevations which fit into Type IIA, IIB or IV. The other types are rare.

Many physicians feel that treatment should be started if the two preliminary tests show cholesterol levels above 200 or triglyceride levels above 140. In young adults or children, much lower levels may indicate need for treatment. Most doctors continue to treat lipid abnormalities intensively even after age sixty-five. Any triglyceride above 150, or a cholesterol over "200 plus your age" has been suggested as an indication to start treatment by some authorities.[1]

Overweight is very important. Obesity increases predisposition to diabetes and hypertension in addition to abnormal blood lipids.

Step number one in the dietary regulation of blood lipids is correction of obesity by restricting calories *selectively*. Thus, if the patient has an elevated cholesterol and normal triglyceride (Type IIA) the caloric restriction will include cutting out all egg yolks, organ meats, fatty meats, and sources of butterfat. If these measures are not effective by the time overweight has been corrected, more rigid dietary restrictions will be indicated. It may be necessary to restrict cholesterol to as low as 100 milligrams daily. This is difficult, as the average American diet contains about 900 milligrams, and a single egg yolk has about 250 milligrams. Fat intake may have to be restricted to 25 to 30 grams and 25 to 40 percent of the calories from fat should be polyunsaturated. Therefore, egg yolks, glandular meats and shellfish may have to be eliminated and a very lean meat must not exceed 8 ounces a day. Proteins are to be supplied mainly by egg whites, lean poultry, "swimming fish" and skim milk products. No carbohydrate restriction is needed except in the IIB Type (blood cholesterol high, blood triglyceride moderately elevated). In these it may be necessary to lower carbohydrate intake to less than 40 percent of the total caloric intake and to limit alcohol to 2 ounces of distilled liquor a day or 8 ounces of dry wine per day while relaxing a little on the saturated fat and cholesterol restrictions.

Table 1

SUGGESTED WEIGHTS FOR HEIGHTS

Median Weight (pounds)

HEIGHT (INCHES)	MEN	WOMEN
60		109 ± 9
62		115 ± 9
64	133 ± 11	122 ± 10
66	142 ± 12	129 ± 10
68	151 ± 14	136 ± 10
70	159 ± 14	144 ± 11
72	167 ± 15	152 ± 12
74	175 ± 15	
76	182 ± 16	

Source: Recommended Dietary Allowances, Eighth Edition, Food and Nutrition Board, National Academy of Sciences-National Research Council, Washington, D.C., 1974.

In Type IV (high blood triglycerides, normal or slightly elevated blood cholesterol), carbohydrate intake often must be reduced to 40 percent of the total calories (150–250 grams per day), ideal weight must be maintained. Moderate cholesterol restriction (400–500 milligrams per day), alcohol — not over 2 ounces of distilled liquor or 8 ounces of dry wine per day. Shellfish are allowed. Fats restricted for weight control — about 25 percent of these should be polyunsaturated.

The Type III cholesterol high, triglycerides slightly to moderately elevated, but with marked variations in serial tests, and occasionally with chylomicrons (electrophoresis test necessary). Diet is similar to Type IV except cholesterol is restricted to 200 milligrams per day.

This *Fat and Sodium Control Cookbook* by Alma Payne and Dorothy Callahan is an excellent "working cookbook" for guidance in controlling blood cholesterol and triglyceride levels.

The patient's physician will find the excellent summary by Levy, Fredrickson et al.,[1] "Dietary and Drug Treatment of Primary Hyperlipoproteinemia," very helpful for more detailed information about the management of the rare Types I, III, and V. Separate diet pamphlets for strict management of Types I through V, Department of Health, Education and Welfare Publication # (N. S. H.) 73–111 through 73–115 can be purchased by addressing Superintendent of Documents, U.S. Government Printing Office, Washington, D.C. 20402, or your physician may be able to get these directly from his local American Heart Association chapter.

In my experience, most individuals who understand the dietary principles and who are willing to sacrifice some of their dining pleasures can improve their blood lipids by diet.

Drug treatment plus diet is advisable if diet alone fails, but it is usually difficult and disappointing, except in the types associated with blood triglyceride elevation (IIB, III, IV), where clofibrate (Atromid-S) is often very helpful as a dietary supplement.

Sodium Control

Salt (sodium chloride) is one of the most important elements of the human body. Man cannot live without salt in his body fluids and tissues.

It was not until the turn of the last century that comments began to appear in the medical literature to the effect that salt restrictions could be helpful in heart failure. Nevertheless, most physicians relied primarily on restriction of fluids, rather than of salt, for treatment of heart failure and certain types of kidney diseases associated with retention of abnormal amounts of fluid (dropsy) in the body tissues. It wasn't appreciated by most physicians until about twenty-five years ago that salt restriction was the key to the prevention of dropsy, and that salt (sodium chloride) and, specifically, the sodium part of the sodium chloride, if wisely restricted, would give maximum relief from dropsy and at the same time avoid the distressful thirst which dominated the earlier day treatment.

It is now appreciated that in most types of heart failure, the kidneys become unable to excrete sodium adequately from the body, so that it is sometimes accumulated in very large amounts. Sodium in the body, just like salt in the pantry, tends to attract water to it, and holds the water, thus becoming the building stone for the excess fluid which produces the "water logging" in dropsical conditions.

Most physicians believe that the logical way to keep potentially dropsical patients free of excessive accumulations of salt and water is to use diuretics or to restrict the sodium intake in the diet to the point where they will have sufficient sodium for their body needs, yet in an amount restricted to the point where it will not accumulate in the body.

More recently a large number of drugs have been developed

which can be given orally or by injection which are very effective in ridding the body of excess sodium and water. The most widely used of these are commonly referred to as "thiazides." These drugs also lower blood pressure. The blood pressure lowering effect appears to be only in part due to sodium elimination. Though they may bring dramatic relief from the dropsical condition or from excessive blood pressure, these drugs cannot be administered without some dangers. In rare instances sudden lowering of blood pressure may precipitate strokes or coronary heart attack (coronary thrombosis). Furthermore, in removing excessive sodium from the body, they may remove too much sodium, or may remove needed potassium and chloride and magnesium from the body, sometimes with grave danger.

Potassium supplements are usually necessary if a patient is taking more than one standard-strength diuretic tablet a day, and if kidney function is poor, or if the patient is taking digitalis (or Digoxin), frequent blood tests for possible potassium deficiency or digitalis excess must be made. Potassium chloride elixir (10 percent) is most commonly used as a potassium supplement. Unless well diluted and sipped slowly with or just after a meal, it often causes indigestion.

Triamterene and spironolactone, both weak diuretics, are often used because they conserve potassium by causing decreased excretion. They are expensive. Potassium occasionally goes too high, a dangerous and sometimes fatal complication. Spironolactone is apt to cause breast enlargement and tenderness if more than one or two tablets are taken daily. The stronger diuretics (especially furosemide and ethacrinic acid) cause a small percentage of patients to develop diabetes.

About 50 percent of patients on more than one diuretic pill a day eventually develop increased blood uric acid levels. If allowed to continue without supplementary help from one of the drugs which must be taken daily to increase uric acid excretion, they are in danger of developing gout or kidney stones.

Thus, diuretic drugs have obvious "convenience" advantages over low sodium diets, but they have obvious disadvantages of expense and numerous side effects and more complications which are potentially serious. A happy medium often turns out to be a partially restricted sodium diet intake, supplemented by smaller amounts of diuretics.

The average unrestricted diet contains as much as 6000 milligrams or more sodium. Elimination of salt at the table and elimination of salt-preserved foods and the most highly salted foods will decrease the sodium intake to about 2000 milligrams. The additional help from some of the above mentioned diuretic drugs could be the equivalent of decreasing the total sodium intake to some figure between 500 and 2000 milligrams — an amount which would be helpful in some conditions requiring only "mild sodium restriction," provided the kidneys were not diseased. We must remember that the daily body needs for sodium vary from 80 to over 2000 milligrams as a very minimum, depending primarily on the integrity of the kidneys. It becomes obvious that diuretics must be very carefully used in individuals who have severe kidney disease or who need a dietary restriction to as low as 200 milligrams (as required by some of the diets used in the treatment of hypertension or resistant heart failure). The amount of sodium, then, to be advised in a sodium restricted diet for a given individual and the question of diuretic supplementation must be decided by the physician.

Dropsical conditions may occur in some types of kidney disease (as in chronic glomerulonephritis) wherein the blood becomes deficient in protein, primarily due to the excretion of protein in the urine (due to kidney damage) in very large amounts. Judicious sodium restriction can be very helpful in minimizing this type of dropsy. However, it is important to understand that diseased kidneys are often unable to hold a proper amount of salt within the body, so that very large quantities of salt may be excreted in the urine. Some of these patients may excrete many grams of sodium a day. Obviously, if sodium restriction in any patient is carried out to the point where less sodium is given in the diet than the amount excreted in the urine, the patient will develop abnormally low body sodium which may become irreversible or even lead to death. Early symptoms (weakness, muscle cramps, dry tongue, lethargy) may act as warnings; but they may be absent, so that blood sodium, potassium chloride, or blood BUN (test for waste products in the blood) may become necessary for safe continuation of the dietary regimen.

In summary, diuretics continue to improve, but they have disadvantages as a total substitute for sodium restriction in the diet.

Advanced liver disease (cirrhosis) may result in deficiency in blood proteins due to inability of the diseased liver to help with their manufacture in the body, and this may lead to dropsy. Wise restriction of sodium may in these cases help to overcome the inadequacy of the blood proteins so that dropsical conditions may be improved.

Premenstrual swelling, with its associated discomfort, may be minimized or eliminated by restriction of sodium intake the last six or seven days before onset of the menstrual period.

In 1946, Grollman and Harrison, and later, Kempner, showed that diets *very drastically restricted* in sodium could be very helpful to some patients with severe hypertension. Thirty to fifty percent of patients with hypertension can be helped markedly by drastic sodium curtailment.

Hypertension is probably the most neglected of the "coronary risk factors" today. It is estimated there are thirty million Americans with hypertension but less than 10 percent are receiving proper treatment for this. Yet hypertension is practically always controllable with proper medication. The attention now focused on hypertension by the American Heart

Association as its "most neglected child" assures us of a new wave of enthusiasm for this in the next few years. The low sodium dietary approach (200 milligrams per day) is too severe for most people to follow. However, *partial* sodium restriction makes it possible to control pressures with *less medication*. This means less expense and less chance of drug reactions. A marked decrease in daily sodium intake can be made merely by eating no salt-preserved (bacon, ham, et cetera) or visible salted foods, and to use a salt substitute or even learn to "salt skimpily" with real or half strength salt.

Drugs such as benzothiadiazines, spironolactones, methyldopa, hydralazine, triamterine, furosemide, ethacrinic acid, clonidine and many others, especially in combination, control hypertension in most instances. Frequently, they are supplemented by sodium restriction since this usually makes it possible to decrease the aforementioned expensive or potentially dangerous drugs.

Sodium- and fat-controlled diets should meet the following requirements:

1.   The approximate sodium and fat content of the diet should be known and understood by patient and physician. If used in the presence of severe kidney disease, the *exact* sodium content must be known and understood.

2.   The diet *must be palatable* so that the patient will not become discouraged (since it is usually difficult to get a patient to change lifelong habits of eating his favorite foods, unless reasonable substitutes can be found).

3.   The diet *must not be harmful* to the patient. It must not contain a smaller amount of sodium than necessary for body demands. It must supply supplemental fat-soluble vitamins (A and D) to diets severely restricted in total fat.

4.   It *must not be deficient in protein* (a real danger since most sources of protein contain relatively large amounts of sodium).

The authors have met these criteria in a very satisfactory manner. They have made an exhaustive search for reliable analyses of sodium in various foods, and they have conducted sodium analyses to cover essential foods whose previous sodium content had not been determined. They have provided practical information about the handling of various foods in this diet, along with numerous easy-to-follow recipes. They have provided figures as to the sodium content of the various menus so that these can be used easily for patients whose physicians have advised them to use the "count method."

They have repeatedly insisted that *these diets cannot be used with benefit and safety except through a physician who understands the patient's diagnosis* — the status of the patient's heart, blood vessels, and kidneys.

So used, this book would become a *manual for home use* — with space provided for *additions and deletions to be inserted by the physician.*

References

1. A Physician's Guide to Hyperlipidemia by Donald S. Fredrickson. *Modern Concepts of Cardiovascular Disease*, Vol. XLI, No. 7 (July, 1972), pp. 31–36.
2. Dietary and Drug Treatment of Primary Hyperlipoproteinemia, by Levy, R. S., Fredrickson, D. S., Shulman, R., et al. *Annals of Internal Medicine*, Vol. 77, No. 2 (August, 1972), pp. 267–294.
3. Precursors of Coronary Arteriosclerosis in the Pediatric and Young Adult Age Groups by Neufeld, Henry N., M.D., *Modern Concept of Cardiovascular Disease*, Vol. XLIII, No. 6 (June, 1974), pp. 93–96.

FOOD FOR THOUGHT

Eating is the first business of a man. If his food is unpleasant to him, his health suffers, his labour is not so productive, his genius deteriorates, and his progeny dwindles and sickens. A healthy digestion, on the other hand, produces a healthy mind, a clear intellect, a vigorous family, and a series of inestimable benefits to generations yet unborn: and how can you have a good digestion, I ask, without a good dinner? and how have a good dinner, without knowing how to cook it?

— WILLIAM MAKEPEACE THACKERAY in *Punch*

YOUR PHYSICIAN'S
INSTRUCTIONS

1

FAT AND CARBOHYDRATE CONTROL

YOUR DOCTOR HAS ALREADY told you how important you are in putting his diet instructions into effect. What may surprise you are the many aids available to help you in your planning and marketing for unfamiliar food items. With a little study and imagination you can soon be turning out excellent meals without too much extra effort in the kitchen. And they will not only please your dieter but other family members as well, for in many instances only slight modifications are necessary. However, these modifications are of great importance to the dieter's special needs.

A thorough understanding of the whys and wherefores behind restrictions is the best starting point toward success in your new program. Often your first introduction to a restricted diet is a "Do and Don't" list handed to you by the doctor or some family member. Or even if you were present when the diet was instructed, you may have many unanswered questions now that you are back in your own kitchen with only a sheet of mimeographed directions as a guide.

The answers to your questions are important.

For many of you, the preparation of tasty meals controlled in fat and/or carbohydrate may be the major problem. If you have to restrict fat and carbohydrate, you'll be eliminating some of the familiar flavors such as butter or regular margarine and substituting oil or special margarine in specified amounts and nonfat or skim milk in controlled amounts. You will be restricting or eliminating sugar and other concentrated sweets. Yes, there will be changes in ingredients, usual cooking methods, and eating habits. But the biggest thing is attitude.

If your dieter must restrict both the sodium and fat content of meals, you may think your task very difficult, in fact, almost impossible. Once you become acquainted with the allowables, you'll soon discover short cuts and ways to minimize kitchen efforts, and with surprisingly good results.

The success of your new program depends upon a thorough understanding of your diet instructions. You should know what foods are allowed and in what amounts, and the substitutions that can be made. Sometimes knowing why the diet has been ordered makes it easier to put the doctor or dietitian's instructions to work. And why it is so important to follow those instructions that have been planned with respect to your needs and the principles of good nutrition.

The purpose of many fat-controlled diets is to reduce patient weight and/or to lower the *cholesterol* content of the blood. Research scientists have shown that when there is too much cholesterol in the blood, it is more likely to accumulate along the artery walls. This narrows the opening of the blood vessel so that the heart, brain, or other organs may suffer or perish from lack of blood. Sometimes the blood vessel closes completely. This is why people with high blood cholesterol levels are more likely to have heart attacks or strokes caused by blockages in arteries already narrowed by atherosclerosis. *Cholesterol* may be a new term to you. One of the adjectives describing this substance is *fatty*. This is a clue to one reason for restricting fat in the diet.

All would be relatively simple if we could just restrict the foods which contain cholesterol. It is present in foods of animal origin (particularly in organ meats and egg yolk). However, the body makes cholesterol from some of the fats that we eat. The presence of atherosclerosis may be a sign that the body is getting too much fat as well as cholesterol.

Fat-controlled diets are also concerned with the saturated fats. All of the fats and oils that you are familiar with contain *hydrogen* (a chemical element) in varying amounts. *If the fat or oil has all of the hydrogen it can contain, it is called a saturated fat; if it can take on more hydrogen, it is called an unsaturated fat* — the more hydrogen it can absorb, the higher the degree of unsaturation.

Usually the hardness of the fat is a clue to its saturation. Fats that are solid at normal room temperature are generally highly saturated. These include meat fats, butterfat, margarine, lard, and most vegetable shortenings. Fats that are liquid at normal room temperature (vegetable and marine oils) are highly unsaturated. *Coconut and palm oils are exceptions to this rule — they are usually liquid at room temperature, yet are highly saturated.* (You'll find them as ingredients in most non-dairy creamers!)

Research indicates that when *saturated fats are restricted*, the cholesterol content of the blood may decrease. This means that in certain people, if animal fat, butterfat, margarine, lard, and vegetable shortenings are either limited or eliminated, the cholesterol content of the blood will decrease.

Other studies have indicated that in some people, if the *saturated fats are limited and a specified amount of unsaturated fat is added*, the level of cholesterol in the blood may drop even lower. In other words, in this diet, the amount of animal fat, butterfat, margarine, and other high saturated foods is decreased, and specified amounts of vegetable oil, such as corn or cottonseed oil, are added.

It is plain then that no two fat-restricted diets may be exactly alike. Some may restrict the total fat yet allow the use of limited amounts of all kinds of fat. Others may restrict only the amount of saturated fats. Still others may restrict saturated fats and add vegetable oil.

Recent studies have indicated that elevated blood *triglycerides* may be treated with control of the kind and amount of carbohydrate allowed. As indicated in the medical introduction, when blood fats are present, not only may the doctor order a regimen to control the kind and amount of fat and cholesterol but also the amount of dietary carbohydrate the dieter may eat. These nutrients must be balanced with the way the body uses them, and only the physician can determine this and prescribe the appropriate diet.

Additional definitions may help you to understand your regimen more clearly. *Triglycerides* are blood *lipids*. High levels of them can be elevated by overweight and a diet high in *carbohydrates*. *Carbohydrates are the sugars and starches in food.* Concentrated sugars are obtained from sugar itself — honey, sirup, molasses, sweetened beverages and the sugar used in food preparation, especially in jams and jellies. Other sugars come from fruits and some other foods such as milk. These are known as natural sugars.

Starches are found in cereal grains, breads and related products, vegetables, and pastas such as macaroni, noodles, and like products. Starches are converted to sugar by digestion. Very little sugar, as such, is stored in the body. Most of it is converted into the substance known as *triglyceride*.

When fat and carbohydrate must be controlled, you can see that it is very important to follow your diet lists very carefully.

For the rest of the family, cutting down on total fat may pay bonus health dividends. In recent years we have learned that the average American family consumes between 40 to 45 percent of total calories in fat-rich foods. We need about 30 to 35 percent according to the experts. So some reduction in fat intake might be good for most of us. At least this is the idea we get from the various pronouncements of the American Heart Association.

It is easy to see how the restriction of fat, and particularly saturated fat, is going to affect your eating habits. When you consider the sources of fat in your daily foods, you will have little difficulty in naming the *visible* fats — meat fats, butterfat, margarine, lard, vegetable shortenings, and oils. And of these fats, all except the vegetable oils are highly saturated and so are usually restricted or eliminated from the diet.

Perhaps you are wondering why vegetable shortenings are saturated, whereas vegetable oils are unsaturated; after all, vegetable shortenings are made from vegetable oil. Vegetable shortenings are high in saturation because they have been *hydrogenated*. In *hydrogenation*, hydrogen is forced into a liquid oil to make it a solid, thus changing it from an unsaturated oil to a saturated fat.

Many brands of peanut butter are now hydrogenated. This changes their classification from unsaturated to a saturated fat. If you are restricted in saturated fat, read the peanut butter label for *hydrogenation*, or *hardening*, as it is sometimes called.

You are more likely to miss the *invisible* fats. Fat is actually hidden even in lean meats — and in fish, poultry, and egg yolk, too. Even when all the visible fat is trimmed the cooked meat drippings in the broiler will contain additional fat.

For this reason, we emphasize *lean* meats to you homemakers with saturated fat restrictions. Usually you will have to substitute *good* or *standard* grades of young beef for the *choice* grade from older cattle (heavily marbled). It may also mean selecting the leaner cuts of meat — top round or sirloin tip of beef for roasts; top round steak for stews and ground meat rather than some of the other fatter cuts. For example, 1 ounce of lean roasted top of round contains about 2 grams of fat whereas 1 ounce of lean roasted ribs of beef contains about 6 grams of fat. Of course, if the baby beef "catches on" and the consumer buys it in quantities sufficient to warrant its continuance, this could be another beef source lower in fat content than meat from more mature animals.

Similarly with other meats — legs of lamb and lamb chops, pork loin and center ham slices are your best choices. Always select the least marbled meat and trim it of all visible fat before cooking. Do not use duck except wild, ham hocks, luncheon meats, spareribs or tongue.

One bright spot for homemakers with saturated fat restriction is the use of fish. Marine oils are usually unsaturated and are classed with vegetable oils rather than animal fats. You may find that the frequent use of fish (perhaps even once a day) is highly recommended on your diet list. A plus for other family members, too, with its high protein value, lower calories, and high unsaturated fat content.

As to the fats themselves (see page 51), the restriction of butterfat affects not only the use of butter, with its saturated fat content of about 2 grams per teaspoon, but also whole milk, cream (including sour cream), and cheese. This restriction also means that commercial foods made of whole milk, such as ice cream, milk shakes, chocolate milk, malted milk, milk mixes, cheese additions, and bakery items, too, are often not allowed.

Whole milk, either homogenized or family (with the cream at the top of the bottle), contains a required amount of butterfat. Pouring the cream off the top of the bottle is not a satisfactory method of removing the butterfat. (If you have not already done so, observe the ring of cream remaining even when you pour one to two cups from the top.) Therefore, skim, nonfat milk or buttermilk made from nonfat milk must be your choice. Fortunately, milk is readily available either in dried or fresh milk form (low sodium variety, of course, if required).

Egg yolk, too, with its high saturated fat content, must be either restricted or eliminated for those of you with saturated fat controls. One large egg yolk contains 5 milligrams of fat, so you will want to use egg whites in fat-controlled cooking (but watch the amount if sodium must also be counted). Or use one of the low fat, cholesterol-free egg substitutes now available on grocer's shelves or in their deep freeze sections. Just wait until you use them for scrambled eggs, French toast or in your home-baked specialties, and we think you will share our enthusiasm for them as a great big aid to the consumer, if not to his pocketbook as yet.

As to the vegetable fats — ordinary shortenings and margarine (see page 9 for low saturated fat margarine) are taboo because of their saturated fat content. Vegetable oils, such as corn, cottonseed or soybean, saffola or sesame seed should be your choices for baking and other cooking purposes. And you will have to turn out your own baked products and other goodies — perhaps even bread — because the ready-mixes and commercial baked goods contain whole milk, whole egg, shortenings, and other highly saturated fats. In fact, you will have to become a label reader, whether it be bread, regular bakery items, or canned goods. Always be on guard against the use of saturated fats in the ingredients.

Many of the vegetable fats, too, are invisible fats — such as those found in olives, nuts, avocados, coconut, chocolate, and peanut butter. Coconut, chocolate, *hydrogenated* peanut butter and roasted nuts are high in saturated fats and are out. Natural *unprocessed* nut butters and nuts (if no sodium restriction), are low in saturated fats and rich in unsaturated fats and may be allowed in specified amounts if total fat is not restricted.

And now for a look at some of the commercially prepared

foods insofar as fat is concerned. Many foods, that are normally low in fat, are on your Don't list because of the fat added during processing. (*Remember that most of these foods are high in sodium content and may not be used if sodium is restricted.*)

Many canned soups contain less than 2 grams of fat per average serving (3 servings per can) when prepared with water or nonfat milk. Check with your diet list to see if allowed. Often, this 2 grams of fat is saturated fat — added chicken fat, for example. If you are severely restricted in total or saturated fat, a wiser expenditure of your precious fat allowance might prove more beneficial.

Most of the familiar canned meats — luncheon meat, sausage, spiced ham, et cetera — are too high in fat content to be used. It is possible to purchase canned chicken, roast beef, and turkey, in which the visible fat can be removed fairly easily, and the resulting product made satisfactory insofar as fat is concerned. They are more expensive than the fresh product, but they are good to have on the shelf. Creamed meats, meats packed in gravy, and products containing other tabooed items must be omitted.

Canned fish, except dietetic and packed without added sodium, may not be allowed on the sodium-restricted diet. And for lower fat content, buy water-packed varieties rather than those with added oil. As with meats, avoid creamed dishes unless prepared at home with special margarine and nonfat milk, or in a few instances with low sodium milk (for those with severe sodium restrictions).

Most homemakers like to have a hurry-up meal on the shelf for emergency use in the form of a canned casserole, pasta, or stew. Fat restriction does offer a problem here. All canned products of this sort do contain fat. Fortunately, new products limited in fat are coming to the market every year. Some excellent meats and relishes have been put out under well-known labels, and you will find some for the sodium-restricted dieter as well as for the fat-restricted one.

You can also buy several margarines high in unsaturated fat. *When you are looking for a controlled-fat margarine, note that those that list as the first ingredient liquid oil (or safflower or soybean oil, et cetera) are acceptable.*

Cereal grains are low in fat. However, baked and processed items such as quick breads, crackers, cookies, cakes, pastries, usually have added saturated fats in the form of lard, hydrogenated shortenings, butter, and margarine. Many also include whole milk, whole egg or egg yolks. Some dessert items contain chocolate and coconut, usually not allowed.

When it comes to yeast breads, with or without added salt, usually all those made with allowed fats or oils or without added fat will appear on your *use list*. In general, regular bread contains a very small amount of fat (about 1 gram per slice). And some breads, such as English muffins, French, tortillas and others, contain no fat. Once again read the labels to be sure your selection contains only the fat listed under allowed oils on page 51. Similarly for crackers.

You will find that the commercially made sweet breads and rolls, Danish pastries and fruit breads, muffins, waffles, bread stuffing, and other specialties should only be included in your market purchases when they are made with vegetable oil and are within your calorie allowance.

In the main you will have to depend upon homemade products which include the use of vegetable oil, egg white or cholesterol-free egg substitutes (see page 400), and nonfat milk when you want to include hot breads, cakes, cookies and pastries in your menu plan. (Consult Appendix 3(A), for listings of a few sodium- and fat-controlled commercial items.) Homemade products will be your best selection for other dessert items, too, such as puddings and frozen desserts.

But do read labels because food producers are presenting new products to make your kitchen chores lighter every month.

All of the recipes in this book have been kitchen-tested and many of them have been tested in hospital kitchens. Where a recipe calls for "*oil*," *it means polyunsaturated oil.* Where "margarine" is specified, it means a *special margarine* high in polyunsaturated fat. *We have omitted salt from our ingredient lists for those on sodium restriction* but for those of you without such restriction, simply add the amount you would normally use.

One more reminder for dieters who must restrict *carbohydrate* (sugars and starches). As we said before, this can be for the control of high blood fats and/or weight reduction. Very few carbohydrates are stored in the body. Most are changed to a fatty substance called *triglyceride*, which can affect your blood fat and cholesterol levels. *Concentrated sugars are the worst offenders.*

If you must restrict carbohydrates, avoid or eliminate concentrated sources of sugar, such as sugar itself, candies, jellies, sweet desserts, and frozen or canned fruits processed in a heavy sirup. Use fresh or water-pack fruits and a prescribed sugar substitute, as outlined by your doctor or dietitian.

Whatever your diet, follow your physician's recommendations explicitly. Use this book only as a guide, and adapt it to meet your special requirements. Combining it with your list of allowables, we hope you will find the recipes interesting and offering you variety in your food planning. You will see that we have calculated each recipe (in terms of amount per serving) for (approximate) milligrams of sodium, grams of total and saturated fat, grams of carbohydrate, and calories. For some recipes, we have offered general variations and low saturated fat variations, with occasional references to carbohydrate uses. Also you'll find at the end of recipes, wherever applicable, the amount of liquid oil in an individual serving.

We suggest that you now read Chapter 2 (if you are on sodium restriction), and then read Chapters 3, 4, 5, and 18 to become acquainted with general information given, and to get started with herb and wine seasoning. Herbs, lemon, wine, et cetera, help take the place of seasoning without butter or margarine, just as they do in unsalted foods.

Keep the following points in mind as you read for your fat and/or carbohydrate restrictions:

1. Most fruits and vegetables are low in fat so may be used generously on fat-controlled diets. Use unsweetened fresh or canned water-pack fruits if carbohydrate is limited.

2. Favor fish and poultry over meat in menu planning.

3. Among the fats to be used with discretion and only as your diet allows are butterfat (including milk, cream, and cheese), beef, lamb, pork, veal, and poultry. Trim all meats and poultry of visible fats. (See suggestions for Special Gravies, page 121.)

4. Hydrogenated shortenings are taboo on diets restricted in saturated fats. Use special margarine, vegetable oil or oil spread, whichever is on your diet list.

5. Use a specially treated pan (a spray-on coating) for frying food to eliminate use of fat or oil additions.

6. Do not use chocolate, coconut, or hydrogenated peanut butter. But you may use nonhydrogenated peanut butter and nontropical nuts, such as almonds, peanuts, pecans, or walnuts, if total fat is not restricted. Nonhydrogenated peanut butter may be substituted for a meat exchange, as allowed.

7. In general, use only egg white in cooking, or an egg substitute, if on your diet list. Use whole egg or egg yolk only in amounts allowed on your diet. Favor a cholesterol-free egg substitute.

8. Avoid special preparations being offered as "protection against heart and artery disease." Use only medications, preparations, and diet recommended by your doctor.

9. In adapting your own "bakery" recipes for diets restricted in saturated fat, you cannot substitute oil on a one-to-one basis — usually a little less oil is needed than solid fat.

Nor can you substitute a sugar substitute on a one-to-one basis. Follow manufacturer's suggestions and use only substitutes as specified by your physician or dietitian.

Until you have time to experiment, choose one of our tested recipes.

10.   When carbohydrates are severely restricted, desserts (except unsweetened fresh or canned water-pack fruits) may be completely eliminated, and bread and cereal products drastically reduced. It may be necessary to eliminate gravies, sauces, and such cooking processes as flouring of meats or other foods. Milk, too, may be restricted. Refer to and follow your diet instructions carefully. Draw a line through "offending" recipes in this book.

11.   Read labels of commercial products for additions of saturated fats. And for consumer aids, consult your local Heart Association.

12.   If you have no sodium restrictions, whenever the recipe lists low sodium dietary products such as baking powder, milk, canned goods and so on, you may substitute regular or salted products; you may also add salt to taste.

13.   The American Heart Association issued four statements for the medical profession and the public between December 1960 and April 1973 on dietary fat and its relation to heart attacks and strokes. The Association endorses with increasing firmness dietary manipulation to decrease saturated fats and to increase polyunsaturated fats (while decreasing total fat consumption) in individuals with or threatened by coronary heart disease. In addition it encourages the public "to eat less animal fat and to increase the intake of vegetable oils or other polyunsaturated fats, substituting them for saturated fats wherever possible; to eat less food rich in cholesterol; and if overweight to reduce caloric intake so that desirable weight is achieved and maintained." In another statement it speaks of dietary modification as influencing serum cholesterol and triglyceride levels in the blood, thus pointing up the importance of the right food

choices as prescribed by the doctor as preventive and therapeutic measures. "Moreover," this statement concludes, "it is possible to plan changes in diet which are palatable, effective, economically feasible, nutritionally sound, and applicable throughout most of life."

Of course it stresses the importance of professional guidance where radical modifications in diet are contemplated, and to make good eating habits a family affair for the benefit of each and all family members. It concludes with recognition of the need for additional research in this entire field.

2

SODIUM CONTROL

YOUR PRIMARY CONCERN may be dietary sodium control. You must learn to cook without some of your familiar "indispensables." You must be able to satisfy the dieter's highly cultivated taste buds, and at the same time meet the requirements of the diet. Your chief concern may be limiting or excluding the use of salt.

Before we get into diet particulars, let's clear up the meaning of some terms that may be new to you. Perhaps your diet is called "low salt" or "salt-free." "Low sodium" and "low salt" have been used so commonly, in the past few years, to express the same diet that many people believe them to be synonymous. Actually, "sodium-restricted" is the more correct term, as it is the sodium content of your diet that is significant. Salt is restricted only because it is approximately 40 percent sodium.

All low sodium diets are not identical. They may vary in the *amount* of sodium that they contain. The diet that you must prepare may be mildly, moderately, or severely restricted in sodium content — ranging anywhere from 200 to 4500 milligrams of sodium daily. Possibly, 1000 milligrams sounds like a lot of sodium to you. Perhaps even 200 milligrams seems like an ample amount. But when you consider that the average "salt-lover" (and how many of us fall into this class!) may consume as much as 6000 or more milligrams of sodium each day, radical changes in both cooking and eating habits are necessary to cut down to a 200 milligram level. That pinch of salt (150 milligrams of sodium) that you may be tempted to use, or that one slice of regular bread (120 or more milligrams of sodium), does make a difference.

No doubt, you will be discussing your diet with some friend or relative "who has been on the low sodium diet for years" or knows someone who has been on it. You may be surprised or confused by the many differences in sodium-restricted diets. These differences are generally due to the degree of sodium restriction necessary. Since a diet too low in sodium as well as one too high may be harmful, do not make any changes in your diet. Your doctor is the only person who can determine if a sodium-restricted diet is necessary and the amount of sodium you require for your health needs. Follow your doctor's directions explicitly. The recipes in this book may be readily adapted for any level of restriction.

There are two methods commonly used for instructing low sodium diets. For simplicity, we will call them the *list method* and the *list-count method*.

If your diet is the *list method*, your physician has given you a list of foods that you may use in any amounts; a list of foods that you may use in limited amounts; and a list of foods that you must avoid. Substitutions should be made only as specified. When you follow this plan you will have a balanced diet considerate of your special requirements.

If your diet is the *list-count method*, you have received a "Do" and "Don't" list, but may also be allowed up to 500 milligrams of sodium daily in free choice items.

Both methods are good. Either one may be used with this book.

For ready reference, you will find not only the sodium but also the potassium, carbohydrate, and calorie content of many common foods listed in Appendix II. However, a more general background of the sodium content of foods and how it is affected in processing or cooking is both helpful and necessary in planning sodium-restricted meals. Why must you be especially careful when you use meat stock? Why can't you use all kinds of frozen foods? What must you look for in the new labeling of foods? And why is it so important for the person with sodium restrictions to become a label reader?

We are ready with the answers to most of these questions because of studies reported by the Food and Drug Administration (whose new regulations went into effect in January, 1975), the Food and Nutrition Board of the National Research Council, the Council on Food and Nutrition of the American Medical Association, and the American Heart Association. Their work has done much to lighten your job in the kitchen.

Unfortunately, most of the hearty, substantial foods that form the backbone of our menus are high in sodium content: meat, fish, poultry, eggs, milk, cheese — in fact, *most foods from animal sources are medium or high in sodium* and must either be used in restricted amounts or eliminated. You will have to learn to make a little of them go a long way. Meat-stretching recipes providing portions with a limited sodium content may have to become your standbys.

The sodium-restricted dieter has to limit not only the *amount* of meat, poultry, or fish he may use, but also the *kinds* allowed. You will find that you can include fresh, frozen, or dietetic canned meat or poultry, except salty or smoked meat, such as bacon, chipped or corned beef, bologna, luncheon meats, salt pork, sausage, and smoked tongue.

A great deal of sodium is added during the processing of these products — most frequently in the form of salt. Take beef as an example. As a sirloin steak or a boneless chuck pot roast, 1 ounce of beef contains approximately 18 milligrams of sodium. After it goes through the brining process and emerges as corned brisket, 1 ounce contains approximately 487 milligrams of sodium. If it has been koshered, 1 ounce of beef contains approximately 454 milligrams of sodium. It is plainly evident that such items would work havoc to a sodium-restricted diet.

On your fish market list, you may include all fresh fish except shellfish. Strangely enough, in general, a salt-water fish contains no more sodium than its fresh-water cousin.

Unfortunately for most of you inland housewives, *frozen fish is taboo, unless it is frozen whole.* Most of those handy frozen fillets and steaks are chock-full of sodium because brine is used in the processing. One ounce of halibut steak jumps from 15 milligrams of sodium when it is fresh to approximately 101 milligrams of sodium when it is frozen. Look before you buy and make sure that your fish fillets are fresh.

Perhaps the greatest change in your market habits will be in the amounts of milk, eggs, butter, and cheese you may buy. Analyses for the sodium content of these foods show that in many instances they are even higher than meats. Milk, for example, contains nearly 500 milligrams of sodium per quart. If you are on a severely restricted allowance, it is obvious that you will have to use a commercial low sodium milk (fresh, frozen or powdered, whole or nonfat) or dialyzed milk rather than the familiar whole or nonfat milk. Use only the kind of milk listed.

With one egg consuming more than an eighth of your daily allowance on the 500 milligram diet, you will have to watch that sodium count when planning menus around soufflés, omelets, or the like. It is well to remember, too, that most of the sodium is concentrated in the egg white. Although you may be able to include some of those delicious fruit whips or meringues, try to favor the egg yolk most often in your cooking or baking, unless otherwise instructed. Just the opposite for saturated fat restriction — you pay court to the egg white. However, if you are on one of the more liberal sodium allowances, you may find that your list includes one of the relatively new cholesterol-free egg substitutes — lower, too, in fat than the barnyard egg.

With cheese and butter, it is the salt added for flavor which puts them in the taboo class. One Swiss cheese and rye sandwich packed in the lunch box or taken as an evening snack will raise your sodium count as much as 600 or more milligrams. Unsalted butter may be on your list, but you may find that unsalted margarine is the choice if saturated fat must also be curtailed.

Fortunately, *most foods from a vegetable source are low in sodium content.* Fruits, vegetables, nuts, grains, and legumes — fresh from the garden or otherwise unprocessed by freezing or canning — have just a trace of sodium. These foods must make up the bulk of many of your meals and can often be used in abundance. Your task will be to serve them in many and tempting ways so that your menus will be appetizing and satisfying.

There are a few exceptions, however, to this rule regarding the low sodium content of foods of vegetable origin. *Some vegetables are so high in sodium that they must be entirely eliminated for those with severe sodium restriction.* Artichokes, beets, carrots, celery, hominy, many of the greens — such as beet tops, chard, dandelion greens, kale, mustard greens, and spinach — and frozen vegetables processed with salt, also sauerkraut, white turnips, and most canned vegetables (except low sodium dietetic) are not allowed.

Of course, if you are lucky enough to be on *mild sodium restriction,* you may be allowed any fresh, frozen, or canned vegetables or vegetable juices, except sauerkraut, pickles, or other vegetables heavily salted or prepared in brine.

Fruits, bless them, *are as a group low in sodium content* and can add much to your menus. Read labels to be sure that no artificial color, flavor, or corn sirup has been added. Do not use dried fruit if sodium sulfite has been added. And, if the carbohydrate or calorie content of your diet has also been limited, you may need to select fresh or water-pack fruits and sweeten as necessary with an allowed sugar substitute.

Pure fruit jellies without added preservatives, jams, and conserves, whether from your own preparation or commercially prepared, fall within your use allowance and can add much to meal flavor. But do remember to read jelly and jam labels, and use nothing but pure fruit jelly and preserve. For you calorie- and carbohydrate-counters, look for dietetic jellies and jams made with allowed sugar substitute.

Now back to salt again — that much overworked seasoning. Salt is our major dietary source of sodium, and by now you can see why so many sodium-restricted diets are called "low salt" diets.

Used as seasoning, ¼ teaspoon salt adds more than 500 milligrams sodium to the diet. Even "salting to taste" in home cooking may add as much as 800 milligrams sodium to a half cup of food, and "salting to taste" in manufactured foods has the same result. Regular dressings, sauces, pickles, processed meat and fish, canned vegetables and soups, and a long list of other products may be on your "Don't" list because of their added salt content. Consult Appendices 2 and 3(A) for additional information.

Now consider the effect of salt with grains. As grains enter the factories, their sodium content is insignificant, but by the time they reach the store counters, many of their products are on your "Don't" list. Most dry cereals (approximately 200 milligrams of sodium per dish), quick-cooking and enriched cereals, crackers (one soda cracker contains about 60 milligrams of sodium), breads, cookies, cakes, and other baked specialties, except low sodium dietetic, have to be banned because of the addition of salt.

Some bakery items are double offenders — in using *both* salt and a leavening agent. One teaspoon baking powder (408 milligrams sodium) or one teaspoon baking soda (1232 milligrams of sodium) can do untold damage to even the moderately restricted sodium diet.

Fortunately, *most of our flours* (except the self-rising varieties), *some of the ready-to-eat cereals*, and *many of our cooked cereals* are *low in sodium content*, so that they will not be wanting in our menus. But do read labels, for many of the ready-to-eats are too high in sugar content for you carbohydrate- and calorie-watchers.

Many manufactured foods are not salted for seasoning, but use salt in processing. Brine is used to sort peas before freezing them, to prevent toughening of vegetables before canning, and to prevent the discoloration of fruits.

As if this were not enough, sodium is often added to foods in forms other than salt. Sodium bicarbonate (baking soda) is used in ready mixes and self-rising flour. Sodium benzoate is used as a preservative. Other sodium compounds are used in water-softening, preventing mold, drying fruits — to name just a few from a lengthy list.

You can see that regular manufactured foods must be used with extreme care. Read and reread labels for the addition of salt itself or any of the sodium compounds. See the list of Available Products in Appendix 3(A) for those that have been laboratory tested for your use.

Your physician has probably told you that your method of preparing foods is important, too.

High sodium foods, such as meat or salty foods, lose some sodium when boiled. The amount of this sodium or salt that is lost will depend partly upon the amount of water used — more salt being lost in a larger quantity of water. Thus, stewed or boiled meats will contain less sodium if the cooking water is discarded.

On the other hand, low sodium foods may gain some sodium from the tap water in which they are cooked. This makes the sodium content of the water supply important, too. Most water softeners leave a large amount of sodium in the water and therefore may not be used with this diet.

You may consume, you know, as much as 2½ quarts of fluid a day in your food and drink. If your water supply contains under 2.5 milligrams of sodium per cup, this amount is not too significant. But if it contains as much as 5, 10, 15 milligrams, or more, as it does in some cities, then water, as a source of sodium in the diet, is important. It may have to count toward the 500 milligram, free choice on the *list-count* diet.

For local information, consult your water purveyor, Heart Association, or Public Health Department. If you must depend upon well water for water, perhaps your doctor will want to run this simple color test made available to us by the Western Branch of the National Canners Association Research Laboratories:

REAGENTS

1. Potassium chromate 10 percent
2. Silver nitrate 0.74 percent

PROCEDURE

Measure out 40 drops of water in a small test tube. Add 1 drop of reagent 1 and 1 drop of reagent 2 and mix with water.

A reddish precipitate will form. If this does not disappear on mixing, water is satisfactory. If red color disappears leaving a bluish white precipitate, water contains more than 3 milligrams sodium per ½ cup.

Medications are often another overlooked source of sodium. Use only the medicine prescribed by your doctor. Some medicines that may contain sodium are: "alkalizers," antibiotics, cough medicines, laxatives, pain relievers, and sedatives. Toothpastes and powders, as well as mouthwashes, may also contain harmful amounts of sodium. If you don't swallow the toothpaste, you don't have to worry. But be sure to rinse your mouth thoroughly with water after brushing your teeth.

Perhaps, by this time, you are getting discouraged and are wondering how anyone can possibly cook an appetizing meal with so many Don'ts.

All is not as bleak as it would appear. Whereas some manufacturers have added to your Don't list, others have stepped in to lighten your task.

If your diet is severely restricted in sodium content, ordinary milk probably heads your list of Don'ts. There are several good sodium-restricted substitutes on the market, available in drugstores, some supermarkets, and health food stores. Or, you may dialyze milk (remove the sodium content) at home, but this is a tedious process.

Many of the chain stores and independent grocers now stock sodium-restricted bread. But be sure when you buy this to read the label for the amount of sodium in 1 slice or serving. Not long ago, we were shopping in a big health store where so-called low sodium bread contained 55 milligrams of sodium per slice. Sure enough, the analysis was stamped on the jacket, but the sales force was urging this product on its consumers as a low sodium item.

Low sodium crackers and bread sticks, sodium-restricted cookies, and canned cake (and mix), and the Jewish Passover matzoth (made with flour and water), are now on the market. Consult your doctor, local Heart Association, and Appendix 3(A) and (B) for brands and availability of sodium-restricted bakery items.

Sodium-free baking powder is available commercially (Cellu brand) for homemade low sodium baked goods. It may also be ordered by prescription at your neighborhood druggist's.

The formula for your druggist is as follows:

Potassium Bicarbonate	79.5 grams
Cornstarch	56.0 grams
Tartaric Acid	15.0 grams
Potassium Bitartrate	112.25 grams

The powders are mixed thoroughly and sifted several times. These baking powder substitutes make it possible for you to add many delicacies and old favorites to your menus.

Some permissible canned goods and other processed items may now be found on your grocer's shelf. Low sodium dietetic canned salmon, shrimps, chicken, and tuna are available, as is a low sodium peanut butter — cashew butter, too. Low sodium cottage cheese, several low sodium dietetic cheddar-type cheeses such as the popular Cellu Dietetic Cheese (cheddar type) may be found locally or ordered direct from mail order supply houses.

A few low sodium soups and bouillon cubes are available (although they are not allowed unless they contain less than 5 milligrams of sodium if you are on a severely restricted regimen).

A few low sodium dietetic-pack meats may be found in large health food stores, some cooperatives, and catalogue ordering houses. We have located sodium-restricted ham, bacon, and other specialties.

In fact, all kinds of specialties are now flooding the market to ease your kitchen problems. There are even condiments restricted in sodium, such as low sodium dietetic mustard, pickles, catsup, chili sauce, tomato paste, and even Worcestershire sauce.

The parade is not limited to such items. You can find melba toast, bread sticks, crackers, cookies, honey and other cakes, mayonnaise, waffle and pancake mixes, and desserts, all dietetically packed and low in sodium.

It will take a while for you to become familiar with your diet principles and available sodium-restricted items. You may have to read and reread your guide sheet the first few weeks as you translate directions into action in the kitchen. Don't get discouraged. There are many wonderful products to help you. And very soon you will find out that you can prepare meals for the dieter and other members of the family with little extra effort. With good planning and imagination you can make them zestful, eye-appealing, and sometimes with a gourmet flair.

The following summary may prove helpful:

1. Whether your diet is called "sodium-restricted," "low sodium" or "low salt," it is the sodium content of the diet that is significant. Only the doctor can determine how much sodium the dieter should be allowed.

2. There are no foods, not even ordinary drinking water, completely free of sodium. Consequently, distilled water for drinking, cooking, and preparation of soups and beverages must be used in some areas to keep the sodium intake within the allowable level.

3. If you are on severe sodium restriction or are taking a diuretic, be sure to check with your physician to determine whether your diet should star high potassium foods and in what amounts you should include them. (See Appendix 2.)

4. Most animal foods are high in sodium content. Use them carefully.

5. Most foods from a vegetable source are low in sodium content. Plan your meals around them.

6. Most canned or processed foods contain more sodium than the fresh product. Know your product before you buy.

7. Many special low sodium products are available on the market, but buy manufactured products only with your doctor's approval.

8. In the chapters that follow, both fat and sodium restrictions are considered because often your medical program calls

for the dietary restriction of both. You may also have to modify our recipes for lower carbohydrate content by using unsweetened foods and allowed sugar substitutes.

3

GETTING TO WORK

— BENJAMIN FRANKLIN
One should eat to live, not live to eat.

Now you are ready to begin your work.

The visits to the physician, the tests, and the diagnosis are in back of you.

The mimeographed instructions on the sodium- or fat-restricted diet are in front of you — but only you can make them work.

Gone from the list, as we have shown, are most of the familiar labor-saving food preparations used in the modern kitchen; but the laboratory has stepped in to give you help in your task of cooking meals without benefit of such aids.

First of all, it has given you research findings on the sodium and fat content of many foods, as presented in Appendices 2, 3(A), 7. You will come to see just how important this material is as you do your daily planning of diet meals.

Then there are the synthetic products of the laboratory — the substitutes you may use, such as salt and baking powder substitutes, low sodium milk, and such other items as may be prescribed by your physicians.

Various state and local Heart Associations affiliated with the American Heart Association, as well as health departments, the Council on Foods and Nutrition of the American Medical Association, the Food and Drug Administration, the National Canners Association, and various governmental agencies — all of these agencies are carrying on studies and putting out materials or products to improve the quality and variety of your daily fare. For the most part, these materials are available only to physicians, but where distribution is general you will perhaps find them included with your instructions.

For general use, try checking your meals against the guide drawn up by the United States Department of Agriculture Leaflet FNS 13. Foods are classified according to their contribution of several nutrients, although the emphasis is placed on key foods as important sources of these nutrients. The daily food plan gives a basis for an adequate diet for the entire family but permits the individual wide choice in his food selections. Adjust the dieter's requirements to meet his medical needs and ensure adequate nutrition for other family members by frequent checking against the following:

MILK GROUP. Some milk daily:
 Children under nine — 2 to 3 cups
 Children nine to twelve — 3 or more cups
 Teenagers — 4 or more cups
 Adults — 2 or more cups
 Pregnant women — 3 or more cups
 Nursing mothers — 4 or more cups
 Cheese can replace part of the milk

MEAT GROUP. Two or more servings (2 or 3 ounces of lean cooked meat): beef, veal, pork, lamb, poultry, fish, eggs, with dry beans and peas and nuts as alternates

VEGETABLE-FRUIT GROUP. Four or more servings, including:
  A dark green or deep yellow vegetable important for
    Vitamin A, at least every other day
  A citrus fruit or other fruit or vegetable important for
    Vitamin C, daily
  Other fruits and vegetables including potatoes

BREAD-CEREALS GROUP. Four or more servings — whole
  grain or enriched.

This fundamental plan will provide the adult with most of his daily nutrient requirements except calories. The basic guide can be supplemented by other foods not specifically noted. Such foods as butter, margarine, other fats and oils, sugars, dessert, jams, and jellies, plus additional servings of food from the basic groups, if desired, serve to fulfill the caloric and nutrient allowances for those members of the family not on a restricted diet. Proper selection and preparation of foods go hand in hand in providing the family an adequate diet — and in these days, with a myriad of choices on the supermarket shelves, it offers a real challenge to the homemaker.

It is obvious that the person on a restricted diet will not be able to have all of the foods listed in this guide nor in the amounts listed, in many cases. In order to plan adequate nutrition for all the family, why not post a copy of the U.S.D.A. Leaflet FNS 13, *Daily Food Guide*, on the inside door of your food cupboard? You could make notations in each of the food sections to indicate special requirements. By so doing, your planning would be considerate of the needs of *all* family members.

Unfortunately, there is no time to review your nutrition. You must get on the job and will have to learn as you go — *learn by doing*, it is called in modern education.

The suggestions and recipes in this book are directed, in the main, to the 1,000 milligram sodium dietary. However, they should be equally usable for those of you with other allowances. If severely restricted in sodium (250 milligrams), you will need to substitute low sodium nonfat milk in all of our recipes. If only mildly restricted in sodium intake, you may be able to use regular canned vegetables and even add small amounts of salt. Your diet list will specify your requirements, and the dietary patterns on pages 35 to 39 will show you how to put them to work.

Suggestions and recipes are also directed to those of you who are concerned with the planning of menus restricted in fat, whether total or saturated, and to those of you with mild carbohydrate restriction. (Sample dietary patterns for these diets will be found on pages 39 to 42.) *For reduction in saturated fat, our recipes are constructed with special margarine or oil instead of solid shortening or butter because of the emphasis of the polyunsaturated fats in the treatment of certain disease states.*

Each diet is necessarily individualized so you will have to make your own substitutions as you go along. *Our recipes specify nonfat milk, but you may substitute measure for measure whatever form of milk your particular diet calls for, whether it be whole milk, skim milk, or one of the low sodium milks, fresh or powdered.* You will need to count the milk used in cooking in your daily milk allowance and make adjustments as may be necessary.

Similarly with seasonings: we make a special point of giving you recipes that bring out the natural flavors of foods and food ingredients. We use lemon juice, wines, and herbs to accent these natural flavors. We think they improve restricted dishes even more than regular ones. But use these flavor aids only if they appear on your diet list. And use them sparingly in the beginning if they are new to you and the rest of the family.

No doubt you will find a few recipes that violate your special instructions. Perhaps your diet list stipulates "no brown sugar" or "no maple sirup." It is plain to see that no one cookbook can meet all of your individual needs, so why not draw a line

for regular and special needs just before serving, using salt for the "regulars" and substitute for the special diet, if allowed.

Similarly with vegetable preparation – buy only fresh, seasonal, frozen vegetables, or canned without added salt for those of you with sodium restrictions. For best flavor, minister to them with care. Read about vegetable preparation in Chapter 10 if you want to review vegetable cookery.

Fruits are a special bonus for their fine flavor. And for morale's sake, whip up a simple dessert or two. Topping the meal with a good dessert can earn raves for an otherwise very simple meal. It need not be overly sweet to be good, but should complement and round out the rest of the meal. Fruit in wine is a case in point. Simple to do, it lifts the usual flavor to the unusual when you want a little variety.

If you make your own breads, decide right now to turn out a really good loaf of bread in spite of restrictions. The processes involved are simple (pages 247 to 251). Soon you will be branching out from basic breadmaking to the specialties in breads, rolls, and quick breads, all of which can give variety to your meals.

Are you impatient to get started? Well, why not do some planning right now? Read over the suggestions for changing a basic family menu to meet diet limitations, get out paper and pencil and make the necessary changes in your menus to meet requirements and taste. Then check your final results against the U.S.D.A. standards to bring your meals up to the standard of adequacy for everyone in your family according to individual need.

Begin your arithmetic now, too. We will not confound you here with the intricacies of the metric system, but will give the amount of sodium, total fat, saturated fat, carbohydrate, and calories of our recipes in terms of household measurement (such as ½ cup, 6 stalks, 1 teaspoon) for individual and total servings. (If the changeover to the metric system becomes widespread, a conversion table can be found in Appendix 1.)

The saturated fat content of our recipes is based on the total grams of saturated fatty acids as listed in Appendix 7. For general classification of foods as to saturated fat content, see Appendix 5.

Our calculations are *approximate*. There are the variables of foods and ingredients used due to climatic and other differences; the care and preparation of foods; the varying amounts of water used in cooking, as well as the sodium content of waters; and cooking time — to mention just a few of the variables from our kitchens to yours. In certain areas, you will have to add the sodium content of your water supply in calculating your recipes, or cook with distilled water for your dieter, whichever is indicated by your physician. When you want to adapt your own recipes, consult the tables in the Appendices.

As you go along in the planning and preparation of this dietary, you will learn more, just as we have, about the scientific whys and wherefores of the low sodium and low fat diet. In fact, you may find that your written instructions may become the most absorbing textbook you have ever studied.

MENU PATTERNS

To help get you off to a good start, we are listing a basic family menu and indicating how it might be changed to meet diet requirements, whether they be sodium-, fat- or carbohydrate-restricted, limited or unlimited in calories. Remember, in most instances, it is not necessary to cook dieter's food separately or to prepare two recipes. Vegetables, sauces, and the like can be salted and "buttered" for the family just before serving, and oil added or served plain, or with a few drops of lemon juice, to dieter. The family can enjoy the low sodium muffins, low fat rolls, low sodium or low fat desserts, and so on, right along with the dieter. *One of the basic aims of this book is to present recipes modified for special dietary needs that can also be used by the entire family — and thus conserve your kitchen effort.*

Basic Family Menu*

BREAKFAST
Chilled grapefruit
Shredded wheat biscuit
Muffins
Milk
Beverage

LUNCH
Tomato stuffed with halibut
Garnish of green peas
Hard rolls
Fruited Jell-O
Milk
Beverage

DINNER
Cranberry nectar
Baked veal steaks
Orange candied yams
Savory green beans
Whole wheat bread
Lemon ice cream
Sugar cookies
Milk
Beverage

* The size of servings, the kind of milk, the use of butter or margarine, and the use of sugar or sugar substitutes will depend upon the needs of each family member.

1000 Milligram Sodium Menus

The Basic Sodium-Restricted Menus on pages 37 to 39 provide approximately 500 milligrams of sodium. Your diet list will specify substitutions and choices that may be made to make a total of 1000 milligrams. For example, ¼ scant teaspoon of salt equals approximately 500 milligrams of sodium; or, 2 slices of regular bread and 1 teaspoon of salted margarine equals 500 milligrams of sodium.

For the sodium-restricted diet, the Basic Family Menu will need to be modified according to calorie allowance. Limiting calories with a sodium-restricted diet presents the same problem as curtailing calories on a regular diet. Fats, sugars, and starches are decreased; and with the lower total food content, careful planning is necessary to make certain that all of the essential food nutrients are included. Starred foods indicate that the recipe is given in this book.

1200 CALORIE MENU

BREAKFAST

½ chilled grapefruit
1 shredded wheat biscuit
1 low sodium muffin*
½ teaspoon unsalted special margarine
½ cup nonfat milk
Coffee or tea with allowed sugar substitute

LUNCH

Tomato stuffed with halibut (with 1 teaspoon French dressing)*
½ cup fresh* or low sodium dietetic canned peas
1 slice low sodium whole wheat bread*
½ teaspoon unsalted special margarine
¾ cup nonfat milk

* Recipe is given in this book. See index.

1 serving fruit gelatin (with unsweetened fruit and allowed sugar substitute)*
Coffee or tea with allowed sugar substitute

DINNER
½ cup cranberry nectar
3 ounces baked veal steaks*
¼ cup mashed sweet potato*
½ cup green beans*
½ cup fresh unsweetened fruit
¾ cup nonfat milk
Coffee or tea with allowed sugar substitute

1800 CALORIE MENU

BREAKFAST
½ chilled grapefruit
1 shredded wheat biscuit
2 low sodium muffins*
1 cup nonfat milk
2 teaspoons unsalted special margarine
2 teaspoons jelly
Coffee or tea with allowed sugar substitute

LUNCH
Tomato stuffed with halibut*
½ cup fresh* or low sodium dietetic canned peas
2 slices low sodium whole wheat bread*
2 teaspoons unsalted special margarine
½ cup nonfat milk
1 serving fruit gelatin*
Coffee or tea with allowed sugar substitute

DINNER
½ cup cranberry nectar
3 ounces baked veal steaks*
¼ cup mashed sweet potato*

* Recipe is given in this book. See index.

½ cup green beans*
1 slice low sodium enriched bread*
1 teaspoon unsalted special margarine
½ cup fresh unsweetened fruit
1 low sodium sugar cookie*
½ cup nonfat milk
Coffee or tea with allowed sugar substitute

UNRESTRICTED CALORIES

When calories are unrestricted, you may have extra servings of any allowed food on your diet list *except meat and regular nonfat milk.* Extra amounts of low sodium nonfat milk may be added.

Fat-Controlled Diets

Most fat-controlled diets limit the fat intake to approximately 30 to 35 percent of the day's calories and include a higher proportion of polyunsaturated fat to saturated fat. They also limit the cholesterol content to less than 300 milligrams. If caloric intake must also be reduced, sugars and starches will be limited. And in some cases, even when obesity is not a problem, the carbohydrate intake will be curtailed. It is important to follow your doctor's directions carefully.

1200 CALORIE MENU

BREAKFAST
½ chilled grapefruit
1 shredded wheat biscuit
1 low saturated fat muffin*
½ teaspoon special margarine
¾ cup nonfat milk
Coffee or tea with allowed sugar substitute

* Recipe is given in this book. See index.

LUNCH

Tomato stuffed with halibut*

½ cup fresh or frozen peas*

Hard roll

½ teaspoon special margarine

1 serving fruit gelatin (with unsweetened fruit and allowed sugar substitute)*

¾ cup nonfat milk

Coffee or tea with allowed sugar substitute

DINNER

½ cup cranberry nectar

3 ounces baked veal steaks*

¼ cup mashed sweet potato*

½ cup green beans*

1 serving lemon water ice (sweetened with allowed sugar
substitute)*

½ cup nonfat milk

2 teaspoons vegetable oil used in cooking

Coffee or tea with allowed sugar substitute

1800 CALORIE MENU

BREAKFAST

½ chilled grapefruit

1 shredded wheat biscuit

2 low saturated fat muffins*

1 teaspoon special margarine

2 teaspoons sugar or jelly

¾ cup nonfat milk

Coffee or tea with allowed sugar substitute

LUNCH

Tomato stuffed with halibut*

½ cup fresh or frozen peas*

2 hard rolls

1 teaspoon special margarine

* Recipe is given in this book. See index.

1 serving fruit Jell-O
1 rounded teaspoon "whipped cream" topping*
¾ cup nonfat milk
Coffee or tea with allowed sugar substitute

DINNER
½ cup cranberry nectar
3 ounces baked veal steaks*
¼ cup mashed sweet potato*
½ cup green beans*
1 slice bread
1 teaspoon special margarine
1 serving lemon water ice*
2 meringue kisses*
½ cup nonfat milk
1 tablespoon vegetable oil added in cooking
Coffee or tea with allowed sugar substitute

UNRESTRICTED CALORIES

When calories are unrestricted, you may have extra servings of any allowed foods except beef, lamb, ham, eggs, margarines, or vegetable shortenings.

1000 Calorie Fat-Carbohydrate Control Diet†

This restricted fat and carbohydrate diet is used to lower blood cholesterol and triglycerides. The fat is restricted to 30 to 35 grams daily with 25 percent from polyunsaturated sources.

BREAKFAST
½ chilled grapefruit
1 serving Egg Beaters (egg substitute)*
1 slice bread

* Recipe is given in this book. See index.
† For use with Type IV patient with high blood triglycerides and normal or slightly elevated blood cholesterol.

1 teaspoon special margarine
½ cup nonfat milk
Coffee or tea with allowed sugar substitute

LUNCH

Tomato stuffed with halibut*
Low calorie dressing
½ cup peas*
1 teaspoon vegetable oil
1 serving fruit gelatin (with unsweetened fruit and allowed sugar substitute)*
¾ cup nonfat milk
Coffee or tea with allowed sugar substitute

DINNER

3 ounces baked veal steaks*
¼ cup sweet potato*
½ cup green beans*
½ cup tossed green salad (1 teaspoon vegetable oil and vinegar)
½ cup fresh unsweetened fruit
¾ cup nonfat milk
Coffee or tea with allowed sugar substitute

If you use one of the diet booklets published by the American Heart Association, refer to it for free choice items. Or make your selections within your free choice list from recipes listed on the following pages. The American Heart Association booklets give you the kinds of foods and amounts you may use by food categories (as meat, fats, et cetera). This cookbook will show you how to use your allowable foods in interesting ways and how to plan nutritious and well-seasoned dishes.

* Recipe is given in this book. See index.

4

OF HERBS AND GREENS
AND SEASONINGS

HERBS ARE TO RESTRICTED COOKERY what heavy cream is to
old-fashioned strawberry shortcake. They should be considered additional seasoning to the familiar sugar and spice, or
pepper, oil, vinegar, and mustard treatment. Used with care
and understanding, they can bring out the natural flavors of
food and lift your restricted recipes out of the prosaic and
into the gourmet class.

After all, the only way to be creative, in this field, is to plan
and cook by *principles*. One of the best ways to achieve this
is to recognize that a recipe can be flavored in many different
ways and with different results. One good recipe, then, has
the potential of being two, five, or many recipes, with the use
of as many different herbs, their combinations and seasonings.

In order to get the most out of your varying flavors for
new results, you will want to become oriented to the know-
how of herbal cooking. Foreign cookery has given us some
wonderful guides in the development of native dishes with

subtle and aromatic flavors. A review of some of these old and many of the newer recipes can give you some marvelous ideas for your own cookery. In all of the literature on the subject, you will find a word of caution: *Don't overdo.* We add it, too, for restricted cookery. When in doubt, remember the pinch flavor method of Grandmother's time.

All herb seasoning should, of course, bring out the natural flavor of foods and never be so strong as to be dominant. The essential oils in each herb give the food its characteristic flavor. Or perhaps it would be more accurate to say that the release of these oils blends with the food to bring out its unique flavor. It takes time for herbs to do their best work for you. Heat reacts more favorably than cold in releasing these pungent oils. The time element is the reason why so many herb-seasoned dishes are more flavorsome the day following first preparation.

Fresh herbs have a truer taste; but except for salads, dried herbs may be used almost equally well. Salads are definitely improved when garden-fresh herbs are available. If you must depend upon commercially prepared ones, do buy only the leaves or seeds and forget all about the inferior powdered form. Do your own pulverizing with a small home mortar and pestle.

If you are lucky enough to be able to start with fresh herbs, first pick off the leaves and discard all stems. They are apt to be the bitter part of the herb. Make little bunches of the leaves and snip fine with kitchen scissors, or mince with a pestle for most satisfactory results. Seeds and dried varieties can often be pulverized in your hand at time of use. The warmth of the hand works on the essential oils in releasing them to begin their work.

Above all, in restricted cookery, don't become a one-herb cook, no matter how good that herb may be. Think of the flavor of the food itself, and then use your herbs to enhance that flavor. Don't distort it and don't drown it. Think of *relatedness* and *suitability* and do some experimenting. Your use of herbs can make your restricted cookery distinctive and bring you distinction, too.

Start with the six stalwart seasoning plants of which you are most familiar. They are Basil, Marjoram, Mint, Rosemary, Sage, and Thyme.

HERBS

Basil

A native of the Far East, BASIL comes from the Greek word meaning royal. Royal it certainly is — in its contribution to good flavor. It has a faint fragrance of tea and mint, if you smell its subtle odor in garden patch or in dried form.

Use basil in many ways. It will aromate an egg dish so that it is positively delectable — similarly with tomatoes or tomato juice. It is a natural for most Italian dishes, soups, meats (particularly stews, ground beef, and lamb), salads, fruits, and vegetable juices and sauces. It is such a good friend to restricted cookery that it deserves your best ministrations.

Sweet Marjoram

Lovely, fragrant MARJORAM sprigs are often laid among fine linens or woolens to keep them sweet and are no less magical in their contribution to making good food better. The dainty, silver leaves may be used fresh or dried in soups (particularly onion), salads, sauces, mushroom dishes, meats (particularly pot roasts, pork, and veal), strewn over fish to be broiled or baked, or combined with certain vegetables (particularly peas, beans, and tomatoes). It has enjoyed long fame with lamb. An old recipe calls for it combined with onion, summer savory, mushrooms, and lemon, as a "dressing" for lamb.

Its sister-plant, OREGANO, or WILD MARJORAM, is a flavorful addition to many meat, pasta, and vegetable dishes. This is used in practically all Mexican and Spanish dishes, a special addition of savor for soups, and an extra dividend in mushroom specialties.

Mint

This bold one (spearmint) will take over your garden if you give it the least encouragement. But its tender leaves, crushed or whole, lift even a plain, uninteresting dish to something special. It is a fragrant addition to fruit salads and salad dressings, lentil soups, meat broths, potatoes, peas (if you must), tea, and ices. A pretty garnishing too!

Rosemary

Sir Thomas More, in *Utopia*, called ROSEMARY "the herb sacred to remembrance and therefore to friendship." It is a good friend, indeed, to low sodium dishes, for it peps them up and at the same time draws out their natural flavors. It will be one of the hard-working herbs in your new program, we predict, just as soon as you learn its value and many uses.

It does wonders for meat recipes. Just try it and see if you don't like it in chicken dishes, veal stew, meat loaf, or sprinkled over pork or beef roast. If you cultivate a luxurious bush at your back door, it can be used in many other ways for your pleasure.

Mincing it very fine, it adds piquancy to many sauces, stuffings, and poultry. It's a delightful addition to baking powder biscuits (see special recipe), to homemade jams and spices, and to certain vegetables (particularly browned new potatoes). Its aroma is deceptive — so again, you will have to watch your amounts. It's another one of those dominant herbs, if you give it half a chance.

Sage

This perennial is so popular that it is grown in almost every American garden giving any space to herbs. No wonder because of its all-around usefulness in party dishes, particularly special stews and other meat dishes made of veal and beef. Many use it in stuffings, sauces, and with duck and geese. If you like the fresh variety, be sure to use its gray pointed leaves sparingly for sage penetrates and its scent lingers on.

Its cousin herbs, WINTER and SUMMER SAVORY, are kinder to most stuffings when blended with low sodium bread crumbs. Mrs. Mazza* and other writers on herbs and cookery consider sage too strong for poultry stuffing and recommend instead a blend of savory, thyme and sweet basil for all-around use.

Thyme

Kipling speaks of the "blunt, broe-headed, whale-backed Downs covered with the wind-bit thyme that smells of dawn in Paradise." The eloquence was well deserved, for THYME is one of the most satisfactory and usable of the culinary herbs.

There are many thymes in use today for various purposes, and all are true to their name, for thyme means incense. The common garden variety is the most satisfactory for cooking. Its range of usefulness is broad.

The leaves can be pulverized in low sodium milk to "kill" its flavor, if you object to it. Its leaves can be blended with other herbs in making herbal vinegars. It is excellent, also, in sauces and meats (particularly veal and pork), fish, soups and chowders, dressings for meats and poultry, vegetables (particularly onions, peas, and tomatoes in any form), and salads. No other seasoning does quite so much for the lowly egg as does the addition of a little thyme. Taking it all in all, it is a hard-working herb in restricted cooking.

* Mazza, Irma Goodrich, *Herbs for the Kitchen* (Rev.).

MORE HERBS AND SEASONINGS

Once you experiment with herbs for giving added flavor to your special diet dishes, it is a safe guess that you will reach out for others. For the love they give, Irma Mazza tells us, is a love that grows. Certainly their use gives you a chance to individualize your cooking in an ever widening way.

And here are a few in the parade to tempt you to be experimental: DILL WEED for eggs, salads, diet cheeses, fish, potatoes and beans; PARSLEY for flavoring soups, salads, meats and vegetables, and as a garnishing to make many a dish appealing to the eye; CURRY POWDER, not truly an herb, is used as such, and is a marvelous addition to a soup pot, salads featuring chicken or turkey, fish and lamb dishes; GARLIC for a European flavor in salads, meats, and many vegetable dishes.

ONION (for our purposes we will treat it both as a vegetable and an herb): as an herb, count on it to add a hearty pungency to stews and soups, and make a real plus contribution to meat roasts and Italian-type sauces.

Onions and salads just seem to go together; as Sydney Smith has said, "Let onion atoms lurk within the bowl and, half suspected, animate the whole." Spring onions, with their light bulbs and green stalks, are best for this purpose. Their very freshness gives a lift to a salad. You will want to use both the bulb and stalk, relying on the bulb when you want a more robust accent, and using the green stalks for piquancy.

Dried red onions are also very useful in tossed salads. Their swirling slices are juicy, rich, and decorative. They do something very nice for string beans when minced fine and blended with vegetable oil, too. Ditto for zucchini squash.

PEPPER becomes the more important in the absence of salt, it would seem. For that reason, if for no other, invest in a pepper mill and grind your own peppercorns. Only in this way can you get the best that pepper has to give you as a seasoning.

VINEGAR: *remember there's a right one for every use.* Acrid and penetrating, you may even want to dilute some of your vinegars with a little water when using in special ways. CIDER VINEGAR, with its low sodium count will have right-hand use, along with WINE and GARLIC VINEGAR in many of your meats, soups, gravies, and salads.

Herb and wine vinegars contain more sodium than cider vinegar. The daily total will tell you "counters" how much you may include, but for the rest of you, refer to your list of allowables or to your physician. If permitted, use with restraint with other higher sodium foods. Cider vinegar may be substituted in all recipes for a lower count. Do not use malt and spirit vinegars as they make no flavor contribution worthy of consideration.

LEMON JUICE, the last in this small and incomplete parade, deserves a whole section devoted to it for it is a real friend to restricted dishes. Sprinkle its pungent juices over meats, fish, or fowl for added flavor and zest. For sodium restriction, use it as you would salt for an aromatic flavor. Often it will make you forget the need of salt.

Then there are the MEAT TENDERIZERS. Don't overlook these "friends" to restricted cookery. For those of you on sodium restriction, get either the low sodium seasoned or unseasoned and use as you would a regular meat tenderizer.

SPICES

Spices can be one of your best kitchen investments and deserve careful selection and care (keep lids screwed on tightly to preserve pungency), if you want them to work well for you.

Get your spices off the shelf and get acquainted with them

once again in terms of their basic aromas. Smell, then taste-test, so that you will know the flavors you are going to use. The first job to do is to discard all stale spices. They pay poor dividends.

A pinch of spice, rightly used, will do much to pep up some of your low sodium dishes. Have you tried:

A CINNAMON STICK in low sodium blancmange?
A dash of NUTMEG as a topping for rice pudding or in meat pie crust?
A dash of ALLSPICE in a meat loaf?
A half dozen whole CLOVES in your soup pot?
A spoon of NUTMEG in rhubarb?
One-fourth teaspoon CURRY in "creamed" eggs?
A dash of MACE or CARAWAY in a coffee cake?
A sprinkling of CURRY or DILL on fish before baking or grilling?

When you really know your spices, there are almost limitless combinations possible for flavor enrichment. Don't be afraid to try some new ones in your new cooking.

SALT-SUBSTITUTES

Use only as prescribed by your physician. If allowed, season at time of serving unless you are very sure that the salt-substitute which you are allowed does not "cook up bitter." If you learn to add salt-substitute in this way, it will be no trick at all to add salt for the regulars at time of serving.

FATS

Fats are flavors just as much as are spices and herbs. For sodium restriction without low saturated fat requirements, select fats from your diet list.

Where saturated fat is limited, use only the fats and oils on your diet list, such as safflower (the highest in unsaturated fatty acids), soybean, corn, and cottonseed in descending order. Sesame and sunflower oils are also acceptable. (Under new Food and Drug Administration regulations you should find the kind of oil specified on the label.) Olive and peanut oils are monounsaturated oils. They may be allowed in small amounts but do not have the cholesterol-lowering properties of the high polyunsaturates.

Use unsaturated or liquid fats only in the amounts specified. This will be individualized for your special needs so that it is of paramount importance to know your allowance. *Do not use any solid fats, except special margarines in the amounts specified (and select a brand that lists a polyunsaturated liquid oil first on the label)*. You will be surprised at the excellent flavor you can give your vegetables, salads, and casseroles with the liquid oils and special margarines once you become accustomed to their flavors and ways to use them. But any use must be counted in your day's total.

Generally speaking, substitution of an oil for a solid fat in baking should not be made one to one; the oils go farther. If you are adapting your own recipe, "one cup of shortening" may be interpreted as three-fourths of a cup of oil, or a little less.

We have tried all of the different oils in our cooking and for flavor we prefer safflower oil for salads and vegetables (but soybean and peanut are very usable too) and corn or cottonseed oil for baking bread, muffins, cakes and cookies, and pastry. Talk about flaky piecrust, wait until you have tried an "oil"-

crusted pie for tenderness and excellent flavor. Easy to handle, too.

Different oils are not identical in cooking properties, but corn, cottonseed, and peanut oil are very much alike for baking, although they do differ in some ways in frying. Olive oil, if allowed, is a wonderful flavor-aid to salads, vegetables, and meat dishes, and maintains its flavor in baking but loses most of it in frying. We no longer stock it on our own shelves because we find we can get high flavor with safflower oil (or one of the other high polyunsaturated oils) combined with lemon juice or wine or wine vinegar for suitable use.

A WORD TO THE WISE

But now a word to the wise before we get on with the recipes.

1. Palatability is what you are striving for in all cooking. Your selection of foods has been made on the basis of nutritional adequacy, so that each part of the meal is important. Herbs and spices can do much to increase the palatability of many of your dishes and bring out their essential flavors.

2. Don't use herbal seasonings in all of your dishes at any one meal. Rather, consider them as you would the accessories of your costume — an accent. An overdose can be as bad as no use.

3. In general, don't combine more than three herbs in any one dish. Have a preponderance of one so that its savor will predominate. When in doubt, let this be parsley, for it will do wonders for so many restricted dishes. As Irma G. Mazza wrote in her *Accent on Seasoning*, "it helps marry the flavors of the other herbs."

4. Dried herbs are more concentrated than green ones, so

use only half as much of them. In the main, our recipes are constructed and calculated with dried herbs. Not because they are better, because they are not, but because they are more readily available and we have the sodium content for many of them.

We hope the material in this chapter will open new vistas to you in planning taste-wise and health-wise meals for your dieter.

5

HOW TO USE SPIRITS
IN DIET COOKERY

If you want to give diet cookery a real gourmet quality, wines and spirits are a must. Knowingly used, they add zest and sparkle to an otherwise simple dish. They enhance the natural flavor of many foods, add flavor to others, and improve the texture of still others. In other words, wine is considered a flavoring here (like salt-substitute and pepper); one which, when blended with other ingredients, complements and enriches the natural goodness of foods in various ways.

Unlike the other seasonings, wine is not detectable in and of itself (unless you use too much and so defeat the whole purpose of its use in cooking). As with herbs, a little goes a long way, for it is not used to hide the natural flavor of foods.

The amount and way you use it depend a good deal upon the effect you want to achieve. A light dribbling of wine over fish or fowl, blended with other seasonings, will bring out the *natural subtle flavors* of these foods and give them added richness. But for a different effect, wine and seasonings may be brewed together and used as a basting sauce. Still another variation is accomplished when wine is added to gravies or sauces before serving them, or is used as a marinade in preparing tougher cuts.

Similarly with nonfat milk dishes — the addition of wine to your puddings and soups will give them that *added bit of flavor* they so much need. It will lift them out of the bland and listless class to something delicate and delectable. But watch amounts used, sodium dieters. See Appendix 4.

All in all, wine, used in conjunction with restricted cookery, can increase pleasurable eating, no matter how it is used. And there is really no trick to cooking with wine. All you have to do is master a few simple principles and have an adventuresome spirit about restricted cookery. At first, you may want to follow tested recipes, but in many cases you won't need a recipe. Measure a small amount of wine and add with other seasonings and taste-test to your liking. Wine, so used, acts as a flavoring only, so you can feel free to use it, teetotaler or not. It acts in much the same way as does vanilla. The alcohol evaporates, or passes off, as heat is applied, leaving a lingering flavor that is something pretty special to food lovers.

One of the best ways to get started in the use of wine in cookery is to make room right now on your flavoring shelf for a bottle of sherry; port or muscatel; a white wine such as sauterne or Rhine wine; and a red dinner wine such as claret or Burgundy.

As you cook with these artful flavorings in soups, meats, and desserts, and add them to salad mixings, new aromas will arise in your kitchen — and your reputation as a cook will rise, too. In general, it is easier to introduce wine to your dishes than herbs. Experiment, with wine and without, and let taste and flavor decide your usage.

There are a few simple rules to guide you in your use of wine in restricted cookery. We are indebted to the Home Advisory Service of the Wine Institute in San Francisco for these suggestions, and for some of the special recipes in this book which were worked out specifically for these diets.

1. Wine must be used with an eye to its sodium content for those who must reckon with this restriction. The daily total will dictate the amount for those who count; others should refer to their diet lists, dietitian, or physician. Use less wine when it is combined with high sodium foods.

2. Use wine as a flavor *accent*. Do not flavor every dish with it at any one meal.

3. Use wine with caution until you know its gentle savors. Use a little *less* rather than a little more to accent, but not dominate, the food prepared.

4. Do not allow any dish containing eggs and wine to boil, or it will curdle.

5. Wine is usually the last ingredient to be added to a dish (with the exception of meat cookery) to protect its fine flavor. Use it in about the same way you use vanilla, unless recipe otherwise specifies.

6. When using wine with fruits, add the wine several hours in advance, so that the wine will have a chance to fully flavor the food.

7. In general, light and delicate dishes invite the use of the light and more delicate wines (the white wines); while the heavier foods, such as red meats, have a natural affinity for the richness of the red wines to bring out their full-bodied flavor.

The kind of wine partly depends upon the kind of grapes used. The red dinner wines are made from the juice of grapes fermented with the skins on, while the white dinner wines are made from the juices alone (no pulp or skins). From time to time, we will list a table or dessert wine in a recipe and leave the specific choice to you. In the fermentation of the grape juice, most of the sweetness disappears, yielding a "dry" wine, such as claret and Burgundy in the red dinner wines — sauterne and Rhine in the white. When you want a delicate, aromatic, and tangy wine you will select from these four wines, or from the varietals.

WINE TYPE	EXAMPLES	CHARACTERISTICS	FOODS THEY GO WITH BEST
Appetizer	Sherry	Nutty flavor, dry to semisweet	Appetizers and soups Chicken Desserts
Red Dinner	Burgundy Chianti Claret Zinfandel Cabernet	Dry (not sweet) and slightly tart. Blend with hearty foods. Light to ruby red in color	Meat dishes of all kinds — steaks, roasts, chops, games, spaghetti, low sodium cheese
	Rosé	Gay pink, fruity, light-bodied, dry or slightly sweet	Meat dishes, cheese, wine jellies, punches
White Dinner	Sauterne Rhine Riesling Sylvaner Chablis	Delicate flavor and very dry to semisweet, pale to deep gold in color	Fish, chicken, eggs and light main course dishes (casseroles)
Dessert	Port Muscatel	Sweet, full-bodied. Port is red, muscatel is amber in color with pronounced flavor and aroma of muscat grapes	Fruits, cookies, sweet cakes, low sodium cheese, jellies
	Tokay	Pinkish amber	Fruits

On the other hand, when you are adding flavor to a sweet dish, you will turn to the sweeter wines, such as sherry, port, and muscatel. These dessert wines do not have any sugar added to them, so you needn't have any anxieties on that score. They simply are not allowed to finish their fermentation and have a little pure grape brandy added to them to arrest the fermentation and hold the natural sweetness of the grapes.

There are natural affinities between certain foods and wines just as there are among herbs and foods. Some of the most usable ones in restricted cookery are shown in the table on the preceding page.

We are omitting the sparkling wines, inasmuch as they are not cooking wines.

NOTES

You will note, from the above chart, that in addition to the familiar-sounding table wines we have listed a few of the *varietal* wines, but we cannot give you individual analyses for the various varietal wines because of wide variation in winery practices. This results in variation in sodium content. If you are on a strict sodium restriction be sure to consult with your physician before using any wine in your recipes. These varietals are named after the grape varieties from which they are made. Some are lower in sodium content than the standard table wines. Vermouth, Champagne, port and sherry have the lowest sodium content. But even they can be so variable, because of present manufacturing processes, that patients on severely restricted sodium diets are advised to have special analyses on wines to be used.

If wines are allowed on your dietary, you may use the white dinner wines interchangeably and you may use the red dinner wines interchangeably without any taste loss. Choose the type of wine that blends with the particular dish you are going to create and stay within your sodium allowance especially if you have to work your arithmetic every day on sodium content totals. For saturated fat restriction, you have no worries here.

In our recipes calling for a "white dinner wine" or a "red dinner wine," our calculations are based upon the listing as presented in Appendix 4. You may alter the selection to suit your requirements and palate. Consult Appendix 4 for sodium content of wines and other alcoholic beverages.

Start right now, won't you, to discover how easy it is to improve the flavor of your restricted cookery with wine?

6

START THE MEAL
WITH SOUP

THE SOUP TUREEN of Grandmother's time is reappearing in antique shops and on dining room tables today. Can it be that with its return there will be an upsurge in the fine old art of soup-making, too?

The "ready-mades" are not for you (with a few exceptions) who are concerned with sodium-restricted or low fat cooking. The commercial products, you will remember, are seldom low in sodium. Many are high in fat content too.

But you may as well face it. Man wants his soup, whatever his diet limitations. You will have to tackle the problem in your own kitchen, whether or not you have a tureen to glamorize your efforts.

SUGGESTIONS FOR SOUP-MAKING:

1. Plan soups in relation to the rest of your meals. The lighter soups combine with a hearty meal; the pottages and

chowders as meat substitutes; the chilled soups as lunch or warm-day stand-bys.

2. Be consumer-wise in your choice of ingredients. For sodium restriction, do not buy ready-to-use packets of vegetables, as they often contain celery, other greens, and carrots allowed only in limited amounts on some regimens. Make your selections in terms of the importance of the soup in the meal, the blending quality of the various ingredients, and cost.

3. Save all leftover vegetables, and juices from cooked vegetables to use in soup for flavor enrichment.

4. Use herbs in various combinations for a plus-value in flavor. Try:

Bay leaf and parsley in low sodium pea soup and fish chowders

Curry and onion in fish chowders and chicken soups

Summer savory and cloves in minestrone

A pinch of oregano in meat-flavored soups

Thyme and cayenne in milk-base soups

Thyme and marjoram in meat-vegetable combinations

5. Vary the seasonings, too. Try:

A pinch of mustard in bean soups

1 fat-trimmed pork chop, cut small, in place of salt pork (if sodium and fat count allows)

A half-dozen cloves in chowders

A dash of allspice in vegetable-base soups

1 teaspoon vinegar to each quart vegetable soup (use cider, tarragon, or wine for variety)

A dash of cayenne

Peppercorns (whole pepper) for chowders and pottages

A little fat, in the form of unsalted special margarine, or vegetable oil, to add body and richness of flavor if allowed

6. Experiment with the addition of wine in some of your

soups. Try a small amount at first to test its flavor. A word to the wise: add wine just before serving soup for best results. Be sure to calculate the sodium content of wine if you are adapting your own recipe. It is included in calculations calling for wine in our recipes.

Herb brandies offer still another savor.

7.   Pay special attention to soup accompaniments and garnishings. Eye appeal and taste appeal march side by side. Try:

Thin lemon slices for tomato bouillons
Finely chopped parsley or chives as toppings for "cream" soups
Paprika sprinkling for pale soups
A topping of freshly cooked unsalted popcorn
Slivers of toasted almonds as floaters
Leftover low sodium pancakes, cut in strips and floated on thick soups
Low sodium croutons
A slice of toasted low sodium bread, lightly coated with paprika — floated on the top of steaming minestrone
Unsalted matzoth
Onion or garlic croutons

FOR SODIUM-RESTRICTED DIETERS

You may use meat, poultry, and fresh fish in your soups only when you can calculate the sodium content accurately — remembering to portion both the meat and broth carefully. You may use vegetable stock and vegetables in quantities; fresh mushrooms; nonfat milk; herbs; wines — to mention some of the most important ingredients for your consideration. Low sodium, nonfat milk is available and may be used to decrease sodium content.

You will want your soups to be something more than a combination of leftovers carelessly tossed into an ever-present soup kettle on the back of the stove, whose yawning depths seem to have no other purpose than to receive the castoffs of the day. This is not to suggest that there is no place for leftovers. To the contrary, they can be a lifesaver to you. Planned and creative use of leftovers — vegetable juices drained from vegetables when served, vegetable peelings, and the outside leaves of lettuce and cabbage — can greatly enrich and so improve the flavor of many of your soups.

But the real task in soup-making for sodium-restricted diets is to bring out the *natural flavor* of ingredients used and to enhance them by every known cooking trick. This means you will have to think through the prevailing flavor of the soup you want to make and select ingredients for their blending qualities. Take, for instance, a fish chowder. Milk, butter, fish, salt, and pepper are the old familiars. On this diet nonfat milk may be allowed. We have constructed all of our recipes with it. But if your diet list calls for low sodium milk, use it. *If you do use regular nonfat milk, you must deduct it from your daily allowance.*

The best way to bring out the prevailing flavor of fish in combination with milk is to add a little wine for richness and for its blending qualities, and a bit of parsley with your choice of herbs to sharpen flavor. These additions strengthen the prevailing fish flavor without detracting from it in any way.

Recipes in this chapter are based upon the restrictions listed below for the sodium-restricted diet. Check them against your own list and make such changes as may be necessary.

FOR SODIUM RESTRICTION, DO NOT USE:

Canned meat or poultry unless low sodium dietetic
Canned salmon or tuna unless low sodium dietetic

2 cups dried beans (cranberry or navy preferred)
2 quarts water
1 green pepper, chopped
4 mashed peppercorns
1 chopped garlic clove
1 cup chopped onions
3 tablespoons minced parsley
½ cup water
¼ teaspoon dry mustard
2 tablespoons vinegar
½ teaspoon sugar
6 whole cloves
1 teaspoon summer savory
1 teaspoon sweet basil
2 cups cut-up tomatoes
1 cup finely chopped zucchini
1 cup peeled and cubed potatoes

Soak beans overnight; drain and put into large soup kettle. Add fresh water, peppers, and peppercorns; cook slowly until soft (about 1½ hours). Drain 2 cups of beans; mash or press through coarse sieve or purée in blender. Return to soup kettle and stir well. Meanwhile, combine garlic, onions, and parsley in saucepan with ½ cup water; cook over low heat for 10 minutes. Add to soup kettle. Add seasonings. Bring soup to a boil. Add vegetables and water to make desired thickness. Cover and simmer until vegetables are fork-tender. Serve in a tureen from the table, with paprika-coated croutons, or onion or garlic croutons. A sprinkling of Parmesan cheese may be added for "regular" family members, and salt for all except sodium-restricted dieters.

ONE SERVING (1 cup)	TOTAL RECIPE	
WITHOUT CROUTONS		
16	124	milligrams sodium
1	8	grams total fat
trace	trace	gram saturated fat
41	330	grams carbohydrate
219	1749	calories

VARIATION

To make this soup really authentic and a whole meal if served with bread and a tossed salad, add 1 cup cooked pasta (spaghetti or macaroni broken into small pieces). Prepare and add to soup just before serving.

ONION CROUTONS
8 Servings

Combine 1 tablespoon corn oil and 1 teaspoon onion. Add 1 cup soft ¼″ low sodium bread cubes and stir until each one is coated with the oil mixture. Spread on a cooky sheet and toast under low broiler heat for about 10 minutes or until golden brown. This will give you onion croutons for your soup.

ONE SERVING	TOTAL RECIPE	
trace	2	milligrams sodium
2	16	grams total fat
trace	1	gram saturated fat
3	26	grams carbohydrate
40	321	calories

One serving: ¼ teaspoon vegetable oil.

CHOWDERS

We don't have to look to Europe for all of our good thick soups — our pottages — as our own New England has given to us bountifully in this field of cookery. The old chowders were originally made of milk and fish. As vegetables abounded in home garden patches, chowders came to include vegetable-milk combinations, too. Many of the old-time recipes have been handed down from generation to generation. These chowders were so chock-full of good ingredients they were meals in themselves.

For you dieters, the adapted chowders are still fine one-dish meals, if you combine them with low sodium bread sticks, a tossed salad, beverage, and fruit dessert.

NEW ENGLAND VEGETABLE CHOWDER
8 Servings

The New England vegetable chowder, like the minestrone, is a vegetable soup, thick and flavorsome if well prepared. It lacks some of the body of the minestrone, due to the bean base of the Italian soup, but is quite palatable even without salt.

1 teaspoon unsalted special margarine
½ cup sliced fresh mushrooms
6 string beans, cut up
¼ cup finely cut onions
1 cup diced potatoes
1 cup cream-style corn, canned low sodium dietetic
Water to cover (about 2 cups)
6 mashed peppercorns

½ teaspoon sugar
Bouquet of herbs
½ cup fresh peas
3 cups nonfat milk
2 tablespoons chopped parsley
¼ cup sauterne
1 tablespoon grated low sodium cheese; 1 tablespoon
Count Down Cheese Spread cubes for low saturated fat
dieters; Parmesan cheese for regulars (optional)
Paprika

Melt fat in small skillet; add mushrooms and sauté for 5 minutes. Prepare vegetables and combine with mushrooms and water in saucepan. Heat to boiling; then simmer for 10 minutes. Add seasonings, peas, and milk. Cook for 10 minutes, stirring from time to time. Fork-test vegetables for doneness. Add parsley and wine; heat slightly. Serve at once, with or without cheese, and a dash of paprika on top of each serving. Salt for regulars. (Deduct milk from the day's allowance or use low sodium nonfat milk.)

ONE SERVING (1 cup)	TOTAL RECIPE	
WITHOUT CHEESE		
54	432	milligrams sodium
1	8	grams total fat
negligible	1	gram saturated fat
18	147	grams carbohydrate
101	806	calories

VARIATIONS

Float a piece of low sodium toast sprinkled with paprika on top of chowder. Or sprinkle with low sodium onion or garlic croutons.

Many substitutions may be made with this basic recipe. It may be made thinner or thicker according to preference, depending upon the amount of liquid used. Many different combinations may be used.

Follow Basic Recipe and Variations except substitute vegetable oil, if required, for special margarine, and use Count Down if cheese is desired. When not restricted in sodium, use regular canned vegetables and add salt to taste.

One serving: negligible saturated fat; ⅛ teaspoon vegetable oil.

CODFISH CHOWDER

8 servings

Our original recipe called for salt pork which must be eliminated for diet purposes. We think the chowder remarkably zestful in this new form. With low sodium bread sticks or bread toasted, a tossed salad, and simple fruit for dessert, you will have a well-balanced meal, and one that is not too hard on the budget.

When you are going to use chowder as a main dish, you may leave fish chunk size instead of flaking. Do not use salted or dried cod.

2 pounds fresh cod
1 quart boiling water
1 bay leaf, crumbled
¼ cup chopped onions
2 cups diced potatoes
2 tablespoons chopped parsley
6 whole cloves

6 peppercorns
2 cups nonfat milk
½ cup Rhine wine (optional)

Place cleaned and washed fish in stewing pan; cover with boiling water. Add bay leaf, cover pan, and simmer fish until fork-tender (about 15 minutes). Drain, saving broth. Flake the fish, removing skin and bones; set aside. Strain broth; measure 3 cups into stewing pan. Add onions, potatoes, 1 tablespoon parsley, and seasonings. Simmer until potatoes are nearly tender (about 10 minutes). Add fish and milk; simmer to heat thoroughly but do not boil. Add wine; garnish each serving with parsley and serve at once. Add salt for those without sodium restrictions. (Use low sodium nonfat milk for a lower count.)

ONE SERVING (1¼ oz. fish, cooked weight)	TOTAL RECIPE	
With wine		
79	633	milligrams sodium
trace	2	grams total fat
trace	trace	gram saturated fat
13	101	grams carbohydrate
100	800	calories

VARIATION

Other fish on your diet list, such as haddock or halibut, may be substituted for the cod. Canned salmon (low sodium dietetic for sodium-restricted dieters) may be used for a hurry-up chowder. Fresh salmon is delicious, too. Vegetable variations may be made to suit individual preferences.

SHRIMP-OKRA GUMBO
6 Servings

Like the minestrones, fish-okra gumbos are almost as numerous as there are good cooks in the Deep South. We have taken an old family recipe and have adapted it for sodium and fat restrictions. Rich and luscious, it is really a meal in itself ladled over steaming rice with raw vegetable accompaniments.

6 chicken-flavored low sodium bouillon cubes
6 cups boiling water
3 cups chopped, peeled fresh tomatoes (or 3 cups canned without added sodium)
2 tablespoons chopped parsley
1 cup chopped green pepper
1 cup chopped onions
2 cloves garlic, chopped fine
10-oz. package frozen okra (or 1 pound fresh okra, washed and trimmed)
Pinch of thyme
2 (5 oz.) cans low sodium dietetic shrimp
½ cup Chablis (optional)
Paprika
¾ cup hot, cooked rice

Dissolve bouillon cubes in boiling water. Add vegetables and thyme (cutting okra into ¾-inch lengths). Cover and heat to boiling; simmer for 10 minutes. Add shrimp and simmer until gumbo slightly thickens from the vegetables and fish, breaking into pieces and mingling with the liquid. Add wine just before serving. Serve in soup bowls with 2 tablespoons hot rice lining bottoms or dropped into each serving. Garnish with paprika; add salt for those without sodium restrictions. (A dash of cayenne gives a red-hot gumbo.)

ONE SERVING	TOTAL RECIPE	
With rice and wine		
58	346	milligrams sodium
1	5	grams total fat
trace	trace	gram saturated fat
17	104	grams carbohydrate
132	793	calories

LOW SATURATED FAT VARIATION

If not restricted in sodium, use regular bouillon cubes and canned shrimp; add 1 cup sliced celery and 10-oz. package frozen ready-cut Alaska crab or an equal amount of fresh crab meat; add salt to taste. If you like a very hot gumbo, add 6 to 8 drops tabasco sauce just before serving.

One serving: negligible grams saturated fat.

SOME OTHER SOUPS

HAMBURGER-VEGETABLE SOUP
8 Servings

This is a man's soup, hearty and complete in itself. It is a very thick soup and is so loaded with vegetables and meat that there is little liquid, as such, at time of serving. If you want a thinner soup, simply increase the amount of liquid used.

1 tablespoon vegetable oil
½ cup minced onion
1 minced garlic clove
1 pound *lean* ground beef, made into small balls
4 whole cloves
1 tablespoon vinegar

½ teaspoon thyme
1 teaspoon marjoram
Black pepper
1 cup shredded cabbage
1 cup cut-up fresh tomatoes
4 cups boiling water
1 cup fresh, cut string beans
1 cup fresh peas

Put oil into warm skillet; heat. Add onion and garlic; lightly brown. Drain off any remaining oil. Add meat balls; simmer gently for about 10 minutes. Remove to soup pot. Add seasonings, cabbage, tomatoes, and water. Bring to a boil; add string beans and peas. Cook until soup thickens and vegetables are fork-tender. You may take out a cup of vegetables, mash them and return to kettle if a thick pottage is wanted. Salt for the regulars before serving.

ONE SERVING (1½ oz. meat, cooked weight)	TOTAL RECIPE	
43	341	milligrams sodium
7	56	grams total fat
3	20	grams saturated fat
7	54	grams carbohydrate
141	1125	calories

LOW SATURATED FAT VARIATION

Use top round steak for ground meat choice, selecting *good* or *commercial* grade of meat; brown meat in ribbed-bottom skillet and discard drippings. Chill soup before serving, and remove hardened fat; then reheat. Add salt to taste if not restricted in sodium.

One serving: 1 gram saturated fat; ⅜ teaspoon vegetable oil.

BASIC CREAM SOUP, SODIUM-RESTRICTED
Base for 4 Servings

1 tablespoon unsalted special margarine
1 tablespoon flour
⅛ teaspoon white pepper
½ teaspoon onion powder
½ cup vegetable water
1 cup nonfat milk
2 tablespoons Riesling
Paprika

Melt margarine; blend in flour and seasonings. Stir in vegetable water, mixing until smooth. Add milk. Cook over low heat until thickened, stirring constantly (about 10 minutes). Add 1 cup vegetables (page 76); blend and heat. Add wine just before serving; sprinkle with paprika and add salt for those without sodium restrictions. (Use low sodium nonfat milk for lower count.)

ONE SERVING	TOTAL RECIPE	
Without vegetable		
34	136	milligrams sodium
3	12	grams total fat
1	2	grams saturated fat
5	18	grams carbohydrate
57	229	calories

BASIC CREAM SOUP, FAT-RESTRICTED
Base for 4 Servings

½ cup vegetable water
1 tablespoon flour
⅛ teaspoon white pepper
½ teaspoon onion powder
1 cup nonfat milk
2 tablespoons Riesling
Paprika

Pour cold vegetable water into small jar; add flour and seasonings. Cover; shake until smooth and pastelike. Add milk gradually, stirring to avoid lumps. Transfer to saucepan and cook over low heat until thickened, stirring constantly (about 10 minutes). Add salt to taste if not restricted in sodium. Add 1 cup vegetable (see below); blend and heat. Add wine, if allowed, and sprinkle with paprika. For a lower sodium content, use low sodium nonfat milk.

ONE SERVING	TOTAL RECIPE	
Without vegetable		
trace	trace	gram total fat
5	18	grams carbohydrate
32	129	calories

Vegetables to use: add to the Cream Soup Base 1 full cup of any of the following (*check against your allowable*) vegetables, mashed, put through a coarse sieve, or minced very fine: Asparagus, broccoli, cauliflower, corn, onion, or potato (add green and white parts of 1 leek and ¼ cup chopped cooked onion).

If you are lucky enough to have a blender, prepare vegetables and blend according to instructions. Then add all ingredients for Basic Cream Soup and blend according to directions.

SPLIT PEA SOUP
4 Servings

¾ cup dried split peas
Dash of nutmeg
4 crushed peppercorns
3½ cups water
½ cup sauterne
Paprika

Soak peas in water overnight. Drain; put into soup kettle with nutmeg, peppercorns, and 3½ cups water. Cover and bring to boil. Simmer for about 2 hours, or until mixture is soft and thick. Add wine; reheat. Garnish with paprika at time of serving. Salt for those without sodium restrictions.

ONE SERVING (1 cup)	TOTAL RECIPE	
19	74	milligrams sodium
trace	2	grams total fat
trace	trace	gram saturated fat
25	100	grams carbohydrate
156	623	calories

Note the carbohydrate content, you carbohydrate counters.

TOMATO SOUP
2 Servings

12-ounce can unsalted tomato juice
¼ teaspoon thyme
1 teaspoon chopped parsley
1 teaspoon grated onion
1 small bay leaf
Pepper to taste

Heat unsalted tomato juice (use only approved brand). Add spices. Do not bring to a boil, but simmer gently. Serve at once with a thin slice of lemon in each cup, and add a sprinkling of salt for those without sodium restrictions.

ONE SERVING	TOTAL RECIPE	
6	12	milligrams sodium
trace	trace	gram total fat
trace	trace	gram saturated fat
8	15	grams carbohydrate
38	75	calories

VARIATIONS

Use cloves with thyme.

Use ½ garlic clove in juice while heating. Remove before serving.

TOMATO CORN SOUP
3 Servings

2 tablespoons unsalted special margarine
¼ cup finely chopped onion
½ small bay leaf
1 tablespoon flour
Pepper
1 cup chopped fresh tomatoes
1 cup cream-style corn, canned (low sodium dietetic)
1 cup water
3 parsley sprigs

Melt margarine over low heat. Add onions; cook for about 5 minutes. Combine all ingredients in soup kettle. Cover; bring to boil and simmer for 30 minutes. Mash through sieve or purée when thick soup is your choice. Add salt for those without sodium restrictions.

ONE SERVING	TOTAL RECIPE	
6	18	milligrams sodium
9	26	grams total fat
1	4	grams saturated fat
22	66	grams carbohydrate
165	496	calories

LOW SATURATED FAT VARIATION

Follow Basic Recipe except to substitute vegetable oil for margarine. Or omit all fat, combine other ingredients in soup kettle and continue as directed. If not restricted in sodium, use regular canned corn and add salt to taste.

One serving, with vegetable oil: 1 gram saturated fat; 2 teaspoons vegetable oil.

COLD SOUPS

HOT WEATHER FRUIT SOUP
8 Servings

With summer's climbing thermometer, you may have to do some extra planning to tempt jaded appetites. Cold plates, a jellied fish or vegetable-fish salad, an iced beverage and a cold, savory soup may be just the answer you are looking for. Here's an unusual one and easy to prepare, too, but very high for you carbohydrate watchers.

3 cups water
½ cup pitted prunes
½ cup seedless raisins

2 medium apples, pared, cored, and thinly sliced
1 medium orange, peeled and sliced
1 can water-packed dark cherries (8 ounces)
½ cup sugar
1 tablespoon pure honey
¼ cup quick cooking tapioca
1 cinnamon stick
2 cups grape juice, without added sugar

Combine water, prunes, and raisins in a saucepan. Bring to a boil. Reduce heat and simmer gently, covered, for 10 minutes. Add fruits, sugar, honey, tapioca, and cinnamon. Simmer covered for 10 minutes until apples are tender and mixture is slightly thickened. Stir in grape juice. Remove cinnamon stick. Chill. Sprinkle with cinnamon, if desired, at time of serving.

	ONE SERVING
5	milligrams sodium
trace	gram total fat
trace	gram saturated fat
54	grams carbohydrate
209	calories

CHILLED TOMATO MADRILENE
2 Servings

Heat a 12-ounce can low sodium dietetic tomato juice. Meanwhile, soften 1 scant tablespoon gelatin in ½ cup cold water. Add 1 tablespoon lemon juice and 1 teaspoon *minced* parsley. Add hot juice; add dash fine black pepper and cayenne. Blend. Chill until ready to serve. Cube lightly with knife, and pile into bouillon cups. Top with a slice of lemon. Sprinkle with salt for those without sodium restrictions.

ONE SERVING (¾ cup)	TOTAL RECIPE	
8	15	milligrams sodium
trace	trace	gram total fat
trace	trace	gram saturated fat
8	16	grams carbohydrate
58	115	calories

7

MEAT'S SPECIAL ROLE

Some have meat but can not eat;
Some could eat but have no meat;
We have meat and can all eat;
Blest, therefore, be God for our meat.
— UNKNOWN: The Selkirk Grace
(From MS. of about 1650)

THIS OLD-TIME GRACE BESPEAKS the sentiments of thousands of people who are on restricted diets. Meat is to them one of the bright spots of their "allowables," because of its fine flavor and appetite appeal, with or without salt.

Meat has been the mainstay of man's diet since the beginning of time. "Protein" comes from the Greek verb meaning to take first place, and of all the proteins meat ranks first in flavor and high in nutritive value. Do treat it well in the way you cook it.

Although it is the most expensive food in our diet, it is such a high quality protein, and a good source of vitamins and minerals to boot and has such fine flavor, that we are sometimes willing to pay for it.

The principal reason meat is limited on the low sodium diet is the high sodium content of foods of animal origin, and on the low saturated fat regimen, to limit the amount of animal fat.

When servings must be small, it is particularly important that selection and preparation be undertaken with care. Avoid buying *prime* and *choice* grades with their high marbled fat. Select instead from *good* or *standard* grades, "maturity bracket A." They have less marbling. Buy beef that is bright because there is less fat in younger animals. Select firm, dry, and fine textured meat for it is superior to soft, moist, and coarsely textured meat. And of course you will want it to be lean and well trimmed. Young veal is light pink; older animals produce meat that is darker grayish-pink. Both are acceptable choices. Young lamb, yearling lamb, is bright pink, older lamb, sometimes known as mutton, is dark pink to red. There is less fat in younger animals. The best quality of fresh pork is firm and bright grayish-pink.

Many of your fat-controlled menu plans will call for more frequent use of fish and poultry than of the higher-fat meats. So when you are going to feature meat, choose carefully and build your menu around one of the most lean cuts rather than the heavily marbled ones. This means a sirloin tip roast in place of a standing one; a sirloin, lean T-bone or lean tenderloin steak instead of a filet mignon. The London broil is an excellent choice for broiling if tenderized or prepared in advance with an acceptable marinade. Round and flank steaks may be prepared in the same way.

The full-bodied flavor of meat allows you to cook it with little added seasoning. But for variety, try the juice of a lemon squeezed over it with a sprinkling of freshly ground peppercorns. And for barbecuing, be ingenious in your marinades. Red wine and water combined with your choice of herbs makes a good starter. And lemon or orange juice also serves as an excellent base for your concoctions.

Our calculations are approximate for the recipes that follow. There are many variables that cannot be controlled from our kitchen to yours. The leanness of meat; amount of fat trimmed; shrinkage of about 25 percent in the cooking process; the variation of sodium content in the different water supplies in the country; the actual amount of water used in meat cookery; the length of time involved in the cooking process and its effect upon the sodium and fat content of the meat itself; the temperature; cooking time; and size of surface of the cooking utensil used in recipes in which dry wines are ingredients; the concentration of sodium and fat in the drippings and juices in prolonged cooking and in repeated boiling of meat — all of these and other factors make it impossible to rule out all of the variables.

Most of the recipes, catering to the very restrictive dietary, are based on 3 ounces of cooked meat or less per serving. If this portion is not satisfying to your "regulars," or if your dietary allowance is more generous, you can plan on 1½ or 2 servings for these members of the family.

For those of you on sodium restriction who find it difficult to stay within your meat allowances, you might like to investigate the interesting article by George Ornstein, M.D., of New York City, in the April, 1951 issue of the *Journal of the Medical Society of New Jersey* on the effect of the repeated boiling of meats (and certain vegetables) on their sodium content.

MEATS TO USE:

Selected lean cuts of:

Beef	Pork
Lamb	Veal

The amount to be used will be determined by your physician, depending upon your particular needs. In general, it will be between 3 and 5 ounces cooked, as specified. Three ounces is about 4″ × 4″ × ½″.

FOR SODIUM RESTRICTION, DO NOT USE:

Bacon

Bologna

Brains

Canned meats, except low sodium dietetic

Chipped or corned beef

Frankfurters

Gravies (unless allowed on your diet list)

Ham, except low sodium dietetic

Kidneys

Luncheon meats

Meats koshered by salting

Salt

Salted or smoked meats

Sausage

Sweetbreads

Tongue, smoked

FOR SATURATED FAT RESTRICTION, DO NOT USE:

Bacon, except Canadian; salt pork, spareribs

Beef, except lean cuts; lamb, except leg cuts; pork, except lean loin, and lean, well-trimmed ham; avoid high fat and "marbled"

Butter, hydrogenated shortenings, or regular margarines in sauces

Canned meats, except allowed dietetic

Cream, fresh or sour; whole milk, or cheese made from whole milk in sauces

Frankfurters, sausage, cold cuts

Gravies, except as specially prepared, page 121

Meat high in cholesterol, as brains, sweetbreads, and liver*

Visible fat from any meat

* Sometimes your physician will allow you to substitute 2 ounces shellfish, ½ cup crab or lobster, 6 to 8 shrimps, oysters, clams, or scallops, or 2 ounces liver, sweetbreads, or heart for 1 egg.

THINGS TO REMEMBER:

1.   Allow approximately 1 pound of meat, without bones, for 3 to 4 servings, or 2 servings with the bone. The amount of fat will alter the number of servings you can get to a pound of raw meat. Meat-stretcher recipes will yield another serving or two to each pound of meat.

You will have to account for the differences in appetites in your family group. Grandma won't need as much meat as your sixteen-year-old footballer.

2.   *Buy meat that has the least amount of marbling, whatever its grade,* and trim it of all visible fat.

3.   Loose-wrap meat and keep in refrigerator until an hour or so before use.

4.   Slow-cook for best insurance of full meat flavor and least amount of shrinkage.

5.   Use a meat thermometer for guaranteed cooking results.

6.   If restricted in fat or fat-carbohydrate, avoid frying of meats as this seals in fat. Broil, pan-broil (in cast-iron ribbed-bottom skillet), bake, braise, pressure-cook, or roast meats. Do not rub meats in flour and pan-brown, as this too seals in fats (and flour is high in carbohydrate, too). Rather broil in oven or ribbed skillet so that fat may drip out, if this is your method choice. Use Teflon treated pan for meat dishes requiring greasing of pan. Do not baste with pan drippings, plain or combined with other liquids.

7.   Use meat tenderizer, seasoned or unseasoned (low sodium for sodium-restricted dieters), on tougher cuts of meat to make fork-tender.

8.   Use lemon juice to point up the natural flavor of meats to be broiled. Or add vinegar to stews and pot roasts for flavor and texture improvement.

9.   Or, substitute wine for some of the liquid in your meat recipes when you want extra flavor richness.

10.   Don't forget herbs — a marvelous addition to meat cookery.

11. Gravies, if allowed at all, must be used in very limited amounts and must be calculated for sodium, fat and carbohydrate content. They must be portioned with same care as you do meat.

AN ADMONITION: Choose your method of meat cookery with the same care you do your meat.

Broil meats when you want their fine, natural flavors.

The *pan-broil or pan-fry* method is less desirable as it tends to seal in juices, and thus store the fat content of the meat.

Braise meats when you use cuts that require special ministrations — such as pot roasts, rolled roasts, shoulder cuts, and cutlets, to mention only a few (such cuts invite your ingenuity in seasonings, too).

Pressure cooking is a real timesaver for stews, rolled roasts, and combination dishes, but don't expect quite the same texture fineness as you will get with the slower methods of preparation.

Roasting is an art all itself; it involves much more than proper temperature and time control, although they are important. The selection of the right size pan (open and low-sided, of course), preparation, appropriate seasoning for desired results — all must play their part.

For roasting or braising meat, use red or white wine, wine and water, or wine and vegetable oil as your basting sauce. To the sauce, add tomato juice (unsalted for sodium restriction), desired herbal combinations, garlic, or spices. Simmer all together to blend flavors before basting. Keep warm during period of use, but do not boil. Never add a cold sauce to cooking meat.

HERBS AND SEASONINGS
TO USE

Although there are no hard-and-fast rules here, there are certain combinations that are traditional in meat cookery and they are good starters. For the nonce, try:

With beef: Basil, bay, caraway, curry, dill, garlic, onion, parsley, rosemary, sage, savory, sweet marjoram, thyme, turmeric, Worcestershire sauce (low sodium dietetic is available)

With pork: Basil, caraway, chives, curry, garlic, ground ginger, lemon peel, nutmeg, onion, rosemary, sage, sweet marjoram, thyme

With lamb: Whole cloves, curry, dill, garlic, onion, oregano, parsley, rosemary, sage, sweet marjoram

With veal: Basil, garlic, nutmeg, onion, parsley, sage, summer savory, tarragon, thyme

BEEF

So full-flavored is fine beef that you will want to cook it many times "as is" with, perhaps, a little lemon juice and pepper. But with meat limited in quantity in both the fat- and sodium-restricted diets, beef deserves special preparation and seasoning once in a while to avoid the monotonous. Herbs and wines can be used alone or in combination to give that special savor. Herbs can be brewed in a wine base as suggested before or can be scattered directly over the meat. The results are very different. Wine can be used in basting sauces as suggested, or poured directly over the meat, or used to flavor the gravy only.

BRAISED SIRLOIN TIPS
8 Servings

1 tablespoon vegetable oil
2 pounds lean sirloin of beef cut in ½-inch strips
½ cup red table wine
1 cup water
½ teaspoon onion salt substitute
½ teaspoon garlic salt substitute
1 tablespoon cornstarch
½ cup water

Slightly warm oil in a large skillet. Add meat and brown on all sides. Stir in wine, water, onion and garlic salt substitutes. (If sodium is not restricted, you may use regular onion and garlic salt.) Heat over medium heat until liquid begins to bubble. Reduce heat, and simmer until fork-tender — about 30 minutes.

Blend cornstarch and water. Add a little of the hot liquid very gradually to the cornstarch mixture, stirring vigorously to promote smooth blending. Add to meat, and continue to stir until mixture again bubbles and liquid thickens. Cook 1 more minute. Serve over hot rice.

ONE SERVING
(3 oz. meat, cooked weight)
Without Rice

75	milligrams sodium
17	grams total fat
7	grams saturated fat
2	grams carbohydrate
244	calories

VARIATIONS

Tomato juice (canned without salt) may be substituted for wine and water for those with severe sodium restrictions. One-half cup low-fat yogurt may be substituted for the corn-starch and water.

✓ SIRLOIN OF BEEF

3 pounds *lean* roast, 9 Servings

Where saturated fat is restricted, choose a sirloin of beef or a top of round (using meat tenderizer) for your beef roast as they contain much less fat than a prime rib roast.

Trim meat of all visible fat; wipe thoroughly with a damp cloth. Season with a light sprinkling of freshly-ground pepper and pure garlic powder or low sodium dietetic garlic salt. Place on a rack in a low-sided pan. For robust flavoring, put 3 slices of onion on top of roast, fastening with tooth picks. Put into a preheated 325° (slow) oven and roast according to your temperature chart. For those without sodium restriction, salt after meat is cooked and sliced, as salt penetrates meat when hot.

ONE SERVING
(3 oz. meat, cooked weight)

52	milligrams sodium
6	grams total fat
3	grams saturated fat
negligible	grams carbohydrate
174	calories

VARIATIONS

Meat may be marinated (page 141) before cooking. Or you may want to baste for added flavor using a sauce made of:

1 cup claret
½ teaspoon thyme

Dash lemon peel
1 tablespoon vegetable oil

Heat sauce and baste at least 4 times during the roasting period.

BEEF JULIENNE
6 Servings

There are many ways to use leftover roast beef. It is good cold and served with a garnish; it is good in low sodium bread sandwiches spread with unsalted special margarine and a dash of mustard, or with garlic "butter"; and it is excellent in a julienne.

½ cup Chianti wine
¼ cup chopped onion
1 tablespoon chopped parsley
1 cup water
6 slices roasted sirloin of beef (2 oz. per slice)

Simmer wine, onion, parsley, and water over low heat until onion is tender (about 5 minutes). Add meat, cover, and let simmer until thoroughly heated (about 30 minutes). Remove meat to platter and thicken liquid with 1 to 2 tablespoons flour. If no sodium restriction, add salt to taste. If dieter is allowed gravy, portion carefully.

ONE SERVING
(2 oz. meat, cooked weight)
With wine gravy

37	milligrams sodium
4	grams total fat
2	grams saturated fat
3	grams carbohydrate
136	calories

STEAK

✓LEAN TOP ROUND STEAK

Trim meat of all visible fat; wipe with damp cloth. Sprinkle with seasoned or unseasoned low sodium meat tenderizer; let stand for 45 minutes. Put into preheated very hot ribbed-bottom skillet. Brown on under side; turn and brown. Remove to warm platter. Season with light sprinkling of freshly ground pepper; salt for those without sodium restrictions.

ONE SERVING
(3 oz. meat, cooked weight)

51	milligrams sodium
6	grams total fat
3	grams saturated fat
none	grams carbohydrate
195	calories

VARIATIONS

Meat may be oven- or pan-broiled and braised in ½ cup water or Chianti. Or tomato juice (low sodium dietetic) may be substituted as the liquid. If a more robust flavor is desired, add ½ teaspoon sweet basil or thyme with ¼ cup finely chopped onions to liquid. Simmer gently; then add to browned meat. Cover and let simmer until fork-tender (from 30 to 45 minutes). If gravy is allowed, cool with an ice cube and skim off surface fat; portion carefully.

LOW SATURATED FAT VARIATION

Never dredge steaks in flour and pan-brown, as this seals in fat. Your method must be to prepare meat so that invisible fat drips out as much as possible. Pan-broil in ribbed-bottom skillet, or oven-broil on rack so that fat drips away from meat. If gravy is allowed, chill with ice cube and remove hardened fat, or make according to special recipe (page 121). If no sodium restrictions, salt meat and gravy before serving.

STEWS

Twenty-five minutes in the kitchen and the main part of your meal is prepared — that is if you have a pressure cooker and are not on low saturated fat restriction. We do not like a quick-stew method as well as the slow-simmer method for those who must limit fat.

Pressure cooking is a time-saving way of cooking not only stew but those cuts of meat which require moist heat cookery. In addition to stews, for sodium restriction try this method for pot roasts, Swiss steaks, short ribs of beef, pork shoulder steaks and hocks, flank steaks, and brisket of beef. The addition of meat tenderizer will cut cooking time, too, and help to assure a tender product from these tougher cuts of meat.

Pressure-cooked meats have a high retention of nutrients, so in addition to being time-savers, they are nutrition-savers, too.

For finest flavor, when pressure cooking is your election, flour and brown meat before adding liquid and seasonings for the final cooking process. *For those of you on fat or fat-carbo-*

hydrate restriction, do not dredge meat in flour but sear in ribbed-bottom skillet; drain all fat and then place in pressure cooker, but remember flavor will be finer using the slow-simmer method.

BEEF STEW
8 Servings

2 tablespoons vegetable oil
2 pounds *lean* stew beef
3 tablespoons flour
¼ cup chopped onion
1 minced garlic clove
Pepper
¼ cup water
¼ cup red table wine
¼ teaspoon thyme
1 tablespoon parsley
1 small bay leaf, crumbled
6 medium potatoes, cubed
1 cup cubed rutabaga
2 cups peas, fresh or canned without added sodium

Heat oil in pressure cooker. Meanwhile wipe meat with damp cloth and trim excess fat. Put flour into bag; add cut-up stew meat and shake vigorously to coat. Put meat, onions, and garlic into pressure cooker and lightly brown; turn as needed. Sprinkle lightly with pepper. Heat water, wine, and seasonings in small saucepan; then add to pressure cooker. Cover and cook as directed for your particular cooker (about 15 to 20 minutes). Add vegetables and cook 5 minutes longer. (Canned peas should be heated separately and added just before serving.) Add salt for regulars.

ONE SERVING (3 oz. meat, cooked weight)	TOTAL RECIPE	
80	637	milligrams sodium
19	149	grams total fat
7	58	grams saturated fat
21	164	grams carbohydrate
361	2885	calories

VARIATIONS

Tomato juice (low sodium dietetic) may be substituted for wine and water.

Sweet basil may be substituted for thyme. Omit bay leaf.

LOW SATURATED FAT VARIATION

Use only top round for stew meat. Trim cut-up meat of all visible fat. Do not dredge in flour but broil or pan-broil in ribbed-bottom skillet. Pour off fat; then proceed as in Basic Recipe. After meat is cooked, swirl ice cube in liquid and remove hardened fat. Add vegetables and cook 5 minutes longer. If desired, thicken gravy with flour mixed with cold water. If no sodium restrictions, regular canned or frozen peas may be used, and add salt to taste.

One serving: 3 grams saturated fat.

ACCOMPANIMENT

HERB DUMPLINGS
6 Servings

Are you looking for something pungent and different for that pot roast or stew dinner? If so, why not try herb dumplings, keeping the seasoning of your meat on the light side, in so far as herbs are concerned.

1 cup all-purpose flour
2 teaspoons low sodium baking powder
Pinch sugar
½ teaspoon powdered savory
¼ teaspoon thyme
½ cup nonfat milk

Sift dry ingredients together and blend in liquid. Drop by spoonfuls onto your meat. (Not on the liquid of the meat if you would avoid soggy dumplings.) Cook 10 minutes with kettle uncovered; 10 minutes with cover. Serve at once with a light sprinkling of salt for the regulars.

ONE SERVING	TOTAL RECIPE	
11	67	milligrams sodium
trace	1	gram total fat
trace	trace	gram saturated fat
16	96	grams carbohydrate
74	445	calories

VARIATION

Herbs may be omitted for plain dumplings. Increase sugar to ¼ teaspoon. For a low sodium count, use low sodium nonfat milk.

GROUND BEEF

The good old "ground round" can be worked overtime on this diet. Moderate in sodium content, it lends itself to any number of combinations when you tire of it plain. It is one of the first to get started with when the rules and regulations all seem a bit confusing. Its good flavor and ease of preparation recommend its use. Of course, ground beef need not be ground top round steak, except for low saturated fat diets. Stew meat, neck, rump, flank, and foreshank, all can be ground for use for general sodium-restricted diets. Have your butcher trim beef before grinding. Be sure to specify the grind you want for your particular meat dish. In addition to the recipes given below, see Tamale Pie in the Veal section.

BEEF PATTIES
4 Patties

1 pound *lean* ground beef
½ teaspoon thyme
½ teaspoon rosemary
1 teaspoon minced parsley
½ teaspoon black pepper

Blend ingredients in a mixing bowl. Shape into patties and broil. Turn once. Sprinkle with salt for the regulars; serve. Or you may pan-broil in ribbed-bottom skillet.

ONE SERVING
(3 oz. meat, cooked weight)

51	milligrams sodium
10	grams total fat
5	grams saturated fat
negligible	grams carbohydrate
185	calories

VARIATION

Put a slice of Bermuda onion and a slice of tomato on top of shaped beef patties. Lightly season with pepper and broil.

LOW SATURATED FAT VARIATION

Use only top round steak and trim off all visible fat. Oil may be used according to daily allowance.

One serving, without oil: 3 grams saturated fat.

MEAT BALLS

5 Servings

We are indebted to Mrs. Finn Taaje, of Los Gatos, California, for this old Norwegian recipe, adapted to the purposes of this dietary. The spices give it an unusual flavor.

1 pound *lean* ground beef, ground twice
½ cup low sodium bread crumbs (at least 1 day old)
2 tablespoons minced onion
⅛ teaspoon ginger
⅛ teaspoon nutmeg
½ teaspoon black pepper
1 tablespoon vegetable oil

Mix all together in a mixing bowl and shape into small, round balls. Brown in heavy skillet, lightly oiled with 1 tablespoon vegetable oil. Cover with water (about 2 cups). Cover pan tightly and let simmer for 1½ hours. Salt for regulars when you serve portions.

ONE SERVING
(2½ oz. meat, cooked weight)

60	milligrams sodium
12	grams total fat
4	grams saturated fat
5	grams carbohydrate
215	calories

LOW SATURATED FAT VARIATION

Use top round of beef, trimmed of all visible fat before grinding. Brown under broiler or in ribbed-bottom skillet. Oil may be added to mixture according to daily allowance. If gravy is allowed, swirl ice cube in liquid and remove hardened fat. *One serving, without oil: 2 grams saturated fat.*

HERBAL MEAT LOAF

6 Servings

It is particularly important to make a good meat loaf in restricted cookery, because it is not only good hot when first prepared, but is a welcome addition for a sandwich filling and for cold cuts. There is a real herb accent to this meat loaf.

1 pound *lean* ground beef
1 shredded wheat biscuit, crumbled fine
¼ cup minced onion
1 egg (optional)
¼ teaspoon summer savory
½ teaspoon sweet basil
½ teaspoon black pepper
¼ cup nonfat milk
¼ cup red table wine

Put ingredients in a mixing bowl, mix thoroughly and shape into a loaf. Put in a lightly oiled baking pan, or bread pan. Bake in a preheated 325° (slow) oven about 60 minutes, depending upon size of loaf and degree of doneness wanted. This makes a fairly moist loaf. Sprinkle salt on portions for the regulars when meat is served.

ONE SERVING
(2 oz. meat, cooked weight)
With egg

66	milligrams sodium
9	grams total fat
4	grams saturated fat
6	grams carbohydrate
195	calories

VARIATIONS

A tomato-base sauce may be made and served over the meat for variety.

One-half teaspoon allspice may be substituted for savory and basil.

Low sodium dietetic chili sauce may be substituted for milk and wine.

Then there is dill to substitute for the savory, rosemary, thyme combination.

For curry lovers, 1 teaspoonful added to meat and other ingredients will give it a rich and aromatic flavor.

LOW SATURATED FAT VARIATION

Use only ground top round steak or chuck when an all-beef meat loaf is your choice. To help the pocketbook as well as the fat content, try the recipe with ½ pound ground top round steak and ½ pound ground veal. Be sure to have butcher trim meat of all visible fat. Use egg white only for binding loaf. For an interesting variation, omit shredded wheat biscuit and use ¼ cup chopped walnuts with an equal amount seedless raisins. Use ½ teaspoon savory and ½ teaspoon allspice in place of seasonings in Basic Recipe.

One serving, all-beef with nuts and raisins: 2 grams saturated fat; ½ teaspoon vegetable oil.

PIN WHEELS

6 Servings

Pin wheels are sometimes called "porcupine meat balls" because of the rice "bristles." They are ever so pretty and are as tasty as they are attractive. If you have unexpected guests and are a little short on meat, remember Pin Wheels because they do stretch that meat.

For 6 balls you will need:

1 pound *lean* ground beef
¼ cup minced onion
¼ cup raw brown rice
¼ teaspoon vegetable oil
¼ teaspoon thyme
1 teaspoon parsley, minced
¼ teaspoon black pepper
2 tablespoons flour

Mix well and form into balls. Lightly flour with 2 tablespoons flour. Now put into a Dutch oven, or heavy skillet, 2 tablespoons vegetable oil. Brown the meat mixture in it until golden in color. Remove from pan, but do not remove drippings, as they form the sauce base.

You will need:

¼ cup onion, minced
1 garlic clove, split lengthwise and put on wooden pick
¼ teaspoon thyme
⅛ teaspoon mace
4 peppercorns
2 cups low sodium dietetic tomato juice
¼ cup Chianti

Put onion, garlic, and thyme into drippings and cook slowly for 5 minutes. Add liquids and other seasonings and bring to gentle boil. Now add meat so that sauce is distributed evenly. Cover and let simmer slowly for 40 minutes. Remove garlic and serve with rice. Add salt for the regulars.

ONE SERVING
(2 oz. meat, cooked weight)

56	milligrams sodium
13	grams total fat
4	grams saturated fat
14	grams carbohydrate
247	calories

LOW SATURATED FAT VARIATION

Omit flouring of meat balls. Oven- or pan-broil in ribbed-bottom skillet until brown. Place in Dutch oven or other heavy-duty pan and cover with sauce as outlined. Oil may be added to meat ball mixture according to daily allowance.

One serving, without oil: 2 grams saturated fat.

HAMBURGER-CORN LOAF
6 Servings

This is a change from the good old meat loaf, and as good cold as it is hot.

1 pound ground *lean* beef
1 cup cream-style corn, canned low sodium dietetic
1 teaspoon minced onion
1 egg
1 tablespoon vegetable oil

1 tablespoon parsley
½ shredded wheat biscuit
¼ teaspoon rosemary
¼ teaspoon black pepper
½ cup sauterne

Put ingredients in mixing bowl and mix together well. Put into an oiled loaf pan and bake in a preheated 325° (slow) oven about 60 minutes. This makes a solid loaf. It may be served plain or with a tomato sauce. Add salt for the regulars.

ONE SERVING
(2 oz. meat, cooked weight)
Without sauce

63	milligrams sodium
11	grams total fat
4	grams saturated fat
11	grams carbohydrate
229	calories

LOW SATURATED FAT VARIATION

Follow Basic Recipe except substitute 1 egg white for whole egg. If no sodium restriction, use regular canned corn and add salt to taste.

One serving: 2 grams saturated fat; ½ teaspoon vegetable oil.

LAMB

So good in almost any form, but higher in sodium count than beef. Plan to serve lower count vegetables when lamb is on the menu. Those of you with saturated fat restrictions will want to choose leg of lamb for your recipes because of its lower fat content. Allow 2 servings per pound of uncooked *lean* meat with bone or 4 servings per pound if boned.

LEG OF LAMB
5-pound *lean* leg, 10 Servings

Wipe meat with damp cloth and cook in open baking pan, fat side up. Cut a few slices of onion over top to give color to your drippings for gravy (these can be removed before making). Roast in a preheated 325° (slow) oven, following the directions for your range for cooking time per pound. For gravy, skim off fat and allow 3 tablespoons flour to 1 pint liquid. One tenth equals dieter's share, if allowed. Add salt for the regulars.

ONE SERVING
(3 oz. meat, cooked weight)
Without gravy

61	milligrams sodium
6	grams total fat
3	grams saturated fat
negligible	grams carbohydrate
158	calories

VARIATIONS

Have your butcher remove the tiny glands at the shank end and into this hole put your herbs, Italian-fashion. A sprig of fresh rosemary, a slice of onion, and a clove of garlic are excellent used in this fashion.

Or, if you prefer to baste, the following sauce is one of our favorites:

½ cup water
½ cup sauterne wine

1 teaspoon dried rosemary
⅛ teaspoon thyme
½ clove garlic
1 teaspoon chopped onion

This is sufficient for a 5-pound roast. Baste at least 4 times during the roasting period. Remove garlic before thickening for gravy — and be sure to portion that gravy carefully, if it is allowed.

SHISH KABOB
(Lamb Kabob; adopted from the Armenian)
8 Servings

Allow 2 servings per pound of lean raw meat with bone or 4 servings if boned.

When using leg of lamb, remove fat, gristle, and bone. Cut meat into squares 1½ to 2 inches in size. Put into a large flat bowl or pan, and add:

1 cup fresh onions, cut in squares, or small canned onions,
   low sodium dietetic
2 tablespoons vegetable oil
¼ cup white table wine (or sherry is excellent)
½ teaspoon pepper
½ teaspoon rosemary

Marinate overnight. Put meat with or without onions on skewers and broil over charcoal fire until crisp and brown on all sides, or broil in oven or rotisserie. Serve with rice. Pass the salt for the regulars.

ONE SERVING
(3 oz. meat, cooked weight)
With onions; without rice

63	milligrams sodium
10	grams total fat
3	grams saturated fat
2	grams carbohydrate
205	calories

One serving: ¾ teaspoon vegetable oil

VARIATION

Other vegetables may be threaded onto skewers with meat. Try cherry tomatoes, fresh mushrooms, green pepper slices, or squares of new potatoes seasoned with dill weed.

LAMB-IN-FOIL DINNER
4 Servings

Another Sunkist Growers' kitchen-tested recipe — delicious, a complete meal in itself, so easy to prepare, and only one pan to wash.

1 pound *lean* boneless lamb
1 medium onion
2 medium potatoes
1 zucchini squash, or 2 summer squashes
½ clove garlic, minced
½ teaspoon oregano
½ teaspoon sweet basil
2 tablespoons chopped parsley
Aluminum foil, cut into four 9 x 15-inch rectangles
4 slices lemon, ¼ inch thick

Cut meat into 1-inch cubes; cut each of the vegetables diagonally into 4 slices. Sprinkle meat and vegetables with seasonings and divide equally into 4 portions; pile or layer in center of each foil rectangle. Top each with lemon slice. Bring up lengthwise sides of foil. Seal together by making 2 folds toward center of package. At each end make 2 folds toward the center. (Be sure packages are airtight to avoid loss of steam and juices.) Lay them in shallow baking pan; bake in a preheated 450° (very hot) oven for 1 hour or until meat is tender when pierced with a fork. Salt for those without sodium restrictions.

ONE SERVING
(3 oz. meat, cooked weight)

67	milligrams sodium
6	grams total fat
3	grams saturated fat
15	grams carbohydrate
225	calories

PORK

Pork is lower in sodium content than beef, lamb, or veal, but it is relatively fat. If you are on a restricted fat diet, you may find pork on your Don't list, or may be limited to the use of loin only, trimmed of all visible fat. If you are one of the lucky ones and can have it on your fare, you have exciting eating indeed. The rich flavor of pork, whether it be choice roast of pork or one of the lesser dishes, offers you an opportunity to use many of your own recipes and perhaps experiment with herbal seasonings. Pork lends itself particularly well to such treatment.

BAKED PORK CHOPS WITH RICE
6 Servings

1 cup brown rice
6 *lean* pork chops (about 2 pounds)
6 slices Bermuda onion
6 thick slices tomatoes
6 slices green bell pepper
Freshly ground pepper
2 cups hot tomato juice (low sodium dietetic)

Cover rice with cold water and soak for at least 3 hours. Then place over low heat and bring to a boil to tenderize. Meanwhile, trim chops of all visible fat and lightly brown in skillet or broiler. Arrange chops in a large casserole or skillet and top with slice of onion, tomato, and green pepper. Lightly pepper. Cover each chop with drained rice, making a little mound on each one. There will be extra rice to fill spaces between chops. Pour tomato juice around meat-rice combination. Cover and bake in a preheated 325° (slow) oven, 50 to 60 minutes. Do not undercook. Add salt for those without sodium restrictions at time of serving. *Those with saturated fat restrictions will want to brown chops in ribbed-bottom skillet or in broiler so as to allow fat to drip away from meat.*

One of the beauties of this dish is that it can be prepared sometime before use and baked when the rest of the meal is under way. Peas or asparagus combine well with it. Add a piece of broiled fruit, a tossed salad, and a light dessert, and you have a company meal at minimum effort.

ONE SERVING
(3 oz. meat, cooked weight)

66	milligrams sodium
13	grams total fat
3	grams saturated fat
21	grams carbohydrate
380	calories

White or wild rice may be substituted for brown rice. Ala, the new Fisher Flouring Company's bulgur wheat, is a delicious substitute for rice in this recipe.

Basil, caraway, or thyme may be sprinkled over chops when an herbal flavor is desired.

AMERICAN CHOP SUEY

3 Servings

Chop suey has become legend in the various Chinatowns of the country, and yet it is not a native dish in the true sense of the word. In fact, it is unknown in the Chinese language, and is considered the corruption of culinary tradition.

Its characteristic ingredients are bean sprouts, onions, meat, and soy sauce. We have to leave out the soy sauce because of its salt flavor. Substitute lemon juice for zest, if desired.

2 tablespoons vegetable oil
½ cup chopped onions
2 cups fresh bean sprouts
1 tablespoon lemon juice
½ pound *lean* loin of pork, shredded crosswise
1 teaspoon sugar
1½ tablespoons cornstarch
¼ cup water
¼ cup blanched almonds, slivered

Warm oil in heavy skillet. Add onion and cook 10 minutes, stirring occasionally to prevent scorching. Wash bean sprouts; add them, dripping, to skillet. Sprinkle with lemon juice. Stir to prevent scorching, and add a tablespoonful or so of water if necessary. Cook just until tender (about 5 minutes). Pour onto warm platter and set in warming oven. Fry pork slivers in remaining oil mixture. Cover and let simmer until thoroughly done. Return bean sprout mixture to skillet and reheat. Meanwhile, make a glaze by blending sugar, cornstarch, and water; cook for 5 minutes. Pour over meat-bean sprout combination. Stir in almonds. Serve onto platter. Rice is a natural accompaniment for chop suey. Add salt and soy sauce for the regulars. *Those with saturated fat restrictions will need to brown pork in broiler or in ribbed-bottom skillet to allow fat to drip away from meat; then add to vegetables.*

ONE SERVING
(2 oz. meat, cooked weight)
Without rice

60	milligrams sodium
15	grams total fat
7	grams saturated fat
14	grams carbohydrate
349	calories

One serving: 2 teaspoons vegetable oil.

VARIATIONS

Broccoli may be substituted for the bean sprouts.
Veal, chicken, or turkey may be substituted for pork.

SWEET-AND-SOUR PORK, SAN FRANCISCO STYLE

6 Servings

1 pound boneless, *lean* pork loin
¼ teaspoon low sodium meat tenderizer
1 tablespoon vegetable oil
1 large, firm tomato

1 fresh onion
½ cup green pepper, cut into ½-inch squares

Trim all visible fat from pork; cut into ¾-inch squares. Sprinkle with seasoned meat tenderizer (or use ½ teaspoon salt and 1 teaspoon light soy sauce if sodium is not restricted). Heat oil in skillet, and brown meat on all sides, using a ribbed-bottom skillet. Cut tomato and onion into 8 sections. Remove meat from skillet and in a small skillet brown onion in pan drippings (or vegetable oil). Add meat, tomato, and green pepper; cook until fork-tender and there is no pinkness in pork pieces. Remove from heat, and let stand while you prepare Sweet-and-Sour Sauce.

SWEET-AND-SOUR SAUCE

½ cup vinegar
½ cup light brown sugar
1 tablespoon cornstarch
¼ cup pineapple juice
¼ cup fresh or frozen orange juice
¼ cup dietetic low sodium tomato juice or paste
12 pineapple chunks

Blend first three ingredients until they are a smooth paste, using one of the new lower-in-calorie brown sugars if sodium regimen requires. Gradually blend in pineapple and orange juice, stirring thoroughly to blend. Add tomato juice. Add to meat skillet. Cook over low heat until pork is done. Toss in pineapple chunks; let heat through, about 5 minutes.

Serve over steamed rice. Pass the soy sauce for the regulars. Let them salt to taste.

ONE SERVING
(2 oz. meat, cooked weight)
With sauce, but without rice

64	milligrams sodium
11	grams total fat
3	grams saturated fat
31	grams carbohydrate
287	calories

VARIATION

For dieters having to observe carbohydrate restriction, use fresh or water-pack pineapple.

VEAL

Veal is one of the meats highest in sodium content but is low in fat content. Many cuts offer you variety in the way you serve it. The rump is usually considered the most flavorsome and coveted piece for roasting. It can be cooked plain or with herbs to enrich its natural good flavor. Boneless rolled shoulder, rib or loin chops, Frenched cutlets, steaks, shank, and breast all lend themselves to braising. Chops, cutlets, and steaks may, of course, be pan-broiled or oven-baked.

VEAL STEAKS, BAKED
8 Servings

Have your butcher cut 2 or 3 lean steaks (round or cutlets) weighing 2 pounds. Prepare as follows:

½ cup flour
½ teaspoon fresh pepper
Steaks cut in 8 pieces
5 large mushrooms, sliced
½ cup nonfat milk

Put flour, pepper, and steaks into a brown paper bag. Shake until well blended. Remove from bag. Meanwhile lightly oil a shallow baking dish and place steaks in it. Sprinkle mushrooms and nonfat milk over the top. Bake in a preheated 325° (slow) oven for 45 minutes, or until thoroughly cooked. Add salt for those without sodium restriction.

ONE SERVING
(3 oz. meat, cooked weight)

62	milligrams sodium
9	grams total fat
4	grams saturated fat
7	grams carbohydrate
120	calories

VARIATIONS

For variety, serve with low sodium dietetic tomato juice heated and slightly thickened. Add ⅛ teaspoon thyme for extra flavor.

Or substitute 1 crumbled shredded wheat for the flour and ¼ cup chopped onion for the mushroom. Add ⅛ teaspoon sweet basil.

Or substitute low sodium dietetic tomato juice for the nonfat milk. Sprinkle with 3 tablespoons chopped parsley and 1 teaspoon chopped chives, 1 tablespoon lemon juice.

Or substitute ¼ cup dry white wine and ¼ cup low sodium dietetic tomato juice for the nonfat milk. Gently heat. Add ½ teaspoon thyme and a dash of cayenne. Pour over meat and baste at least 3 times during baking period. (Cover your pan for this method.)

Or put a slice of Bermuda onion on the top of each steak and drip lightly with white wine and proceed as above with the basting.

Or use bread steaks in crumbled shredded wheat, dip in non-fat milk and bake to doneness.

VEAL CUTLETS IN WINE
6 Servings

6 small cutlets (about 1½ pounds *lean* boneless meat)
½ cup flour
½ teaspoon pepper
2 tablespoons vegetable oil
1 cup sliced fresh mushrooms
1 clove minced garlic (optional)
2 cups cut-up fresh tomatoes *or* 1½ cups canned tomatoes
   (low sodium dietetic)
1 tablespoon minced parsley
1 cup sauterne

Allow 1 cutlet for each serving; wipe with damp cloth. Dredge in flour seasoned with pepper and place in hot skillet with 1 tablespoon oil. Turn to brown on both sides. Sauté mushrooms in 1 tablespoon oil in small skillet for 5 minutes; add garlic and simmer for 5 minutes longer. Combine with cutlets and add remaining ingredients. Cover skillet and gently simmer for 45 minutes. (Check to avoid scorching.) Add salt for regulars.

ONE SERVING
(3 oz. meat, cooked weight)

65	milligrams sodium
14	grams total fat
4	grams saturated fat
13	grams carbohydrate
222	calories

LOW SATURATED FAT VARIATION

Brown cutlets in ribbed-bottom skillet or in broiler. Drain off drippings, then proceed as in Basic Recipe.

One serving: 4 grams saturated fat; 1 teaspoon vegetable oil.

PINEAPPLE-VEAL PATTIES
6 Servings

2 cups ground leftover cooked veal
¼ cup crumbled low sodium bread crumbs
¼ cup tomato juice, canned low sodium dietetic
¼ cup minced onion
⅛ teaspoon black pepper
⅛ teaspoon thyme
1 egg, lightly beaten
6 pineapple slices
3 tablespoons vegetable oil
⅓ cup light brown sugar
½ cup pineapple sirup

Combine meat, bread crumbs, tomato juice, seasonings, and egg; mix all together. Shape into 6 medium patties. Place on pineapple slices in lightly oiled casserole. Combine vegetable oil, brown sugar, and pineapple juice; spoon over patties saving some for basting. Cover; bake in a preheated 325° (slow) oven for 30 minutes. Uncover and bake for 10 minutes longer, or until lightly browned. Baste once or twice with liquid mixture. Add salt for regulars at time of serving.

For a lower carbohydrate content, use water-pack pineapple and a few drops of substitute sugar for brown sugar in dieter's portion.

ONE SERVING
(2⅔ oz. meat, cooked weight)

76	milligrams sodium
16	grams total fat
5	grams saturated fat
29	grams carbohydrate
357	calories

LOW SATURATED FAT VARIATION

Follow Basic Recipe except substitute 1 egg white for 1 whole egg. If no sodium restrictions, use regular tomato juice and add salt to taste.

One serving: 5 grams saturated fat; 1½ teaspoons vegetable oil.

TAMALE PIE
6 Servings

This tamale pie has a very Mexican flavor and is a morale builder for the person on restricted eating because it makes him feel he can have one of the good old standbys. It can be popular with you, too, because it's a good dollar stretcher, in that only three quarters of a pound of meat is used to serve 6. (You may substitute low sodium milk, if restrictions require, or subtract milk from your daily allowance.)

3 cups nonfat milk
1 cup brown granular wheat cereal, uncooked

1 tablespoon vegetable oil
3 tablespoons grated onion
½ pound *lean* ground beef
¼ pound *lean* ground veal
1 cup fresh tomatoes, cut small
⅛ teaspoon black pepper
1 teaspoon curry powder

Heat nonfat milk. Add cereal slowly, stirring constantly to prevent lumping. Cook until thickened; then place over boiling water. Cover and continue cooking for 15 minutes.

Meanwhile sauté onion in oil about 5 minutes, until lightly brown. Add meat and cook until browned. Stir in tomatoes, pepper, and curry powder.

Line a lightly oiled casserole with three-fourths of the cooked cereal. Add meat mixture, and top with remaining cereal. Bake in a preheated 350° (moderate) oven 30 to 40 minutes, until topping is golden brown. Add salt to regular portions.

ONE SERVING
(1½ oz. meat, cooked weight)

107	milligrams sodium
10	grams total fat
3	grams saturated fat
21	grams carbohydrate
227	calories

SCALLOPINI
4 Servings

Strips of veal steak, combined with fine seasonings, offer you a tasty and rich morsel for your meat dish. Scallopini rates top billing with us even with its restrictions (and they are not many). The secret of this delicacy rests with the cooking. It must simmer at very low heat so the herbs and sauce have ample time to permeate the whole.

Have butcher cut thin *lean* veal steaks, allowing ⅓ pound per person, or ¼ pound if boneless.

8 2-inch strips lean veal steaks
¼ cup flour
½ teaspoon pepper
2 tablespoons vegetable oil
1 clove garlic on wooden stick
¼ cup chopped onion
½ cup water
½ cup sauterne
1 cup low sodium dietetic tomato juice
½ teaspoon rosemary
¼ cup minced parsley

Wipe meat with damp cloth; pound out each piece until it is half its original thickness. Roll in peppered flour and let stand for an hour or more. Put oil into heated skillet. Add meat; brown. Remove meat to warm platter. Put garlic and onion into skillet and gently simmer for 10 minutes. Return meat to skillet. Add ½ cup water slightly warmed. Meanwhile simmer over low heat the remaining ingredients; then pour over meat. Cover and simmer for at least 1 hour, or until meat is fork-tender. Add water if necessary to keep from scorching. The sauce will be thick at time of serving when you may add salt for the regulars if you think they will require it. This is so flavorsome that it may never be missed by dieter or the regulars.

ONE SERVING
(3 oz. meat, cooked weight)

60	milligrams sodium
16	grams total fat
4	grams saturated fat
10	grams carbohydrate
218	calories

LOW SATURATED FAT VARIATION

Substitute regular tomato juice for low sodium dietetic. Do not roll in flour or use oil for browning. Rather, pan-broil in ribbed-bottom skillet or oven-broil; pour off drippings. Oil may be added according to diet requirements.

One serving, without oil: 4 grams saturated fat.

MEAT STRETCHERS

With the sodium and fat content of meat as high as it is, it just seems plain prudent to use meat stretchers often. By so doing, the person on the restricted program does not feel that he is being deprived of too much, and you, on the planning end, are able to save some of the precious count.

Stretcher devices have been used for long years by good homemakers. Some of the popular ones are:

1. *Hash* with potatoes, onions, and leftover vegetables
2. *Stew* with vegetables, macaroni, dumplings, or rice
3. *Meat pies* with vegetables and a biscuit or mashed potato topping

4. *Meat loaf* with low sodium bread crumbs, or crumbled shredded wheat, low sodium dietetic tomato juice, and egg
5. *Casserole dishes*, combining meat with vegetables
6. *Patties* with low sodium bread crumbs, mashed, or ground potatoes
7. *Hearty soups* with meat or fish stock base
8. *Rice* with meat balls, such as Pin Wheels, and accompanying sauce
9. *Curries* served over rice or with baked potatoes
10. *Meats stretched with sauces,* as in Scallopini
11. *Meats stretched with low sodium white sauce,* as in croquettes

WHAT TO SERVE WITH MEATS

Think of the sauces, conserves, and specialties which combine with meats for appetite appeal, color and texture contrasts, and flavor pleasure. If carbohydrate is restricted, use fresh or water-pack fruits and sweeten with allowed sugar substitute. Listed below are some of the combinations we have enjoyed:

With beef: Try cranberry sauce, broiled fruit, plain or with jelly centers

With lamb: Try currant jelly, mint sauce or jelly, cucumber sauce, wine jelly

With pork: Try spiced apple sauce, broiled pineapple slices or chunks, candied apples

With veal: Try cranberry jelly, currant jelly, mushroom sauce, broiled fruits

FAT-RESTRICTED BROWN GRAVY
1 Cup

3 tablespoons flour
1 low sodium beef bouillon cube
¼ teaspoon onion powder (not salt)
¾ cup boiling water
¼ cup red table wine

Brown flour in skillet. Combine crumbled bouillon cube, onion powder, and water; add slowly to browned flour to make smooth paste. Cook, stirring constantly to avoid lumping. When gravy begins to thicken add wine and reheat, but do not boil. If no sodium restrictions, use regular bouillon cube and add salt and other seasonings to taste.

TOTAL RECIPE
With wine

23	milligrams sodium
trace	gram total fat
18	grams carbohydrate
131	calories

VARIATIONS

Wine may be omitted and ½ teaspoon low sodium Worcestershire sauce substituted for the wine (regular Worcestershire sauce may be used if no sodium restrictions); or you may substitute herbs of your choice (sweet basil, garlic, and oregano are some of our favorites); or a sprinkling of seasoned low sodium meat tenderizer (regular meat tenderizer may be used if no sodium restrictions) may be added for zest.

8

CHICKEN EVERY SUNDAY

No WONDER BEST-SELLERS are written about it and restaurants selected for gourmet listings because of it! Chicken is just that good. It has been, for the stretch of our memories and more, the *pièce de résistance* of the Sunday dinner, whether that be on Sunday or some other day. In other words, chicken is a special occasion delicacy — to be served the most honored guest or as a family treat. Henry IV of France said at his coronation, "I wish every peasant may have a chicken in his pot every Sunday."

Chicken is good *au naturel,* yielding its succulent juices for good eating, and is out of this world when combined with a bit of garlic, herb, and wine. In other words, chicken is good — whether it be boiled, baked, or broiled, plain or with the enrichment of added seasonings — any time you want fine and pleasurable eating.

SUGGESTIONS:

1. Since chicken is lower in fat than meat, plan to use it often. The American Heart Association states in its *Planning Fat Controlled Meals for 1200 and 1800 Calories*, revised, 1972, that poultry without skin — chicken, turkey, cornish hen, and squab — fish, and any lean veal should be served at eleven out of the fourteen lunches and dinners each week where fat control is essential to the dietary regimen.

Measure the amount of chicken and gravy to be served with respect to the total sodium or fat content allowed on your list.

2. An average serving is 3 ounces, cooked weight. This equals half a breast of chicken or a leg and thigh of a 2½ to 3 pound chicken. Allow an extra ounce or so, raw weight, as shrinkage occurs in cooking.

3. Never serve poultry skin to a sodium-, fat-control, or fat-carbohydrate control dieter. Dark meat contains more sodium and fat than light meat but most diets allow a choice of either or a combination. For best results, skin before cooking and marinate, or baste during cooking. Use dry heat for young and tender poultry, moist heat for the old and lean.

4. Use moderate heat for tender and juicy chicken. This holds for poultry of all ages, from the youngest bird to the oldest hen. High heat hardens and toughens the protein of the chicken, shrinks it more, and lessens its juiciness.

5. Do not start cooking chicken too long before it is to be served.

6. Vary your cooking method according to age and fatness of the chicken. Broiling, frying and oven-roasting lend themselves to *young* and *well-fattened* chickens. Braising or casserole dishes should be the choice if poultry is *young* and *lean.* *Old hens* take to the stew pot, for fricasseeing or steaming. On diet programs where gravy must be omitted, steam, rather than fricassee, as most of the flavor goes into the liquid.

7. When roasting a chicken, cut an unpeeled lemon into

four wedges and place inside cavity. When baking chicken pieces, vary the flavor by the addition of lemon-cartwheel slices on top.

8. Try some of the herbs or herb-wine combinations for high flavor and juicy goodness, if your count will permit. Green pepper, bay leaf, onion, and unsalted tomato juice; thyme, rosemary, and parsley; curry powder, onion, and vegetable oil; sherry-herb basting sauce or lemon juice-herb sauce; a pinch of cinnamon, ginger, or pitted prunes with dry red or white wines — many combinations of herbs, seasonings, and wines will add rich goodness to your chicken dishes. Give the chicken that European flair by using herbs and wines for flavor — stretch it (and so cut down the sodium and fat content) by combining with macaroni, rice, corn, or a macédoine of mixed vegetables and fruits.

9. From this day on, never let it be said that you use sage in stuffing for chicken or turkey. Try the gentler summer savory just once to become a convert to its subtle goodness. Combine with sweet marjoram, thyme, onions, green pepper, and vegetable oil. Above all, avoid mixed "poultry seasoning" as if it were a plague. It is much too strong for your chicken dishes.

10. Wrap chicken in aluminum foil before cooking to seal in the juices and eliminate all basting, if you like a steamed bird. Unwrap the last 20 minutes of cooking, if you want a brown outside.

11. Have handy the good old metal tongs, while cooking, for easy handling of the chicken.

Your method of cookery will depend upon the dish you want to concoct. We say "concoct" advisedly, because chicken cookery allows all kinds of interesting specialties. And these specialties are a boon to you, if you want to make your dieter's portion appear big, and yet remain within the allowable amount.

When you elect to *fry* or *broil* those young tender birds from 6 to 12 weeks old, weighing 1½ to 3 pounds, remove skin, wipe with a damp cloth, and dry; brush lightly with unsalted special margarine or vegetable oil (depending upon your diet restrictions) and cook.

For the still young (5 to 9 months old) and well-fleshed chickens, try *stuffing and roasting* in an open pan. Place chicken breast side down in pan, and cover lightly with aluminum wrap (or follow suggestion #10, page 124). Follow your own cooking directions as to temperature and cooking time.

REMEMBER: *Braising and fricasseeing* are the time-honored methods of chicken cookery for birds past their prime. When you stew your bird, you do so to tenderize it; in so doing you cause the chicken to give up some of its characteristic flavor to the liquid. *This can be recaptured only through the gravy, which, if allowed to your diet, must be calculated and measured carefully.*

FOR SODIUM RESTRICTION, DO NOT USE:

Chicken gravies, without consent of physician, except Fat-Restricted Chicken Gravy (page 133)

Eviscerated frozen chicken, unless you first make sure it has not been treated in a light salt bath before freezing

Salt

"Spanish" sauces of the commercial sort

Worcestershire sauce, except low sodium dietetic

Skin of chicken or turkey

FOR SATURATED FAT RESTRICTION, DO NOT USE:

Commercially prepared chicken dishes or canned chicken unless packed without gravy or fat (without added salt, too, if on sodium restriction)

Regular gravies, as these are fat-rich. If drippings are to be used, chill gravy in refrigerator until fat solidifies and then remove and skim off fat, or better still, use recipe on page 133

Skin of chicken, turkey, Cornish hen or squab

BROILERS

4 Servings — (2-pound broiler — dressed weight)

Skin chicken and wipe dry. Rub with cut garlic clove and sprinkle with 2 teaspoons lemon juice. Brush lightly with ½ teaspoon vegetable oil and ¼ teaspoon fresh black pepper. Spray the bottom of your baster with a nonstick vegetable "spray-on," and put the chicken on it, "skin side" away from the heat. Sprinkle with ⅛ teaspoon savory and ⅛ teaspoon rosemary for each half to be cooked.

As you turn broilers, baste with wine sauce made from ½ cup Riesling and 1 tablespoon vegetable oil. This should be done at 10- to 15-minute intervals. Keep your basting sauce warm but not boiling.

Allow between 30 and 40 minutes for cooking. Fork-test for tenderness and doneness. It is important that chicken be thoroughly cooked.

Skim drippings of excess fat by swirling ice cube in liquid. Thicken for gravy. Allow 1½ tablespoons flour to 1 cup liquid for 1 cup gravy; cook at least 5 minutes over low heat. If dieter is allowed gravy, portion carefully. One-fourth equals special dieter's share. Add salt for those without sodium restrictions.

ONE SERVING
(3 oz. white and dark meat,
cooked weight)
Without gravy

60	milligrams sodium
7	grams total fat
1	gram saturated fat
negligible	grams carbohydrate
189	calories

VARIATIONS

Scatter minced herbs directly on broilers when high flavor is wanted. An epicurean treat.

Many herb-wine combinations will add character to your broiled chickens. For starters, try savory and thyme; rosemary and garlic; onion, vegetable oil, and garlic with wine — slightly warmed. Never add cold blends. Vary your wine-base sauces, too. Sherry is a wonderful substitute for the dry, white wines, when you tire of them, and gives body and richness to broilers.

BAKED CHICKEN

4 Servings — (2-pound fryer — dressed weight)

2-pound fryer, cut into serving pieces or quartered, and skinned
1 teaspoon vegetable oil
¼ teaspoon black pepper
½ teaspoon tarragon
½ teaspoon paprika
1 teaspoon vegetable oil
1 tablespoon water
¼ cup Chablis
Parsley sprigs

Place chicken on rack in baking pan. Brush pieces lightly with 1 teaspoon oil; sprinkle with pepper, tarragon, and paprika. Bake 40 minutes, or until tender and done in a preheated 350° (moderate) oven. Baste at least 4 times with warm white table wine. If gravy is allowed, skim off all fat by swirling ice cube in liquid or chilling in refrigerator; or make special gravy (page 133). Garnish with parsley sprigs and salt for those without sodium restrictions.

ONE SERVING
(3 oz. white and dark meat,
cooked weight)
Without gravy

67	milligrams sodium
5	grams total fat
1	gram saturated fat
negligible	grams carbohydrate
162	calories

VARIATIONS

Substitute 2 teaspoons lemon or lime juice for wine.

Combine 2 teaspoons lemon or lime juice with ½ tablespoon of chopped parsley and green pepper, 2 teaspoons chopped onion, 1 clove finely chopped garlic, and 1 teaspoon vegetable oil. Mix well; baste over chicken.

Foil-wrap and bake for 30 minutes; unwrap for last 10 minutes of baking for browned outside.

One teaspoon paprika and ½ teaspoon dry mustard may be rubbed over chicken before baking.

For herb flavor, ½ teaspoon marjoram, rosemary, or basil, or your own favorite combination.

LOW SATURATED FAT VARIATION

Follow Basic Recipe and Variations except omit flour as it absorbs fat which you want to drip away. Oil may be increased, reduced, or omitted according to your diet needs. Salt to taste if not restricted in sodium. Serve only breast meat to dieter.

One serving, with oil, without gravy: 1 gram saturated fat; ¾ teaspoon vegetable oil.

PRIZE WINNING BAKED CHICKEN AND PRUNES

3 Servings

Here is a prize winning chicken recipe developed by a young northern California homemaker named Jane Greer. Its secret goodness is the blending of the fruit and chicken by slow cooking. This gives it an old-world flavor reminiscent of French cassoulets or mid-European tzimmes casseroles. We are indebted to the California Prune Advisory Board for sharing this tested recipe with us so we may pass it on to you. The prunes give it a high energy level because of their natural fruit sugars (but do increase the carbohydrate level). Their richness in iron, vitamin A, and potassium gives additional pluses. Quick to make too!

1 can (10 oz.) tomatoes, low sodium dietetic
⅛ teaspoon black pepper
⅛ teaspoon each bay leaf, sweet basil, and oregano
1½ teaspoons vegetable oil
1 large onion, thinly sliced
1½ teaspoons flour
1 whole chicken breast, skinned and cut in bite-size pieces
9 pitted prunes (3 oz.), cut in bite-size pieces

Chop tomatoes coarsely, add spices, and heat slowly, stirring occasionally. Cook until tomatoes lose their shape to form a sauce-like consistency, and are reduced to about half in amount. Pour vegetable oil into a Dutch oven or casserole with cover. With paper towel, rub oil around the sides and bottom of the utensil. Arrange onion slices on bottom of utensil. Sprinkle with flour. Place half of chicken pieces on top; add half of the prunes. Repeat layers of chicken and prunes. Slowly pour tomato sauce over chicken covering all parts of the chicken. Cover and bake 2 hours in a preheated 350° (moderate) oven.

ONE SERVING
(3 oz. meat, cooked weight)

70	milligrams sodium
4	grams total fat
1	gram saturated fat
30	grams carbohydrate
175	calories

ROAST CHICKEN

8 Servings — (4-pound roaster — dressed weight)

Oven-baked chicken (or turkey) can be a gourmet's delicacy, or a dry disillusionment.

STUFFING AND COOKING:

In planning your stuffing, allow about 1 cup of (low sodium) bread crumbs for every pound of chicken (dressed weight). So if you have a 4-pound roaster, allow 3 cups of bread crumbs. A standard size loaf of bread makes a full 4 cups of crumbs.

Many recipes call for trimmed loaves. Very good indeed, if you like a soft dressing, moist or not. For full flavor, however, try a loaf as is, and see if you don't like the flavor of the crunchy crust. It adds variety and texture to the dressing, as well as flavor.

Now for seasoning. If celery is not allowed on the sodium-restricted diet, think through new flavor combinations. We think a little green pepper and parsley, with herbs, give a dressing both tasteful and harmonious savor which add to the chicken itself. Or combine ½ cup diced prunes with 2½ cups of low sodium crumbs.

Amount of fat must also be considered on some programs, to further limit the flavor of your dressing. Be sure to remove "pockets" of fat under the skin and near the tail. Roast with skin on to give a moist product. Remove skin, at least for the dieter, before serving. If you can manage, do use a little un-salted special margarine for flavor-plus values.

For a 4-pound roaster, these proportions will give you a general guide to follow:

1 tablespoon vegetable oil
1 teaspoon unsalted special margarine
½ cup finely cut onion
1 garlic clove, minced fine
1 teaspoon finely minced green pepper
3 cups flaked low sodium bread crumbs
1 tablespoon minced parsley
1½ teaspoons summer savory
½ teaspoon thyme
¼ teaspoon sweet marjoram
¼ teaspoon fresh black pepper

Heat oil and margarine in skillet. Add onion, garlic, and green pepper; lightly brown. Combine bread crumbs, parsley, and seasonings in bowl. Add oil-onion mixture to bread crumbs and thoroughly blend; cool. Do not stuff until ready to cook.

Meanwhile, put 2 tablespoons dry white wine into cavity and let stand until ready to stuff for roasting. Drain before stuffing.

Stuff bird, being careful not to pack stuffing in too tightly. Lace skewers to hold stuffing in place. Brush chicken surface lightly with 1 teaspoon vegetable oil; wrap in aluminum foil; put on rack in baking pan with low sides. Place chicken either sideways or on its breast, depending on its shape and other oven demands. Follow your range directions for cooking, but remember that low-temperature cooking will preserve juices and minimize shrinkage.

Roast uncovered, or with a light aluminum tent covering if desired. If this is your choice, unwrap and turn chicken the last 20 minutes of roasting for golden brownness.

Make gravy for regulars and use special recipe (page 133) for your dieter.

ONE SERVING
(3 oz. white and dark meat,
cooked weight)
With dressing; without gravy

66	milligrams sodium
28	grams total fat
8	grams saturated fat
21	grams carbohydrate
492	calories

VARIATIONS

One cup mushrooms may be added to stuffing for variety; or 1 tablespoon sliced mushrooms may be added to gravy.

Chicken may be marinated in a marinade given on page 141.

LOW SATURATED FAT VARIATION

Skin chicken. Dressing for dieter should be cooked separately in a custard cup, as bread crumbs absorb animal fat during roasting. Oil and margarine may be increased, decreased, or omitted from stuffing according to your requirements. If oil is omitted, parboil onion, garlic, and green pepper in ¼ cup water or white table wine. Add salt if not restricted in sodium.

One serving, with oil, and dressing cooked separately: 1 gram saturated fat; ½ teaspoon vegetable oil.

FAT-RESTRICTED CHICKEN GRAVY
1 Cup

3 tablespoons flour
1 low sodium chicken bouillon cube
½ teaspoon onion powder
¾ cup boiling water
¼ cup Rhine wine (optional)

Brown flour in frying pan. Combine crumbled bouillon cube, onion powder, and water. Add slowly to browned flour to make smooth paste. Cook, stirring constantly, to avoid lumping. When gravy begins to thicken, add wine and reheat. If no sodium restrictions, use regular bouillon cubes and add salt to taste. (For fat-carbohydrate control dieters, gravy can be used only if flour is allowed on diet list.)

TOTAL RECIPE
With wine

18	milligrams sodium
trace	gram total fat
19	grams carbohydrate
130	calories

BARBECUED CHICKEN

4 Servings — (2-pound fryer — dressed weight)

Whether you cook this in the oven, on the revolving spit of your broiler or outdoor barbecue, or over a homemade grill, the flavor of barbecued chicken is something very special and deserves your good efforts any time of the year.

2-pound fryer, cut into serving pieces
1 teaspoon low sodium Worcestershire sauce
¼ cup water
½ cup low sodium catsup
2 tablespoons vegetable oil
2 tablespoons vinegar
½ teaspoon freshly ground pepper

Wipe cut-up fryer with a damp cloth and dry; place on rack in baking pan. Make a barbecue sauce by combining remaining ingredients in a small saucepan; simmer for ten minutes. Cool; brush half of sauce over chicken. Let stand at least one hour. Bake in preheated 350° (moderate) oven for about 50 minutes, until tender, basting every 15 minutes with remaining sauce. Add salt for those without sodium restrictions at time of serving.

ONE SERVING
(3 oz. white and dark meat,
cooked weight)

82	milligrams sodium
13	grams total fat
1	gram saturated fat
8	grams carbohydrate
240	calories

VARIATIONS

For high flavor, California red wine, such as Burgundy, may be substituted for the wine vinegar, but for the most part, when wine flavor is desired, substitute dry sauterne.

Lemon juice or herb wine may be substituted for the wine vinegar.

When you are going to barbecue, use marinade on chicken for at least two hours. Turn at least once and brush sauce over all parts. Baste from time to time when cooking over charcoal or on electric spit.

LOW SATURATED FAT VARIATION

If no sodium restrictions, use regular catsup and Worcestershire sauce in barbecue sauce and add salt to taste.

One serving: 1 gram saturated fat.

BRAISED CHICKEN WITH VEGETABLES

6 Servings — (3-pound fryer — dressed weight)

3 tablespoons flour
¼ teaspoon pepper
3-pound fryer, skinned and cut up
1 tablespoon vegetable oil
1 cup sliced fresh mushrooms
½ cup cubed green pepper
2 tablespoons minced parsley
1 cup boiling water
½ cup fresh peas

Combine flour and pepper in paper bag; add chicken pieces and shake well. Brown chicken in oil in heavy skillet, then remove pieces to a casserole. Using the same skillet and oil, add washed mushrooms, green pepper, and parsley. Stir, to avoid scorching, then put into casserole with chicken. Add boiling water. Cover, and let simmer slowly about 1½ hours, or until fork-tender. Add peas about 15 minutes before done. If cooking in oven, preheat to 275° (very slow) and cover the casserole. Bake for 1½ hours. Uncover and add peas as above. For those without sodium restrictions, add salt just before serving.

ONE SERVING
(3 oz. white and dark meat,
cooked weight)
With gravy

81	milligrams sodium
9	grams total fat
1	gram saturated fat
8	grams carbohydrate
216	calories

LOW SATURATED FAT VARIATION

Follow Basic Recipe except omit flour and pan-browning; instead lightly broil chicken pieces. Parboil mushrooms, green pepper, and parsley and add them with boiling water after chicken has been placed on rack in Dutch oven or heavy-duty saucepan. Cover and simmer or oven bake as in directions. Chill liquid and remove hardened fat before thickening cooking liquid with flour for gravy, if desired. If not restricted in sodium, add salt to taste. Chicken may be rubbed in oil according to diet requirements.

One serving, without oil: 1 gram saturated fat.

CHICKEN CURRY

6 Servings — (2 whole chicken breasts —
approximately 2 pounds)

2 whole chicken breasts
1 tablespoon vegetable oil
½ pound sliced fresh mushrooms (stems and caps)
¼ cup chopped onion
Approximately 1 tablespoon curry powder
½ cup homemade chutney (optional)
¼ cup chopped parsley
1 low sodium chicken bouillon cube
1½ cups boiling water

Skin and bone chicken breasts and cut into 1-inch pieces. Sauté chicken, mushrooms, and onions in oil until lightly browned on all sides. Stir in curry powder, chutney, and parsley. Dissolve bouillon cube in boiling water; add to chicken mixture. Simmer for about 15 to 25 minutes until chicken is thoroughly cooked and seasonings have melded, stirring often, as curry burns easily. Add salt for the regulars, salt substitute for the sodium-restricted dieter, when serving. Serve over rice, cooked with a pinch of turmeric if extra flavor is desired.

ONE SERVING
(3 oz. white and dark meat,
cooked weight)
Without rice or chutney

91	milligrams sodium
5	grams total fat
1	gram saturated fat
5	grams carbohydrate
224	calories

VARIATIONS

Substitute 3 cups cooked diced chicken or turkey for the chicken in the basic recipe.

One-fourth cup Rosé wine may be substituted for one-half cup water in the recipe.

One-half cup cubed apple and 1 tablespoon raisins may be substituted for the chutney.

If fat must be sharply curtailed, use a Teflon skillet or spray regular one with nonstick substance before adding chicken, and skim any fat from accumulated liquid before serving.

After sautéing ingredients, they may be poured into a prepared casserole and baked in a preheated 350° (moderate) oven for thirty minutes.

LOW SATURATED FAT VARIATION

Follow Basic Recipe but omit browning of onion and chicken in oil; instead, lightly broil chicken pieces. Place on rack in heavy skillet with other ingredients (lightly salt if not restricted in sodium). Cover and simmer for 1½ hours or until tender. Chill liquid and remove hardened fat; thicken.

One serving, without oil: 1 gram saturated fat.

✓ CHICKEN NAPOLI

6 Servings — (3-pound fryer — dressed weight)

The Wine Institute, San Francisco, has given us permission to use this tested recipe with its fine Italian savor.

3-pound fryer, skinned and cut up
¼ cup flour
¼ teaspoon pepper, freshly ground
¼ teaspoon marjoram (scant)
1 tablespoon unsalted special margarine

1 tablespoon vegetable oil
¼ cup chopped parsley
1 clove garlic, minced (optional)
1 cup fresh tomatoes (or canned dietetic low sodium)
½ cup Cabernet
¼ cup fresh mushroom stems and pieces
1½ cups fresh peas (or canned dietetic low sodium)

Dredge pieces of chicken with flour, seasoned with pepper and marjoram. Heat margarine and oil in a large, heavy skillet; brown chicken on all sides. Add parsley, garlic, tomatoes, and wine. Cover tightly and simmer gently for about 45 minutes, or until chicken is tender. Add remaining ingredients; simmer 5 minutes longer. Serve with boiled or steamed rice. Add salt for those without sodium restrictions.

ONE SERVING
(3 oz. white and dark meat,
cooked weight)
Without rice

79	milligrams sodium
11	grams total fat
1	gram saturated fat
12	grams carbohydrate
274	calories

LOW SATURATED FAT VARIATION

Follow Basic Recipe but do not dredge chicken pieces with flour or pan-brown with margarine and oil; instead lightly broil. Place on rack in skillet, add other ingredients and continue as directed. Before serving sauce, chill and remove hardened fat. (As flour was not used to dredge chicken, you may want to thicken slightly with flour before serving.) If no sodium restrictions, use fresh, frozen, or regular canned vegetables and salt to taste. Oil may be added to sauce according to your diet needs.

One serving, without oil: 1 gram saturated fat.

CHICKEN PAPRIKA

6 Servings — (3-pound fryer — dressed weight)

For fine flavor and something exotic, it is hard to beat Chicken Paprika.

3-pound fryer, skinned and cut up
1 tablespoon vegetable oil
½ teaspoon white pepper
1 teaspoon imported paprika
1 teaspoon tarragon leaves, finely crumbled
1 tablespoon white table wine or lemon juice

Wash and dry chicken parts. Rub lightly with oil. Place on a rack in a shallow baking pan, sprinkle with seasonings, then dribble wine over each piece, being careful not to dislodge seasonings. Bake in preheated 350° (moderate) oven about 50 minutes or until tender. Serve at once on a heated platter or directly onto serving plates.

When diet allows, a gravy may be made of ½ can mushroom soup, diluted with 2 tablespoons white table wine; add ½ cup sautéed mushrooms and heat. Serve a spoonful or more over each piece. Taste before adding salt for those without sodium restrictions as the mushroom soup is salty.

ONE SERVING
(3 oz. white and dark meat,
cooked weight)
With wine; without gravy

80	milligrams sodium
9	grams total fat
1	gram saturated fat
negligible	grams carbohydrate
180	calories

Chicken breasts may be substituted for the parts of a whole chicken. Split each breast and bone, if desired.

LOW SATURATED FAT VARIATION

Follow Basic Recipe except broil chicken parts on rack in baking pan; then continue as directed. If no sodium restrictions, add salt to taste.

One serving: 1 gram saturated fat; ½ teaspoon oil.

POULTRY IN MARINADE

Roasters or fryers gain wonderful savors when put into a marinade for 6 to 8 hours before cooking with the marinade used for basting during the cooking. If you are roasting a whole fowl, rub the marinade inside the chicken and over the skinned surface; if preparing pieces of chicken, "anoint" each piece. Wrap marinated fowl in oiled paper and put in refrigerator for at least 6 hours. Remove 1 hour before cooking. Place on rack in a shallow baking pan; bake in preheated 350° (moderate) oven for 45 to 55 minutes, until fork-tender. Baste at least once. Serve immediately garnishing with parsley.

MARINADE

Here is a marinade particularly good for chicken or turkey which we have adapted from Irma Mazza's recipe in *Accent on Seasoning:*

½ teaspoon rosemary or tarragon
¼ teaspoon black pepper

Rind of ½ lemon
2 tablespoons vegetable oil
2 tablespoons lemon juice
1 tablespoon finely chopped parsley
Dash paprika
¼ cup dry sauterne

Mix and crush herbs and lemon rind in a mortar with pestle. Combine and blend with remaining ingredients. Add ½ teaspoon salt if there is no sodium restriction.

TOTAL MARINADE RECIPE

9	milligrams sodium
28	grams total fat
2	grams saturated fat
3	grams carbohydrate
305	calories

CHICKEN PILAU

4 Servings

A pilau is an Oriental dish made with rice combined with meat, fowl or fish, and spices. It is boiled or oven baked. Some of the old pilaus were made with cracked wheat. We make ours with Fisher's American bulgur wheat. If this is not available, contact your local milling agent and use his product. Or use rice.

2 tablespoons vegetable oil
1 cup bulgur wheat
1 tablespoon finely chopped onion
1 low sodium chicken bouillon cube
2 cups boiling water
¼ teaspoon oregano
Few grains pepper

1 tablespoon minced parsley
1 cup chopped chicken
Paprika

Warm oil in heavy-duty skillet; add bulgur wheat and onion. Stir and cook until golden brown. Dissolve bouillon cube in the water; add seasonings. Pour over bulgur wheat. Cover, bring to boil. Reduce heat and simmer 10 minutes. Add chicken and simmer 5 minutes more. Add a little hot water if necessary. Sprinkle each serving with a few grains of paprika. Add salt for those without sodium restrictions.

ONE SERVING
(2 oz. meat, cooked weight)

47	milligrams sodium
10	grams total fat
1	gram saturated fat
30	grams carbohydrate
298	calories

VARIATIONS

Substitute brown rice for Ala.

For oven-baked pilau, brown Ala or rice on top of range. Add other ingredients. Put into lightly oiled casserole. Cover with ½ cup crumbled low sodium bread crumbs and bake in a preheated 350° (moderate) oven 45 minutes or until golden brown.

With the chicken omitted, bulgur wheat is an excellent accompaniment to any chicken.

For variety, substitute 1 cup fresh tomatoes or unsalted tomato juice for 1 cup of water.

LOW SATURATED FAT VARIATION

Follow Basic Recipe and Variations. If no sodium restrictions, use regular bouillon cube and add salt to taste.

One serving: 1 gram saturated fat; 1½ teaspoons vegetable oil.

OTHER DELICACIES

TURKEY-BROCCOLI AU GRATIN
8 Servings

2 cups fresh broccoli (or 1 package frozen)
¼ teaspoon vegetable oil
2 cups cooked minced turkey
⅓ cup unsalted special margarine
⅓ cup flour
Few grains black pepper
2 cups nonfat milk
1 cup Rhine wine
¼ cup grated low sodium cheddar-type cheese

Steam broccoli over boiling water until almost fork-tender; drain. Lightly oil casserole with vegetable oil. Place ½ broccoli in casserole; cover with ½ turkey. Repeat with layer of broccoli and turkey. Make a white sauce of melted margarine, blended flour, pepper, and milk. Stir constantly to keep smooth. Cook 5 minutes. Add wine. Blend, and remove from heat. Cover turkey-broccoli with sauce. Top with grated cheese. Bake in a 350° (moderate) oven about 30 minutes, until mixture is bubbly. Salt for those without sodium restrictions. (Count milk in day's allowance or use low sodium nonfat milk.)

ONE SERVING
(2 oz. white and dark meat,
cooked weight)

98	milligrams sodium
11	grams total fat
3	grams saturated fat
10	grams carbohydrate
272	calories

Chicken or veal may be substituted for turkey.

LOW SATURATED FAT VARIATION

Follow Basic Recipe except omit margarine, and make white sauce by blending 1 bouillon cube (low sodium, if restricted in sodium) with ¼ cup boiling water; add ¼ cup cold milk. Blend flour with bouillon mixture to make a smooth paste. Slowly add remaining milk, stirring constantly to blend; cook 5 minutes. Continue as directed in recipe but use Count Down Cheese Spread cut in small pieces; top with crumbs. If no sodium restrictions, add salt to taste.

One serving: 1 gram saturated fat.

RABBIT

6 Servings — (3-pound rabbit — drawn weight)

3-pound rabbit, disjointed
2 tablespoons vegetable oil
3 tablespoons flour
1 cup hot water
2 cups raw vegetables

MARINADE

½ cup white table wine
1 teaspoon strained lemon juice
1 tablespoon pure honey
¼ teaspoon pepper
1 small bay leaf, crumbled
3 whole cloves

¼ teaspoon marjoram
½ cup onion, diced small
¼ cup green pepper, cut in small cubes

Combine marinade ingredients and blend well. Wash and dry rabbit pieces; place in a large container. Pour marinade over rabbit so that all parts are "covered." Cover and set in refrigerator. After 4 hours turn and recoat with marinade; allow to stand 4 more hours in the refrigerator.

Remove rabbit and blot dry with paper toweling. Strain marinade into a bowl and set aside. Heat oil in a Dutch oven. Roll rabbit pieces lightly in flour and brown on all sides in oil. Pour the marinade over the rabbit, and add 1 cup or more hot water to cover the rabbit. Cover, and simmer for 1½ to 2 hours, basting twice during the cooking period. Test with fork for tenderness. Do not undercook. Fifteen minutes before serving time, add the prepared raw vegetables. Cook until they are fork-tender. Arrange the rabbit in the center of a warmed platter and border with steamed rice and vegetables. Thicken gravy, if desired, with a smooth paste of flour and water, adding salt for regulars.

ONE SERVING
(3 oz. meat, cooked weight)
Without rice and vegetables

53	milligrams sodium
14	grams total fat
4	grams saturated fat
8	grams carbohydrate
270	calories

LOW SATURATED FAT VARIATION

Follow the Basic Recipe but do not flour and pan-brown the marinated rabbit in oil. Instead, broil it slightly to brown. For minimal fat in gravy, chill it with an ice cube and skim off any hardened fat that appears on the surface. Thicken as desired.

Oil may be added to gravy according to your diet requirements. If no sodium restrictions, add salt to taste.

One serving, without oil: 3 grams saturated fat.

PRUNE-SPANISH RICE
3 Servings

Another California Prune Advisory Board tested recipe. We think you'll agree it is an excellent accompaniment for many plain chicken dishes and for cold cuts, particularly cold roast beef or pork. (Dieters controlling carbohydrate may have to bypass this recipe.)

¼ cup prunes (5 prunes)
1 tablespoon vegetable oil
¼ cup chopped onions
¼ cup chopped green peppers
½ cup rice
¾ cup water
½ small bay leaf
⅛ teaspoon thyme
¼ teaspoon black pepper
1 cup tomatoes, canned low sodium dietetic, or fresh peeled ones
1 tablespoon shredded almonds (optional)

Pit and chop prunes and set aside. Heat oil in saucepan or skillet, add onions and peppers, and sauté until soft but not brown. Stir in rice. Add water, bay leaf, thyme, pepper, tomatoes, and chopped prunes. Bring to a boil, cover and simmer for 45 minutes or until rice is tender. For special occasions, sprinkle with almonds and put under broiler 1 minute to toast them.

ONE SERVING	TOTAL RECIPE	
10	29	milligrams sodium
6	19	grams total fat
trace	1	gram saturated fat
41	122	grams carbohydrate
236	707	calories

SPANISH RICE WITH WINE
6 Servings

A savory accompaniment for that special chicken dish, we think this especially good when served with simple chicken dishes, not the highly seasoned ones.

1 tablespoon vegetable oil
½ cup chopped onion
½ cup finely chopped green pepper
1 minced garlic clove
1 tablespoon flour
1 cup tomatoes, cut in small pieces
1 cup water
½ cup Rhine wine
3 tablespoons minced parsley
¼ teaspoon thyme
Few grains black pepper
⅓ teaspoon cayenne
½ bay leaf, crumbled
1½ cups uncooked brown rice

Warm skillet and add oil. Heat over low heat; add onion, green pepper, and garlic. Cook slowly 5 minutes. Add and blend flour. Add all other ingredients except rice. Bring to a boil and gently simmer for 5 minutes. Slowly add rice, stirring with fork to blend. Cover and let simmer for 30 minutes or until rice is tender and liquid is absorbed. Salt for those without sodium restrictions. Use very small portion or omit for fat-carbohydrate restricted diet.

ONE SERVING

13	milligrams sodium
4	grams total fat
trace	gram saturated fat
45	grams carbohydrate
247	calories

LOW SATURATED FAT VARIATION

If total fat is restricted, follow Basic Recipe but do not brown onion, pepper, and garlic in oil. Rather, simmer gently for 5 minutes in ¼ cup water. Salt to taste if not on sodium restriction.

One serving, with oil: negligible saturated fat; ½ teaspoon vegetable oil.

9

TRICKS WITH FISH

Fish must swim thrice — once in the water, a second time in the sauce, and a third time in wine of stomach.

— JOHN RAY
English Proverbs (1670)

SOME EPICUREANS WOULD AGREE one hundred percent with this old proverb and would argue that a fish without its sauce is no fish at all. Thank goodness, many of us have learned that the delicate and bland flavor of fish is a treat in itself, when seasonings are delicately used to bring out its characteristic taste.

More good fish is spoiled by the way it is cooked than is almost any other food. Its natural juiciness is all but cooked right out of it, leaving us a dry, flat something to chew on. It is far too valuable in our diet for any such treatment, particularly for those of you on restricted programs. (Most fish is low in total fat content, and all fish is low in saturated fat.) Shellfish, however, is somewhat higher in cholesterol and may be restricted on some diets. Fish has fewer calories than meat, and an average serving supplies one-third to one-half our daily protein requirement. Except for shellfish, fresh fish is also low in sodium.

The albuminous or protein part of fish may be likened to the white of egg. Fish should be cooked only until this albuminous substance is "set" and no longer. Generally speaking, fish is cooked when it separates from the bones and may be "flaked" with a knife.

Fish for dieters may be broiled, baked, or boiled (steamed or poached). Fried or sautéed fish is not recommended because of added fat content. Small lean fish, such as trout, fillet of sole, and flounder may be broiled or baked in parchment. Larger lean fish, as carp and haddock, may be baked or broiled and may be served with a sauce (pages 168 to 174) if desired. Cod and haddock are particularly good choices for you on fat restriction.

The so-called fat fish, as bluefish, halibut, and mackerel, may be baked or broiled in smaller pieces. They are delicious with a wedge of lemon or tangy sauce, such as Tomato (page 173).

Today you can usually buy fish dressed and ready for your ministrations. *Fillets* are the sides of the fish cut lengthwise away from the backbone and are ready to cook as purchased. *Steaks* are cross section slices from large dressed fish cut about ⅝ to 1 inch thick; a cross section of the backbone is the only bone in the steak. *Chunks* are cross sections of large dressed fish; a cross section of the backbone is the only bone in a chunk. *Dressed whole fish* are fish with scales and entrails removed, and usually the head, tail, and fins are removed. The fish may then be cooked, filleted, or cut into steaks or chunks. The smaller size fish are called *pan-dressed* and are ready to cook as purchased.

Some years ago, Evelyn Spencer, the Fish Cookery Expert for the United States Bureau of Fisheries, described a Hot-Oven or Spencer method of fish cookery which lends itself to restricted cooking to special advantage. It cuts down the cooking fat or oil by more than one half and produces a better looking product. It is useful for fish weighing up to a pound; for larger amounts, cut fish into strips or slices, as sea bass, sole, et cetera.

This is Miss Spencer's way of doing it: Place cut pieces of fish to your extreme left; next place a bowl of low sodium nonfat (or regular nonfat, depending upon diet regulations) milk, and seasoning. Next to this place a low-sided pan with finely sifted low sodium bread crumbs. Lastly, place a lightly oiled baking sheet with a teaspoon or more vegetable oil in a small measuring cup for "dabbing" the top of fish. With the left hand, put a piece of fish into the bowl of milk; then put into pan of crumbs. Now, with the right hand cover the fish with crumbs and place it in baking pan. Be sure to keep the left hand for the wet work, the right one for the dry. In this way you can keep the crumbs dry. After all of the fish pieces have been treated in the above manner sprinkle each piece with a little vegetable oil. This is the only fat used in this method of preparation. The same results cannot be obtained if a flour, cornmeal, oatmeal, or general unsalted cracker dip is used. She states that with cracker or other dips, fish will be browned in splotches where fat has touched them; with bread-crumb dip and the addition of a little oil — about 1 tablespoon to a pound of fish — the product will be uniformly golden brown after cooking.

Preheat oven to specified temperature for 10 minutes; then place fish in oven. Most fish will cook in 10 minutes. Do not be afraid it will burn, and don't add water to fish cooked this quick way.

The 1972 edition of *Let's Cook Fish** gives the following timetable for cooking fish:

* Fishery Market Development Series No. 8, Department of Commerce, National Oceanic and Atmospheric Administration, National Marine Fisheries Service, Washington, D.C.

METHOD OF COOKING	MARKET FORM	COOKING TEMPERATURE	APPROXIMATE COOKING TIME IN MINUTES
Baking	Dressed	350° F	45 to 60
	Pan-dressed	350° F	25 to 30
	Fillets or steaks	350° F	20 to 25 depending on form and size
Broiling	Pan-dressed		10 to 16 (turning once)
Poaching	Fillets or steaks	Simmer	5 to 10
Steaming	Fillets or steaks	Boil	5 to 10

Experiment and see which method you prefer for your specialties.

If herbs and seasonings are to be used in your fish dishes, add about 4 minutes before fish is done. Garnish with lemon wedges or sauce (pages 168 to 174).

HOW TO SERVE FISH:

As most fish are light and pallid in color and mild in taste, strive for contrast in choice of vegetables and salads. Have flavorsome and colorful vegetables, as red cabbage, tomatoes, cucumbers, radishes, broccoli. Acid flavors make a good contrast for "fat" fish. This is one of the reasons that lemon is such an indispensable for your fish dishes. Use the juices to give a tangy savor to sauces; use a wedge per serving as a garnish.

FOR SODIUM RESTRICTION, DO NOT USE:

Canned fish, except low sodium dietetic

Shellfish, except approved low sodium dietetic

Unrinsed fresh fish

Frozen commercial fish fillet (usually treated in a salt bath in processing)

Regular milk in cooking, without deducting from day's allowance

FOR SATURATED FAT RESTRICTION, DO NOT USE:

Butter, margarine (except special margarine in amounts specified on your diet list), or vegetable shortenings

Canned or commercially prepared fish with butter, whole milk, whole egg

Egg yolk or whole egg

Whole milk or cream

If you must control carbohydrate as well as fat, the amount of milk, flour, bread crumbs, and other high carbohydrate foods will be restricted on your diet list and so add some limitations to your fish cookery.

SUGGESTIONS TO SPEED YOU ON YOUR WAY:

1. Serve fish as soon as cooked. It becomes soggy and unpalatable when allowed to stand.

2. Try parchment or aluminum foil for boiled or baked fish when you want to keep all of the juices "in."

3. Try Bakon Yeast for smoked flavor.

4. Basil, bay, crushed fennel, onion, thyme, dill, ginger root, nutmeg, paprika, green pepper, garlic, and white pepper do nice things for some fish dishes. Of course, lemon juice and white wines are naturals, too. And parsley is a love for garnishing and flavoring, as is curry when lightly sprinkled over fish before cooking.

5. Dry, white wines, such as Sylvaner, blend well with the delicate flavor of fish. Sherry is a zestful addition to scalloped fish and fish sauces.

6. Fish cookery allows you many methods. Choose from baking or broiling when you want oven methods; from boiling, steaming, or pan-frying for top-of-the-stove methods. Leave the deep-frys for those who have cast-iron digestions and no overweight problems.

7. Do not serve sweet salads with fish, but choose crisp,

crunchy greens with sharp dressings for flavor, color, and texture contrast.

8.   If you object to the odor of fish in the kitchen when you are preparing it, try placing several light squeezes of lemon juice in the pan before cooking. This will help to keep the kitchen smelling fresh.

9.   You can remove fish odor from hands, too, by rubbing them with lemon and rinsing. Save lemon shells to scrub pan after cooking fish to keep the fish flavor from lingering in the pan.

STEAMED BLUEFISH
4 Servings

2 pounds bluefish, cleaned and cut in pieces
1 tablespoon vegetable oil
1 garlic clove
¼ teaspoon basil
2 tablespoons finely minced leek tops *or* chives
Paprika

Wipe pieces of fish with damp cloth. Oil fish with vegetable oil in which garlic has soaked for an hour or two. Put fish on steamer rack. Set in place with boiling water in lower part. Sprinkle basil and minced leek tops over fish. Cover tightly and steam for about 30 minutes, or until fork-tender. Serve with Cucumber Sauce (page 171). Garnish with paprika. Add salt for regulars and fat-restricted dieters without sodium restrictions.

ONE SERVING
(3 oz. fish, cooked weight)
Without sauce

86	milligrams sodium
7	grams total fat
trace	gram saturated fat
trace	gram carbohydrate
169	calories

One serving: ¾ teaspoon vegetable oil.

FISH IN CREOLE SAUCE

8 Servings

Another tested recipe from the Home Service Department of the Corn Products Company.

1 recipe Creole Sauce
3 cups cooked fish, cut in small pieces

Prepare Creole Sauce; add fish. If desired, serve on hot platter lined with mashed potatoes.

CREOLE SAUCE

⅓ cup corn oil
1 green pepper, cut in strips
1 cup sliced onion
1 clove garlic
1 teaspoon sugar
1 whole clove
¼ teaspoon pepper
⅛ teaspoon celery seed
3½ cups canned tomatoes without added sodium

2 tablespoons cornstarch
2 tablespoons water

Heat oil in saucepan; add green pepper, onion, and garlic; cover and cook slowly until slightly tender but not brown. Add sugar, whole clove, pepper, celery seed, and tomatoes; cook over low heat, stirring occasionally, about ½ hour. Blend cornstarch with water and add to sauce. Continue cooking 10 minutes, stirring constantly, until sauce thickens. Remove garlic and clove before serving. Add salt for those without sodium restrictions.

ONE SERVING
(3 oz. cod, cooked weight)
Without potatoes

85	milligrams sodium
10	grams total fat
1	gram saturated fat
8	grams carbohydrate
209	calories

One serving: 2 teaspoons vegetable oil.

FISH SOUFFLÉ

3 Servings

1 cup cooked fish, flaked
¼ teaspoon dill weed
¼ teaspoon paprika
1 tablespoon lemon juice
Dash cayenne
⅓ cup low sodium bread crumbs
⅓ cup nonfat milk
1 egg, separated
1 tablespoon sherry

Flake fish. Add dill, paprika, lemon juice, and cayenne; blend. Add bread crumbs which have been soaked in milk until soft (being sure to count dieter's daily milk allowance, or use low sodium nonfat milk). Stir lightly to mix. Blend in 1 egg yolk, lightly beaten. Beat egg white until stiff but not dry. Add sherry; blend. Fold into fish mixture.

Turn into a casserole dish, lightly oiled with vegetable oil.

Set casserole in pan of hot water, and bake in 350° (moderate) oven for 30 minutes, or until soufflé is firm. Serve at once. Salt for those without sodium restrictions.

ONE SERVING
(2⅔ oz. bass, cooked weight)

107	milligrams sodium
4	grams total fat
1	gram saturated fat
9	grams carbohydrate
170	calories

VARIATION

Any fish on your diet list such as haddock, cod, and halibut may be used in this recipe.

LOW SATURATED FAT VARIATION

Follow Basic Recipe except substitute 2 egg whites or ¼ cup liquid cholesterol-free egg substitute, for whole egg. If no sodium restriction, use regular bread and add salt to taste.

One serving: negligible saturated fat (with egg whites).

STEAMED HADDOCK IN COURT BOUILLON

A particularly good choice for those of you with fat restriction.

6 Servings

3 pounds whole haddock, cleaned and cut in pieces
1 tablespoon chopped onion
1 tablespoon chopped parsley
1 teaspoon vegetable oil
3 peppercorns
1 clove
¼ bay leaf
1 tablespoon wine vinegar
1 quart water (about)
Parsley

Wipe haddock and wrap in cheesecloth so that you can lift it from pan without having it fall apart. Set on rack in large kettle. Simmer onion and chopped parsley in small amount of water for 15 minutes. Add remaining ingredients to onion mixture; bring to a boil. Simmer 15 minutes longer. Pour over fish. Add water to kettle, if necessary, so that there are at least 2 inches liquid in bottom of pan. Cover tightly; simmer, being sure to keep liquid below boiling point. Cook until fork-tender. Allow from 24 to 30 minutes for a 3-pound fish. Lift fish carefully from pan. Strain liquid and thicken for sauce (2 tablespoons flour per cup of liquid) if desired. Garnish with parsley. Add salt for regulars or fat-restricted dieter without sodium restrictions.

ONE SERVING
(3 oz. fish, cooked weight)
Without sauce or parsley garnish

70	milligrams sodium
1	gram total fat
trace	gram saturated fat
trace	gram carbohydrate
94	calories

Fish may be poached in water or tomato juice (canned without added sodium for sodium-restricted dieters).

Wine may be used for the poaching liquid by substituting 2 cups red or white dinner wine for 2 cups water.

Other fish may be prepared in this way, as sea bass, halibut, and salmon.

We like to cut fish into serving pieces before boiling for better table appearance, avoiding that chopped-up look.

HALIBUT CASSEROLE
6 Servings

Steam or poach 2-pound halibut steaks as in recipe on page 155. Cool and flake. Make a white sauce, using 1½ cups nonfat milk, 4 tablespoons special margarine, and 3 tablespoons flour. Add to it ½ cup white wine for flavor. Season with ¼ teaspoon pepper and a pinch of thyme. Brush casserole lightly with vegetable oil. Now, put a layer of fish in casserole. Top with white sauce and repeat. Top all with ½ cup low sodium bread crumbs and sprinkle with paprika. Bake 10 minutes in a preheated 400° (hot) oven, then reduce to 375° (moderate) oven for about 15 minutes. Salt for those without sodium restrictions. (Subtract milk from dieter's daily allowance or use low sodium nonfat milk.)

ONE SERVING
(3 oz. fish, cooked weight)
With Sylvaner

95	milligrams sodium
10	grams total fat
1	gram saturated fat
13	grams carbohydrate
298	calories

Substitute Basic Nonfat White Sauce (page 169) for the White Sauce given in recipe. Add salt to taste if no sodium restriction.

One serving: negligible saturated fat.

HALIBUT CONTINENTAL
6 Servings

½ cup seedless grapes (*skins removed*)
⅓ cup sherry
2-pound halibut steaks, cut into 6 slices
Few grains black pepper
1 tablespoon lemon juice
½ cup sliced onions
Few grains cayenne
1 cup Basic Medium White Sauce (page 168)
¼ cup seedless grapes (for garnishing)

Put grapes into a small bowl; pour the sherry over them. Let stand for 30 minutes. Meanwhile, wipe the halibut slices with a damp cloth. Sprinkle with pepper and lemon juice. Cook onion slices in small amount of boiling water for 5 minutes; drain. Lightly oil a casserole; arrange fish slices in it. Top with drained onions; add cayenne to white sauce and pour over fish. Cover and bake in a preheated 350° (moderate) oven, 25 to 35 minutes, until fork-tender. (Do not overcook.) Remove casserole from oven and strain off sauce. Drain grapes; add to the low sodium white sauce. Take 2 tablespoons sherry in which the grapes were soaked and blend with sauce. Reheat; pour over fish. Garnish casserole top with ¼ cup grapes. Add salt for those without sodium restrictions.

ONE SERVING
(3 oz. fish, cooked weight)

85	milligrams sodium
6	grams total fat
1	gram saturated fat
8	grams carbohydrate
244	calories

LOW SATURATED FAT VARIATION

Follow Basic Recipe except substitute Nonfat White Sauce (page 169). If no sodium restriction, add salt to taste.

One serving: negligible saturated fat.

BAKED SALMON IN TOMATO SAUCE
6 Servings

1 ¾ pounds salmon steak cut into 6 slices
1 cup white table wine
1 teaspoon vegetable oil
⅛ teaspoon curry powder
⅛ teaspoon freshly ground peppercorns
6 slices lemon
1 large onion sliced into 6 pieces
3 small tomatoes sliced into 12 pieces
1 green pepper cut into 6 swirls

Put fish slices into a shallow pan and let soak for ½ hour in wine. Meanwhile, brush bottom of baking pan lightly with vegetable oil and place fish in it. Sprinkle each slice with a pinch of curry powder and fresh black pepper. Top each with a slice of lemon and a slice of onion. Place on top of onion 2 small slices of fresh tomatoes and a swirl of green pepper. Bake about 30 minutes in a preheated 375° (moderate) oven until flaky to fork-test. *Baste every 10 minutes* during cooking period with

the wine in which the fish was soaked. As the cooking pro-
gresses, bits of tomato and pepper will break away and become
parts of the sauce, to add to its wonderful flavor. Salt for regulars and fat-restricted dieters without sodium restrictions.

ONE SERVING
(3 oz. fish, cooked weight)
With Sylvaner

62	milligrams sodium
18	grams total fat
trace	gram saturated fat
6	grams carbohydrate
315	calories

VARIATION

Haddock, halibut, cod, bass, or other white fish may be used.
Bass and salmon are higher in fat content than other fish except
tuna, canned in oil, so should be used sparingly if total fat is
restricted.

BROILED SWORDFISH
4 Servings

1 pound swordfish cut into 4 cross-section steaks
2 teaspoons lemon juice
2 teaspoons thyme
1 teaspoon dill weed
¼ teaspoon freshly ground peppercorns
4 teaspoons sauterne wine
2 teaspoons parsley, finely minced
Lemon wedges

Wipe each steak with damp cloth. Sprinkle each with ½ teaspoon lemon juice, ½ teaspoon thyme, and ¼ teaspoon dill.

Pepper lightly. Drip 1 teaspoon sauterne over each steak and put in broiler about 2 inches under heat. Cook 15 to 20 minutes until tests done. Sprinkle with minced parsley when served onto platter, and garnish with wedges of lemon. Serve at once. Salt for regulars and fat-restricted dieters without sodium restrictions.

ONE SERVING
(3 oz. fish, cooked weight)
With sauterne

90	milligrams sodium
5	grams total fat
trace	gram saturated fat
trace	gram carbohydrate
142	calories

VARIATIONS

For variety, try sliced fresh mushrooms on top of your fish fillets or steaks, or serve with nonfat milk-wine sauce (low sodium for sodium-restricted dieters).

A dash of allspice will give your swordfish an unusual flavor. It is particularly good with salmon or halibut, which may be prepared in the same way.

Ditto for curry powder.

In using such seasonings, scatter them over fish before broiling.

Or make an oil-herb sauce by soaking 2 split and crushed cloves of garlic in 2 tablespoons vegetable oil for 2 hours, then discard the garlic and brush fish with oil. Be sure to brush all sides for full flavor. Here we like a hot broiler so that steaks will cook in about 5 minutes for each side. Serve at once onto heated plates; if desired add your favorite sauce.

CREAMED TUNA SUPREME
4 Servings

We are indebted to the Home Advisory Service of the Wine Institute, San Francisco, for this excellent recipe.

¼ cup unsalted special margarine
¼ cup flour
1¾ cups nonfat milk
¼ cup sherry
2 (6½ oz.) cans low sodium dietetic tuna
1 tablespoon finely chopped green pepper

Melt margarine and stir in flour, add milk and cook, stirring constantly, until mixture boils and thickens. Add sherry, tuna, and green pepper. Heat thoroughly. Just before serving, add salt for those without sodium restrictions. Subtract milk from the day's total allowance or use low sodium nonfat milk.

ONE SERVING
(3¼ oz. fish, cooked weight)

94	milligrams sodium
12	grams total fat
2	grams saturated fat
11	grams carbohydrate
253	calories

VARIATIONS

Instead of dietetic low sodium tuna, dietetic low sodium shrimps may be used. Or, 1½ cups diced cooked chicken or veal may be substituted for tuna.

LOW SATURATED FAT VARIATION

Substitute the Basic Nonfat White Sauce (page 169) for the margarine-flour-milk sauce in Basic Recipe. Add a sprinkling of dill weed or crushed fennel to heighten flavor. If no sodium restriction, use regular canned tuna (brine pack) or shellfish, if allowed, and add salt to taste to white sauce.

One serving: negligible saturated fat.

Here are two more tuna dishes, easy on the pocketbook and in preparation time, and excellent in flavor. The first is from the tested recipes of the Wine Institute, the second from our own kitchens.

TUNA TETRAZZINI
6 Servings

4 ounces spaghetti, broken into 4-inch lengths
1 quart water
¼ pound fresh mushrooms
¼ cup green pepper, chopped
1½ teaspoons vegetable oil
1 tablespoon special margarine
1 tablespoon flour
⅛ teaspoon white pepper
1¼ cups nonfat milk
8 ounces flaked, canned tuna, low sodium dietetic
½ cup white table wine

Cook spaghetti in boiling water. Drain. Rinse under cold water unless mixing right away with sauce. Sauté mushrooms and green pepper in oil until fork-tender. Add special margarine, flour, and white pepper. Stir to blend. Cook over low heat for 5 minutes. Heat milk and tuna, drained of liquid, in double boiler or over low heat. Add flour mixture and stir until blended. Cook until thickened, stirring often to prevent scorching. Stir in wine. Mix in spaghetti. Spread mixture in a Teflon baking pan. Bake in a preheated 350° (moderate) oven until thoroughly heated through, but do not let bubble. Serve at once with a green salad, a green vegetable, and toasted French bread. Add salt for regulars when serving. Deduct milk from dieter's daily allowance or use low sodium nonfat milk.

ONE SERVING (1⅓ oz. fish, cooked weight)	TOTAL RECIPE	
52	311	milligrams sodium
4	21	grams total fat
1	3	grams saturated fat
21	125	grams carbohydrate
199	1191	calories

VARIATION

One-fourth cup specified cheese, low in sodium or fat (as required), may be grated or cut in small cubes and sprinkled over top of mixture for added flavor.

One-half teaspoon dill weed may be added for zest.

If no sodium restriction, add 1½ teaspoons chopped pimiento.

HURRY-UP TUNA CASSEROLE

3 Servings

1 can (6½ oz.) low sodium tuna
1 package (12 oz.) frozen chopped broccoli
1 can low sodium dietetic mushroom soup
¼ cup white table wine
9 baking powder biscuits (See recipe, page 264)
Parsley

Line the bottom of a 1-quart casserole dish with tuna. Top with broccoli which has been almost completely thawed. Spoon soup blended with wine over the top. Cover; bake in preheated 350° (moderate) oven for 30 minutes, until mixture bubbles. Remove from oven and arrange biscuits over top of mixture and return to oven. Advance to 400° (hot) oven for about 12 minutes, until biscuits are golden brown. Garnish with a sprig of parsley.

ONE SERVING (2 oz. fish, cooked weight)	TOTAL RECIPE	
56	169	milligrams sodium
10	31	grams total fat
1	2	grams saturated fat
40	121	grams carbohydrate
373	1119	calories

SAUCES

And now for a few sauces, so fish may come "swimming" in them to your table.

BASIC MEDIUM WHITE SAUCE
4 Servings

2 tablespoons unsalted special margarine (1 for thin, 4 for thick)
2 tablespoons flour (1 for thin, 4 for thick)
1 cup nonfat milk
⅛ teaspoon pepper

Melt the margarine and blend with flour; gradually add the milk. Cook over hot water, or direct flame if you can stir constantly until mixture thickens. Add pepper and such other seasonings as you may wish (being sure to add sodium count of your choice of seasonings to total). This basic sauce has little flavor unless you "pep" it up. Count milk in dieter's serving or use low sodium nonfat milk.

ONE SERVING (Medium)	TOTAL RECIPE	
33	130	milligrams sodium
6	23	grams total fat
1	4	grams saturated fat
6	22	grams carbohydrate
82	329	calories

Note: Vegetable oil may be substituted for margarine.

BASIC NONFAT WHITE SAUCE
4 Servings

1 low sodium chicken bouillon cube
¼ cup boiling water
2 tablespoons flour (1 for thin, 4 for thick)
Few grains black or white pepper
1 cup nonfat milk
Seasonings various (optional)

Dissolve bouillon cube in boiling water. Let cool slightly; blend flour and pepper with bouillon to make smooth paste. Slowly add milk, stirring after each addition to ensure smooth sauce. Stir constantly until mixture thickens (at least 5 minutes after bubbles appear). If no sodium restrictions, use regular bouillon, and add salt to taste. Be sure to count nonfat milk in the day's allowance or use low sodium nonfat milk.

ONE SERVING (Medium)	TOTAL RECIPE	
35	138	milligrams sodium
trace	trace	gram total fat
6	22	grams carbohydrate
35	139	calories

VARIATIONS FOR BASIC WHITE SAUCES

Herb Sauce: Add ½ teaspoon of any of the following dried herbs: dill weed, fennel, gumbo file, powdered mushrooms, garlic powder, oregano, onion powder, paprika, or tarragon. Blend thoroughly. Pour over fish. Garnish as desired.

Mushroom Sauce: Sauté ½ cup sliced, fresh mushrooms in 1 tablespoon vegetable oil for 5 minutes. Add to sauce and cook all together for another 5 minutes. Add 2 tablespoons white wine just before serving. One tablespoon lemon juice and ½ teaspoon dry mustard may be added when a sharper flavor is wanted.

Parsley Sauce: Add ½ teaspoon grated onion and 3 teaspoons parsley when sauce is thickened. Add 1 tablespoon white wine just before removing from heat. When serving, sprinkle lightly with paprika and garnish with sprigs of parsley.

Mock Cheese Sauce: Add 1 teaspoon Bakon Yeast with flour.

Cheese Sauce: Add 4 tablespoons grated low sodium cheese and ½ teaspoon paprika. Use low fat cheese if on saturated fat-restricted diet without sodium restrictions.

HOT TARTAR SAUCE
6 Servings

½ cup Basic Medium White Sauce (page 168)
⅓ cup low sodium mayonnaise
½ teaspoon chives, minced fine
¼ tablespoon scraped onion
½ teaspoon tarragon vinegar *or* wine vinegar
½ tablespoon chopped parsley
½ tablespoon low sodium pickles
Paprika

To Basic White Sauce, add the above ingredients in order. Stir constantly until well blended, but do not let boil.

TOTAL RECIPE	
145	milligrams sodium
76	grams total fat
14	grams saturated fat
22	grams carbohydrate
725	calories

LOW SATURATED FAT VARIATION
Use Special Never-Fail Mayonnaise (page 239) or Eggless "Mayonnaise" (page 238) with Basic Nonfat White Sauce (page 169). If no sodium restrictions, use dill pickles and add salt to taste.

One serving: negligible grams saturated fat.

CUCUMBER SAUCE
6 Servings

2 cucumbers pared, grated, and thoroughly drained
1 teaspoon chopped parsley

1 teaspoon minced chives
Vinegar

Season cucumbers to taste for a fish accompaniment. If no sodium restriction, add salt to taste.

ONE SERVING	TOTAL RECIPE	
5	28	milligrams sodium
trace	trace	gram total fat
3	16	grams carbohydrate
9	52	calories

ALMOND SAUCE

For every serving of fish allow:

1 teaspoon vegetable oil
3 almonds blanched and slivered
½ teaspoon lemon juice
½ teaspoon parsley, minced fine
Few grains cayenne

Warm oil in small pan. Add almonds and cook slowly until they just turn color but do not brown. Add to other ingredients or pour over fish, as sole or Rex sole, when extra richness is desired.

ONE SERVING	
trace	milligrams sodium
7	grams total fat
trace	gram saturated fat
trace	gram carbohydrate
64	calories

Wine may be substituted for lemon juice.

TOMATO SAUCE
4 Servings

If you don't like the milk sauces, no matter what you add for extra flavor, try a tomato sauce. Excellent when you want a Spanish tang to your fish dish.

2 tablespoons unsalted special margarine
2 tablespoons flour
1 small bay leaf
¼ teaspoon pepper
1 tablespoon lemon juice
1 cup low sodium dietetic tomato juice

Melt margarine and blend in flour and seasonings. Add tomato juice and stir until sauce thickens. Pour at once over fish, and garnish with parsley for color contrast. Curry powder may be used in place of bay leaf.

ONE SERVING	TOTAL RECIPE	
3	10	milligrams sodium
6	23	grams total fat
1	4	grams saturated fat
5	20	grams carbohydrate
76	304	calories

LOW SATURATED FAT VARIATION
Vegetable oil may be substituted for margarine; or fat may be omitted. Combine flour and seasonings. Blend slowly with tomato juice. Cook, stirring constantly, until sauce thickens. If

no sodium restrictions, use regular tomato juice and add salt to taste.

One serving, with oil: negligible saturated fat; 1½ teaspoons vegetable oil.

10

A PARADE
OF VEGETABLES

WHERE CAN YOU GET SO MUCH for so little in restricted cookery? There are vegetables in abundance to use, and many of them have the good grace to be low in sodium and fat content and are generally high in minerals and vitamins. Broccoli, green beans, turnip greens, tomatoes, sweet potatoes, and many other dark green vegetables are rich sources of vitamins A and C. They also contain iron and other important minerals.

So it would seem that you will be able to pay court to vegetables on this diet and use them with a feeling of abandon (well, not quite all of them). If you want to make them appealing and nutritionally good you will have to dream up something better than the old boil-and-butter method of cookery. Good as that method may be for some of the young and tender vegetables of early spring, it is hardly the treatment for all in all seasons. As with fish, many cooking sins are committed in the guise of vegetable cookery.

First of all, select only fresh vegetables and treat them to proper refrigeration once you get them home, if you want good results. You can't leave them standing around on your sink from time of purchase to preparation time. And they don't like to be prepared in the morning for evening use. Such treatment results in loss of vitamins as well as of flavor.

As for the cooking itself: most vegetables yield up their subtle flavors to the water in which they are cooked. When they are cooked in a bath of water, in other words when too much water is used, little of their true flavor remains when they come to the table.

GROUP A	GROUP B	GROUP C*
Based upon ½ cup servings, each of these vegetables contains about 9 milligrams sodium, and negligible carbohydrate, calories and fat.	Based upon ½ cup servings, each of these vegetables contains about 9 milligrams sodium, 7 grams carbohydrate, 35 calories, and negligible fat.	Based upon ½ cup servings unless otherwise specified, each of these vegetables contains about 5 milligrams sodium, 15 grams carbohydrate, 70 calories, and negligible fat.
Asparagus	Onions	Beans, Lima or navy (fresh or dried)
Broccoli	Peas (fresh or dietetic low sodium canned only)	¼ cup beans, baked (without pork)
Brussels sprouts		⅓ cup or ½ small ear corn
Cabbage		
Cauliflower	Pumpkin	½ cup cooked lentils (dried)
Chicory	Rutabaga (yellow turnip)	⅔ cup parsnips
Cucumber		
Eggplant	Squash, winter (acorn, Hubbard, et cetera)	½ cup cooked peas, split green or yellow, cowpeas, et cetera (dried)
Endive		
Escarole		
Green beans		
Lettuce		1 small potato, white
Mushrooms		
Okra		

GROUP A	GROUP B	GROUP C*
Peppers, green or red		½ cup potatoes, mashed
Radishes		¼ cup or
Squash, summer (yellow, zucchini, et cetera)		½ small sweet potato
Tomato juice (low sodium dietetic only)		
Tomatoes		
Turnip greens		
Wax beans		

* Generally restricted on fat-carbohydrate control diets.

Neither do they like to be cooked for so long that they are mushy in consistency when served. They invite a careful bit of timing in this department. All in all, they require careful handling.

There are many little cooking tricks to help bring out the natural flavors of vegetables. But before we go into that, let's take a look at the Do and Don't list on the opposite page.

Use as desired (fresh, frozen or dietetic canned without added sodium, as permitted by your physician).

See Appendix 2 if you are using list-count method of menu planning.

DO NOT USE:

Artichokes, beet greens, beets, carrots, celery, Swiss chard, dandelion greens, kale, mustard greens, sauerkraut, spinach, turnips (white), canned juices, except low sodium dietetic packed without added salt. Fat-restricted dieters, without sodium restrictions, may use all kinds of vegetables — fresh, frozen, and regular canned — except baked beans prepared with added pork, or other vegetable combinations with added fat.

VEGETABLE COOKERY

A know-how of vegetable cookery involves a knowledge of the combining quality of vegetables with meats they so often accompany. We think of high-flavored meats with high-flavored vegetables. Let's see just how the principle does work out when the sodium count is so all-important.

Beef: With its fine flavor, beef invites such vegetable combinations as corn, string beans or Lima beans, broccoli, eggplant, sprouts, cauliflower, parsnips, yellow turnips, tomatoes, mushrooms, and onions.

Pork: This, too, is a high-flavored meat and is tasty with many of the vegetables listed above for beef — plus cabbage, succotash, parsnips, and sweet potatoes.

Lamb: Now let us turn to the milder meats. Young, succulent lamb is such a treat in the spring of the year that you will surely want to include it somehow if you can, and you can by using very low count vegetables with it. Peas, bless their low sodium content, are the most natural accompaniment to roast lamb, and hard to beat. Squash, asparagus, yellow turnips, cucumbers, baby Lima beans, may all take their turn. In serving lamb, be sure to remember that leg of lamb is lower in fat content than lamb chops.

Veal: With its delicate flavor, veal is a good choice for those of you on fat-restricted diets (but highest of the meats and poultry in sodium content) when you want to serve such vegetables as asparagus, succotash, squash, mushrooms, baby Lima beans, string beans, peas, young green corn.

Chicken (turkey, too): You will have to be pencil-wise again if you are restricting solid fats. Although light and dark meat are allowed, breast meat does contain less sodium and less fat. The vegetables that seem to combine most appropriately with chicken all have very low sodium content. They are corn, baby Lima beans, peas, sweet potatoes, and pearl onions.

Rabbit: Takes the same natural combinations in vegetables as does chicken, but because of its low sodium content, you can select vegetables of higher count, for variety's sake.

HINTS ON COOKING VEGETABLES:

1. Select only fresh vegetables to use. Wash them quickly, and store in closely covered jar or refrigerator container.

2. Prepare vegetables just before cooking for best flavor and nutrition. Under no condition let them soak in water. Whenever it is necessary to string beans, shell peas, or otherwise prepare vegetables before time of use, store in tightly covered jar and fill to top of container.

3. Cook vegetables in as little water as possible; steam whenever possible.

4. Do not overcook. Vegetables are better for you when they are undercooked rather than overcooked. When overcooked or held warm for too long, they suffer loss of color, texture, and nutrients.

5. Save any remaining vegetable liquid for later cooking use in gravies, soups, and sauces.

6. You can get along very well without adding unsalted butter or margarine to cooked vegetables, particularly if you use lemon juice or wine to heighten flavor. But if you must add a fat, use small amounts (vegetable oil only, or special margarines in specified amounts, for restricted-fat diets).

7. For variety in flavoring, try herbs, too. In general, they should be sprinkled over tops of vegetables at end of cooking period. Cover utensil and let stand not more than 5 minutes. Some particularly good *vegetable-herb* combinations are:

Cauliflower with *tarragon* and *low sodium dietetic prepared mustard* (use regular mustard if no sodium restriction)

Summer squash with *nutmeg, mace,* or *sweet basil*

Green beans with *marjoram, savory,* or *dill*

Peas with *thyme* or *marjoram*

Broccoli with *dill weed, oregano,* or *garlic*

8. The red and white table wines for which you have sodium content (Burgundy, the clarets, Rhine, and sauterne) combine with many vegetables for improved flavor. The white wines blend well with light-colored vegetables, the red with the darker ones. Experiment with small amounts and let your own taste guide your use.

9. A *pinch* of sugar is a good accent where salt is omitted. Do not use if on fat-carbohydrate control.

10. Don't overseason. Vegetables have fine flavors in their own rights.

Let us take a look at the methods of cooking vegetables and see what they have to offer.

Pressure Cooking: Preserves the bright color, natural flavor, and best in nutrition to the highest degree. Vegetables cook so quickly by this method that they require only about ⅓ of the usual boiling time.

Steaming: One of our favorite methods of vegetable cookery because of the consistency of good results — colorful and tasteful vegetables, with all of their natural flavor preserved and none of that mushy, all-boiled-out flavor. Place vegetables on rack, with just enough boiling water in the bottom of pan to generate steam. Cover and steam for length of time required for individual vegetable. In general, this will be from 5 to 15 or more minutes longer than for boiling.

A variation of this method and one that brings vegetables to the table chock-full of their true flavors is the lettuce leaf "cover." All you have to do is to place vegetables on rack as with ordinary steaming and cover them with a large piece or two of dripping lettuce. Do not use more than ¼ to ½ inch of water in bottom of utensil. A real flavor-saver.

Pan-frying, also called sautéing and frying: Depends upon fat for the liquid in which the vegetable is to be cooked and is quite a favorite in Chinese cookery. Put a little vegetable oil in the bottom of your skillet, and add your vegetable, shredded or sliced thin, with 1 or 2 tablespoons of water. Stir occasionally and cook until fork-tender — from 5 to 15 minutes. Cabbage, lettuce, broccoli, and sprouts all lend themselves to this treatment (may not be your choice if total fat is restricted).

Baking: Will preserve the food values of your vegetables to a high degree. Beans, potatoes, and tomatoes lend themselves particularly well to direct oven cookery. Eggplant, cauliflower, or mixed vegetables and mushrooms are naturals for the oven casserole.

Boiling: This is the least desirable method of vegetable cookery. When you do elect to boil your vegetables, cook them covered in the smallest possible amount of *boiling* water. Bring your vegetables to a boil quickly, then turn down the heat and simmer gently. Do not overcook, and serve as soon as they are cooked. Save every bit of water left over for sauces and soups. Store it in a covered jar until time of use. Better still, cook in a low sodium dietetic beef bouillon cube liquid in place of water, if your sodium allowance will permit. (Use regular bouillon cube liquid if sodium is not restricted.)

Broiling: The method used for very young and tender raw vegetables, particularly when you are serving a broiled meat and want to conserve heat and cook your vegetables right along with the meat. It can sometimes be used for reheating cooked vegetables, too.

ASPARAGUS

This vegetable is altogether too often spoiled by improper cooking. It can arrive on the table limp and listless when cooked too long, or in too much water. Under such conditions, it is a doubtful addition especially without salt. On the other hand, it can be simply delicious if panned or steamed.

HOT ASPARAGUS
3 Servings

Prepare by breaking off all tough ends and removing scales of 1 pound. Put the stalks standing upright on a rack in saucepan or directly into pan if you are going to pan-cook it. Cover tops with dripping lettuce leaf to hold in moisture, and cut down amount of water needed for boiling or steaming. Whatever you do, use a minimum amount of water. Boil 10 to 20 minutes, steam 12 to 30 minutes; for tips only, boil 5 to 15 minutes, steam 7 to 15 minutes in a tightly covered pan. Serve plain, with lemon juice, "Butter," (page 207) or with sauce of choice. Add salt for those without sodium restrictions.

6 STALKS

Without "butter"

2	milligrams sodium
trace	gram total fat
5	grams carbohydrate
26	calories

ASPARAGUS CHINESE STYLE
6 Servings

2 pounds fresh asparagus
¾ cup low sodium bouillon, chicken-flavored
1 tablespoon cornstarch

1 tablespoon cold water
1 garlic clove, finely chopped
Few grains black pepper
2 tablespoons vegetable oil
1 teaspoon lemon juice

Wash asparagus and break off tough lower stalks. Using a sharp knife, cut diagonally in very thin slices. Make chicken bouillon, stir in a mixture of cornstarch and water. Cook until thickened, stirring constantly to prevent scorching. Add garlic and pepper. Sauté asparagus slices in hot oil for about 3 minutes, until fork-tender. Blend lemon juice and sauce; pour over asparagus. Stir and cook 1 minute. Serve at once. Salt for those without sodium restrictions.

ONE SERVING	TOTAL RECIPE	
3	18	milligrams sodium
5	29	grams total fat
trace	2	grams saturated fat
5	32	grams carbohydrate
70	419	calories

One serving: 1 teaspoon vegetable oil.

VARIATION

Follow directions for preparation of asparagus, and steam over boiling water until fork-tender (about 20 minutes depending upon the size of asparagus and container).

FRESH OR FROZEN STRING BEANS
4 Servings

Pressure-cook, steam, pan-cook, or broil. Allow from 20 to 35 minutes for boiled whole string beans; 15 to 25 minutes for cut.

To 1 pound of beans try adding a pinch of sugar, 1 teaspoon vegetable oil to water or bouillon. When ready to serve, add ⅓ teaspoon dill weed and ½ teaspoon lemon juice. Salt for those without sodium restrictions.

ONE SERVING	TOTAL RECIPE	
Without low sodium bouillon or oil		
7	28	milligrams sodium
trace	1	gram total fat
trace	trace	gram saturated fat
7	28	grams carbohydrate
32	129	calories

VARIATIONS

Marjoram or savory will accent the flavor of beans pleasantly.

For variety, add a few slivers of toasted almonds as you serve your string beans and 1 tablespoon dry red wine in place of lemon juice.

Prepare green beans as outlined above. Wipe a small skillet with 1 teaspoon vegetable oil and slightly warm. Add 1 tablespoon minced onion and 1 small clove of garlic, minced, or pressed through a garlic press. Cook for 5 minutes, stirring to avoid scorching. Add to beans the last minute of cooking.

Instead of the onion-garlic addition, substitute 1 tablespoon browned, slivered almonds. Add and stir them into beans at time of serving.

LIMA BEANS
2 Servings

Baby Limas are delicious whenever available. Use 1½ pounds unshelled or ½ pound shelled beans. Simply cut off their outer rims and shell-like peas. Boil 20 to 30 minutes; steam 25 to 35 minutes. Season with ½ teaspoon unsalted special margarine and 1 teaspoon minced parsley. (Savory may be used in place of parsley.) Salt for those without sodium restrictions.

ONE SERVING	TOTAL RECIPE	
4	7	milligrams sodium
2	4	grams total fat
trace	1	gram saturated fat
30	60	grams carbohydrate
176	352	calories

LOW SATURATED FAT VARIATION
Substitute vegetable oil for special margarine or serve without fat. Salt to taste if no sodium restriction.

One serving, without fat: negligible grams saturated fat.

BROCCOLI

Now, here is a versatile vegetable, distinctly flavorsome and equally good hot or cold. Its green flowers lend a decorative quality to the salad bowl; and flowers, stems, and leaves may be cooked. It will yield a marvelous flavor if you will only cook it pan or steam method.

Ms. Lois Marr introduced us to it, Chinese-fashion, some years ago, and here we adapt it for diet cookery.

PANNED BROCCOLI
3 Servings

1 pound broccoli
2 tablespoons vegetable oil
1 tablespoon water
1 cup low sodium chicken bouillon
1 teaspoon cornstarch
¼ teaspoon oregano

Wash the broccoli; cut stems from flowering tops. Peel stems and cut crosswise. Heat the oil until very hot in a heavy skillet or Chinese wock. Add broccoli stems and stir constantly for 5 minutes. Add water and cut-up flowers; cook fast for 2 minutes. Heap to one side of utensil and stir into oil mixture the blended low sodium bouillon and cornstarch. (The amount specified provides a lot of sauce; reduce amount if desired.) Let cook slowly over low heat until it thickens. Now blend in broccoli; mix thoroughly and stir to prevent scorching. Cook until just fork-tender, about 10 minutes or less. Sprinkle oregano over top, cover and let stand 2 minutes. Serve at once. Salt for those without sodium restrictions.

ONE SERVING	TOTAL RECIPE	
21	63	milligrams sodium
10	29	grams total fat
1	2	grams saturated fat
8	23	grams carbohydrate
125	376	calories

One serving: 2 teaspoons vegetable oil.

VARIATION

Prepare 1 pound broccoli as outlined above. Parboil about 10 minutes or, better still, pressure-cook 1½ to 3 minutes. Meanwhile, put 2 teaspoons vegetable oil into your skillet and heat. Add 1 tablespoon minced onion, and 1 garlic clove split lengthwise and fasten on a wooden pick. Brown slowly and add drained broccoli. Sauté all together for about 10 more minutes or until done. Sprinkle with ⅛ teaspoon pepper and stir in 1 tablespoon lemon juice. Remove garlic and serve at once, adding salt for those without sodium restrictions. Vinegar or red table wine may be used in place of lemon juice.

CABBAGE

For variety's sake, when you want to serve cabbage raw, don't always depend upon a cabbage slaw. Use wedges, white savory or red, for that raw addition of the day. Its crunchy goodness is good to the last taste, served in just its natural state.

HOT CABBAGE
4 Servings

Shred a 1-pound head cabbage thin and wash thoroughly. Put the dripping cabbage into your saucepan, adding enough water to keep from scorching. Add ½ teaspoon unsalted special margarine, ½ cup sugar, ½ teaspoon caraway seed, and 2 tablespoons vinegar to make the whole tart. Boil only until tender. This takes from 3 to 10 minutes. Salt for those without sodium restrictions; omit with carbohydrate restrictions.

ONE SERVING	TOTAL RECIPE	
21	83	milligrams sodium
1	3	grams total fat
trace	1	gram saturated fat
31	124	grams carbohydrate
126	504	calories

Substitute vegetable oil for unsalted special margarine in Basic Recipe. Add salt if no sodium restrictions.

One serving: negligible grams saturated fat; ⅛ teaspoon vegetable oil.

CAULIFLOWER

It is delicious raw, and its dainty flowerets should be served in this form often.

Whatever you do, don't overcook cauliflower. Its flowerets need only 8 to 15 minutes, if you choose to boil them, while 10 to 20 minutes will give desirable tenderness if steamed. For real conservation of flavor and texture, try steaming this vegetable. Once tried, it's safe to predict you'll be a convert.

STEAMED CAULIFLOWER
3 Servings

Wash and cut up 1-pound cauliflower and steam 10 to 20 minutes, depending upon the size of your flowerets. Season with ¼ teaspoon tarragon and a dash of cayenne, and let stand 5 minutes. Spread flowerets lightly with low sodium prepared mustard, using a brush to spread quickly. Use regular mustard and add salt for those without sodium restrictions.

ONE SERVING	TOTAL RECIPE	
15	60	milligrams sodium
trace	1	gram total fat
trace	trace	gram saturated fat
8	24	grams carbohydrate
42	125	calories

SPANISH CAULIFLOWER
6 Servings

1-pound head cooked cauliflower
½ teaspoon thyme, minced
Few grains pepper
Dash allspice
2½ cups fresh tomatoes, cut up
½ cup soft low sodium bread crumbs (100 percent whole wheat bread is particularly good)
1 teaspoon unsalted special margarine

Put cauliflower in a shallow, lightly oiled casserole. Add seasonings to the tomatoes and bring to a rapid boil. Pour over cauliflower, top with crumbs, and dot all with 1 teaspoon unsalted special margarine. Bake in 350° (moderate) oven 15 to 30 minutes, and serve at once. Add salt for those without sodium restrictions.

ONE SERVING	TOTAL RECIPE	
13	79	milligrams sodium
1	8	grams total fat
trace	1	gram saturated fat
11	68	grams carbohydrate
64	385	calories

LOW SATURATED FAT VARIATION
Follow Basic Recipe except substitute vegetable oil for unsalted margarine. Put bread crumbs and oil into jar and shake to

blend; add to cauliflower mixture. If not restricted in sodium, add salt to taste.

One serving: negligible grams saturated fat; ⅛ teaspoon vegetable oil.

GREEN CORN

The vegetable marts not only strip corn of some of its husks and therefore reduce a considerable part of its nutritional value, but let the ears stand around on the counters so long that kernels are withered often before you can make your purchase. Enough said. Don't purchase. The ideal way, of course, is to be able to get corn on the cob fresh from the field with its golden tassels gleaming. Hurry it home and set in a shallow pan of water so that its stubby bases are kept moist and fresh until time of husking. The natural sugars in corn begin to change to starch within one-half hour after picking. If you can't buy this vegetable fresh in your market, you may want to resort to the frozen variety that is packed under favorable conditions.

FRESH OR FROZEN CORN

Good on the cob, boiled or barbecued; cut from the cob and mixed with a little unsalted special margarine and pepper or made into fritters; with green peppers, or combined with an assortment of vegetables — fresh or frozen corn is good in so many ways! (By the way, frozen corn is the one vegetable that needs to be partly thawed before cooking. Follow the directions on your package for best results.) Put shakers of salt on the table for individual use of those without sodium restrictions.

One pound of cut corn will yield 4 servings.
Substitute a little vegetable oil for low saturated fat dieters.

CUCUMBERS

Perhaps you reserve cucumbers for salads when you want
their crunchiness to add texture contrast. For variety, try them
hot sometime and see if you don't like their "different" taste.

CUCUMBERS IN MILK
6 Servings

1 teaspoon unsalted special margarine
3 cucumbers
⅔ cup sliced radishes
¼ teaspoon grated onion (or sliced thin)
¼ cup nonfat milk
¼ teaspoon pepper

Melt margarine and add cucumbers, radishes, and onions. Cover
and cook rapidly 10 minutes, adding 2 tablespoons of water if
necessary to prevent scorching. Uncover and continue cooking
to let some of the juice evaporate. Add nonfat milk and pepper;
reheat, but do not boil. Add salt for the regulars. Count the
dieter's portion of milk in the daily allowance or use low
sodium nonfat milk.

ONE SERVING	TOTAL RECIPE	
16	96	milligrams sodium
1	5	grams total fat
trace	1	gram saturated fat
5	32	grams carbohydrate
27	169	calories

LOW SATURATED FAT VARIATION

Substitute vegetable oil for margarine. If not restricted in sodium, add salt to taste.

One serving: negligible saturated fat; ⅛ teaspoon vegetable oil.

BAKED EGGPLANT
4 Servings

This easy-to-do vegetable recipe came to us from the San Joaquin, now Central California, Heart Association and is so good we hope you will try it often.

Preheat oven to 350° (moderate). Remove skin from eggplant. Cut into slices ⅜-inch thick. Place slices close together on a lightly oiled cookie sheet. Brush tops of the slices with 1 tablespoon vegetable oil. Bake 12 minutes. Turn slices and bake about 10 minutes longer. Serve at once with a light sprinkling of salt and white pepper for the regulars; or sprinkle with lemon juice for all.

ONE SERVING	TOTAL RECIPE	
Without lemon juice		
2	8	milligrams sodium
4	15	grams total fat
trace	1	gram saturated fat
6	22	grams carbohydrate
55	219	calories

One serving: ¾ teaspoon vegetable oil.

Bake whole eggplant in preheated 350° (moderate) oven until it turns color and can be pierced with fork (about 30 minutes). Slice in half lengthwise and cut off stem piece, being careful not to tear skin. Scoop out the flesh, and mash with a potato masher. Add ¼ cup cholesterol-free egg substitute, 1 teaspoon dehydrated onion flakes, and ⅛ teaspoon pepper. Add salt if sodium is not restricted. Mix thoroughly, and blend in ⅓ to ½ cup fine low sodium bread crumbs, so that mixture is quite firm. Return to shells. Bake in preheated 350° (moderate) oven 30 minutes or until golden brown.

BROILED MUSHROOMS
2 Servings

Remove stems from ½ pound large mushrooms and clean caps. Brush lightly with 1 tablespoon vegetable oil. Place caps, top side up, 3 inches below broiler unit. Broil 5 to 8 minutes. Fork-test, and do not overcook, as mushrooms toughen with too much and too long heat. Add a light sprinkling of salt for those without sodium restrictions.

ONE SERVING	TOTAL RECIPE	
17	33	milligrams sodium
8	15	grams total fat
trace	1	gram saturated fat
5	10	grams carbohydrate
93	186	calories

One serving: 1½ teaspoons vegetable oil.

ONIONS

You may want to skip right over this section, believing that too much emphasis has already been given to onions as a flavor. True, they do appear frequently in this connection because they heighten the flavor of many dishes when salt is not used. As a seasoning, they can be cleverly used and disguised so that the taster is aware only of the flavor and not at all of onions.

As a vegetable, they add their hearty bit to many a meal. The small white pearl onions, boiled and buttered, are a natural combination with turkey or duck. Good with veal, too. The larger and lustier varieties lend themselves to baking. They combine well, also, with other vegetables where an onion, in combination flavor, is desired. Boiled, baked, pan-fried, or sautéed — onions offer you interesting vegetable variety.

BAKED ONION RINGS
6 Servings

Peel and slice 1 pound large onions crosswise, ¼-inch thick, and separate into rings. Dip in 1½ cups Fritter Batter (page 274) and put into shallow pan, coated with vegetable oil. Bake about 30 minutes in a preheated 400° (hot) oven, or until lightly brown. Check at half time to see whether additional oil is needed. Sprinkle lightly with paprika and serve with salt added for the regulars (without sodium restriction). Subtract the amount of milk used from the daily allowance or use low sodium nonfat milk for the dieter.

ONE SERVING	TOTAL RECIPE	
32	190	milligrams sodium
3	17	grams total fat
trace	3	grams saturated fat
23	140	grams carbohydrate
138	826	calories

LOW SATURATED FAT VARIATION

Follow Basic Recipe except use Low Saturated Fat Variation for Fritter Batter (page 275).

One serving: negligible grams saturated fat; ⅓ teaspoon vegetable oil.

GLAZED PEARL ONIONS
6 Servings

1½ pounds pearl onions
2 tablespoons vegetable oil
Few grains pepper
2 tablespoons sugar
¼ teaspoon fresh grated nutmeg

Peel onions and steam over water in covered pan for 25 to 35 minutes. Remove from heat before they are quite ready to serve. Drain. Meanwhile, heat 2 tablespoons vegetable oil. Add other ingredients and stir to blend. Add onions and cook slowly until they are golden in color, turning as needed to ensure uniform golden color and glaze.

ONE SERVING	TOTAL RECIPE	
10	62	milligrams sodium
5	29	grams total fat
trace	2	grams saturated fat
13	78	grams carbohydrate
97	580	calories

One serving: 1 teaspoon vegetable oil.

PARSNIPS

Parsnips may be sautéed or baked with unsalted special margarine or oil. If quartered lengthwise, they boil in 20 to 30 minutes; bake in 30 to 45 minutes in 350° (moderate) oven. Remember to remove the parsnip cores when you prepare them, so you will not get woody shreds.

BOILED PARSNIPS IN SAVORY SAUCE
2 Servings

½ pound parsnips
1 tablespoon flour
1 tablespoon unsalted special margarine
⅓ cup parsnip liquid
¼ teaspoon low sodium dietetic Worcestershire sauce
¼ teaspoon onion powder
Scant ¼ teaspoon low sodium dietetic prepared mustard
1 teaspoon minced parsley

Wash and scrape parsnips and cut into lengthwise strips. Barely cover with water and boil 20 to 30 minutes until just tender. Drain liquid and save. Combine flour with heated special margarine in small skillet. Add parsnip liquid and stir until mixture boils and thickens. Add remaining ingredients except parsley. Pour sauce over parsnips and serve garnished with parsley. Salt for those without sodium restrictions.

ONE SERVING	TOTAL RECIPE	
13	25	milligrams sodium
6	12	grams total fat
1	2	grams saturated fat
20	39	grams carbohydrate
136	272	calories

VARIATION FOR SODIUM RESTRICTION

One tablespoon low sodium dietetic cheddar-type cheese may be added to sauce.

LOW SATURATED FAT VARIATION

Follow Basic Recipe but omit margarine from sauce. Slowly blend parsnip liquid with flour, stirring constantly; or substitute vegetable oil for the unsalted margarine. If no sodium restrictions, use regular Worcestershire sauce, prepared mustard, and add salt to taste.

One serving: negligible grams saturated fat; 1½ teaspoons vegetable oil.

FRESH PEAS

Peas may be panned, steamed, or boiled, although the last method is certainly the least desirable. Small and tender, the first peas of spring need little seasoning, except perhaps a pinch of sugar and a small amount of vegetable oil or unsalted special margarine. Do not add butter or margarine if you are on saturated fat restriction.

PEAS

2 Servings

Shell 1 pound of peas just before cooking, to preserve every bit of the goodness. Minister to their cooking time, lest they be overcooked and spoiled both in appearance and taste. For best results, pressure-cook or steam them with dripping leaves of lettuce lining saucepan and covering peas. Cook at the very last moment and serve piping hot. Add salt for those without sodium restrictions.

ONE SERVING	TOTAL RECIPE	
2	4	milligrams sodium
trace	1	gram total fat
trace	trace	gram saturated fat
13	25	grams carbohydrate
101	201	calories

VARIATION

Prepare and cook as outlined above. When tender, add ½ teaspoon savory, thyme, or onion powder. Stir well, so herbs blend with all of peas. Cover and let stand for 5 minutes for further blending, and serve at once. If you wish, you may cut up lettuce and serve with peas, for it is quite tasty. Also, you may place a few pea pods on top of lettuce leaves when you cook peas to add to flavor.

PEPPERS (GREEN)

A colorful addition to our lengthening list of vegetables. The green bell pepper, a perennial favorite for its color, taste, and texture, a buoyant addition to a plate of raw vegetables, is equally at home when cooked. In this connection, it is usually served whole, with some stuffing, and baked; or cut in slivers or rings, and sautéed.

STUFFED GREEN PEPPERS
6 Servings

6 bell peppers
1 tablespoon vegetable oil
2 tablespoons chopped onion
¼ teaspoon thyme
Dash savory
Few grains black pepper
2 cups cooked brown rice (or Ala)
½ cup tomato juice, canned low sodium dietetic

Remove stem, seeds, and membrane from peppers. Wash inside and out. Cover with boiling water and cook 5 minutes to parboil. Meanwhile heat oil and lightly brown onion. Remove from heat; add seasonings, rice, and tomato juice. Fill peppers with rice mixture. Place in baking dish and bake in a preheated 400° (hot) oven about 20 minutes, until thoroughly heated and fork-tender. A tomato sauce may be added, if desired. Salt for those without sodium restrictions.

ONE SERVING	TOTAL RECIPE	
With rice; without sauce		
10	62	milligrams sodium
3	18	grams total fat
trace	1	gram saturated fat
14	85	grams carbohydrate
103	617	calories

One serving: ½ teaspoon vegetable oil.

VARIATIONS

Chopped or ground leftover meat (veal or chicken are particularly good) may be substituted in whole or part for rice. Ground lean beef is also an interesting filling.

POTATOES
(White)

A well-cooked potato adds enjoyment and balance to a well-planned meal, and with its low sodium and low fat content is a welcome addition. Mashed potatoes are perhaps the least savory of the many ways they may be prepared without salt, and where low sodium milk must be used as a liquid, they are apt to be pretty flat. If your meal just seems to call for them in this form, try adding a little finely minced parsley and a bit of grated onion to bolster them. Buttered, baked, fried, or scalloped, they make wonderful contributions to our meals. For nutrition's sake, leave skins on whenever possible during cooking, or pare very thin.

NEW POTATOES
3 Servings

Use 1 pound for 3 servings.

Scrape and wash 1 pound potatoes. Boil whole about 25 minutes until fork-tender (depends upon the size of the potato). Instead of pan-frying in vegetable oil and sprinkling with parsley, which is a delicious treatment, try sprinkling with ½ teaspoon crumbled dill, 1 teaspoon vegetable oil, and ¼ teaspoon freshly ground pepper. Blend and serve with a sprinkling of salt for those without sodium restrictions.

ONE SERVING	TOTAL RECIPE	
4	11	milligrams sodium
2	5	grams total fat
trace	trace	gram saturated fat
21	63	grams carbohydrate
107	320	calories

One serving: ⅓ teaspoon vegetable oil.

STUFFED POTATOES

4 Servings

2 medium-sized potatoes
¼ cup nonfat milk, warmed
½ teaspoon vegetable oil
¼ teaspoon tarragon
Dash onion powder
Dash garlic powder
Few grains black pepper
Paprika

Select 2 potatoes of similar size; scrub thoroughly. Wrap in aluminum foil in individual packages. Bake 45 to 60 minutes in a 350° (moderate) oven until tender. Remove from oven and cut lengthwise. Scoop out potatoes and blend in warmed milk. Beat until snowy white and as fluffy as your whipped cream in the days before restricted cookery. Stir in oil and seasonings; blend thoroughly. Give one more beating to keep fluffy. Lightly spoon mixture into potato shells, heaping full. Sprinkle with paprika and lightly brown if crusty top is desired. Otherwise, serve at once. Add salt for those without sodium restrictions. So little milk is in the dieter's portion that you may not have to count this unless restriction is severe.

ONE SERVING	TOTAL RECIPE	
10	38	milligrams sodium
1	3	grams total fat
trace	trace	gram saturated fat
9	37	grams carbohydrate
48	193	calories

SODIUM RESTRICTED VARIATION

Top each filled potato shell with a slice of low sodium dietetic cheese.

LOW SATURATED FAT VARIATION

Cut 1 slice Count Down Cheese Spread into small cubes and fold into potato mixture or dot tops. Sprinkle with paprika and set under broiler for 5 minutes until golden brown.

MASHED SWEET POTATOES
2 Servings

Wash and boil ½ pound sweet potatoes, unpeeled. Remove from stove and peel. Mash thoroughly and add ½ teaspoon orange peel (or fresh, grated), two dashes Angostura Bitters, and ½ cup orange juice (or less) for piquant flavor. Beat until fluffy. Serve at once. Add salt for those without sodium restrictions.

ONE SERVING	TOTAL RECIPE	
10	20	milligrams sodium
1	1	gram total fat
trace	trace	gram saturated fat
31	61	grams carbohydrate
133	265	calories

VARIATIONS

One-half cup crushed pineapple and pineapple juice may be substituted for the orange juice.

CANDIED YAMS
6 Servings

Because any fancy treatment of yams increases their carbohydrate and calorie content to such high levels, they must only be used when calories and carbohydrate are not restricted.

Wash and boil 1½ pounds yams, unpeeled, until tender. Meanwhile, make a sirup of 1½ cups water, 1 cup light brown sugar, 1 tablespoon vegetable oil, and ⅛ teaspoon nutmeg. Heat all together and simmer gently. Remove yams from fire, peel and slice. Arrange in lightly oiled baking dish. Pour sirup over yams and bake in a preheated 400° (hot) oven until a light golden brown. No salt or substitute needed.

ONE SERVING	TOTAL RECIPE	
20	122	milligrams sodium
3	16	grams total fat
trace	1	gram saturated fat
60	357	grams carbohydrate
262	1573	calories

One serving: ½ teaspoon vegetable oil.

SPROUTS

Brussels sprouts, with their moderate sodium content, can be combined with beef, pork, or veal to their advantage because of their high flavor. One pound sprouts will give 4 servings.

BRUSSELS SPROUTS
4 Servings

Try cooking 1 quart with a pinch of sugar and sprinkle lightly with 1 teaspoon lemon juice; then serve. Add salt for those without sodium restrictions.

ONE SERVING	TOTAL RECIPE	
12	48	milligrams sodium
1	2	grams total fat
trace	trace	gram saturated fat
9	35	grams carbohydrate
41	165	calories

VARIATION
Use vinegar in place of lemon juice; or dress with a low sodium hollandaise sauce (but not for those with saturated fat restrictions).

SQUASH

Squash is "in" every season, fortunately so, with its very low sodium and fat content. Whether you choose to serve on your menu the crookneck or zucchini, the delicate green or white scallop of summer, or the Hubbard of winter, you have a mild and versatile vegetable. Sliced or cut in wedges, the spring and summer varieties can be steamed to advantage and are delicious combined with a small dribbling of oil or unsalted special margarine, sugar, or cinnamon. Winter Hubbard is best baked or mashed.

ZUCCHINI–ITALIAN STYLE
4 Servings

1 tablespoon vegetable oil
1 tablespoon chopped onion
1 chopped garlic clove
½ teaspoon rosemary
4 medium-sized zucchini squash (about 1 pound)
1 tablespoon slivered blanched almonds
1 teaspoon lemon juice

Put oil into skillet; warm. Add onion, garlic and rosemary. Stir and cook until oil is absorbed and onion-garlic is tenderized. Add washed and sliced zucchini (unpeeled). Add 2 to 4 tablespoons water. Cook about 10 minutes just until tender. Blend in almonds and lemon juice. Toss lightly. Serve at once. Add salt for those without sodium restrictions.

ONE SERVING	TOTAL RECIPE	
1	5	milligrams sodium
5	19	grams total fat
trace	1	gram saturated fat
5	19	grams carbohydrate
64	255	calories

One serving: ¾ teaspoon vegetable oil.

TOMATOES

Universally liked, tomatoes, fortunately, can be used often on restricted dietaries. Conveniently low in sodium and fat content, they can be used as wedges, in salads galore, and as a vegetable. Boiled, baked, or broiled, alone or in combination, they will do much to add zest to your meals. They combine with such other vegetables as string beans (with a little rosemary and thyme), with corn and green peppers, with Lima beans — yes, and with okra too. We have already seen in meat cookery how tomatoes are used as a seasoning as well as a vegetable accompaniment. There is scarcely a vegetable which will work harder for you.

Thyme, curry, dill, marjoram, and parsley are herbs that combine favorably with this vegetable.

BAKED TOMATO SLICES
3 Servings

Use 3 tomatoes weighing about 1 pound.

Wash and cut in slices, ¼ inch thick. Bread in crumbled shredded wheat (about 1 biscuit). Sprinkle lightly with ½ teaspoon thyme, ⅛ teaspoon fresh black pepper, and a pinch of sugar. Place on baking sheet lightly oiled. Bake in 350° (moderate) oven for 15 to 30 minutes. Sprinkle with salt for the regulars.

ONE SERVING	TOTAL RECIPE	
5	16	milligrams sodium
1	2	grams total fat
trace	trace	gram saturated fat
15	44	grams carbohydrate
67	202	calories

VARIATION

Broiled tomatoes may be prepared in exactly the same way as Baked Tomatoes. Cut slices thicker, of course, for broiling.

BAKED STUFFED TOMATOES
6 Servings

6 tomatoes of even size (2 pounds)
¼ cup onion, minced
2 tablespoons vegetable oil
⅛ teaspoon black pepper
1 cup soft low sodium bread crumbs
⅛ teaspoon allspice
½ teaspoon sugar

Wash and scoop out unpeeled tomatoes. Sauté onions in vegetable oil. Stir in tomato pulp, bread, and seasoning. Stuff and place in lightly oiled baking dish. Add a little hot water to cover the bottom of the dish. Bake in a preheated 350° (moderate) oven for 20 minutes. Add salt for the regulars.

ONE SERVING	TOTAL RECIPE	
6	33	milligrams sodium
5	32	grams total fat
trace	trace	gram saturated fat
15	44	grams carbohydrate
111	665	calories

One serving: 1 teaspoon vegetable oil.

"BUTTERING"

Unsalted special margarine may be used in moderation in many of these vegetable recipes for the fine seasoning that it is, if allowed on your diet. Be sure to count it in your fat allowance if you include it. Vegetable oils may be substituted for unsalted margarine in the lemon, garlic, wine sauces (without egg), allowing ½ teaspoon oil per serving, for those with saturated fat restrictions.

Lemon Butter: Fastest way to perk up the flavor of sodium-restricted foods is with Lemon Butter or oil. Like the wave of a magic wand, a pat of this seasoned margarine will transform a flat-tasting food into something pretty special. Versatile, too, with four variations on the basic mix:

BASIC "LEMON BUTTER"
4 Servings

A Sunkist tested recipe, used by permission from Sunkist Growers.

1½ teaspoons boiling water
2 tablespoons unsalted special margarine
1 tablespoon fresh lemon juice

Add boiling water to softened special margarine. Mix well. Add lemon juice and whip mixture until smooth and creamy. Makes enough for two cups of vegetables.

VARIATIONS

Add 1 tablespoon chopped fresh parsley for sandwich spread. Also fine for meats and vegetables.

Add 1 tablespoon chopped fresh herbs or 1½ teaspoons dried herbs (approximate, due to individual taste). Use on meats and vegetables. Begin with small additions, such as basil, garlic, or onion *powder*, mustard, rosemary, thyme.

Add 1 tablespoon grated onion or chopped chives. Excellent on baked potato. Try also on green beans and squash.

Add ½ teaspoon dry mustard and ¼ teaspoon marjoram. Very good on steamed cabbage.

Browned Butter: This is delicious with corn on the cob, steamed squash (particularly summer), string beans, and plain sweet potatoes. Melt the amount of unsalted special margarine to be used until it darkens. Add 2 tablespoons lemon juice or vinegar. Herbs of choice may be added for another variety.

Garlic Butter: Melt unsalted special margarine and add 1 garlic clove, split lengthwise and fastened on a wooden pick. Let this stand until you are ready to add to vegetables. Remove garlic, blend, and serve. Minced parsley may be added to garlic butter for another variation.

Browned Butter Crumbs (*au beurre*): These are called for in many scalloped vegetable dishes and as a topping in others. Melt 2 tablespoons unsalted special margarine and stir in 1 cup fine, dry low sodium bread crumbs. Cook over low heat until crumbs are lightly browned. Season as desired.

Wine-Butter Sauce: Beat 1 egg yolk or 1 tablespoon cholesterol-free egg substitute and add 2 tablespoons water, 1 teaspoon lemon juice, ⅛ teaspoon freshly ground black pepper, and 1 tablespoon dry white wine. Cook slowly in double boiler until about the consistency of custard. Add 2 tablespoons unsalted special margarine and dash nutmeg. Stir and heat but do not boil. Pour at once over hot vegetables and serve. In general, this can be used only for those of you on mild sodium restriction with a whole egg allowance. Remember when you use the yolk of an egg in cooking you must subtract it from your daily or weekly allowance.

Where fat is not restricted closely along with your sodium, you may elect to use "butter" seasonings as sauces and serve them in a pitcher at the table.

LOW SATURATED FAT VARIATION

Substitute the following spread from the Home Service Department of Corn Products Refining Company as your basic mix for herb mixtures or use plain as a "butter" substitute. Spreads well but does not melt as do the "butters." Be sure to include amount used in your daily oil or total fat allowance, and use low sodium nonfat milk if your dieter is severely restricted in sodium.

CORN OIL SPREAD

1 tablespoon cornstarch
⅔ cup nonfat dry milk powder
1 tablespoon lemon juice
⅔ cup water
2 cups corn oil
Few drops yellow food coloring

Sift cornstarch and instant nonfat dry milk powder together into top of double boiler. Combine lemon juice and water; gradually add to starch mixture stirring until smooth. Cook over boiling water, stirring constantly, until mixture thickens, about 4 minutes. Remove from heat. Add corn oil, ¼ cup at a time, beating with rotary beater after each addition. Add coloring to give desired shade. Do not use electric blender. Makes about 1 pound 5½ ounces.

Add salt if no sodium restrictions.

One level tablespoon: 1 gram saturated fat (2½ teaspoons vegetable oil).

11

WITH A CRUET
IN EACH HAND

Oh, herbaceous treat!
'Twould tempt the dying anchorite to eat;
Back to the world he'd turn his fleeting soul,
And plunge his fingers in the salad bowl;
Serenely full the epicure would say,
"Fate cannot harm me, — I have dined today."
— SYDNEY SMITH
A Receipt for a Salad (*c. 1810*)*

AND TREAT INDEED is a succulent salad for persons on the sodium-restricted or fat-restricted diet. It is refreshingly good and adds much to the pleasure of eating. The health benefits also abound in its store of minerals and vitamins.

You can be in style, too, for the approved way of serving many of the best salads is to bring all ingredients and mixings to the table and assemble them in full view of all, respectfully and with care. This little ceremony of mixing the salad is not without its psychological benefits. The dribbling of oil and vinegar, the addition of seasonings, and the final tossing of the salad can stimulate appetites for the good food to come. With so many limitations in the choice and preparation of food, the very appearance of salad in its many garbs can set the stage for complete acceptance of the entire meal.

* From *A New Dictionary of Quotations*, selected and edited by H. L. Mencken; New York, Alfred A. Knopf, Incorporated, 1942. Quoted by permission of Alfred A. Knopf, Incorporated.

Discount it, if you will, but salad, from its inception to the last mouthful eaten, can be a plus-value to you, if you give it Number One billing at your festive board. Select it with care in relation to the rest of the meal, and prepare it with all the skill you have. Its rewards will be worth your "trouble."

There are some limitations in salads, of course, but no one but yourself need be aware of them. You have many tools (ingredients) with which to concoct good salads. Gone are the dandelion greens, nasturtium, celery, chard, and spinach for those with sodium restriction. So what? You still have a wide selection of lettuces and greens — butterhead, roseleaf, Boston and Los Angeles head lettuce, as well as the delectable romaine; and endive, cabbage, zucchini squash, and broccoli. Cucumbers, radishes, and parsley are available, too. Besides which, a wealth of fruit is at your disposal when a sweet salad is the choice.

When you are planning your menus, don't make the mistake of thinking any salad will do for any meal. There is the ever-present matter of the sodium and fat content of its ingredients; you may be surprised to see how those lettuce leaves and other makings add to the meal's total. Salad must, therefore, be thought of in relation to the count of a particular meal as well as for its eating qualities. It should be planned in the context of the meal in its entirety and *should complement the whole*.

Taking it by and large, vegetable salads are better appetite-stimulants than sweet fruits. This is also true when salads are to be served with the main course. Vegetable-tossed salads, the raw combinations, seem to combine naturally with most meats. Perhaps the outstanding exception is veal and fowl. You can use almost any light fruit combination with them and have a good effect, taste-wise, if you must have your fruit in salad form.

The fruit and molded salads should be considered primarily

dessert salads, to follow the main course or be used as the main interest in a lunch meal.

THINK through the different flavors you have used in your recent salads, and evaluate their contribution to your meals before you do too much new planning. Then make up your mind that you will turn out good salads without making too much extra work for yourself. The women's magazines are full of good time-saving suggestions and recipes for you to adapt.

FOR SODIUM RESTRICTION, DO NOT USE:

Prepared dressings, such as mayonnaise or French, except low sodium dietetic

Prepared fruit gelatin except dietetic low sodium

Salt

Shellfish except canned, dietetic low sodium

Vegetable salts (such as garlic, celery, and so on); pure powders may be used or low sodium dietetic

FOR SATURATED-FAT AND FAT-CARBOHYDRATE RESTRICTION, DO NOT USE:

Salad dressings which contain fresh or sour cream

Olive oil, unless specifically allowed

Cheese-flavored dressings

Regular prepared dressings, all varieties, unless made with an oil listed on your "allowables" (one teaspoon mayonnaise equals one teaspoon oil)

HINTS ON SALAD MAKING:

1. Have a work center for salad-making and keep your standbys always ready to use.

This should include such indispensables as a mixing tray, measuring spoons and cups, a *wooden* salad fork and spoon for dressing the salad, a large salad bowl, a pepper mill and peppercorns, sugar, paprika, salt for those without sodium restrictions. You will also want to have, on a tray or nearby, curry powder, cayenne, dry mustard, fresh or dried herbs (fresh are much better), garlic buds, young onions, and parsley sprigs, various salad oils, and vinegars.

2. Regardless of how you plan to serve your salad, do have your plates or bowls thoroughly chilled. You can't serve a crisp, chilled salad on tepid plates. That's right: set salad bowl and serving plates in the refrigerator to cool before using. Ditto for salad servers.

3. Pay special attention to your dressings. They add quality to your salad flavor.

4. Include the sodium content of lettuces and dressings if you must "do the count."

5. Be generous in your use of herbs and use fresh ones if possible for salads. Avoid blended seasonings and herbs. Concoct your own combinations and so make your salads distinctively your own creations.

6. Our recipes are developed with safflower or corn oil, but you may substitute any oil on your diet list. (Walnut oil will give you a French-tasting oil while olive oil emphasizes the Italian, but use them only if they are on your list.)

7. Let your own palate dictate use of lemon juice or vinegar. For steady use it is hard to beat a straight wine vinegar blended with an herb one when you want a tangy, robust flavor. But when you want the subtle savors of fruit juices, try lemon, lime, or orange. We like to rub our fruit salad bowls with the rind of citrus fruit to be used.

8. Always consider the color, texture, and shape of your salad "makings" in relation to the rest of the meal. For eye and taste appeal use only crisp, dry greens.

MAKING A TOSSED SALAD:

Whether you like the modern emphasis in home decorating or not, you can be grateful to it for the increase in large salad bowls and platters. All salad fanciers emphasize the point that a tossed salad can be well made only in a huge bowl. For best results, you will want one that has some depth as well as width, so you can gently lift your greens up and down and round-about in the tossing period.

When you harvest your greens from your garden patch, or bring them home from the store, trim off all inedible leaves and cut away brown spots. Store your greens in tightly covered containers in refrigerator until time of use. Before salad-making time, cut out core of head lettuce and hold the cavity under cold running water until its leaves separate and all are thoroughly washed. For the leaf lettuces and endive, put in a deep mixing bowl, separate each leaf, and wash thoroughly. This may require more than one water if much sand is imbedded. Dry greens by putting them in a clean towel, then transfer to lettuce bag and place in refrigerator until you are ready to use them. *Be sure they are completely dry before use.*

To assemble: Put greens and other salad ingredients into large bowl, and add garlic — not directly, as we pointed out in the chapter on herbs, but split in two, and rubbed over the heel of a piece of low sodium bread and tossed into the salad bowl with the greens. Dress greens with this *chapon* and remove it at time of serving.

Now you are ready for the oil. For good tossed salad, it is imperative that oil and vinegar be used separately and that you forget all about your homemade mixtures so carefully stored on your shelf. The reason for adding oil first is to seal the tiny pores in the leaves and protect them from quick wilting. The amount of vegetable oil to use will depend upon your particular medical restrictions, your own taste, and the size of the salad.

As a beginning, allow 1 teaspoon to 1 tablespoon per person, according to your allowance. Let the oil *dribble* slowly over the greens, then take wooden fork and spoon and lift gently.

Toss until each leaf is coated with the oil, and "so sealed from the invaders."

Add bits of "bruised" herbs, discarding bitter stems as you use them.

Now grind a sprinkling of fresh black pepper over your greens. Invest in a pepper mill if you do not already own one, and use peppercorns freshly ground at each making for improved salad flavor. Now you are ready for vinegar or lemon juice. Allow ½ teaspoon or more per serving.

Use any good vinegar to bring out the taste you want. There is nothing like wine vinegar for epicurean results. The amount, again, is a matter of taste and the brand you use. Allow about 1 teaspoon per serving in the beginning and increase if you want greater sharpness.

Toss salad again, after this addition, until seasonings and vinegar are well blended with the greens. Taste before you ask others to sit in judgment. When your salad is dressed to your liking, remove the garlic bread and serve at once.

Add salt for those without sodium restrictions.

SOME SIMPLE TOSSED SALADS

BASIC TOSSED SALAD
6 Servings

½ head romaine lettuce
½ head red crinkle lettuce
1 chopped garlic clove *or 1 chapon*
3 tomatoes, peeled and cut in wedges
½ cup thinly sliced onion rings
½ cup wafer-thin cucumber slices
4 tablespoons vegetable oil

¼ teaspoon freshly ground peppercorns
2 tablespoons wine vinegar

Wash each leaf of lettuce and thoroughly dry. Break leaves
into bite size and toss into large salad bowl. Add garlic and
vegetables. Drip oil over entire surface and toss with salad
fork and spoon, lifting and turning mixture to be sure that
oil has a chance to coat all surfaces. But use a gentle hand to
avoid any bruising of greens. Now grind pepper and blend.
Add vinegar and toss again. Taste for desired tartness. (With
tomatoes you may use less vinegar than with other vegetable
combinations because of their tartness.) Serve the sodium-
restricted dieter's portion; add salt for those without sodium
restriction.

ONE SERVING	TOTAL RECIPE	
13	79	milligrams sodium
10	58	grams total fat
1	4	grams saturated fat
7	41	grams carbohydrate
117	703	calories

One serving: 2 teaspoons vegetable oil.

VARIATIONS

We favor the fresh, uncooked vegetables for their crispness.
You may combine any of the vegetables on your list that
appeal to you, raw flowerets of broccoli or cauliflower, slices
of green pepper or squash (summer or zucchini), leeks — tops
and all — are good choices.

Cooked vegetables — leftovers or freshly cooked — may be
substituted for all or part of the fresh vegetables in the Basic
Recipe.

Orange, grapefruit, or tangerine sections combine with
greens when a more delicate and piquant tossed salad is the
choice. An excellent accompaniment to a veal dinner.

Lemon or lime juice may be substituted for wine vinegar in Basic Recipe.

For special ingredients, try *garbanzos*, slivers of cold veal, chicken, or beef, dietetic low sodium tuna or shrimps (regular for fat-restricted dieters who do not have to limit sodium), onion or garlic croutons (made of low sodium bread for sodium-restricted dieters), red beans, or a topping of dietetic low sodium cheese. For fat-restriction use small cubes of Count Down, 99 percent fat-free.

ZUCCHINI-RADISH SALAD
4 Servings

Combine two lettuces, such as ½ head romaine and ½ head Los Angeles head lettuce. Add ¼ cup sliced radish and ½ cup zucchini, slivered thin and quartered, a garlic heel of low sodium bread, and a bulb of a new onion. Dress with 3 tablespoons vegetable oil, freshly ground pepper, 2 tablespoons white wine vinegar. Add salt for those without sodium restriction. See previous directions for tossing.

ONE SERVING	TOTAL RECIPE	
14	56	milligrams sodium
11	43	grams total fat
1	3	grams saturated fat
5	20	grams carbohydrate
114	457	calories

One serving: 2¼ teaspoons vegetable oil.

VARIATION
Dress with French Dressing or Italian variation (pages 234–235) spiked with 1 teaspoon or less fresh or dried dill leaves.

OTHER SALADS

CABBAGE SLAW
4 Servings

Wash in ice water 2 cups finely shredded cabbage. Drain, wrap in towel. Dry and chill. Now put cabbage into a mixing bowl. Add 3 tablespoons Cooked Salad Dressing (page 235) and an extra pinch of mustard. Toss all lightly with a fork to blend and serve immediately on beds of lettuce. Add salt for those without sodium restrictions.

ONE SERVING	TOTAL RECIPE	
12	47	milligrams sodium
2	7	grams total fat
trace	trace	gram saturated fat
9	37	grams carbohydrate
48	191	calories

VARIATION

Add 1 cup crushed pineapple to the above (6 servings) or ½ cup crushed pineapple and ¼ cup yogurt (nonfat for fat-restriction).

POTATO SALAD PIQUANT
8 Servings

We are indebted to the Home Advisory Service of the Wine Institute, San Francisco, for this excellent recipe.

4 cups diced, cooked potatoes
2 hard-cooked eggs, chopped
1 cup diced cucumber

¼ cup chopped onion
¼ cup chopped parsley
1½ cups California white table wine
1 tablespoon white wine vinegar
2 teaspoons dry mustard
1 teaspoon dill seeds
½ cup low sodium mayonnaise
½ teaspoon pepper, freshly ground

Combine potatoes, eggs, cucumber, onion, and parsley in a mixing bowl. Add wine. Cover and chill in the refrigerator for 1 to 2 hours. Drain thoroughly. Add remaining ingredients, using just enough mayonnaise to moisten the mixture. Mix gently to avoid mashing the potatoes. Chill again until time to serve. Serve in crisp lettuce cups. This salad makes a delicious filling for a low sodium tomato aspic ring. Add salt for those without sodium restrictions.

ONE SERVING	TOTAL RECIPE	
With Rhine wine		
31	245	milligrams sodium
3	104	grams total fat
3	20	grams saturated fat
15	121	grams carbohydrate
182	1454	calories

LOW SATURATED FAT VARIATION

Omit eggs and substitute ½ cup Cooked Salad Dressing (page 235) for mayonnaise. Add salt for those without sodium restrictions.

One serving: negligible grams saturated fat; ⅜ teaspoon vegetable oil.

MAIN-DISH SALADS

When we think of more elaborate salads, we immediately think of shellfish and avocados. Avocado, fish, chicken, and meat are all important ingredients for the low sodium dietary when a rich main-dish salad is the choice. And don't neglect the dietetic low sodium shrimps, salmon, tuna, chicken, and ham, as well as the fresh varieties.

When fat is restricted, avocado may not be allowed on some regimens. But you have many choices from the above, and when sodium is not restricted, you will not have to use the dietetic items processed without salt. Fish and poultry are your best choices and they offer you great variety. The recipe below is an excellent one.

ALL-PURPOSE FISH SALAD

6 Servings

1 pound halibut, cut into small pieces
1 large tomato, chopped fine
1 small onion, chopped fine
½ green pepper, chopped fine
¼ cup vegetable oil
1 tablespoon white vinegar
¼ cup parsley, chopped
¼ cup lemon juice
¼ teaspoon oregano
6 sprigs parsley

Blanch fish in boiling water for 3 minutes. Remove from water. Cool. Place in large mixing bowl and combine with remaining ingredients. Marinate at least 3 hours in refrigerator. Drain and serve on bed of lettuce. Garnish with parsley sprigs.

ONE SERVING (1½ oz. fish, cooked weight)	TOTAL RECIPE	
37	223	milligrams sodium
10	60	grams total fat
1	4	grams saturated fat
5	31	grams carbohydrate
177	1063	calories

VARIATION

Any cooked white fish may be substituted for the uncooked halibut; allow about ½ cup loosely packed fish per serving.

VARIATIONS

Substitute salmon, cod or turbot for halibut and vary your seasonings. Dill is an excellent substitute for oregano in the marinade, and lemon juice may be used in amount desired. If sodium is not restricted, add ¼ teaspoon of tabasco sauce and ½ teaspoon salt.

MEAT SALAD
6 Servings

In Mrs. Irma Goodrich Mazza's delightful book *Herbs for the Kitchen,* she gives adaptations of very old French salads using cold meats for "the most inspired way of serving cold roast one can imagine."

Meat leftovers can be adapted to the sodium-restricted and fat-restricted diet in the following way:

Chop ¼ cup parsley into small bits; put in a bowl with 1 tablespoon vinegar, 2 tablespoons vegetable oil, ½ teaspoon dry mustard, and mix. Add, by degrees, 6 slices cold beef roast (about 1 ounce per serving), cut *very thin* and narrow. Put in a few strips at a time. Then add ¼ teaspoon rosemary, ½ teaspoon sage; shake, and stir well. Cover the bowl, and let meat marinate a good 3 hours before serving. For each serving, garnish with parsley sprig and serve with crunchy accompaniment such as 1 radish, 1 small wedge of lettuce, and 1 thin slice green pepper. Let those without sodium restrictions salt to taste.

ONE SERVING (1 oz. meat, cooked weight)	TOTAL RECIPE	
24	145	milligrams sodium
7	41	grams total fat
1	8	grams saturated fat
3	19	grams carbohydrate
108	647	calories

One serving: 1 teaspoon vegetable oil.

VARIATIONS

Sliced roast lamb, veal, or chicken may be used in place of beef. Use chives or rosemary in your marinade.

STUFFED TOMATOES
4 Servings

Peel and scoop out 4 medium tomatoes. Cut the amount scooped out into small bits and combine with 1 cup flaked halibut. Try using ¼ cup small cubes of zucchini squash instead of the usual celery. Marinate by dribbling ¼ cup homemade French Dressing (page 234). Fill tomatoes. Chill thoroughly and serve on romaine lettuce. Add salt for those without sodium restrictions.

ONE SERVING (2 oz. fish, cooked weight)	TOTAL RECIPE	
50	201	milligrams sodium
1	5	grams total fat
1	3	grams saturated fat
10	39	grams carbohydrate
153	611	calories

One serving: ¾ teaspoon vegetable oil.

VARIATIONS

Use ¼ cup thinly sliced radishes in place of zucchini. Tuna, salmon, or other cooked fish may be used in place of halibut. Or use 1 cup cut-up chicken instead of fish as a tasty variation.

MOLDED AND FRUIT SALADS

Although we lean toward vegetable salads for many meals, there are times when fruit salads play their part as introductory or accompanying salads.

The appetizer salads should be light in flavor and texture. A tangy sharpness is pleasant in such a salad. Such selections as citrus fruits alone or in combination with thick onion slices, or melon combinations, are delicious first courses, and avoid the sweetness of many fruits that cloy rather than sharpen appetites.

Molded salads — apple with lemon juice, cabbage, and citrus fruits — are good combinations with cold meats provided their dressings are kept on the tart side, when you want to get fruit into your meal in this way.

Dessert salads can use avocados, if allowed, bananas, prunes, pineapple, peaches, and other sweet fruits. In both flavor and consistency, they seem to go *after* rather than *before* the main part of the meal.

If you are on a fat-carbohydrate controlled diet, omit sugar as an ingredient in any recipe and substitute an artificial sweetener, in amounts allowed and following manufacturer's directions for equivalent amounts. Do not use canned fruits packed in a sirup. Instead, use water-pack fruits and use artificial sweetener as a substitute. In general, one serving is ½ cup of unsweetened fruit juice, fresh unsweetened fruit, or unsweetened frozen or canned fruit; ¼ cup cooked, unsweetened dried fruit.

BASIC RECIPE FOR MOLDED SALAD

6 Servings

The ready-made flavors are out, as you know, for sodium restriction, except low sodium dietetic ones. You must be content to build flavor into your molded salads. Wonderful for buffets, for luncheons, for hot weather coolness — molded salads have the proverbial 1001 uses. Most of the molded salads are computed without the addition of dressing, because the choice is so often a matter of individual preference. Be sure to add the dressing count to your daily total.

Prepare unflavored gelatin according to directions on the package, using one package or 1 tablespoon to stiffen one pint of liquid, as a general rule. However, when fruits or nuts are added, a jelly may require more gelatin. This also applies if the recipe is enlarged and is to be molded in a large container. Be sure to measure gelatin with care, remembering that an overly stiff, rubbery jelly is most unappetizing. Should your jelly be too quivering to hold its shape, serve in dessert glasses.

Gelatin dissolves more evenly if first softened in cold liquid. Measure the amount of cold liquid specified into a bowl and sprinkle gelatin over it; let stand 5 minutes. Then add hot liquid and stir until gelatin is completely dissolved. *Do not let mixture boil* after gelatin has been added as this affects the gelatin so that it will not stiffen.

Prepare unflavored gelatin according to direction on package, using one package of gelatin, dissolved in ½ cup cold water, or ¼ cup liquid if fruit juice and fruit additions are to be used. Add 4 tablespoons lemon juice or vinegar, when you want a sharper flavor, and 1½ cups boiling water, vegetable, or fruit juices. Chill, and when partially set, add about 1½ cups strained and cut-up fresh or canned fruit, leftover vegetables, chicken, or fish.

When partially set again, pour into a ring mold (8 inches), and chill until firm (about 4 hours). Unmold onto a large platter or chop plate, and garnish with any of the lettuces.

APPLE CIDER RING
6 Servings

We are indebted to Mrs. Frederick Bauer, formerly of Berkeley, California, for this delicious recipe, and for the Cranberry Pie which appears in the dessert chapter (page 337). Mrs. Bauer, a sodium-restricted dieter herself, believes in sharing from one homemaker's kitchen to another's — to widen selection for all.

    1 package unflavored gelatin
    ½ cup apple cider
    ½ cup pineapple juice
    1 scant cup apple cider
    1 tablespoon sugar
    1 tablespoon lemon juice
    1 teaspoon orange rind, grated
    ¼ cup broken walnuts

½ cup crisp-cut canned pineapple bits
¾ cup diced apple

Put ½ cup cider into a mixing bowl and add gelatin to soften. Heat pineapple juice, scant cup apple cider, sugar to boiling point and add to the gelatin mixture. Stir thoroughly until gelatin is dissolved. Add lemon juice and orange rind and let stand until jelly begins to thicken. Then add walnuts, pineapple bits, and diced apple.

Rinse mold with cold water, or lightly oil, and fill with mixture.

Chill until gelatin is set. Unmold onto a bed of lettuce greens and serve with dressing of choice.

ONE SERVING *With walnuts*	TOTAL RECIPE *Without walnuts*	
	Without dressing	
4	20	milligrams sodium
3	1	grams total fat
trace	trace	gram saturated fat
19	114	grams carbohydrate
113	512	calories

SHERRIED AVOCADO AND GRAPEFRUIT RING

6 Servings

We are indebted to the Home Advisory Service of the Wine Institute, San Francisco, for this excellent recipe.

1½ envelopes (1½ tablespoons) unflavored gelatin
¼ cup cold water
1½ cups grapefruit juice
½ cup California sherry

⅓ cup sugar
1½ cups well-drained grapefruit segments
1 cup diced avocado
1 tablespoon grated green pepper

Soften gelatin in cold water 5 minutes; dissolve over hot water. Add grapefruit juice, wine, and sugar, stirring until sugar is dissolved. Chill until mixture begins to thicken, then fold in grapefruit, avocado, and green pepper. Turn into slightly oiled ring mold; chill until firm. Unmold on crisp salad greens and serve with dressing of choice.

ONE SERVING	TOTAL RECIPE	
Without dressing		
6	38	milligrams sodium
4	25	grams total fat
2	6	grams saturated fat
23	138	grams carbohydrate
155	932	calories

CHICKEN MOLD WITH WALNUTS
6 Servings

Follow the preceding Basic Recipe (page 225) substituting ½ cup lemon juice for the water and add 1 cup diced cooked chicken, ⅓ cup Special Never-Fail Mayonnaise (page 239), ¼ cup toasted slivered nuts. Serve on lettuce cups. Sprinkle lightly with salt for those without sodium restrictions.

ONE SERVING (1⅓ oz. chicken)	TOTAL RECIPE	
34	203	milligrams sodium
17	101	grams total fat
2	12	grams saturated fat
4	22	grams carbohydrate
217	1299	calories

One serving: 2⅔ teaspoons vegetable oil.

VARIATION

Substitute salmon for chicken in the preceding recipe.

MOLDED CRANBERRY SALAD
6 Servings

2 cups fresh cranberries
½ cup sugar
1 package unflavored gelatin
½ cup cold water
½ cup boiling water
¾ cup orange juice
1 tablespoon lemon juice
1 teaspoon grated orange rind
½ cup walnut pieces (optional)

Put raw cranberries through food chopper. Add sugar. Make gelatin according to Basic Recipe (page 225). Chill gelatin until slightly thickened. Add cranberries; nuts, too, if extra richness is desired. Pour into molds and chill in refrigerator until firm.

ONE SERVING *With walnuts*	TOTAL RECIPE *Without walnuts*	
4	21	milligrams sodium
6	2	grams total fat
trace	trace	gram saturated fat
27	151	grams carbohydrate
163	654	calories

WHITE FISH MOLD
6 Servings

Follow the Basic Recipe for molded salad (page 225), substituting ½ cup lemon juice for the water. Use 1 cup flaked halibut, ½ thinly sliced or cubed cucumber, ½ teaspoon dry mustard, and follow as outlined. Serve on crisp lettuce cups and sprinkle with salt for those without sodium restrictions.

ONE SERVING (1⅓ oz. fish, cooked weight)	TOTAL RECIPE	
32	194	milligrams sodium
1	4	grams total fat
trace	trace	gram saturated fat
3	20	grams carbohydrate
69	415	calories

LIME-CUCUMBER MOLDED SALAD
6 Servings

1 envelope granulated gelatin
½ cup cold water
1 tablespoon sugar
1 cup hot water

¼ cup lime juice
1 cup cucumber, minced fine
½ cup Special Never-Fail Mayonnaise (page 239)
Paprika

Soften the gelatin in cold water. Add sugar and boiling water, and stir until dissolved. Add the lime juice, mix well, and pour into mixing bowl that has been rinsed with cold water. Let stand until mixture begins to jell slightly. Add mayonnaise and cucumber, stirring thoroughly. Pour into individual molds, or a ring, or melon mold (rinse mold in cold water before using), and put in refrigerator to set and chill. To serve, turn out onto shredded lettuce; sprinkle with paprika. Dress to taste, being sure to include your choice of dressing in daily count. (Excellent, as is, for family use, too.)

ONE SERVING	TOTAL RECIPE	
9	56	milligrams sodium
18	111	grams total fat
2	11	grams saturated fat
5	31	grams carbohydrate
185	1112	calories

One serving: 4 teaspoons vegetable oil.

VARIATION

One-fourth cup lemon juice may be used in place of lime.

LUNCHEON SALAD OF FRUITS
4 Servings

Use 1 large red-skinned apple, 1 peeled avocado, cut in wedges, and 1 grapefruit, sectioned. Arrange in mixed order on lettuce bed for flavor and eye appeal. Serve with ½ cup Cooked Salad Dressing (page 235). See introductory statement (page 224) on use of fruits and size of servings for fat-carbohydrate controlled diets.

ONE SERVING	TOTAL RECIPE	
5	20	milligrams sodium
11	45	grams total fat
2	9	grams saturated fat
31	122	grams carbohydrate
185	738	calories

VARIATIONS

Unsalted nuts, as walnuts, pecans, and almonds, add flavor and texture to fruit salads. For total fat restriction, use only if allowed on your diet.

Orange chunks and pineapple chunks may be added to the Basic Recipe for variation. Top with equal amounts of sugar and lemon juice for a light, piquant dressing.

TOMATO ASPIC

4 Servings

Follow the Basic Recipe for Molded Salads (page 225), substituting unsalted tomato juice for boiling water.

Add . . . .
1 teaspoon sugar
1 tablespoon scraped onion *or* ½ teaspoon onion powder
Dash paprika
¼ teaspoon thyme *or* sweet basil
1 tablespoon vinegar *or* lemon juice

Proceed as outlined in the preceding recipe and pour into individual or small mold. Unmold on salad greens, and serve with dressing of choice. Sprinkle with salt for those without sodium restrictions. Fat-restricted dieters without sodium restrictions may use regular tomato juice and add salt to taste.

ONE SERVING	TOTAL RECIPE	
Without dressing		
6	24	milligrams sodium
trace	trace	gram total fat
trace	trace	gram saturated fat
6	25	grams carbohydrate
34	135	calories

DRESSINGS

You will want to experiment with basic dressings and modify their flavors in terms of basic salad ingredients. Experiment with wine, cider, and herb-flavored vinegars, the ever-popular citrus additions — lemon, grapefruit, and orange juice — and a galaxy of herbs for your choice flavors. Remember to dilute vinegars with a little water if their tartness is too sharp.

BLENDER MAYONNAISE
1½ Cups

This is an excellent recipe adapted from the recipe on the Fleischmann's Egg Beaters container. Quick to make, low in saturated fat, it has a lot going for it.

½ cup Egg Beaters
¼ teaspoon salt, if allowed
½ teaspoon dry mustard

¼ teaspoon paprika
2 tablespoons wine vinegar
1 cup vegetable oil

Combine Egg Beaters with seasonings, vinegar, and ¼ cup oil in blender. Cover and whirl on medium high (mix) speed just until blended. Without turning off blender, pour in remaining oil in a steady stream. If necessary, use rubber spatula to keep the mixture flowing to blades. Continue until dressing is desired thickness.

ONE SERVING
½ tablespoon
(Without salt)

5	milligrams sodium
5	grams total fat
1	gram saturated fat
trace	gram carbohydrate
45	calories

FRENCH DRESSING
1 Cup

If the idea of French Dressing without salt sounds impossible to you, you haven't tried this one! The paprika, dry mustard, and onion combined with lemon juice or vinegar makes as tangy a dressing as anyone could wish:

½ cup fresh lemon juice
½ teaspoon paprika
⅛ teaspoon black pepper
¼ teaspoon dry mustard
1 teaspoon finely chopped onion

1 tablespoon sugar
½ cup vegetable oil

Combine the lemon juice, paprika, pepper, dry mustard, onion, and sugar. Mix well. Slowly add vegetable oil, beating constantly with rotary or electric beater. Makes 2 cups. Add salt for those without sodium restrictions.

ONE TEASPOON	TOTAL RECIPE	
trace	2	milligrams sodium
2	110	grams total fat
trace	11	grams saturated fat
trace	22	grams carbohydrate
22	1052	calories

One tablespoon: ¾ teaspoon vegetable oil.

VARIATIONS

Substitute ¼ cup vinegar and increase oil to about ¾ cup in the Basic Recipe.

Catsup, chili sauce, or relish (dietetic low sodium for those with sodium restrictions) may be used to spark dressing.

For an Italian slant with plenty of tartness, use ⅓ cup fresh lemon juice or vinegar with ⅔ cup vegetable oil. Here we like to put oil in bowl first, then add lemon juice or vinegar *slowly*, beating vigorously to emulsify. Add freshly ground pepper and other seasonings as desired.

COOKED SALAD DRESSING
2 Cups

Good with most any kind of salad and a change from the perennial "pour" type dressing, here's a cooked one that is clear and thick yet delicate. Lemon juice is skillfully combined with mustard and paprika to result in a delicious tart flavor in this tested Sunkist Growers' recipe.

1 cup sugar
2 tablespoons flour
2 teaspoons dry mustard
1 tablespoon paprika
1 cup fresh lemon juice
1 tablespoon grated onion
¼ cup vegetable oil

Mix sugar, flour, mustard, and paprika. Add lemon juice and mix well. Cook 8 minutes; cool. Add grated onion. Beat oil slowly into the mixture. Chopped parsley may be added when served. Makes 2 cups. Add salt to taste for those without sodium restrictions.

ONE TABLESPOON	TOTAL RECIPE	
trace	6	milligrams sodium
2	56	grams total fat
trace	4	grams saturated fat
7	230	grams carbohydrate
43	1370	calories

One tablespoon: ⅜ teaspoon vegetable oil.

VARIATION

Diluted wine vinegar may be substituted for the lemon juice.

CRANBERRY DRESSING
4 Servings

This is particularly good with orange salads because of the blending qualities of cranberry and orange. Use dietetic cranberry jelly for carbohydrate control.

Beat with a fork ½ cup cranberry jelly. Add 4 tablespoons vegetable oil, 2 tablespoons lemon juice, ¼ teaspoon finely grated onion. Blend all together until smooth.

ONE SERVING	TOTAL RECIPE	
With wine vinegar		
1	2	milligrams sodium
14	56	grams total fat
1	5	grams saturated fat
15	58	grams carbohydrate
195	779	calories

One serving: 1 tablespoon vegetable oil.

"EASY-MIX" SALAD DRESSING
1½ Pints

Another Corn Product Company tested recipe

¼ cup nonfat dry milk
3 tablespoons sugar
1½ teaspoons dry mustard
⅓ cup water
2 cups vegetable oil
½ cup wine vinegar *or* lemon juice

Combine first four ingredients in deep bowl. Beat with rotary beater until thoroughly mixed. Add vegetable oil, ¼ cup at a time. Beat after each addition until oil is blended and mixture is smooth. Add vinegar, all at once, and beat until smooth and thick. (After vinegar is added, dressing thins slightly but thickens immediately when beaten.) Store in refrigerator in covered jar. Add salt to taste, if allowed.

ONE TABLESPOON	TOTAL RECIPE	
	With wine vinegar	
1	66	milligrams sodium
9	440	grams total fat
1	44	grams saturated fat
1	47	grams carbohydrate
85	4071	calories

One serving: 2 teaspoons vegetable oil.

EGGLESS "MAYONNAISE"
1 Cup

⅓ teaspoon paprika
¼ teaspoon dry mustard
Dash cayenne
½ cup double-strength nonfat milk
1 teaspoon plain gelatin
½ cup hot nonfat milk
¼ cup lemon juice

Mix dry seasonings in cold milk and dissolve gelatin. Add hot milk and blend. Add lemon juice. Chill in refrigerator until half congealed. Beat until fluffy. Return to refrigerator and chill until firm. Remove, and beat once again. Store in covered jar in refrigerator. Stir vigorously before serving. Thin with lemon juice as desired. This recipe is not suitable for sodium-restricted diets unless low sodium nonfat milk is used. (If no sodium restriction, add salt to taste.)

TOTAL RECIPE	
194	milligrams sodium
trace	gram total fat
23	grams carbohydrate
157	calories

SPECIAL NEVER-FAIL MAYONNAISE

1 Cup

We are indebted to the Home Service Department of Corn Products Refining Company for this tested egg-white mayonnaise made with their product, Mazola.

½ teaspoon sugar
½ teaspoon dry mustard
Few grains red pepper
1 egg white
1 cup corn oil
4½ teaspoons vinegar

Combine first three ingredients in a bowl. Mix well. Add egg white; beat well with rotary beater. Continue beating and add corn oil a little at a time, beating continually until ½ cup is used. Then add 1½ teaspoons vinegar, and continue adding remaining corn oil a little at a time. Beat in last tablespoon vinegar. Add salt if not restricted on sodium.

ONE TABLESPOON	TOTAL RECIPE	
3	47	milligrams sodium
14	220	grams total fat
1	22	grams saturated fat
trace	3	grams carbohydrate
123	1971	calories

One tablespoon: 1 tablespoon vegetable oil.

TRANSPARENT SALAD DRESSING
6 Servings

This dressing is particularly good with cabbage or cabbage-fruit slaws and with cooked vegetable salads. The mustard and vinegar are the sources of its authority.

    2 tablespoons flour
    1½ teaspoons sugar
    1 teaspoon mustard
    Few grains cayenne
    ⅔ cup water
    1 egg yolk
    2 tablespoons vegetable oil
    ¼ cup mild cider vinegar

Mix flour, sugar, mustard, and cayenne in the top of a double boiler. Stir in water and egg yolk. Stir until thick, about 10 minutes. Add vegetable oil and cider vinegar. Mix well and chill. Add salt for those without sodium restrictions.

ONE SERVING	TOTAL RECIPE	
2	10	milligrams sodium
6	33	grams total fat
1	4	grams saturated fat
3	20	grams carbohydrate
65	389	calories

LOW SATURATED FAT VARIATION
Substitute 1 egg white for egg yolk.

One serving: Negligible grams saturated fat; 1 teaspoon vegetable oil.

12

THE STAFF OF LIFE

Here is bread, which strengthens man's heart, and
therefore called the staff of life.

— MATHEW HENRY
Commentaries. Psalm CIV

THIS IS ONE AREA in which you need make no apologies for
the product. Low sodium breads can be so good you will have
a hard time keeping them on hand.

They may never take blue ribbons at county fairs; they may
be a little coarser in texture than the commercial breads we
use today; they may "tear" occasionally due to absence of salt;
but they are still so good you will even have family members
clamoring for them. And they are low in saturated fats, too,
when made with nonfat milk and vegetable oil. Of course,
you will have to keep an eye on your carbohydrate allowance
as bread products do include flour, sugar, milk, and other ingredients high in carbohydrate.

It's a wonderful family experience to introduce bread making to the modern home. The fragrance of freshly baked
loaves offers a cheap but treasured excursion for many old-
sters into the memories of childhood, when Mother's bread

making was taken for granted and held to be one of her most popular tasks. If you missed out on sifting her carefully measured flours and stirring the mixings in your yesteryears, you have a most exciting cooking experience ahead of you. It is one the family may want to share in, too.

There is also an inner secret to bread making for the maker. Dough can be to her what Plasticine and clay are to the young child. Do you remember how he punches and pulls, stretches and pats his material? Well, these very same manipulations are part and parcel of good bread making. The very plastic qualities of dough make it a live thing to handle, and the rhythm of kneading can relax and heal tired or anxious feelings or muscles. There can be such inner satisfaction in this kneading process that baking days can become adventures in contentment for you.

We say baking day advisedly, for there is little economy of effort in making just one loaf of bread, particularly if you have a home freezer. You may as well make a batch of dough while you are about it. The same dough can be used for bread, pan rolls, raised biscuits, or certain sweet breads. You can make up the dough all at once, or shape dough for different purposes, lightly bake, store in freezer, and complete baking at time of need. And don't forget that bread is a good source of vitamins, particularly if it is made with whole grain or enriched flours.

If eggs and milk are used in your bread making, the saturated fat, carbohydrate, and cholesterol content of the bread will increase, but a slice of bread will only contain one-sixteenth to one-twentieth of the total of each loaf.

Our recipes are constructed with polyunsaturated oils and nonfat milk. For those of you with sodium restriction, you may have to favor the egg yolk (or whatever your list specifies). For those of you with fat restriction, favor the white of egg or cholesterol-free egg substitute. For those of you with fat-carbohydrate restrictions, occasionally you may want to favor a bread recipe made with water. Make your selections from your allowables. And remember, as in all our recipes, you may substitute low sodium nonfat milk powder for nonfat dry milk powder in equal amounts to lower the sodium content of bread.

Now for a quick review of the sodium and fat prohibitions and suggestions as to ingredients to speed you on your way.

FOR SODIUM RESTRICTION, DO NOT USE:

Baking powder, except low sodium

Bicarbonate of soda

Cheese, except low sodium dietetic

Commercial products, except low sodium

Corn sirup

Milk, except kind specified on diet list

Molasses

Ready-mixes, except low sodium

Salt

Self-rising flours

FOR SATURATED FAT RESTRICTION, DO NOT USE:

Margarine, except special margarine as allowed

Cheese, except specially made fat-controlled

Cream

Hydrogenated fats

Whole egg, or egg yolk; instead use one of the new egg substitutes

Whole milk

FOR FAT-CARBOHYDRATE CONTROLLED DIET,
DO NOT USE:

Breads made with butter and eggs

Chips and flavored crackers

Commercial bakery products and mixes

Cheese, except specially made fat-controlled

Cream

Hydrogenated fats

Margarine, except special margarine as allowed

Sugar or other concentrated sweets except as allowed

Whole egg, or egg yolk; instead use one of the new egg substitutes

Whole milk or nonfat milk except in amounts allowed on diet list

YEAST

There are two types of yeast for your use — just as in ordinary bread making. The older and more familiar variety is the little cake of compressed yeast, which must be stored in the refrigerator and used within a few days of purchase. To use compressed yeast successfully, you must crumble it into water that is just *lukewarm*. We consider this to be 85° to 95°. With compressed yeast, it is better to be on the cold side, rather than the hot, for good fermentation to take place.

More than half the yeast now being used by American homemakers is the new active dry yeast — the granular type. It has only been available to us in our kitchens since the end of World War II, but is certainly popular today. And no wonder, for it is packaged in a moisture-proof container, and may be kept as long as four months if stored in a cool, dry place. It must be used, however, fairly soon after being opened.

Unlike compressed yeast, granular yeast must be dissolved in water that is a little warmer than lukewarm water (115°). If the water is too cool, the active dry yeast will be "shocked" and will not give you its best fermentation.

Either yeast may be used interchangeably in recipes and in the same amounts (1 package equals 1 cake) — just remember the slight difference in temperature of water to use: *lukewarm for the compressed; warm, not hot, for the active dry yeast.* Crumble yeast in ¼ cup water (temperature regulated to type used) or sprinkle granular yeast over the water and proceed with mixing directions. It is no longer necessary to let yeast stand in water before mixing.

And now to introduce you to some of the substitutes and supplements available for low sodium bread making. Some of the most important ones are:

MILK

Use nonfat milk unless your list calls for another type. This comes in liquid and dry form. We have used dry in our bread recipes, not because it is better but for ease of use. However, those of you with sodium restriction may find some other form of milk specified. Nonfat, "skim milk," and low sodium milk, dry or liquid, are interchangeable, and nonfat buttermilk may be allowed for some of your quick-bread recipes. For a lower sodium count per slice or serving, use low sodium nonfat milk, especially with quick-bread recipes.

FLOURS

Wilma Lord Perkins points out in the Fannie Farmer *Boston Cooking-School Cook Book* (9 ed.) that flours rich in gluten make the best bread, because they make the dough strong and elastic as the yeast causes it to expand. Special bread flours are high in gluten, but all-purpose flours make good breads. All-purpose flour need not be sifted; just spoon lightly in measuring cup, and do not tap or shake cup. Unbleached flours are high in flavor and nutrition, so deserve to be used often in low sodium breads. But don't overlook the dark flours — rye, graham, and wheat — for their fine flavor and rich nutrients. If a flour is marked 100 percent whole-grain, it must be just that, according to Federal Food and Drug Administration regulations. In the case of wheat, the 100 percent means that the germ of the wheat is included. When you use whole grain flour, buy in small quantities and store in a covered container in the refrigerator or freezer. Enriched flour, less nourishing than whole grain despite its name, has a longer shelf life and need not be refrigerated.

When you elect to add wheat germ to your flour, use about 1 tablespoon for each cup of flour. You may toast it before adding it to dry ingredients, if it seems to retard rising when used in its natural state.

FATS

Because many of our readers are restricted in the use of the saturated fats — butter, hydrogenated shortenings, margarine — most of our recipes are tested using vegetable oils. Those of you who are allowed the use of saturated fats may want to substitute unsalted special margarine, or shortenings such as Crisco or Spry if on your allowable list for the vegetable oils. In general, to change recipes from solid fat to oil, allow ¾ cup oil for each cup of solid fat; on the other hand, to change recipes from oil to solid fat, allow about one-third more fat.

A small amount of unsalted special margarine mixed with the sugar-cinnamon topping of coffee cake, or spread as the filling of sweet rolls, does add plus-flavor to these breads.

GENERAL RULES FOR YEAST BREADS

If it is results you are concerned with in making yeast breads:
1.   Do read the recipe carefully. If you are using your own recipe, rather than a special one, sit down with pencil and paper and make necessary modifications before you begin preparations.
2.   Check your shelves to see that you have adequate equipment. You will need:

Baking pans

At least 1 liquid measuring cup with lip and line above the cup line

Graduated measuring cups in ¼, ⅓, ½, and 1 cup amounts for dry ingredients and shortening

Graduated measuring spoons for amounts less than ¼ cup

Mixing bowl 3 times the bulk of dough

These kitchen aids will save you time, effort, and failures.
3.   Get mixings together at work center before you begin preparations. This goes for utensils, too.

4.   Measure carefully for best results in texture and taste. All measurements in our recipes are level.

5.   Sift dry ingredients as outlined in the various recipes. An easy way to do sifting is to use a double square of wax paper as a receiving base. Store in flour drawer for frequent use.

6.   Watch the temperature of water in all yeast recipes.

7.   Take short cuts only after you have mastered basic recipes. Every effort has been made to think through shorter steps in bread making, but no one kitchen or one homemaker has all the answers.

8.   Spend effort now for later timesaving. Double your recipe whenever practicable. Bake what you need; freeze the remaining dough, or bake all and freeze the finished product.

9.   Compressed yeast or dry granular yeast may be used interchangeably in all recipes and in equivalent amounts. Compressed yeast cakes must be stored in refrigerator and be used within a few days. Granular yeast will keep as long as four months, properly stored. Note expiration date on package.

10.   Do not let yeast doughs rise more than double in size for "good" bread.

11.   After you have mixed yeast dough, round up, and let stand for 10 minutes to tighten for easy kneading.

12.   Don't handle dough any more than necessary — and keep light and easy to handle.

13.   Oil your hands lightly before kneading dough to avoid stickiness.

METHOD OF BREAD MAKING:

We use the straight dough method in the recipes in this chapter — that is, adding the flour all at once. Let the dough rise once in the bowl, shape into loaves, put into pans, let rise again, and bake.

KNEADING:

Turn dough onto a lightly floured board, cover with a bowl, and let stand 10 minutes to tighten up. Oil hands lightly with vegetable oil to make handling easier. Knead dough by folding it toward you, then pushing away from you with "heel" of hand. Turn the dough as you work it. These two actions in manipulating the dough are all there is to kneading. Repeat until dough is smooth and elastic and you can see little bubbles forming beneath (about 40 turns). Your dough will be free of the board and light enough so you will be able to hold it in your hand a few seconds without any sticking.

RAISING LOW SODIUM DOUGH:

Use a large mixing bowl for bread that is to rise — one about 3 times the size of dough. Place the dough after kneading it in the bowl, lightly oiled with vegetable oil. Turn dough once, so top is greased. Cover with a *damp* cloth and let rise in a warm place (about 85°) until double in bulk (45 to 60 minutes). If your kitchen is very warm in midsummer, place a pan of water at 75° under the bowl. If the temperature of the room is less than 80°, put bowl of dough over a pan of hot water (do not let it touch bowl) and cover with a damp cloth. Remember that the water you used in dissolving it started the yeast's work — and the temperature you keep around the dough will complete it. When your room is too cold, the growth of the yeast is retarded; when too hot, the yeast is killed.

For perfect bread, let the dough rise just the exact time needed. Salt, you may remember, is used in regular bread making to give flavor and to slightly retard yeast action. Without it, dough will rise in about half the time required for ordinary bread making. If you let dough rise too long, your product will be coarse and full of holes; if not long enough, it will be heavy.

Perhaps you are thinking you will have to set the minute

hand on your stove to achieve this exactness in rising. But this is not the case; the best method to determine when to shape dough is the finger indention method. With the variables in different flours, temperature of water, and room temperature, this method will give you most uniformly good results. To test for handling, press two fingers deeply into dough. If indention remains when fingers are withdrawn, the dough is double in bulk and ready to handle.

Punch dough down with fist to let gas escape and let fresh oxygen into the yeast.

TO MOLD BREAD:

Turn onto a lightly floured board again and cut dough in two with a sharp knife. This breaks any remaining bubbles. Make into 2 balls — cover with a cloth and let stand for 10 minutes.

Now you are ready to shape the dough into loaves and rolls. To shape for bread, flatten out dough and press all air out of it with closed fists. Fold dough lengthwise, and stretch and pull to lengthen. (Slap against table to stretch out if necessary.) Bring the two ends to center and overlap together tightly. Have seam on the underside to give a smooth top. Place the shaped loaf, side down, in lightly oiled bread pan (use 9 × 5 × 3″). Fill pan about two thirds full.

Cover and let rise again until dough comes to top of pan with center rounding. Finger test in 25 minutes. If indentation remains, loaves are ready to bake.

BAKING AND CARE OF BREAD:

Bake bread in a preheated 400° (hot) oven about 30 to 40 minutes or until golden brown, or at 375° if a glass baking dish is used; plain yeast rolls, 400° to 425° for 15 to 25 minutes; sweet yeast rolls, 375° for 20 to 30 minutes.

Bread will shrink from sides of pan and be light brown in color when done. A good test is to remove bread from oven at minimum time, loosen from sides of pan, and tap bottom of loaf. A good hollow sound indicates that bread is done. Turn onto a rack to cool.

For a *soft crust*, cover top of loaf with a damp cloth for 5 minutes.

For a *shiny top*, brush lightly with ½ teaspoon vegetable oil or melted unsalted butter (if you are not restricted on saturated fat). Cover with a towel for a few minutes to soften crust.

For a *crisp crust*, do not grease or oil bread. Allow it to cool uncovered.

To keep breads fresh, wrap in wax paper or save bread wrappings from bakery bread. Store in refrigerator or cool bread box. Low sodium bread without salt must be carefully cared for; otherwise, it will mildew.

BASIC BREAD AND ROLL RECIPE

Good ingredients go into this bread, and with proper mixing and handling of dough, the product can merit raves. Note the addition of wheat germ (optional) for improved flavor and nutrition. (If no sodium restrictions, add ¾ teaspoon salt per loaf of bread.)

For One Loaf
   16 slices
¾ cup hot water
1½ tablespoons sugar
1 tablespoon vegetable oil
¼ cup warm, not hot, water (cool to lukewarm for compressed yeast)
½ package or ½ cake yeast, active dry or compressed

¼ cup nonfat dry milk powder
2½ to 3 cups *sifted* all-purpose flour
2 tablespoons wheat germ
For Two Loaves
  32 slices
1¾ cups hot water
3 tablespoons sugar
2 tablespoons vegetable oil
¼ cup warm water (cool for compressed yeast)
1 package or 1 cake yeast, active dry or compressed
½ cup nonfat dry milk powder
5½ cups, more or less, *sifted* all-purpose flour
¼ cup wheat germ

Combine the hot water, sugar, and oil in a large mixing bowl. Beat to blend and emulsify. Let cool to desired temperature. Meanwhile, put warm water (cool to lukewarm for compressed yeast) into a measuring cup and sprinkle or crumble in yeast. Stir; then add to the large mixing bowl. Add milk powder sifted with one-half of the flour. Stir in wheat germ. Work in remaining flour (reserving some for dusting of mixing board) until there is just enough to prevent sticking to bowl. When dough comes away from sides of bowl, turn onto floured board, round into a ball, and cover with a cloth; let stand for 10 minutes to tighten up to handle. Knead, let rise, mold, let rise in pan(s), and bake in preheated 400° (hot) oven 30 to 40 minutes. If a glass loaf pan is used, set oven at 350° because oven-glass holds heat longer than metal.

ONE SLICE	ONE LOAF	ONE SLICE	ONE LOAF	
Crisp Crust		Shiny Top		
6	100	6	100	milligrams sodium
1	18	1	21	grams total fat
trace	1	trace	1	gram saturated fat
21	331	21	331	grams carbohydrate
100	1606	102	1627	calories

VARIATIONS

2 Loaves

Water: Add 2 more tablespoons vegetable oil to hot water and omit nonfat dry milk powder.

Potato: Substitute potato water for nonfat dry milk powder and water, keeping liquid measurements the same and adding a mashed, sieved potato. As the sieved potato provides some bulk, you may be able to decrease flour by ¼ cup.

Cracked Wheat: Substitute ½ cup cracked wheat and 2½ cups 100 percent whole wheat flour for 3 of the cups white flour. Omit wheat germ. Reduce sugar to 1 tablespoon and add 2 tablespoons honey.

Whole Wheat: Substitute 2 cups 100 percent whole wheat flour for 2 of the cups white flour. Omit wheat germ.

100 Percent Whole Wheat: Substitute 6 cups 100 percent whole wheat flour for white flour. Omit wheat germ. Decrease sugar to 2 tablespoons, and add 4 tablespoons honey.

Soy: Substitute 6 tablespoons soy flour for 6 tablespoons white flour.

1 Loaf

Date: Knead in 1 cup finely chopped dates.

Raisin: Knead in 1 cup raisins.

Herb: Wonderful for stuffing or with special meat dishes and salads. For a stuffing bread, add 1 teaspoon summer savory, ½ teaspoon thyme, and ½ teaspoon rosemary to dry ingredients. For general use, try nutmeg with caraway or savory, or mace with savory.

Cheese: Delicious toasted and served with salads or thick soups, and is good for sandwiches, too. Add ¾ cup grated low sodium cheese, mixing it with the last flour added. *Not for you on fat-restriction.*

STANDARD ROLLS
12 Rolls

Make up your Basic Recipe as for 2 loaves and divide into 2 balls. Reserve 1 for bread, the other for rolls. After the "resting" period, make 1 long roll about 18 inches long, cut into twelve 1½-inch pieces, and shape into round balls. Put into a lightly oiled, round baking pan (you can use a 9-inch deep pie plate, if nothing else is available). Let rise in a warm room until light (about 45 minutes). Bake until a golden brown in a preheated 425° (hot) oven, 15 to 25 minutes. For carbohydrate control, cut roll dough into 18 to 24 pieces.

If you don't want to serve these rolls on the day of making, shape them, let rise, lightly bake, cool, and prepare for freezing. All ready for later light baking to serve.

ONE ROLL
(White, whole wheat, or
cracked wheat)

8	milligrams sodium
2	grams total fat
trace	gram saturated fat
28	grams carbohydrate
134	calories

VARIATIONS

Bread Sticks: Cut dough into 12 pieces, and pull and stretch into long thin sticks. Put in a shallow baking pan, lightly oiled. Cover with damp cloth to rise. Bake as directed above. Good with thick soups, casserole dishes, and as salad accompaniments.

Parker House Rolls: Roll dough ⅓ inch thick and cut with biscuit cutter (12 rolls). Place on a lightly oiled pan and brush tops with ½ teaspoon vegetable oil. Make a crease across each roll with the rounding handle of a knife. Fold over, so top half slightly overlaps. Press edges together at crease. Place close together or separately on pan, depending on crustiness wanted in finished roll. Let rise and bake as directed above.

Clover-leaf Rolls: Cut dough into 12 pieces, and then divide each piece into thirds. Make little balls of each piece of dough. Place 3 balls in each cup of a lightly greased muffin tin. Let rise and bake as directed above.

SWEET YEAST BREADS

For breakfast, tea, and between-meal "snacks," sweet yeast breads get triple star rating. Quick to make and chock-full of good ingredients, they win both homemaker's and eater's approval (but may be out for those with fat-carbohydrate control because of sugar content).

BASIC SWEET YEAST BREAD
12 Servings

1 cup nonfat milk

2 tablespoons vegetable oil

¼ cup sugar

1 package or cake yeast, active dry or compressed

¼ cup warm, not hot, water (cool to lukewarm for compressed yeast)

3 cups (more or less) all-purpose flour

2 tablespoons wheat germ (optional)

Scald milk. Add oil and sugar and beat to emulsify. Cool to required temperature (warm for dry yeast; lukewarm for compressed). Dissolve yeast in water; add to milk mixture and blend. Add 1½ cups flour and wheat germ, if used. Beat thoroughly for 5 minutes with electric beater. Add enough more flour to make dough just barely firm to handle. Knead. Shape immediately into any of the shapes suggested in Variations. Let rise until light (about 30 minutes); then bake in preheated 375° (moderate) oven for 20 to 30 minutes. Frost with confectioners' sugar icing (½ cup sugar moistened with water and flavored with vanilla or grated lemon rind). If no sodium restrictions, add ¾ teaspoon salt.

ONE SERVING	TOTAL RECIPE	
With wheat germ		
12	138	milligrams sodium
3	33	grams total fat
trace	2	grams saturated fat
36	429	grams carbohydrate
174	2082	calories

One serving: ½ teaspoon vegetable oil.

VARIATIONS

Cinnamon Buns: Flavor with ½ teaspoon cinnamon or sprinkle cut shapes with ½ teaspoon cinnamon blended with 2 tablespoons sugar. Cut with 3-inch cutter or fancy shape. Follow Basic Recipe for rising and baking.

Cinnamon Rolls: Proceed with Basic Recipe and flatten dough to ¼-inch thickness. Brush dough with ¼ teaspoon vegetable oil and spread with sugar-cinnamon mixture. Dot with ⅓ cup cut-up dates. (If dates are very sticky, dip in flour before dotting dough.) Or spread dough with applesauce or crushed pineapple, thoroughly drained. Roll as for jelly roll, beginning at wide side. Be sure to pinch edges of roll firmly to seal. Cut to 1-inch slices. Place on lightly oiled baking sheet or in muffin cups. Allow space between rolls for doubling in size. Follow Basic Recipe for rising and baking.

Cinnamon Twists: Add ½ teaspoon caraway to dry ingredients. Follow Basic Recipe and flatten dough to oblong piece, about ⅓-inch thick. Sprinkle half of dough with ¼ cup light brown sugar blended with ½ teaspoon cinnamon and 2 tablespoons raisins. Fold other half over spread half. Cut into 12 strips 1 inch wide. Hold strips at both ends and twist in opposite directions. Place on lightly oiled baking sheet, 2 to 3 inches apart, pressing both ends of twist to baking sheet to seal. Brush with ½ teaspoon vegetable oil. Follow Basic Recipe for rising and baking.

Orange Rolls: Use orange juice in place of milk and add 1 tablespoon grated orange peel. Shape like Parker House Rolls, putting a cube of sugar, dipped in orange juice, in each. Follow Basic Recipe for rising and baking.

Rich Coffee Rolls or Cake: If you are allowed whole egg, you may add 1 medium egg to milk mixture when it is cool; blend thoroughly. But this must be calculated as part of your egg allowance for the day.

QUICK BREADS

You can adapt many of your own favorite recipes for quick breads after you have learned a few basic principles. The milk, eggs, baking powder, salt, and soda of your recipes will have to be altered or eliminated in terms of your dietary requirements.

The total fat and carbohydrate content of quick breads is higher than in plain yeast breads. For this reason, some of you may have to omit these products from your diet. However, by using vegetable oil in place of shortening or butter, and substituting 2 egg whites or ¼ cup liquid cholesterol-free egg substitute for 1 whole egg, the saturated fat content of quick breads is made negligible.

The recipes in this section are worked out with nonfat milk but you can easily make a product lower in sodium content by using low sodium nonfat milk. The quick breads will meet the needs of the severe sodium restrictions, in most instances. As explained before, if you have a more generous allowance of milk and eggs, it is easy enough to make substitutions upward, insofar as the sodium content is concerned.

A low sodium baking powder is used in all quick bread recipes. It may be ordered at drugstores (page 24) or may be purchased commercially at health stores under the name of Cellu, *green label*. Or ordered direct from this big dietetic firm.* (Regular double-action baking powder may be substituted if you do not have sodium restriction.)

* The Chicago Dietetic Supply House, Inc. P.O. Box 40, La Grange, Illinois 60525.

Lida Jamison, former dietitian of the Chicago Dietetic Supply House, tells us she gets best results with their Cellu Baking Powder by sifting it with flour, as usual, using same amount as Calumet. It is always well to shake the jar before measuring baking powder, as special powders tend to separate somewhat. Miss Jamison advises increasing the baking powder approximately 1 teaspoon per cup of flour if whole milk or eggs are omitted from the recipe, or if 2 egg whites are substituted for a whole egg. You need not alter amount if you use an egg substitute.

To make good quick breads you must do good planning. You will have to depend upon the low sodium baking powder and air beaten into your mixtures to *raise* quick breads (soda and acids such as sour milk and molasses are taboo). Where you elect to use your egg allowance in your quick bread, the egg will help keep mixture light. In some of the fruit breads, where neither egg nor whole milk is used, you may get a sticky product. The bread is good to taste but somewhat inferior in quality to that produced when egg is included as an ingredient.

FOR GOOD RESULTS:

1. Read over the recipe carefully before you begin.
2. Assemble all "tools" and ingredients at your work center.
3. Preheat oven to required temperature for baking.
4. Measure dry ingredients and sift.
5. Add shortening (vegetable oil in most of our recipes), egg, if any, and nonfat milk, pouring all at once over entire surface of flour mixture.
6. Mix together with a pastry blender and stir until flour is moist and all of the ingredients are blended. (Don't try to stir out all the lumps in quick breads.)
7. Mix wet and dry ingredients as quickly as possible.
8. Turn into lightly oiled pan and bake at once in middle of oven or as directed in recipe.

MUFFINS
12 Muffins

This excellent Basic Recipe comes from the Home Service Department of Corn Products Refining Company and it offers you many variations. (We have adapted it for diet requirements.)

2 cups all-purpose flour
1 tablespoon low sodium baking powder
2 tablespoons sugar
1 egg, well beaten
1¼ cups nonfat milk
⅓ cup corn oil

Mix and sift dry ingredients. Make a well and add remaining ingredients all at once; stir only enough to dampen flour. Batter will be lumpy. Fill lightly oiled muffin pans ⅔ full. Bake in 425° (hot) oven, 20 to 25 minutes, until golden brown. Count milk in your day's allowance or use low sodium nonfat milk.

ONE MUFFIN	TOTAL RECIPE	
19	225	milligrams sodium
7	81	grams total fat
1	9	grams saturated fat
18	221	grams carbohydrate
150	1798	calories

VARIATIONS

Blueberry Muffins: Increase sugar to ⅓ cup. Add 1 cup fresh, frozen, or drained canned blueberries to mixed, sifted, dry ingredients. (Other fruits may be used, as cherries, peaches, or crushed pineapple.)

Cheese Muffins: Add ½ cup grated low sodium dietetic cheese to mixed and sifted dry ingredients. Sprinkle tops of muffins with paprika before baking. And for special flavors, use ½ teaspoon basil, caraway, dill, *or* sage with dry ingredients. *Cheese muffin variation not to be used by those with saturated fat restrictions.*

Graham Muffins: Use ⅔ cup graham flour with 1 cup all-purpose flour in the Basic Recipe.

Nut Muffins: Add ½ cup coarsely chopped walnuts to mixed and sifted dry ingredients.

Sugared Apple Muffins: Add 1 cup chopped apples to mixed and sifted dry ingredients. Combine ½ teaspoon cinnamon with 2 tablespoons sugar. Sprinkle over tops of muffins before baking.

LOW SATURATED FAT VARIATION

Follow Basic Recipe except to substitute 2 egg whites or ¼ cup liquid cholesterol-free egg substitute for the whole egg. All Basic Recipe Variations may be used except Cheese. Nut Variation should be omitted if total fat is restricted. If no sodium restrictions, use regular baking powder and add 1 teaspoon salt.

One muffin, Basic Recipe: negligible saturated fat; 1⅓ teaspoons vegetable oil.

LOW SATURATED FAT MUFFINS

12 Muffins

Adapted from a Fleischmann Egg Beaters recipe, many of you will find it a perfect basic muffin recipe. You can then make any of the additions listed above or create new variations of your own.

2 cups all-purpose flour
¼ cup sugar
1 tablespoon baking powder
¼ stick unsalted special margarine
¼ cup Fleischmann's Egg Beaters
1 cup nonfat milk

Sift dry ingredients. Cut in margarine until pieces are pea-size. Combine Egg Beaters and milk. Add to flour mixture; stir quickly with fork just until dry ingredients are moistened (batter will be lumpy). Divide mixture between 12 lightly oiled muffin pans, 2½ × 1¼ inches. Bake in a preheated 400° (hot) oven 25 minutes, or until done. Serve hot and split and toast any leftovers.

ONE MUFFIN	TOTAL RECIPE	
20	245	milligrams sodium
5	54	grams total fat
1	9	grams saturated fat
20	244	grams carbohydrate
137	1643	calories

CORNMEAL MUFFINS

12 Muffins

1 cup all-purpose flour
1 cup enriched yellow cornmeal
¼ cup sugar or 3 tablespoons honey
1 tablespoon low sodium baking powder
1 cup nonfat milk
2 tablespoons vegetable oil
1 egg, well beaten

Mix and sift the dry ingredients together three times. Make a well and add remaining ingredients all at once. Mix quickly, just enough to moisten dry ingredients. Batter will be lumpy.

Pour into lightly oiled muffin tins, filling them ⅔ full. Bake in 400° (hot) oven, 20 to 25 minutes. Or pour into lightly oiled 8 × 8 × 2-inch baking pan for 9 servings of corn bread. Increase baking time to 30 to 40 minutes; use a preheated 425° (hot) oven. (For a lower sodium count, use low sodium nonfat milk.)

ONE MUFFIN	TOTAL RECIPE	
With Sugar		
16	192	milligrams sodium
3	35	grams total fat
trace	4	grams saturated fat
20	244	grams carbohydrate
124	1488	calories

LOW SATURATED FAT VARIATION

Follow the Basic Recipe except to substitute 2 egg whites or ¼ cup cholesterol-free egg substitute for the whole egg. If no sodium restrictions, use regular baking powder, and add 1 teaspoon salt.

One muffin: negligible saturated fat; ½ teaspoon vegetable oil.

BAKING POWDER BISCUITS
10 Biscuits

1 cup all-purpose flour
1 ½ teaspoons low sodium baking powder
1 teaspoon sugar
2 tablespoons vegetable oil
⅓ cup nonfat milk

Mix and sift dry ingredients. Combine oil and milk and pour over entire surface of flour mixture. Mix with fork to make a dough light and soft to handle. Shape lightly with hands to make a ball. Place on waxed paper and knead about 10 times or until smooth. Pat out to ½-inch thickness for average biscuits (thinner for Southern type, thin and crusty biscuits; slightly thicker for the tall, fluffy ones). Or roll between 2 squares waxed paper (about 12 inches square). Remove top sheet of paper; cut biscuits with unfloured 2-inch biscuit cutter. Place biscuits on unoiled baking sheet — 2 inches apart for crusty biscuits or close together for soft ones. Bake in a preheated 450° (very hot) oven, 10 to 15 minutes. If no sodium restrictions use regular baking powder and add ½ teaspoon salt.

ONE BISCUIT	TOTAL RECIPE	
5	45	milligrams sodium
3	29	grams total fat
trace	2	grams saturated fat
10	99	grams carbohydrate
77	726	calories

One biscuit: ½ teaspoon vegetable oil.

VARIATIONS

Drop: In a hurry? Try Drop Biscuits by increasing liquid by about 2 tablespoons. Drop by spoonfuls on an oiled baking sheet or put in muffin pan, filling two-thirds full. Bake as outlined.

Cheese: Add ¼ cup grated low sodium cheese to dry ingredients. A real delicacy with salads. *But not for those with fat restrictions.*

Curry: Add ½ teaspoon curry powder to dry ingredients. Something very special when split and topped with "creamed" left-over meats or croquettes.

Herb: Add ¼ teaspoon nutmeg, ¼ teaspoon sage, and ½ teaspoon caraway seeds to dry ingredients. Elegant split for "creamed" chicken or mushrooms. Good with tossed salads, too.

Orange: Add 1 tablespoon grated orange rind to dry ingredients. When biscuits are shaped and on pan, place ½ cocktail cube sugar dipped in orange juice onto top of each biscuit.

Parsley: Cut in 2 tablespoons chopped parsley with dry ingredients.

COFFEE CAKE
9 Squares

2 cups all-purpose flour
1 teaspoon powdered orange peel
½ cup sugar
2 teaspoons low sodium baking powder
1 medium egg, slightly beaten
½ cup nonfat milk
½ cup fresh or diluted frozen orange juice
⅓ cup vegetable oil

Mix and sift dry ingredients. Make a well and add the remaining ingredients. Stir only enough to dampen flour — the batter will appear lumpy. Turn into lightly oiled 10-inch pie pan or a 9-inch square baking pan. Spoon topping over surface and bake in a preheated 375° (moderate) oven, 25 to 35 minutes. Delicious plain or with topping.

MARMALADE TOPPING

¼ cup sugar (more or less)
¼ cup flour
1 teaspoon unsalted special margarine
1 tablespoon water
½ cup pure marmalade

Mix in order given and blend to a coarse mix. Spoon onto batter and spread lightly over surface. The topping will melt down through coffee cake during baking to give it a rich flavor.

ONE SQUARE With marmalade topping	TOTAL RECIPE Without topping	
17	133	milligrams sodium
10	81	grams total fat
1	9	grams saturated fat
54	299	grams carbohydrate
316	2067	calories

VARIATIONS

One-fourth cup white or light brown sugar combined with 1 teaspoon cinnamon may be sprinkled over coffee cake in place of topping.

Thin slices of apple may be substituted for the marmalade.

Combine with ½ cup water and ½ cup sugar. Simmer gently for 5 minutes. Then arrange on the batter. (A few broken walnuts may be scattered over the top if fat content will allow.) This gives a glazed topping.

One teaspoon caraway may be added to the apple mixture.

LOW SATURATED FAT VARIATION

Follow Basic Recipe or Variations except substitute 2 egg whites or ¼ cup egg substitute for 1 whole egg and omit unsalted margarine. If no sodium restrictions, use regular baking powder, and add ¾ teaspoon salt.

One serving: 1 gram saturated fat; 1¾ teaspoons vegetable oil.

FRUIT AND NUT BREADS

No wonder fruit and nut breads are so popular. They are chock-full of good nutrients and are flavorful and appealing in texture — whether plain, thinly spread for tea, or as general sandwich bread when variety is wanted.

Like other quick breads, they are higher in fat and carbohydrate content than plain yeast breads. However, when made with egg white and vegetable oil, the saturated fat content is lowered. When a large loaf of bread is made with as much as a cup of walnuts, little or no oil is needed; but when the nuts are omitted, oil or shortening is necessary to give a good product.

Fruit breads should be cooked with an inverted loaf pan cover for the first 20 minutes of baking; then remove to complete. Allow to stand overnight for best slicing, and whatever you do, use a sharp, straight-edged knife, not a saw-toothed one.

Don't worry if your fruit breads crack in the center. This is quite typical of these heavy, rich breads. They are really half bread, half cake, and may be used in a variety of ways to give interest to your meals.

APRICOT NUT LOAF
1 Loaf (12 slices)

This recipe comes to us from the Home Advisory Service, Wine Institute, San Francisco, California.

1 cup dried apricots
¾ cup water
½ cup California muscatel wine
1 egg, lightly beaten
Liquid from cooking apricots
½ cup nonfat milk
1 tablespoon vegetable oil
2 cups all-purpose flour
½ cup sugar
4 teaspoons low sodium baking powder
1 teaspoon grated lemon rind
½ cup chopped walnuts

Rinse apricots, add water and wine; boil, uncovered, about 10 minutes. Cool; drain, reserving liquid, and slice apricots. Beat egg lightly. Turn liquid from apricots into measuring cup and add nonfat milk to make ¾ cup. (Mixture may curdle slightly, but this will not affect baked loaf.) Combine with egg and oil. Sift flour, sugar, and baking powder. Add lemon rind, walnuts, and liquid mixture, and mix until all of flour is moistened. Carefully blend in apricots. Turn into lightly oiled loaf pan (8½ × 4½ × 2½ inches). Bake in a preheated 350°

(moderate) oven about 1 hour. Turn out onto wire rack to cool.

ONE SLICE	TOTAL RECIPE	
15	175	milligrams sodium
5	55	grams total fat
trace	5	grams saturated fat
34	405	grams carbohydrate
199	2383	calories

LOW SATURATED FAT VARIATION

Follow Basic Recipe except substitute 2 egg whites or ¼ cup cholesterol-free egg substitute for 1 whole egg. If no sodium restrictions, use regular baking powder, and add ½ teaspoon salt.

One serving: negligible saturated fat; ¼ teaspoon vegetable oil.

ECONOMY FRUIT BREAD
18 Slices

This recipe has been developed without eggs or fat for the highly restricted diet.

1¼ cups light brown sugar
3 cups all-purpose flour
5 teaspoons low sodium baking powder
¼ teaspoon nutmeg
1½ cups nonfat milk
1 cup cooked prunes, cut in small pieces

Put light brown sugar into a mixing bowl. Sift together and stir in flour, low sodium baking powder, nutmeg. Stir in nonfat milk. Then blend in and stir well cooked prunes.

Pour into a lightly greased loaf pan and let stand 15 minutes. Bake in a preheated 350° (moderate) oven, 1 hour or until center of loaf is dry to wooden pick test. Turn onto rack to cool and let stand overnight, if possible, for best slicing. This bread is an excellent accompaniment to a salad meal. For lower sodium content use low sodium nonfat milk.

ONE SLICE	TOTAL RECIPE	
16	295	milligrams sodium
trace	4	grams total fat
trace	trace	gram saturated fat
37	668	grams carbohydrate
160	2876	calories

ORANGE BREAD

2 Loaves (20 slices)

3 cups all-purpose flour
1 tablespoon low sodium baking powder
1 tablespoon grated orange rind or powdered peel
½ cup sugar
1 medium egg, lightly beaten
¼ cup orange juice
1¼ cups nonfat milk
2 tablespoons vegetable oil

Mix and sift dry ingredients 2 times. Combine egg, orange juice, milk, and vegetable oil. Add to dry ingredients and mix just enough to blend. Pour into 2 slightly oiled and waxed-paper-lined loaf pans (8 × 3½ inches). Bake in preheated 350° (moderate) oven, 60 to 75 minutes. For a lower sodium count, use low sodium nonfat milk.

ONE SLICE	ONE LOAF	
11	114	milligrams sodium
2	19	grams total fat
trace	2	grams saturated fat
19	194	grams carbohydrate
106	1062	calories

VARIATIONS

Add 1 cup raisins or diced prunes to dry ingredients.

Add 1 cup broken walnut meats to batter.

For a cakelike loaf, increase sugar to ¾ cup.

LOW SATURATED FAT VARIATION

Follow Basic Recipe and Variations except substitute 2 egg whites or ¼ cup cholesterol-free egg substitute for 1 whole egg. If no sodium restriction, use regular baking powder, and add ½ teaspoon salt.

One slice: negligible saturated fat; ¼ teaspoon vegetable oil.

PRUNE BREAD
1 Loaf (12 slices)

1 cup prunes

½ teaspoon grated orange rind

½ cup orange juice

Hot water

2 cups all-purpose flour

4 teaspoons low sodium baking powder

½ teaspoon cinnamon

¾ cup sugar

1 tablespoon vegetable oil

1 medium egg, lightly beaten

Cut prune meat from pits with knife or sharp scissors; add rind. Add enough hot water to orange juice to make 1 cup; pour over prunes and rind. Let stand 10 minutes. Sift dry ingredients 4 times. Add oil and egg to prune mixture; then add dry ingredients and beat to blend well. Pour into lightly oiled loaf pan (8 × 4 × 2 inches); bake in a preheated 350° (moderate) oven, 1 hour, or until fruit bread tests done. Turn out onto wire rack to cool.

ONE SLICE	ONE LOAF	
7	81	milligrams sodium
2	23	grams total fat
trace	3	grams saturated fat
38	457	grams carbohydrate
177	2127	calories

VARIATIONS

One-half to 1 cup broken walnut meats may be added to batter.

Dates may be substituted for the prunes.

LOW SATURATED FAT VARIATION

Follow Basic Recipe and Variations except substitute 2 egg whites or ¼ cup egg substitute for 1 whole egg. If no sodium restrictions, use regular baking powder and add ½ teaspoon salt.

One slice: negligible saturated fat; ¼ teaspoon vegetable oil.

PANCAKES AND WAFFLES

Pancakes, with their few ingredients, are relatively easy to make and are very good with substitutions — so plan to include them plain or dressed up as a special treat for any meal.

The secret of making good pancakes is to combine the liquid and dry ingredients quickly, and stir only until flour mixture is dampened. Of course, the cooking is important, too. A griddle must be "seasoned" right if it is going to cook right. Try two coatings of one of the new long-lasting "surfacings" to condition it. Preheat as directed, and then brush with unsalted fat if necessary. So treated, the griddle can be wiped after each use without washing. Since you can't use a good old salt-in-the-bag rub to clean griddle of batter pieces, you may have to brush lightly with vegetable oil from time to time to keep in shape.

GRIDDLECAKES OR PANCAKES
6 Griddlecakes

1 cup all-purpose flour
2 teaspoons low sodium baking powder
1½ tablespoons sugar
1 medium egg, lightly beaten
⅔ cup nonfat milk
2 tablespoons vegetable oil

Mix and sift dry ingredients. Combine egg, milk, and oil; add to dry ingredients, beating just enough to dampen flour. The batter should be lumpy. Add more milk, if necessary, to make batter just thin enough to pour. Heat griddle or frying pan over moderate heat, lightly oiled if necessary. To ensure pancakes of uniform size, use a ¼-cup measure to dip the batter onto the griddle. Turn pancakes as soon as they are puffy and full of bubbles and nicely browned on under side. Using a spatula, turn to other side to brown. Serve immediately with 100 percent maple sirup or honey. Or top with fruit or confectioners' sugar. Count milk in daily allowance or use low sodium nonfat milk.

ONE PANCAKE	TOTAL RECIPE	
Without sirup or fruit		
25	148	milligrams sodium
6	35	grams total fat
1	4	grams saturated fat
20	118	grams carbohydrate
148	892	calories

VARIATIONS

Whole Wheat: Use ⅔ cup white flour and ⅓ cup whole wheat flour. If desired, omit sugar and substitute 2 tablespoons honey.

Buckwheat, without Egg: Use ¼ cup white flour and ¾ cup buckwheat flour. Increase baking powder to 2½ teaspoons. Two tablespoons of honey may be substituted for sugar.

Wheat Germ: Use ½ cup white flour, ⅓ cup graham flour, 2 tablespoons toasted wheat germ, 2 tablespoons cornmeal, and ½ cup low fat cottage cheese. Increase milk to 1 cup (or slightly more depending upon desired consistency). Omit egg. Follow above preparation steps, except add cottage cheese after you have combined dry ingredients with milk and oil.

Fritters: Useful for leftover vegetables or fruits, but good with almost any combination. Follow Basic Recipe, but reduce baking powder to 1 teaspoon. Separate egg and add beaten egg white after other ingredients are blended. Fold in 1 cup drained fruit or vegetable. This addition may be made to dry ingredients if you prefer a particularly light fritter. Makes 8 medium fritters.

Follow Basic Recipe and Variations for Whole Wheat and Fritters except substitute 2 egg whites or ¼ cup cholesterol-free egg substitute for 1 whole egg. Buckwheat and Wheat Germ Variations may be used without any changes. If no sodium restrictions, use regular baking powder and add ½ teaspoon salt.

One pancake, Basic Recipe: negligible saturated fat; 1 teaspoon vegetable oil.

FRENCH PANCAKES
20 Four-inch Cakes

A real dessert or luncheon delicacy, and so good when cooked to perfection in a small frying pan, or on your griddle. They glamorize many simple leftovers which may be used as fillers. They may be made ½ hour before meal is to be served and kept hot between the folds of a warm towel in warming oven, if you don't want to prepare them at the last moment. Or make ahead of time and freeze until time of use.

1 cup pastry flour
½ teaspoon sugar
1 cup nonfat milk
2 medium eggs

Mix flour and sugar. Add milk and stir until batter is smooth. Add eggs and beat thoroughly. Let batter stand a half hour or more. Heat a 4-inch or other small frying pan. Brush lightly with vegetable oil and cover pan with very thin layer of batter. Tilt pan to spread mixture evenly over surface. When cooked on one side, quickly loosen edges with spatula and toss or turn to cook other side. (French pancakes may be turned again if necessary to brown evenly.) Spread with jelly or jam, roll and sprinkle with confectioners' sugar and serve. Count milk in daily total or use low sodium nonfat milk.

ONE PANCAKE	TOTAL RECIPE	
Without jelly or sugar		
13	252	milligrams sodium
1	13	grams total fat
trace	4	grams saturated fat
5	102	grams carbohydrate
34	678	calories

SPECIAL WAYS OF SERVING PANCAKES

With Chicken: Spread each pancake with 1 tablespoon chopped, cooked chicken. Roll and place in casserole. When ready to serve, pour mustard-cayenne-flavored hot low sodium cheese spread over pancakes. Set in broiler to lightly brown. Or spread each cake with 2 tablespoons nonfat milk "creamed" chicken. Roll and garnish with parsley sprig. (Leftover meats may be used in the same way.)

With Vegetables: Spread with 1 rounded tablespoon cooked vegetables. Sprinkle with paprika to serve with sauce of choice. Set rolls of pancakes in a casserole and place in broiler to heat sauce. Watch carefully so as not to overcook and toughen pancakes.

LOW SATURATED FAT VARIATION

Follow Basic Recipe except substitute 3 egg whites or ½ cup egg substitute for 2 whole eggs; add ½ teaspoon low sodium baking powder. When using Chicken Variation, omit cheese because of its saturated fat content and use Count Down, if desired. If no sodium restrictions, use regular baking powder and add ½ teaspoon salt.

One pancake, Basic Recipe: negligible saturated fat.

WAFFLES

Six Large Waffles or Twelve 3 × 6-inch Waffles

This recipe is straight from the Home Service Department of the Corn Products Company, and thanks to Jane Ashley, we have made the necessary adaptations for this diet.

2 cups all-purpose flour
1 tablespoon low sodium baking powder
2 tablespoons sugar
2 medium eggs, lightly beaten
1 ½ cups nonfat milk
½ cup vegetable oil

Mix and sift dry ingredients. Combine eggs, milk, and vegetable oil (corn oil in the tested recipe). Add to dry ingredients; blend well. Bake in a hot waffle iron about 3 minutes, or until batter stops steaming. Lift from iron with fork and serve at once. Count milk in day's allowance or use low sodium nonfat milk.

ONE WAFFLE *3 x 6 inches*	TOTAL RECIPE	
27	318	milligrams sodium
10	123	grams total fat
1	15	grams saturated fat
19	224	grams carbohydrate
185	2219	calories

Soybean Flour Waffle: Substitute ½ cup *sifted* soybean flour for ½ cup white flour in Basic Recipe.

Whole Wheat Waffles: Substitute *sifted* whole wheat flour for white flour in Basic Recipe.

LOW SATURATED FAT VARIATION

Substitute 3 egg whites or ⅓ cup cholesterol-free egg substitute for whole eggs and increase baking powder to 4 teaspoons in Basic Recipe and Variations. If no sodium restrictions, use regular baking powder, and add 1 teaspoon salt.

One serving, Basic Recipe: 1 gram saturated fat; 2 teaspoons vegetable oil.

MISCELLANEOUS

WHEAT GERM SQUARES
48 Squares

When you want a crisp and nutty-flavored cracker, try this quickie recipe graciously given to us by Ms. Frances Prout, former Home Economics teacher and past member of the Nutrition Committee of the Alameda County Heart Association.

½ cup cake flour
½ cup all-purpose flour
4 teaspoons low sodium baking powder
1½ cups wheat germ

3 tablespoons vegetable oil
⅓ cup water
Pinch sugar, if desired

Sift flours with baking powder; add 1 cup wheat germ. Cut in oil with 2 knives until well blended. Then add water. Turn onto lightly floured board on which has been sprinkled part of the remaining wheat germ. Form mixture into a ball and pat out to ½-inch thickness. Sprinkle with some of the wheat germ; roll until paper-thin. Add more wheat germ as needed. Cut in 1½ inch squares with pastry edger or kitchen knife. Use a spatula to place wafers on unoiled baking sheet. Bake in a preheated 350° (moderate) oven, 12 to 15 minutes, until *lightly* browned. (If no sodium restrictions, use regular baking powder, and add ½ teaspoon salt.)

ONE SQUARE	TOTAL RECIPE	
trace	5	milligrams sodium
1	52	grams total fat
trace	7	grams saturated fat
3	141	grams carbohydrate
24	1171	calories

Three squares: ½ teaspoon vegetable oil.

MELBA TOAST

For authentic Melba toast, slice low sodium white bread (page 251) from ⅛ to ¼-inch thick. Lay on a shallow baking pan and bake in a 250° (very slow) oven until perfectly dry and crisp. Toast should be golden brown and not curled. Good plain or with a spread.

Some of the dietetic supply houses* also make commercial Melba toasts, bread sticks, and zwieback — low in sodium and fat, too.

* The Chicago Dietetic Supply House P.O. Box 40, La Grange, Illinois 60525.
Stella D'Oro Biscuit Co., Inc. 184 West 237th Street, Bronx, New York 10463.

13

DESSERTS FOR
EVERY OCCASION

"I am glad that my Adonis hath a sweet tooth in
his head."
— John Lyly
Euphues and His England

WE AMERICANS DO LIKE to finish off our lunches and dinners
with a sweet. Not a bad idea, nutritionally speaking, if that
dessert is planned to complete and round out the meal. Too
often, we think of desserts only as rich pies, pastries, and
puddings that, inappropriately used, cloy rather than satisfy
at the end of a hearty meal.

Fortunately for sodium- and fat-restricted dieters, fruit is
abundantly available. It has long been the favored dessert of
many epicureans, who use tortes, soufflés, and pastries only
when dessert is to be the featured attraction. The emphasis on
fruit and fruit-made desserts in this book does not mean that
all of the richer desserts have to be forsaken entirely. Not at
all — but they will have to be planned and used with care and
according to your allowables. They often call for large
amounts of eggs and fats to give them their luscious richness.
These ingredients must always be watched and used only as

allowed. But with so many choices, surely there will be enough desserts to tickle your palate and give you variety.

What is left, you ask? There are the presently popular fruits-in-wine and flaming desserts, many of which feature fruit. They are pleasing in color, subtle in flavor, and a real addition to the diet. Then there are the gelatin whips, the delicate, frothy bits of flavor that add delightful piquancy to a hearty meal: simple tortes, low sodium cakes and cookies, puddings old and new, and pies. Do you think you will suffer for want of a toothsome dessert?

Of course, some of you who have calorie and/or carbohydrate restrictions will have to use the recipes in this chapter with caution. You will want to favor fresh fruits, or unsweetened canned fruits, and perk them up with an approved sugar substitute.

FOR SODIUM RESTRICTION, DO NOT USE:

Bakery products of the commercial variety, such as cakes, cookies, doughnuts, pastry

Cake, cookie, pudding, and pie mixes and toppings

Commercial ice cream and sherbet (except low sodium dietetic), candy (except low sodium dietetic)

Canned milk, condensed or evaporated

Cream, except in amounts allowed on your diet list

Crystallized or glazed fruit

Desserts containing baking powder (except low sodium) or baking soda

Prepared desserts such as flavored Jell-O

Fruits canned or frozen in sugar sirup unless on unrestricted calories

Instant cocoa mixes

Maraschino cherries, on some lists

Molasses

Nonfat milk, except in amounts allowed on your diet list

Pudding mixes, except low sodium dietetic

Rennet tablets

Salt

Sweet fountain commercial sirups

Sugar substitute, except low sodium

Whole milk, except if specified on your diet list

FOR SATURATED FAT RESTRICTION, DO NOT USE:

Bakery products, except made with vegetable oil, special margarine, egg white or egg substitute, and nonfat milk

Butter

Chocolate

Coconut

Commercial desserts, mixes, and hydrogenated toppings used on cakes, cookies, ice cream, milk sherbet, pie and puddings

Cream, table or whipping

Egg yolks or whole egg desserts unless kept within your allowance

Hydrogenated fats, such as Crisco or Spry

Lard

Margarine, except special margarine

Whole milk

FOR FAT-CARBOHYDRATE CONTROL, DO NOT USE:

Any of the ingredients or products listed under saturated fat restriction

Cornstarch or flour*

Dried fruits*

Sweetened fruits and fruit juices

Honey

Milk*

Molasses

Rice and other cereal or bread*

Sirup

Sugar (all kinds)

Tapioca*

* Starred items may be used only in amounts allowed on your diet list. It is plain to see that fruits, ices, and gelatins (sweetened with approved sugar substitute) will be the dessert choices for most fat-carbohydrate control dieters. Puddings, cakes, cookies, pastries, and the like (even if homemade) will be taboo for most dieters.

SPECIAL FLAVOR AIDS

A squeeze of lemon or lime juice on bananas, cantaloupe, or peaches for delicious flavor. Add sugar or honey as desired (approved sugar substitute for carbohydrate or calorie control).

Angostura Aromatic Bitters for a spicy tangy flavor; try 2 to 3 drops in center of apples to be baked; 5 to 6 dashes to a pound of prunes or apricots during stewing; 3 to 4 drops per serving to half grapefruit; 5 to 6 drops added to each cup sirup of canned fruits or puddings.

Freshly ground nutmeg over bland puddings.

Sugar substitutes, low in sodium, to sweeten fruits and other desserts when you must be carbohydrate and calorie conscious. In baked goods and frozen desserts, some sugar substitutes do not give the same texture as sugar, so use tested recipes in this book or in material from manufacturer.

FRESH SEASONAL FRUITS

There are times when a bowl of fresh, colorful fruit is just the answer for dessert. Be sure to think of texture and taste differences in making up your selections. Whatever you do, use *fresh* (or frozen) fruit if you expect the plaudits of family or friends.

Fruit combinations, too, are becoming increasingly important in dessert planning. Here, you control color combination, taste, and texture differences, and can produce many different varieties.

A few suggestions to get you on your way:

Avocados, if allowed, with mixed fruit
Orange sections with stewed cranberries
Melon combinations
Pineapple chunks and raspberries
Mixed fruit compotes
Pineapple or watermelon, hollowed out, and filled with a
blend of fruits

CANTALOUPE FRUIT CUP
2 Servings

Cut cantaloupe in half. Remove seeds. Fill centers with ¼ cup orange sections and ¼ cup raspberries. Sprinkle lightly with 1 teaspoon lemon juice and 1 tablespoon sugar. Chill thoroughly.

ONE SERVING	TOTAL RECIPE	
23	45	milligrams sodium
1	1	gram total fat
trace	trace	gram saturated fat
36	72	grams carbohydrate
144	288	calories

CALIFORNIA AMBROSIA
6 Servings

Peel and slice 6 Sunkist oranges. Arrange slices in serving dish; sprinkle with ½ cup confectioners' sugar, and ½ cup chopped walnuts.

ONE SERVING	TOTAL RECIPE	
1	8	milligrams sodium
6	34	grams total fat
trace	2	grams saturated fat
28	167	grams carbohydrate
156	933	calories

FLAMING DESSERTS

We have already stated the importance of presenting sodium- or fat-restricted foods to their best advantage to make the simple diet you have to offer as attractive as possible. Steaming soups ladled from a tureen, the tossing of a green salad for the ceremony as well as flavor improvement, and now exploration with desserts "on fire" served for all to admire. Indulge yourself in a chafing dish, if your budget will allow, or prepare these simple desserts in the kitchen at the last moment — and bring them to the table, *flaming*, in all of their glory.

PEACHES JUBILEE
6 Servings

Use large Elberta peaches (canned) for this delectable dessert. Drain sirup from one 2½ size canned peach halves. Lightly thicken sirup with 1 tablespoon cornstarch (thickness of sirup will alter the amount of thickening you will need). Blend and boil until clear, stirring to prevent lumping. Add peach halves and poach until thoroughly heated. Arrange peach halves in chafing dish or on platter, cut side up. Cover with sirup; add 1 jigger heated brandy; light, and serve flaming.

ONE PEACH	TOTAL RECIPE	
3	18	milligrams sodium
trace	1	gram total fat
trace	trace	gram saturated fat
22	133	grams carbohydrate
99	595	calories

FRUITS IN WINE

There has been an increasing interest in combining fresh fruit (or frozen) in wine the last few years. No wonder, for the delicately blended savors of the fruit in the wine and the wine in the fruit make this a truly gourmet dessert. Easy to prepare, greatly improved with hours of "standing," here is a boon to you who must plan ahead to get everything done.

FRUIT COMPOTE
5 Servings

This sweet dessert is sometimes called "An 'I Love You' Dessert." Perfect for a Valentine Day special or any other special occasion if your diet allows the calories. If not, you can have the delicious flavor blend by using water-packed fruits. Whether you make this with sweetened or unsweetened fruits, give it special treatment at the table and serve it from your best company bowl. And if you are trying to add dietary potassium, just consider the calculations: one serving contains 438 milligrams.

1 cup California prunes
1 cup water
½ can (1 lb. 4 oz.) pineapple chunks
½ can (1 lb. 4 oz.) whole figs
½ can (1 lb.) peeled apricots
1 teaspoon brandy
1 teaspoon grated orange rind
½ teaspoon grated lemon rind

Combine prunes and water in saucepan. Bring to a boil. Cover and simmer for 10 minutes. Cool. Drain prunes, saving 2 tablespoons liquid. Pit prunes. Drain other fruits, reserving 2 tablespoons of sirup from each. Place all fruits in large bowl and pour reserved sirup over all. Stir in brandy and sprinkle with grated orange and lemon rinds.

ONE SERVING	TOTAL RECIPE	
5	23	milligrams sodium
trace	1	gram total fat
trace	trace	gram saturated fat
45	255	grams carbohydrate
177	885	calories

STRAWBERRIES IN PORT WINE

3 Servings

Wash, sort, and stem 1 pint basket of strawberries. Sugar with ¼ cup confectioners' sugar. Sprinkle with ½ cup port. Cover. Set in refrigerator to cool, allowing at least 6 hours for fruit and wine to blend. Many seasonal fruits, or their frozen varieties, may be fixed in this way. Prepared ahead of time, they demand no last-minute effort.

ONE SERVING	TOTAL RECIPE	
4	13	milligrams sodium
trace	1	gram total fat
trace	trace	gram saturated fat
22	65	grams carbohydrate
132	396	calories

VARIATIONS

Substitute honey for sugar; or substitute low sodium sugar substitute in an equivalent amount (read label for this information) for sugar if you must count calories.

Raspberries, pineapple chunks with claret.

Blended fruit with muscatel.

Sliced peaches in port.

FROZEN FRUIT DESSERTS

Frozen Desserts, *by Hilda Faust (Extension Nutritionist, University of California, Agricultural Extension Service), has some excellent suggestions for making homemade frozen desserts. We are indebted to Miss Faust for permission to adapt this material for our purposes, and to share with you her recipe for Cranberry Ice.*

Practically any dessert that can be ice-frozen without stirring can be frozen in your refrigerator tray under the same conditions. Of course, you will want a smooth-grained product. Some of the usual ingredients used to accomplish this are denied you, but egg white, flour, or gelatin will help. Allow about 1 tablespoon of any one of the three for 1 quart of mixture.

HERE ARE SOME OTHER AIDS FOR FROZEN DESSERTS:

1. It is important to thicken frozen mixtures enough to prevent large crystals from forming. Flour, cornstarch, cooked strained tapioca, mashed fruit, and honey will improve your product in this regard.

2. Try making up your frozen fruit desserts with a minimum amount of water.

3. Freeze under highest temperature possible. Have all of your ingredients *equally* cold when you mix them.

4. Try adding sugar to the fruit, instead of making all the sugar into a sirup. Let the sugared fruit stand for a few hours or overnight, then, if your recipe calls for a sirup, make it by boiling fruit juice and adding a little water, if necessary. When menu count permits use of egg white, try adding some of the sugar into the white for texture goodness.

5. Remember that excess sugar prevents freezing. Try substituting honey for some of the sugar in the fruit mixtures. In making this substitution, consider that honey is slightly sweeter than your granulated sugar, so use only two-thirds honey for the sugar called for in the recipe.

6. In making sherbet calling for beaten egg white, freeze the chilled mixture to a mushy consistency (30–60 minutes). Remove to a chilled bowl, beat until product is light; then add the egg white, and return to freezing tray, and freeze.

Now, for some recipes.

CRANBERRY ICE
8 Servings

1 quart cranberries
2 cups water
2 cups sugar
½ cup lemon juice

Poach the cranberries in the water for about 10 minutes, then rub through a sieve. Add sugar and lemon juice. Stir all until sugar is dissolved. Pour into refrigerator tray and freeze until mushy consistency. Remove to chilled bowl and beat until light. Return to freezer tray and freeze. (A second beating during freezing process will improve texture.)

ONE SERVING	TOTAL RECIPE	
1	10	milligrams sodium
trace	4	grams total fat
trace	trace	gram saturated fat
57	457	grams carbohydrate
222	1778	calories

VARIATIONS

Cranberry Ginger Ale Ice: Simply combine 1 can jellied cranberry sauce with ¾ cup ginger ale. Beat until well blended.

Lemon Water Ice: Make a sirup by boiling 1 quart water with 1¾ cups sugar. Add ½ teaspoon lemon rind or 1 tablespoon lemon peel. Cool; add ¾ cup lemon juice and blend.

Grape Ice: Soften 2 teaspoons plain gelatin in ¼ cup cold water; then place gelatin over hot water to melt. Add 2 tablespoons lemon juice, 1 cup grapefruit juice, 1 quart pure unsweetened grape juice, and 1 cup sugar. Stir thoroughly to dissolve.

SHERBETS

When your count permits, add 1 egg white to any of your water ice recipes in the following way:

1. While sirup is still hot, pour gradually over freshly beaten egg white. Cool mixture and combine with fruit juices.

2. When you want to increase the volume and airiness, add to mixture when half frozen, as explained before.

BLACKBERRY VELVA
6 Servings

This recipe, adapted from a U.S. Department of Agriculture bulletin, may be frozen in a crank or electric freezer, or packed at once into a moisture-vapor-resistant container, sealed, and placed in the home freezer.

1 quart blackberries
½ cup (or more) sugar
1 tablespoon lemon juice
2 teaspoons plain gelatin
¼ cup cold water

Sort, wash, and drain blackberries. Press through sieve to make 1½ cups purée. Add sugar and lemon juice to purée and stir thoroughly. Soften gelatin in cold water 5 minutes, then soften over hot water. Add to fruit, being sure that purée is around room temperature when added. If purée is too cold, the gelatin will congeal before it has a chance to bind the fruit. Stir to completely blend. Pour into ice cream freezer or freezer tray; or prepare for quick-freezing. Serve soft-frozen over fruit salads or fruit cups; or reduce freezer temperature to normal when mixture is soft-frozen and let "ripen" for at least an hour.

ONE SERVING	TOTAL RECIPE	
2	10	milligrams sodium
1	6	grams total fat
trace	trace	gram saturated fat
30	181	grams carbohydrate
123	740	calories

VARIATIONS

Any fresh or water-pack fruit may be used. Allow about 1½ cups fruit, such as fresh peaches or apricots, for the purée.

BANANA LOW SODIUM, LOW FAT ICE CREAM
4 Servings

This recipe has been developed by Ms. Lida Jamison, former dietitian for the Chicago Dietetic Supply House, and is built around their low sodium nonfat dry milk. We are indebted to them for permission to use it here. (If your sodium restriction allows you to use regular nonfat dry milk, simply substitute it for the low sodium nonfat milk. The same holds true for those of you with fat restrictions.)

½ cup cold water
2 tablespoons lemon juice
½ teaspoon vanilla
¼ cup sugar
½ cup low sodium nonfat dry milk powder
1 cup mashed or puréed bananas

Put water into bowl; add the lemon juice, vanilla, and sugar. Stir and add low sodium nonfat dry milk powder. Beat vigorously until of a thick foamy consistency. Add bananas and blend. Pour into a refrigerator tray; freeze for ½ hour. Remove mixture to chilled bowl and beat well. Return to freezing unit until ready for use. Allow 3 to 4 hours for freezing. Turn refrigerator to normal for 1 hour of "ripening."

ONE SERVING	TOTAL RECIPE	
5	20	milligrams sodium
trace	1	gram total fat
trace	1	gram saturated fat
27	107	grams carbohydrate
139	554	calories

VARIATIONS

Crushed or sieved berries, drained crushed pineapple, puréed apricots or peaches may be substituted for the banana. Or you may use baby-food purée if there are no additives. Or pineapple, apricot, or loganberry nectar or juice, or a blend of cranberry and orange juice. For a lower calorie dessert, substitute water-pack fruit and sweeten with a sugar substitute. Add 1 tablespoon vegetable oil after ice cream is blended and beat a few seconds longer to mix oil and give smooth-textured product.

Banana-Orange Parfait: Pour 2 tablespoons of honey over 1 cup orange pieces 2 hours before serving. Alternate orange and honey and low-fat ice cream in tall sherbet glasses. A topping of chopped walnuts may be added if desired. This fruit combination makes 4 servings.

FRUIT DESSERTS, COOKED

APPLE TORTE
4 Servings

Beat 1 egg and add ¾ cup sugar. Continue beating until well blended. Add ½ cup broken walnuts, ¾ cup (scant) peeled, sliced thin apples, ½ teaspoon caraway seed, 1 teaspoon vanilla or lemon, 2 tablespoons flour.

Mix all together and add 1¼ teaspoons low sodium baking powder.

Sprinkle this lightly over the surface of your mixture and stir until it is blended well. Pour into an 8-inch baking pan (1 inch deep), lightly greased with vegetable oil. Bake in a preheated 350° (moderate) oven about 40 minutes until a light, golden brown. This is so rich it is apt to crack, and is best served from the kitchen. Serve with "Whipped Cream" Topping (page 320).

ONE SERVING	TOTAL RECIPE	
Without Topping		
16	64	milligrams sodium
10	38	grams total fat
1	4	grams saturated fat
47	186	grams carbohydrate
273	1091	calories

LOW SATURATED FAT VARIATION

Substitute 2 egg whites or ¼ cup cholesterol-free egg substitute for 1 whole egg. If no sodium restrictions, use regular baking powder and add ½ teaspoon salt.

One serving: negligible saturated fat.

BAKED APPLES WITH FRESH ORANGE SAUCE

8 Servings

Two other apple desserts have come to us from our good friends at Sunkist Growers, and we are happy to share them with you.

8 red baking apples, washed and cored
Nutmeg
⅓ cup sugar
½ cup water
Orange Sauce

Starting at stem end, peel cored apples ¼ of way down. Arrange apples in shallow baking dish. Sprinkle centers of apples with nutmeg and sugar. Pour water into bottom of baking dish. Bake uncovered in a 350° (moderate) oven, 40 to 60 minutes (depending on size of apples). Serve warm or cold with Orange Sauce.

ORANGE SAUCE

½ cup sugar
3 tablespoons cornstarch
1 cup water
1 cup fresh orange juice
2 tablespoons grated orange peel
2 California oranges, peeled, cut into bite-size pieces

Combine sugar and cornstarch in saucepan; gradually add water and orange juice. Bring mixture to boil and cook over low heat for 5 minutes, stirring constantly. Stir in grated orange peel and orange pieces. Serve hot or cold over apples. Makes 2⅓ cups sauce.

ONE APPLE
With Sauce

2	milligrams sodium
trace	gram total fat
trace	gram saturated fat
49	grams carbohydrate
190	calories

AUNT NESSIE'S SKILLET BAKED APPLES

6 Servings

3 tablespoons slivered orange peel
6 medium, tart red apples
¼ cup seedless raisins
1 cup freshly squeezed orange juice
1 cup maple sirup or honey

Thinly pare an orange with a sharp knife or vegetable peeler, removing outer peel only; stack 2 or 3 pieces of peel on cutting board. Cut into very thin strips to yield 3 tablespoons orange peel. Wash and core apples; peel about ⅓ of the way down from the top. Place apples in a covered skillet. Fill center of each apple with raisins. Thoroughly combine slivered peel, orange juice, and maple sirup or honey. Pour over apples. Tightly cover skillet. Simmer over medium heat about 20 minutes until apples are just tender. Baste several times. Serve warm or chilled for breakfast or for a dessert.

ONE APPLE
With maple sirup

9	milligrams sodium
negligible	grams total fat
negligible	grams saturated fat
64	grams carbohydrate
240	calories

BAKED APRICOT TAPIOCA

8 Servings

Put 2½ cups cooked dried apricots in an oblong lightly oiled baking dish. Sprinkle lightly with ½ teaspoon caraway seed.

Combine in a saucepan ½ cup minute tapioca, ½ cup honey, 3 cups cold water, and 2 tablespoons lemon juice. Bring all to a boil over medium heat, stirring constantly. Pour over fruit in baking dish. Cover and bake in a preheated 375° (moderate) oven about 15 minutes. Serve plain to dieter and with cream for regulars, if desired.

ONE SERVING	TOTAL RECIPE	
9	71	milligrams sodium
trace	1	gram total fat
trace	trace	gram saturated fat
32	253	grams carbohydrate
174	1388	calories

VARIATIONS

Dried prunes (pitted) may be substituted for the dried apricots.

Canned apricots may be used in place of dried apricots.

Try different fruit combinations with this recipe for interesting and simple tapioca desserts. Apples, peaches, and cherries have been favorites with us. Vary seasonings, too.

BAKED BANANAS
4 Servings

Peel 4 bananas and place in baking pan. Sprinkle lightly with 1 tablespoon lemon juice and ¼ cup light brown sugar. Bake in a preheated 400° (hot) oven for about 15 minutes, or until slightly brown. Baked bananas may be served with veal or as a dessert.

ONE SERVING	TOTAL RECIPE	
5	21	milligrams sodium
trace	1	gram total fat
trace	trace	gram saturated fat
37	146	grams carbohydrate
138	552	calories

BROILED GRAPEFRUIT
2 Servings

There are times when your meal calls for a hot fruit dessert. This is one of the best.

Cut medium grapefruit in half and separate the sections. For each grapefruit half, sprinkle the top with 1 tablespoon light brown sugar, ¼ teaspoon cinnamon, dash of mace, or a dash of Angostura Aromatic Bitters in center of cavity. Place under broiler and cook until lightly browned.

Or bake in a preheated 350° (moderate) oven until thoroughly heated and sections rise up in shells. Serve at once.

ONE SERVING	TOTAL RECIPE	
5	10	milligrams sodium
trace	trace	gram total fat
trace	trace	gram saturated fat
28	56	grams carbohydrate
110	219	calories

Honey may be substituted for light brown sugar for a slightly different flavor.

One tablespoon sherry may be sprinkled over top of each grapefruit in place of bitters.

ORANGE-STRAWBERRY ROYALE
8 Servings

A piquant dessert for a hot summer day and as pretty to look at as it is to taste.

4 cups strawberries
1½ cups sugar or equivalent amount of sugar substitute, as allowed
1 cup fresh squeezed orange juice
½ cup water
2 tablespoons quick-cooking tapioca
1 fresh orange, peeled and cut into bite-size pieces
Lemon juice
⅛ teaspoon nutmeg

Wash and hull berries. In medium saucepan, bring sugar, orange juice, water, and tapioca to a boil. Reduce heat and simmer for 5 minutes. Add berries; cook 1 minute. Cool for 20 minutes. Add orange pieces, lemon juice, and nutmeg. Spoon into fruit glasses and chill until serving time, at least 1 hour.

ONE SERVING	TOTAL RECIPE	
With sugar		
1	10	milligrams sodium
negligible	1	gram total fat
negligible	negligible	gram saturated fat
51	411	grams carbohydrate
202	1615	calories

GELATIN DESSERTS

Use only plain, unflavored or approved dietetic low sodium gelatins in your recipes for those of you with sodium restrictions. For fat-carbohydrate control, use an approved artificially sweetened gelatin, or an approved sugar substitute with the plain gelatin. One envelope gelatin (1 tablespoon) will set 2 cups liquid, with the exception of acid fruit, which uses only 1¾ cups liquid. Your basic gelatin recipe on the envelope can be adapted in a variety of ways, for fruits, salads, or desserts.

FRUIT GELATIN
4 Servings

Put 1 tablespoon gelatin into mixing bowl and soften with ¼ cup orange juice. Dissolve with ¾ cup boiling water. Stir in ½ cup sugar (this may be decreased where canned fruit juices are used). When gelatin and sugar are dissolved, add ¾ cup orange juice, 1 tablespoon lemon juice, and ½ teaspoon grated lemon rind. Chill mixture; when it begins to set, add ½ cup fresh strawberries and 1 banana, sliced. Pour into a ring mold or individual molds and chill until set.

ONE SERVING	TOTAL RECIPE	
2	7	milligrams sodium
trace	1	gram total fat
trace	trace	gram saturated fat
39	157	grams carbohydrate
162	646	calories

VARIATIONS

Lemon Gelatin: Substitute ¼ cup sherry for ¼ cup liquid the next time you make Lemon Gelatin. It gives you something pleasingly different. (4 servings.) Other fruits and juices, alone or in combination, may be used.

ORANGE-PRUNE-WALNUT WHIP
6 Servings

We are indebted to the Consumer Service Division of Sunkist Growers for this delicious recipe.

1 tablespoon unflavored gelatin
⅓ cup sugar
½ cup cold water
1 cup fresh orange juice
3 tablespoons fresh lemon juice
1 cup chopped, cooked prunes
½ cup chopped walnuts
1 cup orange chunks, drained (2 medium oranges)

Mix gelatin, sugar, and water in top of double boiler. Heat over hot water until gelatin and sugar dissolve, stirring constantly. Remove from heat; cool, then stir in orange and lemon juice. Chill until mixture is slightly thicker than the consistency of unbeaten egg white. Beat with rotary or electric beater until light and fluffy and double in volume. Fold in chopped prunes, walnuts, and orange chunks. Pour into 1-quart mold and chill until firm.

ONE SERVING	TOTAL RECIPE	
2	14	milligrams sodium
5	32	grams total fat
trace	2	grams saturated fat
29	174	grams carbohydrate
169	1015	calories

PUDDINGS

BAKED CUSTARD
4 Servings

Especially for you readers who want to restrict saturated fat and cholesterol.

½ cup cholesterol-free egg substitute
¼ cup sugar or ⅓ cup pure honey
1⅓ cups nonfat milk, scalded
¼ teaspoon vanilla extract
¼ teaspoon nutmeg

Combine Egg Beaters or other egg substitute and sugar or honey. Stir in scalded milk and vanilla. Pour into four 5-ounce custard cups. Sprinkle with nutmeg. Set cups in a shallow baking pan which has 1 inch of boiling water in it.

Bake in a preheated 350° (moderate) oven 30 minutes, or until a silver knife inserted in center comes out clean. Serve warm or cool.

ONE CUSTARD
With sugar

97	milligrams sodium
4	grams total fat
1	gram saturated fat
18	grams carbohydrate
128	calories

BLANCMANGE
3 Servings

Mix 1½ tablespoons cornstarch with 2 tablespoons sugar, ½ cup nonfat milk, until smooth. Heat 1 cup nonfat milk, then pour a little of it on the cornstarch mixture. Blend smoothly. Add remaining milk and put in double boiler. Stir constantly, until pudding begins to thicken. Cover and let cook 25 minutes, stirring as needed. When pudding is cool, add ½ teaspoon vanilla extract. (If no sodium restrictions, add ⅛ teaspoon salt.) Count milk in dieter's daily allowance or use low sodium nonfat milk.

ONE SERVING	TOTAL RECIPE	
64	192	milligrams sodium
trace	trace	gram fat
18	53	grams carbohydrate
90	271	calories

VARIATIONS
This pudding separates if not used rather quickly, so instead of making just one flavor, divide into three servings and make three different ones for individual servings. Many combinations are possible. These are some that are good:

Jelly or Jam: Into one serving, put 1 teaspoon pure jelly or jam.

Banana: Into a second, substitute ½ teaspoon banana flavor, cut up ½ banana at the time of serving.

Cinnamon: For the third, try chilling with a small cinnamon stick. Remove when serving, and sprinkle lightly with cinnamon on top.

Peppermint flavoring may be used also. Or *Angostura Aromatic Bitters.*

BREAD PUDDING
6 Servings

2 cups nonfat milk
1 cup low sodium bread cubes
1 egg
¼ cup sugar
½ cup chopped prunes
½ teaspoon vanilla extract
½ teaspoon nutmeg

Warm milk; remove from heat. Add bread cubes. Beat egg lightly and add sugar. Add milk mixture, prunes, and vanilla extract. Blend; pour into lightly oiled baking dish and sprinkle with nutmeg. Set in pan of hot water. Bake in a preheated 350° (moderate) oven, 30 to 60 minutes, or until inserted knife comes out clean. Count milk in dieter's daily allowance or use low sodium nonfat milk.

ONE SERVING	TOTAL RECIPE	
56	338	milligrams sodium
2	10	grams total fat
trace	2	grams saturated fat
27	154	grams carbohydrate
131	783	calories

LOW SATURATED FAT VARIATION
Substitute ¼ cup cholesterol-free egg substitute for egg in above recipe.

CALIFORNIA FRUIT PUDDING
6 Servings

A hurry-up dessert, this is a bonus treat for most of you. Do not use, however, if dieter is on severe sodium restriction unless you make your own pudding without salt and either count milk as part of the daily allowance or use low sodium nonfat milk.

1 package vanilla pudding mix
2 cups nonfat milk
1 cup fruit cocktail, canned without sugar or in a light sirup, as allowed
1 tablespoon white port (or sherry)

Prepare vanilla pudding according to package directions. Or make your own pudding, using nonfat (or skimmed) milk. Cool. Before serving, blend in the drained fruit and port or sherry. Serve in individual fruit compotes and garnish as desired.

ONE SERVING	TOTAL RECIPE	
(*With fruit cocktail, canned without sugar*)		
121	726	milligrams sodium
negligible	negligible	gram total fat
negligible	1	gram saturated fat
25	152	grams carbohydrate
117	704	calories

VARIATION

Blend port with pudding after it has been cooked, and at time of serving, spoon drained fruit cocktail or seasonal fruit over it.

RICE PUDDING
4 Servings

½ cup brown rice
½ cup chopped dried apricots
1 cup nonfat milk
½ teaspoon nutmeg
¼ cup sugar
½ teaspoon vanilla extract

Follow directions on package for washing rice. (Some rice does not need washing.) Combine all ingredients. Pour into a lightly oiled baking dish and bake in a preheated 300° (slow) oven, 2 hours or more, until rice and fruit are tender. Stir several times during the first hour. (If no sodium restrictions, add ¼ teaspoon salt.) Count milk in dieter's daily allowance or make with low sodium nonfat milk.

ONE SERVING	TOTAL RECIPE	
40	158	milligrams sodium
1	3	grams total fat
trace	trace	gram saturated fat
48	190	grams carbohydrate
213	853	calories

Uncooked Rice Pudding: Combine 1 cup cooked rice with 1 cup whole cranberry sauce. Add ½ cup confectioners' sugar. Fold in 1 cup "Whipped Cream" Topping (page 320) just before serving. Pile into individual serving dishes and top with a rounded tablespoonful of whole cranberry sauce.

MERINGUE SHELLS
12 Medium

Quick as a whip to make, and delicious with almost any fruit or sherbet, don't overlook these shells for party or family fare.

Beat ½ cup egg whites until foamy but not dry; add slowly 1 cup sugar, beating after each addition. Continue to beat until meringue forms sharp little peaks when you raise beater. Then add 1 tablespoon lemon juice, and beat again.

Shape meringue with spoon or pastry bag on unwaxed paper on oiled baking sheet. Allow space for meringues to spread. Bake in a preheated 250° (very slow) oven 1 hour and 15 minutes, until shells are thoroughly dried and tops are a delicate cream color. Remove from paper carefully, using a wet towel on the hot baking sheet so that meringues can be eased off. Let cool completely before storing.

Fill shells as desired. Makes 8 very large or 12 medium-sized shells.

ONE SERVING (¹⁄₁₂ recipe)	TOTAL RECIPE	
16	194	milligrams sodium
trace	trace	gram total fat
17	200	grams carbohydrate
70	835	calories

SCONES
6 Servings

1 ½ cups all-purpose flour
2 teaspoons low sodium baking powder
2 teaspoons sugar
¼ cup vegetable oil

1 egg, slightly beaten
⅓ cup (more or less) nonfat milk

Sift dry ingredients together. Combine oil, beaten egg, and milk. Pour all at once over entire surface of dry ingredients. Mix with fork to make soft dough. Turn onto lightly floured board or wax paper and knead ten times or until smooth. Stretch into strips and form coils; or keep ¼-inch thick and shape into triangles; or into whatever shape you desire. Place scones on ungreased baking sheet. Bake in a preheated 425° (hot) oven, 10 to 15 minutes. Serve with fresh or frozen fruit or jam of choice.

ONE SERVING	TOTAL RECIPE	
Without fruit or jam		
18	107	milligrams sodium
11	63	grams total fat
1	7	grams saturated fat
24	146	grams carbohydrate
212	1270	calories

VARIATION

Shortcake: Follow Scone recipe, increasing sugar to 1 tablespoon and baking powder to 1 tablespoon. Or use Baking Powder Biscuit recipe (page 264) increasing sugar to 1 tablespoon.

LOW SATURATED FAT VARIATION

Follow Basic Recipe and Shortcake recipe, except omit egg or substitute 2 egg whites. If no sodium restriction, use regular baking powder and add ½ teaspoon salt.

One serving: 1 gram saturated fat; 2 teaspoons vegetable oil.

DESSERT SAUCES

CARAMEL SAUCE
1 Cup

Heat 1 cup sugar in heavy pan over moderate heat until melted and golden brown. Stir constantly. Add 1 cup boiling water gradually. Boil 5 to 6 minutes; cool. Use for custards, and as ice cream topping.

ONE TABLESPOON	TOTAL RECIPE	
trace	1	milligram sodium
trace	trace	gram fat
12	199	grams carbohydrate
48	770	calories

Coffee-Caramel Sauce: Substitute ¼ cup strong coffee for ¼ cup water.

CRANBERRY-PINEAPPLE SAUCE
1¼ Cups

Mix ½ can (1-pound size) whole cranberry sauce with ½ cup crushed pineapple (drained). Add ⅛ teaspoon peppermint extract if desired.

ONE TABLESPOON	TOTAL RECIPE	
trace	4	milligrams sodium
trace	1	gram total fat
trace	trace	gram saturated fat
6	110	grams carbohydrate
21	428	calories

CURRANT JELLY SAUCE
½ Cup

Beat ½ cup pure currant jelly with fork. Add 2 tablespoons hot water and 2 teaspoons lemon juice and blend. (Jelly may be melted for thinner sauce.)

ONE TABLESPOON	TOTAL RECIPE	
3	24	milligrams sodium
trace	trace	gram fat
14	112	grams carbohydrate
55	443	calories

ORANGE SAUCE
4 Servings

This is another of the fine Sunkist Growers' recipes.
¾ cup sugar
3 tablespoons cornstarch
¾ cup water
½ cup fresh orange juice
3 tablespoons fresh lemon juice
1 teaspoon unsalted special margarine

Mix sugar and cornstarch in saucepan; stir in water. Heat until mixture boils for 2 minutes, stirring constantly. Remove from heat; add fruit juices and margarine. Stir well; cool. Serve over slices of unfrosted cake, snow pudding, or any custard-type pudding where citrus flavor is desired.

ONE SERVING	TOTAL RECIPE	
1	2	milligrams sodium
1	4	grams total fat
trace	1	gram saturated fat
47	186	grams carbohydrate
193	771	calories

CAKES

If you like cake, use it as a morale booster in your diet. Perhaps you can remember the World War II days when homemakers were taught to make one-egg and sometimes no-egg cakes. Those cakes weren't as rich and luscious as some of your best recipes, to be sure. But they were cakes; they had some very good ingredients in them — and they were morale boosters as well.

Today the situation is somewhat the same in sodium- and fat-controlled baking. You have already read in earlier chapters that most commercially-made cakes, mixes, cookies, and prepared puddings, pies and other desserts are high in sodium (because salt, baking powder, baking soda and other high sodium ingredients have been used in their preparation), saturated fats, cholesterol, and carbohydrates.

Consider eggs: They must be used sparingly and sometimes not at all (and only as directed by your physician's instructions). In our recipes or in your own favorites, you may substitute 1 egg white for 1 egg yolk; 2 whites for 1 egg; or 3 whites for 2 eggs (if your sodium count permits). Where sodium is not a factor, a cholesterol-free egg substitute may be substituted for 1 egg or more. (Follow directions on container for equivalent amounts.) *Ordinary baking powder, corn sirup, dark brown sugar, molasses, and all of the ready mixed cakes, cookies, and some toppings are taboo for you sodium-restricted dieters.* And for many others of you not only many of the above items will be disallowed, but the kind and amount of fat will be specified. Within the variety of our recipes, however, there should be some for your special use.

If you have sodium but not saturated fat restriction, your list may allow occasional use of shortening, unsalted special margarine, whole egg, or egg yolk (but you must count as part of your daily allowance). We prefer to use vegetable oil, usually saffola or corn, or a special margarine lower in saturated fat than a regular margarine. And we use nonfat milk in our recipes and calculations, but when you so elect, you must count it as part of the dieter's daily allowance. In many dessert recipes that follow, you may very well decide to use low sodium nonfat milk to lower the sodium content of the particular specialty.

If you have saturated fat restrictions, favor egg whites, egg substitutes, such as Fleischmann's Egg Beaters or Second Nature. Nonfat or skim milk, vegetable oil and a special margarine will also be your choices. If you do not have to be concerned with sodium restriction, use regular baking powder in the amounts we have specified as "special" or "low sodium."

The restrictions do not narrow the field as much as you might think, but relatively high or high in calories they are. If you plan lower calorie selections for the rest of the meal, you can include cake for special treats. And you'll find that you can make a good cake, velvety in texture, light and fine, and slightly moist on the surface to please you and the family as well. Where you must get every bit of goodness out of your ingredients, a few suggestions may speed you on your way to success for your occasional treats.

1. Read over the recipe before you begin.
2. Assemble your ingredients and equipment before you start any preparation.
3. Measure carefully. Too much is as bad as too little. Too much shortening, sugar, or baking powder may cause your cake to run over the top of pans or fall. Too much flour is apt to

result in a dry or tough cake. Too little liquid can have the same effect. Our measurements are level.

4. Prepare baking pans before you do any mixing, and have the right size for the recipe. Lightly oil bottoms of pans with pastry brush and flour lightly, shaking out any extra flour. Or lightly oil and line with paper; or do a combination — whichever you prefer.

5. Bake at correct temperature, and for length of time specified in the recipe. And, of course, let oven preheat while you are mixing ingredients.

6. Test for doneness at minimum time. Press cake lightly with finger tip; if cake is done it will spring back.

7. Remove cake from oven and let stand 10 minutes. Loosen sides with spatula; tip and turn gently, and invert onto rack.

8. Let cake cool, and spread with icing and filling.

BASIC LOW SODIUM TWO-EGG CAKE
12 Servings

2 cups cake flour
2 teaspoons low sodium baking powder
1⅓ cups sugar
½ cup vegetable shortening
¾ cup nonfat milk
1 teaspoon vanilla *or*
2 teaspoons grated lemon rind
2 medium eggs, unbeaten

Mix and sift flour, baking powder, and sugar. Add shortening, milk, and flavoring. Beat for 2 minutes (300 strokes). Add eggs and beat for 2 minutes longer. Bake in 2 lightly greased and floured 8-inch layer pans in preheated 375° (moderate) oven for 20 to 30 minutes, or until cake springs back when finger-tested. Let cool 10 minutes; loosen sides with spatula and turn onto rack.

ONE SERVING	TOTAL RECIPE	
19	225	milligrams sodium
9	112	grams total fat
2	29	grams saturated fat
38	454	grams carbohydrate
249	2991	calories

BASIC LOW SATURATED FAT CAKE
12 Servings

2¼ cups *sifted* cake flour
1 tablespoon low sodium baking powder
1¼ cups sugar
3 medium egg whites *or* ½ cup cholesterol-free egg substitute
½ cup vegetable oil
¾ cup nonfat milk
1 teaspoon vanilla *or*
2 teaspoons grated lemon rind

Mix and sift flour, baking powder, and ¾ cup of the sugar. In a large bowl, beat egg whites until foamy; add remaining sugar gradually, beating until mixture forms stiff peaks. Make a well in the dry ingredients and add in order, oil, ½ cup of the milk, and flavoring. Blend; beat 150 strokes (1 minute at medium speed). Add remaining milk and beat an additional 150 strokes (1 minute). Pour batter slowly into the meringue, gently folding until completely blended. Fold, do not stir. Turn batter into 2 lightly oiled and floured 8-inch layer pans. Bake in preheated 375° (moderate) oven for 20 to 30 minutes, or until cake springs back when finger-tested. Let cool 10 minutes; loosen sides with spatula and turn onto rack.

ONE SERVING	TOTAL RECIPE	
(With egg whites)		
20	244	milligrams sodium
9	110	grams total fat
1	11	grams saturated fat
39	462	grams carbohydrate
251	3015	calories

One Serving: 2 teaspoons vegetable oil.

VARIATIONS FOR BASIC TWO-EGG
OR LOW SATURATED FAT CAKE

Cupcakes or Loaf Cake: These Basic Recipes may also be used for cupcakes or loaf cake. Bake cupcakes at 375° (moderate) oven, 15 to 25 minutes; make loaf cake (9 x 9 x 2-inch pan) in preheated 350° (moderate) oven, 45 to 60 minutes.

Glazed Nut: Bake in 9-inch square pan in 350° (moderate) oven for 45 to 60 minutes or until done. Remove from oven and spread with glaze made from the following ingredients:

2 tablespoons melted, unsalted special margarine or vegetable oil
¼ cup light brown sugar
¼ cup chopped walnuts
1 teaspoon cake flour
1 teaspoon water

Return to oven and bake 5 minutes longer.

Orange: Substitute ⅔ cup orange juice for milk in Basic Recipe.

Add 1 tablespoon lemon juice to liquids; and 1 tablespoon grated orange peel to dry ingredients. Bake as for Basic Recipe.

Pink and White: Divide batter in half. Add ¼ teaspoon (or more) red vegetable coloring to one portion. Spoon into 9-inch square pan, alternating white and pink batter. Bake as for Loaf Cake.

Plantation Marble: Decrease sugar to 1 cup and omit vanilla in Basic Recipe. Divide batter in half. To one portion, add the following ingredients that have been well mixed:

¼ cup light brown sugar
1 teaspoon cinnamon
½ teaspoon cloves
½ teaspoon nutmeg

Spoon into 9-inch square loaf pan, alternating white and spice. Bake as outlined for Loaf Cake.

Spice: Follow Basic Recipe and add to dry ingredients, 1 teaspoon cinnamon, 1 teaspoon ground cloves, and ½ teaspoon allspice. Bake as layer or loaf cake as outlined before.

HOT MILK SPONGE CAKE
12 Squares

This sponge cake recipe is simple to make and is a good product. The secret of any sponge cake is beating very well to incorporate just as much air as possible. We have added some baking powder to make up for the decreased amount of eggs. This recipe may be used only by those with whole egg allowance.

2 eggs
1 cup sugar
1 teaspoon vanilla
1 cup cake flour
2 teaspoons low sodium baking powder
½ cup hot nonfat milk

Beat eggs very well, until thick and light in color. Then beat in sugar and vanilla. Mix and sift flour and baking powder; add, alternately with the hot milk, to the egg mixture.

Bake in lightly oiled 9-inch loaf pan in a preheated 350° (moderate) oven for about 30 minutes.

ONE SERVING	TOTAL RECIPE	
16	190	milligrams sodium
1	13	grams total fat
trace	4	grams saturated fat
25	297	grams carbohydrate
117	1409	calories

FROSTINGS AND FILLINGS

BASIC ''BUTTER'' FROSTING

This recipe is for those of you who have unsalted special margarine on your diet lists. Otherwise, use Low Saturated Fat Variation (page 319). Do note how frostings and fillings increase calories.

2 cups *sifted* confectioners' sugar
¼ cup soft unsalted special margarine
2 tablespoons nonfat milk
1 teaspoon vanilla

Blend sugar and special margarine. Stir in milk and flavoring. (Flavoring may be altered to suit.) Stir until smooth.

TOTAL RECIPE

24	milligrams sodium
46	grams total fat
9	grams saturated fat
256	grams carbohydrate
1410	calories

VARIATIONS

Browned Butter: Follow Basic Recipe except brown special margarine in skillet before blending with sugar.

Coffee Butter Frosting: Substitute double-strength coffee for milk in the Basic Recipe.

Fruit Butter Frosting: Substitute fruit juice for nonfat milk.

LOW SATURATED FAT VARIATION

Substitute 1 tablespoon vegetable oil for margarine; increase nonfat milk to ¼ cup. Or use 2 tablespoons Corn Oil Spread (page 210) with 3 tablespoons nonfat milk. Adjust to desired thickness by adding a few drops more of milk. *These variations are negligible in saturated fat content for one serving.*

LEMON FILLING

1 cup sugar or sugar substitute
2½ tablespoons flour
1 tablespoon grated lemon rind or lemon peel
¼ cup lemon juice
1 egg, slightly beaten
1 teaspoon unsalted special margarine

Mix sugar and flour; add lemon rind and juice, then egg. Melt margarine; add mixture and cook, stirring constantly, until it boils. Cool. Orange juice and rind may be substituted for lemon.

TOTAL RECIPE
With sugar

63	milligrams sodium
10	grams total fat
3	grams saturated fat
216	grams carbohydrate
966	calories

LOW SATURATED FAT VARIATION

Omit egg, increase flour to 3½ tablespoons, and substitute oil for special margarine if list requires. Otherwise, use special margarine.

Total recipe: 1 gram saturated fat.

"WHIPPED CREAM" TOPPING
1½ Cups

1 cup double strength nonfat milk (6 tablespoons powder to 1 cup water)
2 teaspoons gelatin
1½ tablespoons cold water
¼ cup sugar
1 teaspoon vanilla

Scald milk. Soak gelatin in cold water. Combine scalded milk, sugar, and gelatin. Stir until dissolved. Place in refrigerator and allow to jell. Whip with rotary beater until consistency of whipped cream. Add vanilla and whip again. Use as topping for cream pies and puddings as well as spread for cakes.

TOTAL RECIPE

141	milligrams sodium
trace	gram total fat
72	grams carbohydrate
307	calories

VARIATIONS

One tablespoon sherry may be used in place of vanilla for flavor change.

Imitation banana extract, peppermint, or almond may also be used for flavoring, allowing 1 teaspoon as with vanilla.

COOKIES

In the beginning days of restricted cookery, when you are trying to get used to the many prohibitions, you may wonder if you will ever be able to turn out any of your specialties again, cookies included. The answer is an unequivocal "yes." Your baked goods may go through many changes, to be sure, but you will add adaptations as you feel more at home with the limitations.

There are quite a few good basic cooky recipes which can be made quickly and with few ingredient changes. These are good starters to give a lift to what might otherwise be a drab meal, or for between-meal munching, if allowed.

BANANA OATMEAL COOKIES
42 Cookies

We are indebted to Miss Grace Fowler, former Nutritionist, San Joaquin County Heart Association, for this interesting vari-

ation of the standard oatmeal cooky. Hearty, and without egg, it should be a plus contribution to many readers.

½ cup sugar
1½ cups all-purpose flour
2 teaspoons low sodium baking powder
¼ teaspoon cinnamon
¼ teaspoon nutmeg
¼ teaspoon mace
¼ cup vegetable oil
⅓ cup water
1 cup mashed bananas
1¾ cups rolled oats
½ cup chopped walnuts

Sift together dry ingredients. Combine oil, water, and mashed bananas; add to dry ingredients. Add rolled oats and walnuts; stir until thoroughly blended. Drop by teaspoonfuls onto lightly oiled baking sheet. Bake in a preheated 350° (moderate) oven, 8 to 15 minutes. Allow space on baking sheet for these cookies to spread. (Puréed fruits, as apricots and peaches, may be substituted for the banana.)

ONE COOKY	TOTAL RECIPE	
trace	12	milligrams sodium
2	100	grams total fat
trace	9	grams saturated fat
9	372	grams carbohydrate
60	2522	calories

One cooky: ⅓ teaspoon vegetable oil.

BUTTERSCOTCH BROWNIES
16 Squares

A tested recipe from the Home Service Department of Corn Products Refining Company.

1 cup light brown sugar
¼ cup vegetable oil
1 egg (or two egg whites or ¼ cup liquid cholesterol-free egg substitute)
½ cup chopped walnuts
1 teaspoon vanilla
⅔ cup cake flour
1 teaspoon low sodium baking powder

Combine sugar and vegetable oil in mixing bowl. Add egg and beat well. Add chopped nuts and vanilla. Fold in mixed and sifted dry ingredients. Bake in lightly oiled pan (8 x 8 x 2-inches) in a preheated 350° (moderate) oven, 25 to 35 minutes. Cut into squares while warm.

ONE SQUARE *With whole egg*	ONE SQUARE *With egg whites*	
8	10	milligrams sodium
6	6	grams total fat
1	trace	gram saturated fat
18	18	grams carbohydrate
125	122	calories

One square: ¾ teaspoon vegetable oil.

VARIATIONS
Omit nut meats when plain, chewy brownie is your choice. Substitute ½ cup raisins for nut meats.

CINNAMON ROUNDS
48 Cookies

⅓ cup egg whites
2 cups confectioners' sugar
½ teaspoon grated lemon rind
½ teaspoon cinnamon
2 cups mixed nuts (walnuts, almonds), ground fine

Beat egg whites until stiff but not dry. Gradually add sugar, blending after each addition. Add lemon rind; continue to beat until completely blended (about 5 minutes). Reserve ¾ cup mixture for filling. Blend together cinnamon and ground nuts; fold into remaining egg white mixture. If batter is too soft to roll, let stand at room temperature until sufficiently stiff to handle. Roll out about ⅛-inch thick on cloth-covered board. (Use confectioners' sugar rubbed on cloth to keep from sticking.) Cut into rounds with cooky cutter. Place ½ teaspoon reserved mixture on center of each round. Bake on lightly oiled baking sheet in a preheated 350° (moderate) oven about 12 minutes.

ONE COOKY	TOTAL RECIPE	
3	128	milligrams sodium
3	141	grams total fat
trace	10	grams saturated fat
6	299	grams carbohydrate
53	2531	calories

DIETETIC CORN FLAKE DREAMS
50 Cookies

Thanks to Kay Chambers, who was always experimenting for the Buff of this book, we have many delectable conversion recipes. This is a great favorite with dieter and the regulars.

3 medium egg whites
⅞ cup sugar
1 teaspoon lemon extract
1 ½ cups low sodium dietetic corn flakes
½ cup chopped walnuts

Beat egg whites until stiff; gradually add sugar, a few tablespoons at a time, beating after each addition. Add flavoring and beat. Fold in corn flakes and nut meats. Drop by teaspoonful on lightly oiled baking sheet. Bake in a preheated 275° (slow) oven about 25 minutes until golden brown and "set."

ONE COOKY	TOTAL RECIPE	
3	150	milligrams sodium
1	32	grams total fat
trace	2	grams saturated fat
4	214	grams carbohydrate
24	1188	calories

MERINGUE KISSES
36 Kisses

3 egg whites (room temperature)
1 cup sifted sugar
1 teaspoon vinegar
1 teaspoon vanilla

Beat egg whites until they form pointed peaks. Add sugar, 2 tablespoons at a time; beat after each addition. Add vinegar and vanilla and beat until meringue forms stiff peaks.

Lay smooth wrapping paper or aluminum foil on baking sheet; do not oil. Drop mixture onto paper by heaping teaspoonfuls. Bake in a preheated 250° (very slow) oven, 25 to 30 minutes, until a pale cream color. Outside will be hard, inside slightly soft, must hold shape. Remove at once from paper and cool on cake rack.

ONE MERINGUE KISS	TOTAL RECIPE	
4	146	milligrams sodium
trace	trace	gram total fat
6	199	grams carbohydrate
23	815	calories

PEANUT COOKIES
36 Cookies

1 egg (or 2 egg whites)
⅔ cup sugar
1 teaspoon water
1 tablespoon all-purpose flour
½ teaspoon low sodium baking powder
1 cup finely ground, unsalted, roasted peanuts

Beat egg until lemon-colored (egg whites until stiff). Gradually beat in sugar and water. Mix flour and baking powder; gently fold into mixture with rubber spatula. Add peanuts, blending gently but thoroughly. Drop by teaspoonfuls, 2 inches apart, on ungreased wrapping paper or foil on baking sheet. Bake in a preheated 325° (slow) oven, 8 to 15 minutes.

ONE COOKY	TOTAL RECIPE	
With whole egg		
2	70	milligrams sodium
2	78	grams total fat
1	18	grams saturated fat
5	166	grams carbohydrate
41	1462	calories

RYE HAPPIES
36 Cookies

This recipe will be a boon to dieters looking for a goody low in saturated fat. We are indebted to Fisher Flouring Mills Company for permission to adapt.

½ cup rye flour, unsifted
½ cup rolled oats
½ teaspoon low sodium baking powder
¾ cup coarsely chopped walnuts
⅓ cup vegetable oil
½ cup sugar
½ cup light brown sugar, firmly packed
1 teaspoon vanilla
3 egg whites

Mix flour, oats, baking powder, and walnuts. Combine oil, sugars, vanilla, and egg whites in mixing bowl; beat until free from all lumps. Stir in dry ingredients. Bake in lightly oiled 9-inch square pan in a preheated 350° (moderate) oven, 30 to 35 minutes. Cool in pan; then cut in squares. You may dust with powdered sugar if desired. Store in covered jar in cool place.

ONE COOKY	TOTAL RECIPE	
5	182	milligrams sodium
3	125	grams total fat
trace	11	grams saturated fat
8	278	grams carbohydrate
63	2278	calories

One cooky: ⅓ teaspoon vegetable oil.

SPICED WINE COOKIES
WITH RAISINS
36 Cookies

We are indebted to the Home Advisory Service of the Wine Institute, San Francisco, for this delicious cooky.

2 cups all-purpose flour
2 teaspoons low sodium baking powder
¼ teaspoon cinnamon
¼ teaspoon nutmeg
1 egg (or 2 egg whites)
1⅓ cups light brown sugar
¼ cup vegetable oil
¼ cup California muscatel
½ cup chopped walnuts
½ cup raisins

Mix and sift first four ingredients. Beat egg; add sugar and oil. Stir until well blended. Add sifted dry ingredients to egg mixture alternately with wine. Stir in walnuts and raisins. Drop from teaspoon onto lightly oiled baking sheet. Bake in a preheated 400° (hot) oven, 10 to 12 minutes.

ONE COOKY	TOTAL RECIPE	
With whole egg		
5	189	milligrams sodium
3	95	grams total fat
trace	8	grams saturated fat
15	542	grams carbohydrate
87	3147	calories

One cooky: ⅓ teaspoon vegetable oil.

White port or sherry may be substituted for muscatel.

One cup unsalted shredded coconut may be substituted for nuts and raisins if saturated fats are not restricted.

SUGAR COOKIES – GRANDMOTHER'S VARIETY

30 Cookies

1 ¼ cups all-purpose flour
1 teaspoon low sodium baking powder
¼ teaspoon nutmeg (optional)
⅓ cup vegetable oil
½ cup sugar
2 egg whites
1 teaspoon lemon juice
½ teaspoon lemon peel
Granulated sugar

Mix and sift first three ingredients. Combine oil and sugar in mixing bowl. Add unbeaten egg whites, one at a time, beating well after each addition. Add lemon juice and peel. Add sifted dry ingredients all at once; blend well. Shape dough into little balls, about ¾ inch in diameter. Dip balls into granulated sugar. Place balls, sugar side up, 3 inches apart, on lightly oiled baking sheet. Press with a flat-bottom glass covered with a damp cloth until dough is ⅛-inch thick. Or crisscross with tines of fork. Bake in preheated 375° (moderate) oven, 8 to 10 minutes. Remove from baking sheet at once. Cool on cake rack.

ONE COOKY	TOTAL RECIPE	
3	100	milligrams sodium
2	74	grams total fat
trace	7	grams saturated fat
9	278	grams carbohydrate
61	1842	calories

One cooky: ½ teaspoon vegetable oil.

VARIATIONS

Sherry may be substituted for lemon juice; vanilla may also be used as the flavoring.

Balls may be lightly dipped in finely ground nut meats.

Balls may be dipped in cocoa or chocolate if saturated fats are not restricted.

One egg or ¼ cup liquid cholesterol-free egg substitute may be used in place of egg whites if diet allows.

WHEAT GERM DROP COOKIES
36 Cookies

Another San Joaquin, now Central California, Heart Association tested recipe.

2 ¼ cups whole wheat flour
1 teaspoon nutmeg
1 teaspoon cinnamon
2 teaspoons low sodium baking powder
½ cup wheat germ
½ cup honey
¼ cup vegetable oil
¾ cup water, less 2 tablespoons

Sift flour, nutmeg, cinnamon, and baking powder. Add wheat germ and blend. Combine honey, oil, and water. Add to other ingredients; blend and beat until well mixed. Drop by teaspoonfuls onto lightly oiled baking sheet. Bake in a preheated 350° (moderate) oven, 8 to 15 minutes until golden brown.

ONE COOKY	TOTAL RECIPE	
1	19	milligrams sodium
2	63	grams total fat
trace	4	grams saturated fat
10	347	grams carbohydrate
57	2048	calories

One cooky: ⅓ teaspoon vegetable oil.

PASTRY

You need make no apologies for your pastries. They should be as tender and flaky — and as flavorsome too — as were your products before the restricted dietary.

True, you will not be able to add salt if sodium is restricted, but a little sugar or spice, depending on the flavor of the filling, will help to make your pastry unique. Try a dash of cinnamon or nutmeg with squash, or a little caraway with apple.

Another trick to add flavor to your pastry is to replace some of the liquid with fruit juice. When you make cherry pie, add some cherry juice to your pastry. Ditto for pineapple.

Invest in a deep-dish pie plate, or "flavor saver," as it is sometimes called. Then, the next time you bake an apple pie, after you have sealed the two crusts, make three or four slits around the outer rim, just below the seal. While the pie is baking, some of the flavorsome juices will flow out and give the outer edge of crust the most delicious flavor. The deep plate will protect your oven.

To prevent soaking of lower crusts in custard-type pies, we advise a 400° to 425° (hot) oven.

For a shiny top on your pies, brush lightly with low sodium nonfat milk before baking.

We have included three recipes for pastry — all meeting the requirements of sodium or saturated fat restrictions. Vegetable oil pastry is tender and flaky, and so easy to make — and delicious enough for anyone to enjoy, too.

Of course, you may prefer to use your own recipes for pastry. *Just omit salt, if you are on sodium restriction, and substitute ½ teaspoon sugar. If you are on saturated fat restriction, you will have to omit solid (hydrogenated) shortening and use a vegetable oil pastry.*

Where milk is an important ingredient of pastry or any of the recipes for fillings that follow, we have used nonfat milk. You may substitute, measure for measure, low sodium nonfat milk to reduce the sodium content of pastry and filling. If you do use nonfat milk, be sure to count it in the dieter's daily allowance.

As with cakes and cookies, the carbohydrate and calories of pie crust are so high that you will have to use sparingly, if at all. One-crust selections will help some. And serve the dieter half portions of pie for lower calorie count.

Our recipes are for 9-inch pies unless otherwise noted.

VEGETABLE OIL PASTRY
6 Servings — (For 1 two-crust pie)

Vegetable Oil Pastry is a quick pastry method, with no guessing as to cutting in shortening or how much liquid to add.

2 cups all-purpose flour
½ teaspoon sugar

½ cup vegetable oil
¾ cup nonfat milk

Mix flour and sugar; add oil and milk all at once. Stir quickly until dough "cleans" bowl. Pat into round ball; wrap in waxed paper, and set in refrigerator for at least an hour to thoroughly chill. Roll between waxed paper squares, working very quickly so pastry remains cold. Fit to pan; reserve ½ for top crust.

ONE SERVING	TOTAL RECIPE	
6	36	milligrams sodium
19	112	grams total fat
2	11	grams saturated fat
30	181	grams carbohydrate
307	1843	calories

One serving: 4 teaspoons vegetable oil.

WHOLE WHEAT PASTRY

6 Servings — (For 1 two-crust pie)

We are indebted to Fisher Flouring Mills Company for this tested recipe, which we have adapted for dietary use.

1½ cups 100 percent whole wheat flour, unsifted
1 teaspoon low sodium baking powder
½ cup nonfat milk
½ cup vegetable oil
⅓ cup (more or less) 100 percent whole wheat flour for pastry board

Mix flour and baking powder. Beat or whip milk and oil together to blend. Add to flour mixture all at once; stir with fork until mixture leaves sides of bowl. Turn onto board sprinkled

334 DESSERTS FOR EVERY OCCASION

with ⅓ cup whole wheat flour; press into ball. Divide into 2 pieces; roll out. Or put ball between wax paper squares and roll to desired size.

ONE SERVING	TOTAL RECIPE	
12	70	milligrams sodium
19	114	grams total fat
2	11	grams saturated fat
27	164	grams carbohydrate
293	1758	calories

One serving: 4 teaspoons vegetable oil.

CORN FLAKE CRUST

6 Servings — (For 1 crust, 8-inches)

1 cup crushed low sodium dietetic corn flakes
⅓ cup vegetable oil
¼ cup sugar

Roll or grind corn flakes to make generous cupful. Combine with vegetable oil and sugar. Press crust firmly on bottom and sides of pan; chill crust. It is not necessary to bake before filling; it may be chilled in refrigerator for later use. However, you may bake at once in a preheated 375° (moderate) oven, 15 minutes. After being chilled or baked, fill with any previously cooked custard-type filling or fresh or dried fruit filling. Top with meringue if sodium allowance permits. Delicious, too, with a chiffon-type pie.

ONE SERVING	TOTAL RECIPE	
	Crust only	
1	3	milligrams sodium
12	73	grams total fat
1	7	grams saturated fat
12	74	grams carbohydrate
156	937	calories

One serving: 2⅔ teaspoons vegetable oil.

PIES

APPLE PIE
6 Servings

Vegetable Oil Pastry (page 332)
¾ cup sugar
2 tablespoons flour
1 teaspoon cinnamon
¼ teaspoon nutmeg
6 medium apples, peeled and sliced
3 tablespoons vinegar

Line pie plate with ½ of pastry. Mix sugar, flour, and spices. Alternate layers of sliced apples with sprinkling of sugar-mix, arranging so that apples are piled slightly higher toward center of pan. Sprinkle with vinegar. Wet edges of undercrust, cover with upper crust, and press edges together. Prick several places with fork. Bake in a preheated 425° (hot) oven, 45 to 55 minutes.

ONE SERVING	TOTAL RECIPE	
7	42	milligrams sodium
19	112	grams total fat
2	11	grams saturated fat
75	451	grams carbohydrate
482	2897	calories

One serving: 4 teaspoons vegetable oil.

APPLE PIE VARIATIONS

Almost as infinite as the imagination of the cook. With highly flavored apples, only a whiff of cinnamon is necessary. But with market-fresh apples, lemon juice and rind may be substituted for vinegar to point up flavor. Caraway may be used in place of cinnamon. And rum or a few drops of Angostura Aromatic Bitters may even be used for extra flavor.

FRESH FRUIT PIE VARIATIONS

Taste-ticklers to be sure but watch those calories if you have to consider overweight. Follow method outlined in recipe for Apple Pie. Sprinkle flour-sugar mixture over fruit; omit vinegar; add spices if desired. Bake in a preheated 425° (hot) oven for 45 to 55 minutes. Reduce baking time 10 minutes if you use canned fruit.

FRUIT	QUANTITY	SUGAR	FLOUR
Apricot	3 cups, sliced	1 cup	2 tablespoons
Berry	3 cups	1 cup	3 tablespoons
Cherry	3 cups, pitted	¾ cup	2 tablespoons
Peach	3 cups, sliced	¾ cup	2 tablespoons
Rhubarb	3 cups, cut	1½ cups	2 tablespoons

CRANBERRY PIE
6 Servings

2 cups cranberries, washed and sorted
¾ cup sugar
½ cup water
1 tablespoon gelatin
2 egg whites, beaten stiff but not dry
2 teaspoons lemon juice
1 teaspoon lemon rind

Put into a saucepan the sorted and washed cranberries; stir in ½ cup of the sugar and ¼ cup water. Cook about 5 minutes, until skins begin to burst. Mash through a large colander. Meanwhile prepare gelatin by putting ¼ cup cold water in a measuring cup and sprinkling gelatin over it. Let stand 5 minutes or until softened. Dissolve by standing cup in a bowl of hot water. Then blend gelatin into cranberry mixture and set aside. To the beaten egg whites add, a little at a time, lemon juice, lemon rind and remaining ¼ cup sugar. Fold into cranberry mixture. Spoon into baked 8-inch pie shell, and let stand in refrigerator until set, allowing a minimum of 4 hours.

ONE SERVING	TOTAL RECIPE	
Without pie crust		
17	101	milligrams sodium
trace	2	grams total fat
trace	trace	gram saturated fat
29	173	grams carbohydrate
125	752	calories

VARIATIONS

Puréed apricots, peaches, and prunes are other fruits particularly flavorsome in this recipe.

GREEN TOMATO MINCEMEAT
20 Pints

1 peck green tomatoes (8 quarts)
½ peck apples (4 quarts)
½ pound suet (optional)
6 cups light brown sugar
2 tablespoons cinnamon
½ tablespoon cloves
1 tablespoon nutmeg
3 pounds raisins
¾ cup vinegar

Chop — or put through meat chopper adjusted to coarse knife — tomatoes, apples, and suet. Put in large kettle. Add remaining ingredients. Cook very slowly until tender (about 2 to 3 hours). Bottle in sterilized jars. Allow 1 pint per pie (6 servings). *Omit suet if restricted in saturated fats.*

ONE PINT	TOTAL RECIPE	ONE PINT	TOTAL RECIPE	
		With suet; without pie crust		
Without suet or pie crust				
49	979	55	1091	milligrams sodium
1	22	12	235	grams total fat
trace	trace	5	101	grams saturated fat
149	2982	149	2982	grams carbohydrate
582	11641	679	13578	calories

MOCK CHERRY PIE

6 Servings

We are indebted to Miss Kathleen Piper of Lynn, Massachu-setts, for this recipe. The tart flavor makes it combine well with a bland menu. Serve it once, and we are sure that it will be a favorite with the entire family.

1 cup washed cranberries, cut in halves
½ cup seedless raisins
1 cup sugar
1 tablespoon flour
½ cup water
½ teaspoon almond flavoring

Combine cranberries, raisins, sugar, and flour in a large bowl. Add water and flavoring; stir to blend, being careful not to bruise cranberries. Spoon into pastry lined pie plate. Top with remaining pastry or arrange a lattice top for a partylike look, following preparation directions in pastry recipe of choice. Be sure to cut slits on top for vent. Bake pie on bottom shelf in a preheated 425° (hot) oven for 15 minutes. Change to middle shelf and continue cooking until fruit is tender (about 20 to 30 minutes).

ONE SERVING	TOTAL RECIPE	
Without pie crust		
4	24	milligrams sodium
trace	1	gram total fat
trace	trace	gram saturated fat
46	278	grams carbohydrate
180	1077	calories

PINEAPPLE PIE
6 Servings

2 tablespoons cornstarch
2 tablespoons sugar
2 cups hot, crushed pineapple
1 tablespoon lemon juice
1 tablespoon grated lemon rind
Baked pastry shell
Meringue (optional)

Mix cornstarch and sugar; add to pineapple. Cook in double boiler 20 minutes, stirring constantly until thickened. Cool; add other ingredients. Fill pie shell. *If sodium count permits,* cover with meringue made of 2 egg whites, ¼ cup sugar, and 1 teaspoon vanilla (add sugar gradually, and continue beating until blended and whites are stiff; add flavoring). Let set, if no meringue is used; if meringue is added, bake in a preheated 425° (hot) oven, 4 to 4½ minutes.

ONE SERVING	TOTAL RECIPE	
Without meringue or		
pie crust		
1	4	milligrams sodium
trace	1	gram total fat
trace	trace	gram saturated fat
23	139	grams carbohydrate
90	537	calories

SQUASH PIE
6 Servings

¼ cup sugar
½ cup light brown sugar

¼ cup flour
1 teaspoon cinnamon
½ teaspoon ginger
½ teaspoon nutmeg
2 cups cooked, strained squash (unsalted)
1 egg
1½ cups nonfat milk

Mix sugar, flour, and spice. Add to squash and mix well. Beat egg slightly and add to squash mixture. Add milk gradually. Bake in one crust in a preheated 400° (hot) oven, 30 minutes, until knife comes out clean. Count milk in daily allowance.

ONE SERVING	TOTAL RECIPE	
Without pie crust		
49	294	milligrams sodium
1	8	grams total fat
trace	2	grams saturated fat
43	260	grams carbohydrate
194	1161	calories

LOW SATURATED FAT VARIATION

Follow Basic Recipe except to substitute 2 egg whites or ¼ cup liquid cholesterol-free egg substitute for 1 whole egg. If no sodium restriction, add ½ teaspoon salt.

One serving, without pie crust: negligible saturated fat.

14

TASTE-TICKLERS

And that's just what they are, taste-ticklers — these morale builders and vitamin boosters and fragrant delicacies of one sort or another. Their primary aim in the diet is to please highly cultivated taste buds, but they can be a plus-value nutritionally and psychologically, too.

Yes, they can make a definite and positive contribution to your emotional climate, if you are on a restricted food program. They represent the "goodies" of eating, and to be able to have at least a few of them may help you to forget or help you to accept the many prohibitions of your sodium- or fat-restricted diet.

If you are on a severely restricted program, your system goes through many changes in adapting from the old to the new food allowances. This is the time to introduce a few "treat times" for nourishment of body and soul. Midmorning coffee or fruit juice with low sodium or regular toast, as allowed —

dietetic cooky or confection, as allowed — can bolster nutrition and you at the same time.

Afternoon tea is quite a custom, when you come to think of it! Too bad that in the hustle and bustle of everyday living most of us pay it such slight homage. Or — is it a shame, since so few of us brew a really good cup of tea?

Why not begin with tea, then, and go on to other beverages and some of their accompanying delicacies?

BEVERAGES

TEA

The first prerequisite in making a good cup of tea is to buy a tea of good quality. Whether you like the decisiveness of the "black varieties" or the more subtle taste of the green is a matter of individual taste. Some of the flower blends are just delightful and are particularly pleasing when iced tea is to be served.

Bring water to the boiling point, meanwhile scalding out your teapot. Prepare tea in a china, Pyrex, enamel, or earthenware pot, allowing 1 teaspoon tea to 1 cup of water. Put tea leaves in the teapot and pour water over them. Now steep for 3 to 5 minutes, and strain into another pot, if you are going to let it stand before serving. We like the old English custom of muffling this pot in a cozy and letting tea stand quietly until serving time. When serving tea, have a pitcher of hot water on your tray, so tea may be diluted to suit individual tastes. Flavor with rose geranium leaves, thin slices of lemon or orange, preserved ginger, cloves, or a piece of cinnamon, and serve with low sodium or regular toast or other goody, as allowed.

ICED TEA

For a long, cold drink, it's hard to beat a tall glass of iced tea or lemonade. There are some simple secrets to good iced tea-making to guarantee a flavorsome result.

Make a tray of tea ice cubes for chilling tea, to preserve both flavor and aroma in your long drink.

Now proceed as outlined above for hot tea. Pour hot tea in glasses filled with ¾ chopped tea ice or cubes. Sweeten to taste and garnish as for hot tea, or with any of your own favorites.

HOW TO MAKE GOOD COFFEE

Some like it strong and some like it weak. All coffee lovers are agreed they want the full flavor of coffee in their drink. Whatever the strength for your taste, you will want your coffee to be clear and completely free of muddiness, that is, if it is on your allowable list.

You just can't make good coffee in an unclean pot, so Principle Number One is a *sparkling clean and scalded pot*.

Start with fresh, cold water, and for each serving allow 1 standard coffee measure (or its equivalent, 2 level measuring tablespoons) of fresh coffee to each ¾ cup of *freshly drawn water*. (Yes, water does get stale.)

Use only coffee ground for your type of coffee maker. You can get best results by using your coffee maker at full capacity. It pays to have a small one for family use to capitalize upon this point.

Timing is important in the making of coffee so don't brew it happenstance. If you are a devotee of instant coffee, do follow label directions for best results. However you make it, serve at once while it is steaming and yields its most aromatic "flavors."

INSTANT ESPRESSO

Unbelievable but at last it's true, you can serve after-dinner coffee with a real deep-roasted, Continental flavor and no more trouble than any other instant coffee. For now espresso is instant, too — Jomar is one brand that should be available in your favorite store.

CAFÉ AU LAIT

Here is your chance to have a gourmet flair to an otherwise simple meal. Serve strong, hot coffee (we like the French Market coffee with chicory for this) with an equal amount of hot nonfat milk. Pour milk and coffee into cup simultaneously — a pot in each hand. And if you want to be very authentic according to Southern custom, you will use after-dinner coffee cups (demitasses) instead of regular size.

ICED COFFEE

For really good iced coffee, make it double strength and pour over iced coffee cubes.

FRUIT BEVERAGES

There is nothing better than a refreshing tall fruit drink on a warm day for a pickup. Minerals, vitamins, and natural sugars of the fruits used, plus the addition of a sweetener, will ensure that energy lift. But be sure to consult your diet list if you are on a fat-carbohydrate controlled diet. (See Variation, page 347.)

FRUIT BEVERAGE SIRUP
1 Cup

Add ¾ cup sugar to ¾ cup boiling water and stir until sugar is dissolved, being careful not to stir sugar onto the sides of the pan, as it will form crystals. Boil over very slow fire for about 10 minutes. Cool and bottle.

ONE TABLESPOON	TOTAL RECIPE	
trace	2	milligrams sodium
none	none	gram total fat
9	149	grams carbohydrate
36	578	calories

SUGGESTIONS FOR
FRUIT BEVERAGES

Lemonade (6 Servings): Combine ¼ cup Fruit Beverage Sirup with ½ cup lemon juice. Add 1 quart cold water. Serve over ice.

Pineapple Lemonade (12 servings): Combine 1½ cups Fruit Beverage Sirup, ¾ cup lemon juice, and 5 cups ice water. Add 2 cups crushed pineapple. Chill thoroughly in tightly sealed jar. Strain (optional), and serve. If unable to chill, serve over ice cubes.

Fruit Punch (8 servings): Combine 1 cup Fruit Beverage Sirup, 3½ cups ice water, ½ cup lemon juice, 1 cup orange juice, and 1 tablespoon grated lemon or orange rind. Chill thoroughly or serve over ice cubes. The addition of ½ cup lightly crushed berries or ½ cup pineapple chunkies is a delightful variation. Garnish each serving with 1 whole berry.

VARIATION

If calories or carbohydrates are restricted, use only as allowed. Omit Fruit Beverage Sirup and use specified sugar substitute to sweeten beverage.

SPICED HOT CIDER
6 to 12 Servings

2 quarts apple cider
1 tablespoon lemon rind
1 small cinnamon stick
6 slices orange
12 cloves

Put cider, lemon rind, and cinnamon into a saucepan. Simmer slowly about 15 minutes. Top with orange slices and cloves. Remove cinnamon before serving.

TOTAL RECIPE	
20	milligrams sodium
trace	gram total fat
244	grams carbohydrate
962	calories

MILK BEVERAGES

Chocolate may not be used if you have saturated fat restrictions. For the rest of you, make your choices from the nonfat milk-fruit or coffee combinations. Puréed apricots, peaches, pineapple, or prunes, strained berries of choice may be combined with milk and sugar or sirup (page 346) for a nutritious and tasty beverage. If you have a blender, follow directions for any milk-fruit combination of choice, always being careful to check against your list of allowables when you elect to have one of these extras. And be sure to include its count in your daily total.

REDUCER'S COFFEE MILK SHAKE
1 Serving

1 cup nonfat milk
1 ice cube
1 teaspoon instant coffee
Allowable sugar substitute

Beat in electric blender until creamy.

ONE SERVING	
128	milligrams sodium
trace	gram total fat
12	grams carbohydrate
90	calories

TREATS TO GO
WITH BEVERAGES

Sweet bread, low sodium toast with homemade jam or jelly, toast sprinkled lightly with sugar and orange juice — all of these and other things are good for a midmorning snack. For tea time treat, try fruit or cinnamon toast, fruit bread or nut, or wee little homemade pastries.

Little pastries are just what their name implies — pies filled with fruit, jam, or custard and handled as for any pie. They can be made in your fluted muffin or 3-inch individual pan, or cut with cooky cutter any desired shape.

Tarts make a particularly nice afternoon sweet, and may appear without top crusting, filled with fruit, jam or a pie filling, or with a gay little top crust in fancy design. If you use individual pudding molds or muffin tins, simply fit pastry over "their backs" and prick to prevent puffing. Put pan upside down on baking sheet and bake in a preheated 450° (very hot) oven for 6 to 8 minutes. Be sure to count them as a part of the daily sodium, fat, carbohydrate, and calorie allowance.

CONFECTIONS

The amount of latitude you have in providing some of these taste-ticklers depends upon your specific diet limitations. Remember that everything eaten must be accounted for, and if you have a "muncher" in your family, you must not neglect to include the "in-betweens" in your day's total. Where weight (or carbohydrate control) is also a factor, most of the suggestions in this chapter will be of little avail. On the other hand, some of you may be confronted with the problem of having a naturally small eater becoming a smaller eater through dietary restrictions. Your physician may suggest you serve 4 or 6 "meals" during the day rather than the usual 3.

APPLETS
36 Squares

2 cups unsweetened applesauce
2 cups sugar
2 tablespoons unflavored gelatin *softened in* ½ cup cold water
1½ cups mixed nuts (walnuts, pecans, almonds)
Few drops of Angostura Aromatic Bitters
¼ cup confectioners' sugar

Put applesauce through sieve; add sugar and cook until very thick (240°). Remove from heat; add gelatin, and stir thoroughly. Add nuts and flavoring. Pour into oiled pan (8 x 8 inches). Let stand overnight until firm. Cut into squares and roll in sugar.

ONE SQUARE	TOTAL RECIPE	
1	26	milligrams sodium
3	110	grams total fat
trace	8	grams saturated fat
14	515	grams carbohydrate
85	3061	calories

FIG-NUT SWEETS
30 Pieces

This is a good candy substitute.
Cover 1 cup figs with boiling water. Let stand 10 minutes.

Drain and cut fine. Mix figs with 1 cup finely cut walnuts. Roll into a long piece, about 1½ inches in diameter, roll in ¼ cup confectioners' sugar (if desired), and slice ⅓ inch thick.

ONE SERVING	TOTAL RECIPE	
With Confectioners' sugar		
2	59	milligrams sodium
2	66	grams total fat
trace	4	grams saturated fat
5	164	grams carbohydrate
41	1234	calories

MIXED FRUIT BALLS
20 Balls

A word of warning: fruit balls are hard to keep on hand.

By this time, you've grasped the idea of using foods only in their natural forms, unless otherwise permitted. This goes for dried fruits, too.

½ cup apricots
½ cup peaches
½ cup pears
¼ cup raisins
½ cup prunes
¼ cup wheat germ
¼ cup confectioners' sugar

Put all ingredients except wheat germ and sugar through fine cut of meat grinder two times. Blend in wheat germ. Shape with hand into balls the size of a large marble. Roll lightly in ¼ cup sifted confectioners' sugar and put in covered serving bowl in refrigerator to keep cool until time of use.

ONE SERVING	TOTAL RECIPE	
3	69	milligrams sodium
trace	5	grams total fat
trace	trace	gram saturated fat
14	317	grams carbohydrate
62	1247	calories

GLAZED NUTS
About 30 Pieces

Although walnuts are an excellent source of polyunsaturates, remember that they are also high in fat — a half cup equals approximately a day's total allowable fat. High, too, in carbohydrate. So choose them as one of your free choice items only as allowed.

2 cups sugar
1 cup boiling water
⅛ teaspoon cream of tartar
2 cups blanched, unsalted almonds, pecans, or walnuts
  (preferred)

Cook sugar, water, and cream of tartar to boiling point. From time to time, wipe sides of pan with pastry brush or cloth dipped in cold water to prevent crystallization. Boil without stirring until sirup begins to turn lightly brown at 310° on candy thermometer. Place pan in larger pan of cold water to stop boiling at once. Remove from cold water and set in pan of hot water while dipping nuts into sirup on long pin or skewer. Or add nuts to mixture; stir to cover. Place on oiled baking sheet or waxed paper to dry.

ONE SERVING	TOTAL RECIPE	
With walnuts	*With pecans*	
trace	2	milligrams sodium
5	158	grams total fat
trace	10	grams saturated fat
14	430	grams carbohydrate
95	3044	calories

VARIATIONS

Orange juice may be substituted for water. Omit cream of tartar. Or you may spice your glaze by adding 1 teaspoon cinnamon and ½ teaspoon vanilla extract. Another good variation is double strength coffee boiled with 3 cups light brown sugar to very soft ball stage (234° to 240°). Remove from heat and add 1 teaspoon corn oil; stir. Blend in nuts. Beat and pour onto lightly oiled candy plate. Cut into squares when cold.

Have a small bowlful of "untreated" walnut or other nut meats (see Appendix 2), and use them plain as a munching extra.

PERSIAN DELIGHTS
24 Pieces

2 packages (2 tablespoons) unflavored gelatin
½ cup cold water
¾ cup boiling water
2 cups sugar
Pure vegetable or fruit juice coloring
Flavoring
¼ cup confectioners' sugar

Soften gelatin in cold water. Mix boiling water and sugar and stir until dissolved. Bring to a boil and add gelatin, stirring until thoroughly dissolved. Boil mixture slowly about 15 minutes.

Remove from heat. Color and flavor as desired. Stir thoroughly, and pour mixture into an oblong pan, 8 x 8 x 2 inches. Do not chill in refrigerator. Ease candy from sides of pan with a wet knife and spread, upside down, on a lightly sugared board (confectioners' sugar). Cut into squares and rub all sides in confectioners' sugar. Put cut pieces on a flat serving dish to avoid any stickiness. A delicious Christmas delicacy made in green and red, but delicate and delectable at any season of the year.

ONE SERVING	TOTAL RECIPE	
trace	10	milligrams sodium
none	none	gram total fat
18	429	grams carbohydrate
72	1731	calories

JELLIES, JAMS, PRESERVES

Jellies, of course, are good taste-ticklers and deserve your attention just as soon as you can get to them. Wine jellies and jams made from frozen fruits make jelly-making an any-month-of-the-year job. If the home jelly is well made, only the *very best* commercial product can compare with it. Jellies on the grocers' shelves often contain sodium citrate as a stabilizer. There might be only a trace of it, to be sure, but you will have to look to your list and your physician's instructions to find out whether or not you may use commercial jellies on your particular diet.

The Farmers' Bulletin No. 1800 of the United States Department of Agriculture, *Homemade Jellies, Jams and Preserves*, has helpful suggestions on basic principles involved in home preservation of fruit with sugar.

To get good jellies — clear, shimmering, and with finest flavor

— and good preserves that are clear, tender, and shapely, you will have to work by known principles.

Cook your jellies and jams a minimum amount of time to ensure the most color and flavor. Time will vary with different fruit-sugar combinations, but will have to be sufficient to "concentrate" this sirup — change the texture of the fruit itself.

Home economists have worked out many aids in this field and it is wise to follow their suggestions for thin or thick sirups, since firm and soft fruits have different sirup requirements.

You have, no doubt, been using a pectin to set your home-made jellies. Since pectin must be present with acid and sugar to make a jelly which sets successfully, you need to know which fruits are particularly rich in pectin and acid and those which may have to have pectin added. Commercial pectin is fairly high in sodium content, so again, in a very tight diet requirement you may have to make your own pectin (page 356) or use fruits which are high in pectin and acid.

Fruits rich in pectin and acid (to 1 cup juice, use ¾ to 1 cup sugar):

> Apples, sour
>
> Blackberries, sour
>
> Crabapples
>
> Cranberries
>
> Currants
>
> Gooseberries
>
> Grapes (Eastern)
>
> Lemons
>
> Loganberries
>
> Plums (not all varieties)
>
> Prunes, sour
>
> Quinces, sour

If you are in doubt about the pectin content, make a simple test by putting 2 teaspoons cooked fruit juice in a glass and adding an equal amount of rubbing alcohol (70 percent or more). If the juice is high in pectin, you will get a gelatinous material in your glass. If only moderately rich in pectin, you will get a few pieces of this gelatinous material, and if poor in pectin (too poor to make a jelly), you will get only a few flaky pieces.

Now, of course, you can add pectin to your liquid juice in the proportion of 1, 2, 3 or more tablespoons to a cup of juice. You can use your pectin test for this or follow any of the good recipes you have.

Jam- and jelly-making is an easy but an exact form of cookery. You must (1) wash, scald, and drain glasses and tin covers; (2) bring mixture to boil, reduce heat, cover, and simmer when recipe specifies simmering time; (3) mix a little water with pulp in jelly bag and squeeze again if there is a slight shortage of juice; (4) be sure to measure accurately, using the same measuring cup for both dry and liquid ingredients; (5) be sure you have a full rolling boil that cannot be stirred down; (6) fill jelly glasses to ½ inch of top so there will be space between the paraffin, and cover to prevent seepage; (7) use only new paraffin. Pour ⅛ inch layer of it over jellies and jams and cover glasses with tin or tightly pasted paper covers; (8) store in cool, dry place.

HOMEMADE APPLE PECTIN EXTRACT*

Summer apples do not have sufficient pectin for such use. Sound culls or apples with surface blemishes are usable. Scrub the

* From U.S.D.A. Farmers' Bulletin No. 1800, *Homemade Jellies, Jams and Preserves.*

apples and cut out the imperfect spots, then slice thin, retaining ends and cores. For each 4 pounds of prepared apples, use 4½ pints of water for the first extraction.

Place 4 pounds apples and the water in a large pan so as to allow rapid boiling. Cover and boil for 20 minutes. Strain through 4 thicknesses of cheesecloth until the juice stops dripping.

Repeat the process, adding the same quantity of water, boiling and straining as before. The two extractions should amount to about 3 quarts. A little lemon juice may be added to the water in order to increase the amount of pectin obtained.

Boil this juice in a pan large enough so that the liquid will be 2 inches deep. Boil rapidly until the juice is reduced to ¼ of its original volume. This usually requires from 30 to 40 minutes. There should be 1½ pints of the concentrated apple juice or pectin extract. If the extract is not to be used at once, pour it while hot into hot sterilized half-pint jars, partially seal, and process on a rack in a boiling water bath for 20 minutes. Complete the seal and store in a cool dry place. Once the canned extract is open, it must be used immediately as it will not keep.

ONE CUP	TOTAL RECIPE	
5	16	milligrams sodium
3	10	grams total fat
trace	trace	gram saturated fat
81	243	grams carbohydrate
323	968	calories

PORT WINE JELLY
Five 6-Ounce Glasses

Wine jellies are delicious with meats, as a spread on low sodium toast, or as a garnish (to be eaten) on a huge fruit salad platter.

Simply combine 2 cups port with 3 cups sugar in a saucepan, and cook over briskly boiling water 2 minutes, until wine and sugar are thoroughly heated. Stir constantly. Now mix in ½ bottle commercial liquid pectin or ½ cup homemade pectin. Pour immediately into five 6-ounce sterilized glasses, and seal with paraffin.

ONE TABLESPOON	ONE GLASS	TOTAL RECIPE	
With homemade pectin			
1	10	48	milligrams sodium
trace	trace	2	grams total fat
11	135	673	grams carbohydrate
52	625	3130	calories

Burgundy, sherry, and sauterne may also be used in this recipe.

RHUBARB PRESERVES
3 Pints

2½ pounds rhubarb (about 6 cups)
1⅓ cups crushed pineapple
3½ cups sugar
1½ small unpeeled oranges, sliced
1½ cups walnut meats, broken into small pieces

Wash rhubarb and cut into ½-inch pieces. Combine with remaining ingredients in saucepan and bring to boil, stirring occasionally. Now reduce heat and simmer, uncovered, over low heat about 1½ hours, or until like a conserve in consistency. Stir only as needed the first hour, but more frequently during last period of cooking to prevent any scorching. Remove from heat. Pour into hot, sterilized jars and seal.

ONE TABLESPOON	ONE-HALF PINT	TOTAL RECIPE	
trace	5	27	milligrams sodium
1	16	98	grams total fat
trace	trace	trace	gram saturated fat
9	140	842	grams carbohydrate
43	690	4138	calories

STRAWBERRY PRESERVES
1½ Pints

4 cups whole washed, drained, and hulled strawberries
2 cups sugar
2 tablespoons water
1 teaspoon lemon juice

Combine sugar, water, and lemon juice in a 2-quart saucepan and place over low heat, bringing to a boil, stirring constantly. Add berries. Stir just enough to combine thoroughly with the sirup mixture. Bring to a rolling boil and boil just 4 minutes — be sure to time this, for good results. Remove from heat and skim carefully. Pour preserves into a shallow platter. Allow to stand a full day. (This is the real secret of this recipe.)

When the preserves are of the proper consistency, ladle into hot, sterilized jars and seal.

ONE TABLESPOON	ONE–HALF PINT	TOTAL RECIPE	
trace	2	6	milligrams sodium
trace	1	2	grams total fat
trace	trace	trace	gram saturated fat
9	150	450	grams carbohydrate
37	587	1761	calories

CALIFORNIAN MARMALADE

2 Pints

2 medium-sized oranges
5½ cups water
1 lemon
2 cups apricots
3 cups granulated sugar

Slice one unpeeled orange very thin. Add 2½ cups water and grated rind from lemon. Boil 1 hour. Wash apricots thoroughly. Cover with 3 cups water and boil until tender. Beat to a pulp. Add sugar, cooked orange slices, juice from second orange, and lemon juice. Boil slowly until very thick (about 1 hour). Stir frequently to prevent scorching. Pour into hot, sterilized glasses and seal with paraffin. Makes 2 pints of beautiful golden, lemon-orange-colored marmalade.

ONE TABLESPOON	ONE–HALF PINT	TOTAL RECIPE	
1	22	87	milligrams sodium
trace	trace	2	grams total fat
13	209	834	grams carbohydrate
51	816	3265	calories

RELISHES

Use cranberry jelly, sauces, and relishes for occasions other than "turkey times," when chicken, veal, and mixed dishes are your selection. Orange and cranberry have a natural affinity for each other, as you will discover in relishes, sauces, salad molds, and frozen desserts.

UNCOOKED CRANBERRY-ORANGE RELISH

Wash 1 quart cranberries. Wash and cut up 1 large orange, being sure to remove the seeds. Grind both fruits coarsely and stir in 1½ cups granulated sugar. Let stand, stirring occasionally, until sugar is dissolved, then cover loosely and keep in refrigerator. Makes 2 pints of relish.

ONE TABLESPOON	ONE-HALF PINT	TOTAL RECIPE	
trace	3	12	milligrams sodium
trace	1	4	grams total fat
trace	trace	trace	gram saturated fat
6	91	363	grams carbohydrate
23	360	1438	calories

SPICED PEACHES
6 Servings

Easy to prepare, colorful, and eye-appealing, spiced peaches are a perfect accompaniment for a platter of cold meats or chicken.

Drain peaches, canned in a light sirup or water-packed, and

arrange on a platter. Sprinkle each half, cup side up, with cider vinegar, allowing about 1 tablespoon for 6 peach halves. Sprinkle ⅛ teaspoon dill weed over each peach. Cover with waxed paper and set in refrigerator overnight.

ONE PEACH HALF
In light sirup

1	milligram sodium
trace	gram fat
9	grams carbohydrate
34	calories

SAUCES

For an added bit of pleasurable eating, try these sauces on your menus.

COLD ORANGE SAUCE
4 Servings

This is a great favorite with lamb and duck and can be used with veal, too.

6 tablespoons pure currant jelly
3 tablespoons sugar
Grated rind of 2 oranges
2 tablespoons California port
2 tablespoons orange juice
2 tablespoons lemon juice
⅛ teaspoon cayenne

Put into a mixing bowl currant jelly, sugar, and the grated orange rind. Beat at low speed to blend, then increase to medium speed and continue for 5 minutes. Stir in port, orange juice, lemon juice, and cayenne, stirring to blend. Chill and serve.

ONE SERVING	TOTAL RECIPE	
5	21	milligrams sodium
trace	trace	gram total fat
32	127	grams carbohydrate
134	537	calories

CUMBERLAND SAUCE
6 Servings

"Dee-licious," with any chicken dish, veal, or duck.

6 tablespoons pure red currant jelly
4 tablespoons port wine
4 tablespoons orange juice
2 tablespoons mustard powder
1 teaspoon paprika
½ teaspoon ground ginger
1 teaspoon cornstarch
2 tablespoons grated orange rind

Stir jelly over low heat until melted. Blend other ingredients, add to jelly and bring to boil. Then simmer, stirring constantly, for 5 minutes. Let stand at least 1 hour before serving.

ONE SERVING	TOTAL RECIPE	
5	28	milligrams sodium
trace	trace	gram total fat
16	98	grams carbohydrate
77	464	calories

15

THE HOME FREEZER
CONTRIBUTES TOO

THE LARGE FREEZING section of your refrigerator, or your home freezer, can be a real bonanza in diet cookery. It makes it possible to do in-season buying for out-of-season use. So utilized, it can make a real contribution to that fast-diminishing food dollar, and at the same time provide you with a larger selection of foods all the way around the calendar. Such foods as roasted meats, poultry, and mixed dishes can be prepared in large quantities, packaged in one-meal portions, and kept in the freezer. This gives you food insurance — a guarantee of always having on hand low sodium or low fat foods for special needs.

Imagine having melon balls for Thanksgiving or New Year's Day dinner; sliced cucumbers, dressed in vinegar, in January; corn on the cob all year long; home-grown cherries in November; chicken every month of the year at spring prices; whole dinners to take out of the freezer at a moment's notice. All of these things and more are possible — if you put your freezer to work for you in creating interesting and unusual meals. You do the planning and let it give its yield.

If you have the large storage space that a home freezer affords, or even the lesser space of a modern refrigerator cold section, try to use your energy and effort in that once-a-week extra cooking and baking to provide supplies for freezer packaging, too.

In the chapter on breads, you may remember that the suggestion was made to make enough dough in one mixing for different purposes and for use even at different times. The same principle is involved in planning, marketing, and preparing ahead to get the best use out of other foods for freezer use. If you are going to have pie for dinner, make an extra one to freeze. Or, convert the extra pastry into tart shells or four individual pies, each with a different filling. Similarly with soups and casserole dishes — double the recipes and have a substantial part of a meal "ahead." The extra effort involved in increasing a recipe is very little in comparison with the dividend you get in variety and delicacies at a later date.

Your freezer is also an asset and economizer in the wise use of leftovers. That "smidge" of soup or sauce adds special flavor to your dieter's menu when saved for future use. Of course, leftovers do require a little special care. You cannot freeze them with safety if they have been allowed to stand around for some time after initial preparation. Wrap and freeze leftover meat the day of preparation — or make it into a vegetable-meat soup, croquettes, hash, or a casserole dish. Label and freeze. In general, it is best not to refreeze foods.

Let your freezer simplify your shopping, too. Quantity buying can save you money and effort. You never run short, once you get the frozen food habit. Even an inexperienced cook can have a feeling of confidence with a supply of frozen foods and meals on hand. Stock up on frozen vegetables and fruits when they are offered at bargain prices, to add to your homemade foods. Frozen fruits and vegetables are clean and uniform and are halfway prepared when they come out of the freezer, so they save precious minutes at meal preparation time.

One of the problems in getting use out of frozen foods is to know just how long they may safely be stored. In the first place, try to budget your food storage and plan menus from frozen food stocks so that foods are used within the recommended storage period. Remember that long storage impairs quality. Use first the food that has been stored longest.

The following storage times are a guide for foods stored at zero Fahrenheit:

Beef, veal, and poultry — 9 to 12 months

Ground meat — 1 to 3 months

Cakes, angel, sponge, chiffon, baked — 4 to 6 months

Cakes, shortened — 2 to 6 months

Cooked meats — 2 to 4 months

Fruits and vegetables — 12 months

Pies:

   Chiffon with gelatin base — 1 month

   Fruit — 6 months

   Pumpkin — 1 to 3 weeks

Pork, fish, and lamb — 3 to 6 months

Sandwiches — 2 to 4 weeks

   Open-face — 1 to 2 weeks

In general, baked goods with any kind of filling and sandwich fillings have the shortest storage periods. Water ices and sherbets will keep indefinitely, but both flavor and texture begin to deteriorate after one month, and they may develop icy crystals if kept too long.

Fish may be kept up to 6 months but fatty fish should not be stored longer than 3 to 4 months. Lake trout gives finest flavor if used within 2 to 3 months. Fresh seafood may be frozen 4 to 6 months; cooked seafood, 2 to 3 months.

Prepare and freeze chickens during the spring season, spacing your freezing so that you guarantee chicken around the calendar at spring's low prices.

If you have had your home freezer for some time you have already experimented and know about its most effective use for your own needs. No two families are exactly the same in what they want their freezers to do for them. One family may want the most economical purchasing of food to be the prime consideration; another may want it for special-occasion delicacies or for hard-to-make dishes ahead of use. One use that almost everyone will agree upon is the storage of the makings of a complete dinner. However, for home use it is recommended that the foods be stored separately, not together on a tray. Make the most of your home freezer restricted items, whether they are fat, carbohydrate or sodium specialties. Follow manufacturer's directions for best results from your home freezer. Above all remember that the food you take from it can only be as good as the food you put into the freezer.

FREEZE-EASY DINNER I

Suppose for one dinner for six you want to serve Tuna and Mushroom Casserole, Peas, Stuffed Baked Potatoes, Frozen Fruit Salad, Dinner Rolls, and Cherry Pie.

To prepare the dinner for freezing:

TUNA AND MUSHROOM CASSEROLE
6 Servings

Place in a lightly oiled casserole alternate layers of dietetic low sodium tuna (2 cans, 6½ oz. each) and sliced broiled mushrooms (about 1 cup slices). Cover with 2 cups low sodium Basic Medium White Sauce (page 168) seasoned with ½ teaspoon dill, 1 teaspoon low sodium Worcestershire sauce, and dash of paprika. Top with ½ cup crumbled or rolled dietetic low sodium corn flakes. Bake in a 350° (moderate) oven 30 to 60 minutes, but do not overbrown topping.

LOW SATURATED FAT VARIATION

Use Basic Low Fat Medium White Sauce (page 169). If no sodium restriction, use regular tuna fish, regular Worcestershire sauce and corn flakes, and add 1 teaspoon salt.

STUFFED BAKED POTATOES
6 Servings

Follow recipe given on page 201. Fill one shell for the dieter; add salt to taste for the regulars. Put a toothpick in the special one to designate it when you take it from the freezer. Wrap all for freezing.

PEAS

Put 1½ packages frozen peas into a single carton for the regulars. Plan to use fresh or approved-brand dietetic canned peas without added sodium for the sodium-restricted dieter.

FROZEN FRUIT SALAD
6 Servings

Make Basic Recipe for Molded Salad (page 225), using ¼ cup sherry in place of that amount of liquid in the recipe.

DINNER ROLLS
12 Rolls

Take ½ dough from 2-loaf Basic Bread Recipe (page 252) and make into a long roll. Cut into 12 slices. Shape as desired or keep as cut. Lightly bake as directed (page 250). Cool on rack. Put onto baking sheet or special freezer pie plate. Wrap for freezing.

CHERRY PIE
6 Servings

Follow directions for making Cherry Pie (page 336), lightly bake; cool, wrap for freezing.

Assemble the complete meal on a cooky tray if you choose, but wrap items separately, and label (being sure to include sodium or fat content); freeze.

TO COOK THE DINNER:

Unwrap potatoes. Arrange on a cooky sheet and place on top shelf of oven, with Tuna and Mushroom Casserole. Bake in a preheated 350° (moderate) oven; bake 45 minutes, or until thoroughly heated. Serve at once. (Do not reheat or refreeze.) Place unwrapped pie and rolls (let them stand at room temperature for 1½ hours first) on bottom shelf of oven. Boil peas for the regulars in ¼ cup salted water until fork-tender (8 to 20 minutes); cook fresh peas for those with sodium restrictions. Just before serving, unmold salads on beds of lettuce greens. Garnish as desired. For a crunchy addition, serve a plate of raw vegetable sticks to round out this meal.

FREEZE-EASY DINNER II

Another freezer meal might consist of Soup, Meat Patties, Corn on the Cob, Mixed Fruit Cup, Basic Cake, frosted.

TO PREPARE THE DINNER FOR FREEZING:

SOUP

Bottle leftover low sodium or low fat soup in special freezer container, and freeze.

MEAT PATTIES

Make individual Beef Patties (page 97), separating each one with a round of laminated paper to prevent sticking. Wrap for freezing.

CORN ON THE COB

Corn on the Cob is easily prepared for freezing. Follow directions for your freezer for parboiling corn. Cool quickly, and pack in freezer bags. These come in various sizes, permitting you to freeze a single ear, 2 or 4 ears in combination. From the standpoint of most efficient use of space, it seems unwise to store more than 4 ears to a package.

MIXED FRUIT CUP

For 4 servings, allow 2 cups blended fresh or combined fresh and frozen fruits. To give flavor and texture delight be sure to include at least 1 crunchy fruit, such as apple or pineapple. Use orange juice, apricot nectar, or liquid of choice to moisten. Sugar (or not) to taste. Pack fruits, cut in edible sizes, in a large-necked jar, especially put out for freezer storage. Pour liquid over all and cover. If necessary, use water-pack fruits and artificial sweetener, as allowed.

BASIC CAKE

See recipe on page 314 or 315. If you want to bake and frost cake, be sure to set it in your cold section *unwrapped* for 1 hour to allow frosting to partly freeze so it will stay in place and not run. Remove from freezer, wrap, label, and put in freezer.

Now wrap other items in separate wraps, label, and put in freezer. By labeling, we mean the complete story — food name; amount and number of servings; sodium and fat content; date.

Make this inventory in duplicate so you will have a copy near your work center for planning purposes.

TO COOK THE DINNER:

Let corn thaw before cooking.

Set soup container in a pan of water to speed thawing. Turn into pan to heat as soon as thawing permits. Now put meat patties on broiling rack of oven and broil at 400° until brown on one side. Turn and brown on other side. Salt the patties for the regulars. Boil the thawed corn 5 to 8 minutes, adding a *pinch* of sugar if you want to emphasize its sweetness. Let fruit cup and cake stand at room temperature to thaw. Add a beverage, low sodium bread, and unsalted butter — and your meal is ready to be served.

Before leaving these dinner meals, we want to remind you that with marked meal packages listing the menu, number of servings, and instructions for reheating, you have an entire precooked meal package and can arrange one you later put unwrapped on a shallow pan (to catch drips), and heat it in the oven, with little fuss.

Generally speaking, you will want to allow 30 to 45 minutes longer cooking time for meals right out of the freezer than for thawed food. Thawed food should be ready to eat in about 30 minutes. You will have to figure your time by the meat you are going to serve, rather than by the vegetables.

To thaw most packaged meals, allow 6 to 8 hours in the refrigerator, or 2 to 3 hours at room temperature.

Work out some kind of inventory (and usually it has to be in duplicate so that one copy can be at the freezer location and one in the kitchen for meal planning) so that you use your frozen food to best advantage.

OTHER FOODS

All kinds of goodies can be made and stored for treats and menu enrichment. Some of the foods we have found particularly adaptable are:

Low sodium, low fat ice cream: Store in container and scoop out portions 20 to 30 minutes before serving time. Can also be used in an ice-cream pie by softening ice cream and filling baked low sodium pie shell. Wrap and return to freezer until ready to use. A fruit sauce may be served with this if desired.

Lunch sandwiches: Make a different sandwich for each of 5 days, using such fillings as meat; low sodium cheese (if no fat restrictions), Count Down for those requiring a lower fat content and not having to respect sodium restrictions; blended peanut butter (unsalted for sodium restriction, nonhydrogenated for saturated fat restriction), and pure fruit jelly; low sodium dietetic tuna; ground date mix. Spread on low sodium bread, lightly "buttered" with unsalted special margarine or oil spread. Sprinkle the meat sandwich with a little Bakon Yeast for gourmet flavoring. Place sandwiches in plastic boxes or sandwich bags, label, and freeze.

Sunday-night treat: Serve frozen "creamed" asparagus on low sodium toast topped with low sodium heated dietetic cheese sauce if cheese spread is allowed. For fat-restricted dieters use Count Down. Truly delectable for the regulars, as well as for the dieter.

Baked apples: Bake apples as usual. Cool and set in paper cups; seal, freeze.

Apple pie: Nothing so very new about apple pies in the larder or freezer in this case. Remember the accounts of old Colonial days when the winter's supply of apple pies was baked and frozen? For longest use, bake, cool, freeze; then wrap and store.

Meat balls: Prepare your favorite way in sauce. Cool and fill freezer container.

Leftovers: Freeze the extra soup, chicken à la king, sandwich spreads, leftover turkey. They will taste wonderful next month, and the family will thank you for their spaced reappearance.

Or, combine that leftover chicken with dietetic peas canned without added sodium, thin semolina spaghetti, and a medium low sodium white sauce. At time of serving, sprinkle each portion with 1 tablespoon low sodium grated cheese if allowed.

FACTS FOR FREEZING

1. Only the finest fruits and vegetables should be frozen and they must be fresh if you want tasteful results. *Freezing retains the quality of the food, but cannot improve it.*

2. Learn about the foods that freeze best. Some give better results than others.

3. Follow the directions for your freezer for best results. Scalding before packaging is necessary for vegetables to inactivate the enzymes that turn food dark and contribute to flavor loss, too. Fruits are usually frozen with cold sirup or crushed and coated with dry sugar. To avoid browning, add an ascorbic acid preparation, following label directions.

4. Always freeze immediately after packaging. Leave packages in cold compartment (quick freeze) until solid, with every package touching a side or coil.

5. Use only recommended packaging materials if you want fine results. Wrappings must be moisture- and vapor-proof if foods are to be stored for more than one month. Cellophane, Pliofilm, aluminum or heavy laminated paper, and waxed locker paper — all fulfill this requirement. A double wrap is usually recommended for meats, fish, and poultry. Use rigid containers for fruits and other somewhat liquid foods. The large-necked jars, plastic boxes with interliners, waxed tubs — all meet the

requirement here. Vegetables are usually packed in rectangular containers, with interliners of cellophane or laminated paper. The liners are heat-sealed with a hand iron before packaging.

6. Protect all packaging materials from dust and insects.

7. If packaging material becomes brittle in the heat, place in a refrigerator for 48 hours before using.

8. Freezing jars must be clean and in perfect condition for getting best results from your frozen food.

9. A word of caution about frozen baked goods with frostings. If you want to frost any kind of baked goods before freezing (the alternative would be to frost just before use), use a confectioners' sugar or so-called "fancy type" frosting. *Don't use seven-minute or egg-white types.* They become spongy and somewhat disintegrated during storage period. No frosted cake holds up any too well in freezing, so plan to use within 3 to 4 weeks from freezing date for best results. On the other hand, unfrosted cakes hold up very well in a freezer and may be kept for several months as indicated.

POSTSCRIPT

Consider your freezer a bank. Deposit every bit of surplus that you can manage to save. Withdraw that surplus as you have need. So conceived, the freezer can be one of the best aids available to you in restricted cookery — to provide variety in your meals, extra dollars in your pocket, and energy and smiles in your disposition.

16

YOU CAN
TAKE IT WITH YOU

MANY OF YOU on sodium- and fat-restricted programs will elect
to take lunch to work with you rather than put up with the
frustrations of restaurant eating at peak hours. Of course, the
fine restaurants in almost every city have à la carte service
which can meet your need – if you have the time to wait for
such service and can pay the price.

If you have decided to pack your own, you are, no doubt,
considering sandwiches first of all. They are the good old
standby of lunch boxes and make a good foundation for an adequate luncheon meal. You may remember that starches produce energy – and it is the energy-producing carbohydrates
that are important for a midday meal, particularly if you are in
an active occupation.

Well, what can you use? You have various breads (sodium-
restricted for those with sodium restrictions, fat-restricted for
those with fat restrictions) to offer variety – so let's take a look

at fillings for sandwiches from the standpoint of allowables, palatability, and contribution to good nutrition.

BUTTER SUBSTITUTES

When we use a special margarine instead of a regular one in a recipe it is specified because it is high in polyunsaturated fatty acids. However for the dieter in your family, use the fat specified, whether this is butter, special margarine, or Corn Oil Spread (page 210).

For a special zest, try any of the following in combination with your allowable fat: dry mustard, lemon juice and grated lemon peel; fruit juice and grated grapefruit peel; minced green bell pepper or chives; onion juice or minced onions; dried or green herbs, such as parsley, marjoram, thyme; dry wine, such as claret; or Bakon Yeast for that smoky bacon flavor; a chopped clove of garlic, or pure garlic powder; chopped onion, or pure onion powder; dill, oregano, or tarragon (allow about ¼ to 1 teaspoon herb to 4 tablespoons spread). You may want to add a half teaspoon of white wine vinegar or lemon juice to some of the herb spreads to sharpen their flavor. You will have to test-taste for these combinations as the base spread will alter the addition possible.

MEAT SANDWICHES

If you are packing a lunch for a man, it's hard to improve on a plain bread, your specified fat spread, and meat sandwich.

The meat allowance, it must be remembered, will have to be relatively small if you are planning to serve meat again at the evening meal.

ROAST BEEF

Sliced sirloin of beef is tasty if spread with Bakon Yeast and a "butter" combination.

When you want something other than plain roast beef sandwiches, try combining one of the following with your meat:

Thin slices of onion, with a sprinkling of medium grained fresh pepper. Delicious on 100 percent whole wheat bread with one of basic spreads

Thin slices of cucumber, with a sprinkling of medium-grained black pepper, dry mustard, and vinegar

Very thin slices of tomatoes, in the same way as cucumbers

Some of your specially prepared pickled fruits (without salt for sodium restriction) as a topping to meat filler

A little chopped green bell pepper

Crisp leaf of your favorite lettuce

A thin spread of mustard (low sodium dietetic for sodium-restricted dieters)

LAMB AND VEAL

Pure fruit currant and cranberry jelly or dietetic jelly, if specified, combine well with lamb or veal — spread with special margarine, lemon "butter," or Oil Spread.

Spiced fruit also combines nicely with veal.

Sprinkle meat with Bakon Yeast for a barbecued flavor.

PORK

Chop raisins or prunes in (low sodium) French dressing as a topping for thin slices of pork.

Use a firm applesauce topping for pork sandwiches.

Grind the end of a pork roast, and mix with dry mustard and Bakon Yeast to taste. Blend with spread of choice, plain or flavored with lemon juice, herbs or wine.

OTHER SANDWICH FILLINGS

Choose with respect to allowables for the dieter. Spread bread with one of the basic spreads, and fill with:

Sliced breast of chicken or turkey, plain or with cranberry relish or jelly (must be paper-thin)

Flaked white fish, marinated in low sodium French dressing for extra flavor

Raisin-nut spread

Mashed avocado, if allowed, blended with (low sodium) French dressing

Low sodium tomato aspic combined with paper-thin cucumber slices

Deviled egg, plain or flavored to taste, and mixed with (low sodium) mayonnaise or with a dash of (low sodium dietetic) tomato catsup or curry powder. Where

the whole egg is limited, substitute scrambled cholesterol-free egg substitute, and season as desired

Ground meats with oregano, sweet basil, curry or other
herbs of choice, or with slivers of onion; or sliced (low
sodium) meat loaf (but not in hot weather unless sandwich is to be eaten soon after preparation)

Low sodium, or for fat-controlled diets, nonhydrogenated peanut butter with Port Wine Jelly (see page
357).

Dietetic salmon, shrimp, crab, or tuna (water-packed for
fat-controlled dieters) with lettuce

Low sodium dietetic cheese, plain or with sprinkling of
Bakon Yeast. Use Count Down for fat restricted dieters,
succulent, paper-thin slices of onion with herbs

Yogurt with lemon, garlic, or herb spread

Low sodium or nonfat cottage cheese with pure fruit jelly

Chopped ginger with honey

Alternating slices of light and dark bread may be used
with any of the above combinations.

GROUND FILLERS

The good old food grinder can be worked overtime in making tasty sandwich fillers. This is a good way to use tag-end
meats and vegetables, too. Combined with other ingredients,
they make some of the best sandwich spreads. Blend them with
one of the special "butters" or low saturated fat spreads for
high flavor.

For planning ground fillers, try:

One-half cup orange marmalade combined with ¼ cup
ground nut kernels

Combined equal amounts of chopped dried dates with chopped walnuts, or filberts (use lemon "butter" as spread for bread)

Dry roasted peanuts (unsalted, of course for those with sodium restrictions) — a good source of Vitamin B complex they combine well with many sandwich fillings, combined with spreads, vegetables, or fruits; do not use "roasted" for fat control

Combined in equal amounts, low sodium peanut butter with ground dates moistened in orange juice (nonhydrogenated peanut butter for saturated fat restriction)

For something on the exotic side, and if it's a man you're pleasing, try sprinkling your buttered bread with ground peanuts and top with thin slices of Bermuda onion.

Or you may want to try a salad filling for bread or rolls:

I. ¼ cup shredded cabbage
¼ cup low sodium peanut butter (nonhydrogenated for saturated fat restriction)
1 tablespoon finely minced parsley
Orange juice
Black pepper

II. ½ cup minced low sodium dietetic shrimps
Dash dill
Lemon juice

ROLLED SANDWICHES

The rolled sandwich is a real lunch-box treat in appearance and taste and is a space saver, too.

Many people think of rolled sandwiches as lots of extra work and consequently use them only for special occasions. They are quite the opposite – and one of their special values is that they may be made ahead of use. They store well in the freezer, too. You do have to be a little more careful in rolling low sodium bread than with regular bread, but it handles well with reasonable care.

All you have to do, to make a delectable rolled sandwich, is to slice bread lengthwise in desired thinness, spread the slices with a seasoned butter or spread, and add filling. Once your slices are spread with their fillers, let stand for a few minutes. Then roll as for jelly roll. Seal edges with unsalted special margarine, or low saturated spread, wrap in wax-paper rolls and store.

When ready to use, unwrap roll, and slice. Such sandwiches make wonderful additions to the lunch box and give it a festive air.

SUGGESTED FILLINGS FOR ROLLED SANDWICHES

Paper-thin slices of meat, chicken, or turkey

Dietetic-pack tuna, chicken, shrimps, or salmon with shredded lettuce

Low sodium dietetic peanut butter (nonhydrogenated for those with saturated fat restrictions) with pure fruit jelly

Low sodium dietetic cheese or cheese spread (Count Down for those with fat restrictions)

Ground cauliflower, tomato, and yellow turnip mixture

Paper-thin slices of cucumber on low sodium peanut-butter spread (nonhydrogenated for those with fat restrictions), or with Bakon Yeast butter spread

Mashed kidney beans (low sodium, prepared) with garlic butter

SANDWICH ACCOMPANIMENTS

Now the next thing to ask yourself is, "What to put into the lunch box to combine with the sandwiches?" For one thing, raw vegetables for color and texture contrast and for good nutrition. Use the crunchy varieties, such as yellow turnip strips, cauliflower flowerets, slices of green peppers, or wedges of lettuce. A whole tomato, although lacking in texture contrast, is juicy and colorful and a welcome supplement, particularly in warm weather.

Make it Rule Number One to include a raw vegetable in some form in every packed lunch. Select from your allowable list.

Fruits are more universally used in traditional lunch boxes than are vegetables — and they are good for our purpose, too. Vary the usual orange, apple, banana treatment with berries in season — and for fun's sake, try leaving them stemmed, including a small carton of sugar for dunking purposes for an occasional treat. The Mixed Fruit Balls (page 351) are a fine goody when your box calls for a rich dessert or confection. Wedges of fresh pineapple, melon in season, and fruit cup, all make good additions to sandwiches when fruit is the choice.

SANDWICH SUBSTITUTES OR SUPPLEMENTS

Salad

There will be times when you want the heartiness and freshness of a salad in place of sandwiches or to supplement them. Look over the chapter on Salads (pages 211–240) and line up the "carrying ones." Salads can be very tempting and refreshing *if* sufficiently chilled before packing, and properly insulated. The best way to ensure this is to pack them well. Use a paper container for a new type of insulator. The paper cup with cover type is good for this purpose — the cup itself is a fairly good insulator.

What do we suggest to put in the container? First of all, there are the vegetable and fruit-vegetable slaws. Cabbage slaw, in its many variations, is one of the best carrying salads. Try it with apple, yogurt, pineapple, berries, fresh pears or peaches, or any of your own favorites.

Potato salad without egg as an ingredient holds up well, too, for lunch-box purposes. Remember to use parsley and a little extra vinegar to give it a lift without benefit of salt. You may like a dash of curry powder, Bakon Yeast, or extra dry mustard for flavor change. We like a little wine vinegar for extra tanginess.

Then there are vegetables to stuff. A good, firm tomato is all right, if properly drained before stuffing, so that it is not leaky and mushy by the time it is to be eaten. Leftover meat, chicken, fish, or vegetables can be used alone or in combination as a stuffing. Don't overlook crunchy raw vegetables for their pleasant blending qualities. You may even want to use your egg allowance by hard-boiling it for the tomato filler. For fat restriction, use the recipe on the carton of Fleischmann's Egg Beaters for Egg Salad filling.

Avocado is also good for any of the above stuffings. It is a little bland and sweet, so needs the sharpness of vinegar and oil to give it character, but should be used only as allowed.

There are, also, the gelatin salads — the molded salads, which may be used occasionally if the weather is not too hot, and if packing conditions and "equipment" are favorable. Salads molded with fruits or fish seem particularly appropriate for the lunch box. *Make your selections only from your allowables.* A tiny little covered container for liquid dressing is a must. These are available in paper or plastic, or you may use well-washed discards from your bathroom shelf.

Casseroles

Indeed they do have a place in the lunch box, if your dieter has a place to warm anything or is fortunate enough to have one of the new cup-shaped insulators just big enough for such an addition. Any of your low sodium or low fat leftovers can go into this — tuna-mushrooms; minestrone; stew with vegetables; rice-turkey or chicken; ground meat casseroles; mock tamale casseroles — in fact, almost any flavorsome *made dish.*

But do not include dishes made with milk sauces or eggs unless they can be refrigerated.

Desserts

Fresh fruit has been mentioned already. It is certainly one of the best desserts for the meal to be taken — from the standpoint of its carrying qualities and its taste appeal. But it should not be considered the only dessert, by any means.

There are the tiny pastries; the tarts; the deep pies; fruit turnovers; scones; low sodium or low saturated fat cakes, cookies, and pies; puddings galore — surely your dieter will not want for a dessert sweet in some allowable form. Don't forget some of the taste-ticklers (pages 349–354). There are the fruit balls, rich desserts in themselves; the dipped walnuts — and ever so many other goodies to add a surprise element to the lunch box, providing calories and other restrictions allow them.

PACKAGING AND PACKING THE LUNCH

Second only to the lunch itself is the packing of it. First of all, you need a box large enough to do the job well. Many shapes and varieties are now being shown in the stores. There are even plastic lunch boxes available. Light to carry, they make attractive food servers. The lunch-box liner fits inside a standard lunch box, makes it easy to pack a lunch the night before to keep in the refrigerator. Two covered compartments have ample space for salads, casseroles, fruits, vegetables, or pudding. The large compartment is planned for sandwiches, pastry, and fruit. A plastic box with alligator finish, equipped with wallet and compact accessories, may even be found — to satisfy milady's whim if she is the dieter.

You will probably want two Thermos bottles — if you hope to put out a balanced and complete lunch. The regular size (1 or 2 cup) will do very nicely for soup or beverage, but you will also want to add one of the new squat-shaped kind of insulator for salad, casserole, gelatin, or dessert.

Package your various foods carefully and attractively. Use enough wax paper to do the job required. There is nothing a man so dislikes in a lunch box, they tell us, as leaky foods. Wrap sandwiches separately. (This goes for vegetable sticks, too.) Don't let them rub against other foods, but protect them with their own wrappings. Think of the order of eating as you put your packages in their place. Relatedness is a factor here as in general food planning and preparation.

Let your freezer or the cold compartment of your refrigerator work for you. Make up sandwiches a week ahead (page 373) so that some of your early morning energy can be spent on careful packaging. Oh, yes, just one last word — for eye appeal, put a gay paper napkin on the very top of all the wrappings to greet the dieter when he or she "opens up."

17

TIPS ON TRIPS
AND EATING OUT

LIFE (as far as eating is concerned) need not be lived within the four walls of your home just because you happen to have some diet restrictions. Eating out and taking trips that involve ordering meals are not very difficult once you have mastered the limitations of your regimen and can deal with them wherever you are.

In the beginning, home fare is sufficient — whether you are preparing it or consuming it. You have to learn to conform to the new and radically different diet, and the homemaker must learn not only the sodium or fat content of foods allowed, but to use cooking skills to make food palatable without salt or the usual fats. Both tasks call for mature acceptance of responsibility. While all of this is taking place, home base may seem particularly attractive.

But the day will come when you are tired of planning, ordering, and preparing or eating home meals and when you will want that "first" meal out. That time may come quite by accident and on the spur of the moment. If such is the case, you may forget to take with you some of your sodium-restricted items, such as unsalted margarine, salt substitute, if allowed, low sodium bread, or other requirements of your dietary. Your dieter may get a pretty slim meal. So what? There is always the refrigerator to forage in when you get home — and the pleasure of the change may have more than compensated for the slimness of the meal.

FOR THE
SODIUM-RESTRICTED DIETER

Once the plunge is made, you will begin to realize that with a little care in the ordering end of things you can eat out as frequently as your inclination and pocketbook will allow. Just remember the more severe the restriction, the more care you must give to your food choices when you are eating out.

Listed below are some general and specific hints to help you in ordering your meal away from home.

1.   Become thoroughly familiar with your diet allowables before you try to eat out.

2.   Choose restaurants having *à la carte* service.

3.   If your diet is only mildly restricted in sodium, you will not find it difficult to eat away from home. For mild restriction, simply avoid the foods you know you cannot have. But if you are on the 1000 or 500 milligrams sodium diet, choose very carefully and specify that no salt is to be added and the method of preparation. Avoid fried foods as many hot plates are treated with salt "rubs."

MAIN COURSE: Your best choices are broiled chops, steaks, chicken, and fish, and boiled or poached (in unsalted water) eggs. Inside cuts of roasts and poultry may also be ordered. Trim one-fourth inch off edges and do not eat skin. Trim any visible fat. Meats should be prepared without salt or seasonings, except lemon juice, wine if allowed, and pepper, and do not order or eat gravy.

POTATOES: Baked without dressing.

VEGETABLES: Fresh, not frozen, in most instances. No sauces.

BREAD: As allowed (no butter, unless unsalted, and unsalted margarine preferred).

SALADS: Head lettuce, unsalted vegetables (raw or cooked), a tossed salad of greens, tomatoes, or fruit, abound on *à la carte* menus. Avoid all molded salads. Specify no dressing; use lemon juice, vinegar, vegetable oils, and herbs of your choice, but do not use *herb salts* or parsley flakes.

DESSERTS: Fresh or frozen fruits or ices, not sherbets, as they are often made with milk. Avoid all commercial desserts made with whole egg, regular butter or margarine, whole milk and fancy sauces. This means that baked goods such as pastries and cake will be tabooed, as well as puddings, pies, ice creams, and most confections.

BEVERAGES: Carbonated, as allowed, cider, coffee, fruit juices, buttermilk, nonfat milk, and tea offer you many choices.

Unless you live and work in a community where there is a very active Heart Association, you may not find low sodium bread, unsalted margarine, or salt substitute in the restaurants of your choice. These are the three indispensables of the severely restricted sodium diet that you will have to carry with you for meals away from home. Of course, if you are on the 500 milligram diet, a glass of milk broadens your selection base. And for you lucky ones with a sodium allowance of 1000 milligrams or more, you can choose a slice of regular bread and a pat of margarine (don't expect to get special margarine). Other choices await you. Your problems are small, indeed.

The severely restricted dieter soon learns to carry some of his own necessities. For these, try a small basket and stock with salt substitutes, a French dressing, matzoth, and unsalted special margarine — the latter put in at the very last moment for each sojourn away from home. Such a carrier might even harbor delicacies for picnics and nibbling en route. One day it might produce sandwiches (low sodium bread and fillers, of course); another, skinned, broiled chicken; and still another, salad mixings, or cocktail goodies, or cookies.

FOR THE
LOW SATURATED FAT DIETER
(WITHOUT SODIUM
RESTRICTIONS)

FIRST COURSE: Clear soup, tomato or blended vegetable juice or fruit cup.

MAIN COURSE: Fish or chicken (no skin), baked or broiled without butter; sliced turkey, veal or beef, trimmed of all visible fat; London broil (flank steak) without gravy.

POTATOES: Boiled, baked, without dressing. Avoid French fries and potatoes au gratin.

VEGETABLES: Any fresh, canned, or frozen if processed without the addition of fats or sauces. Avoid vegetable casseroles and creamed dishes in general as they may contain butter and cream or whole milk and cheese.

SALADS: Tossed green with oil and vinegar; fruit gelatin, but not fruit mousses; fish salad (but watch what you combine it with for your protein choice as you will probably get tuna canned in oil); vegetable plate.

BREAD: Made without added fat such as French or Italian

bread, melba toast, bread sticks, and most regular breads (white, whole wheat, or rye). Avoid muffins, biscuits, and hot breads.

DESSERT: Fresh, frozen, or canned fruit (drained of heavy sirups); unfrosted angel food cake; fruit ice, sherbet, fruit whip made with egg white and puréed fruit. Avoid all commercial desserts made with chocolate, coconut, whole egg, butter, margarine, whole milk, fancy sauces, or cream. This means that baked goods such as pastries and cake will be tabooed, as well as puddings, pies, ice creams, sherbets, and confections.

BEVERAGES: Carbonated as allowed, cider, coffee, fruit juices, buttermilk, nonfat milk, and tea offer you many choices.

FOR THE FAT-CARBOHYDRATE CONTROLLED DIETER

You are probably controlling calories as well as carbohydrates on this diet. You will need to be particularly selective about foods containing sugar and starches and to eliminate concentrated sources of sugar. You may also be reducing foods high in cholesterol and have a specified amount of saturated fat and polyunsaturated fat. Your eating out has special planning features.

1. Become very familiar with your diet before you try it.
2. Plan your day's menu around your anticipated restaurant selections.
3. Avoid casserole and other made dishes with hidden ingredients.
4. In ordering, be specific as to method of preparation.
5. Avoid fatty meats, fried foods, whole milk products, cheeses, pastries — sweet and dessert type, and the other items on your "Avoid" list. Plan around some of the following, as allowed:

FIRST COURSE: Clear soups, tomato juice or blended allowed vegetable juices, or fruit cup.

MAIN COURSE: Baked or broiled fish, veal or lean beef, poultry which has been skinned; low-fat cottage cheese.

VEGETABLES: Plain vegetables without sauces. Margarine, if available, may be used.

POTATOES: Baked or broiled without dressing, plain rice, macaroni or spaghetti, in limited amounts.

BREAD: Bread, bread sticks, French bread, hard rolls, plain tortillas or English muffins, in limited amounts. Do not use butter.

DESSERTS: Fruit, fresh or unsweetened, is your best choice.

BEVERAGES: Select from your list tea, coffee; noncaloric carbonated beverages; fruit juices; nonfat milk; buttermilk; alcohol, if allowed on diet.

CEREAL: Avoid sugar-coated cereals, and serve with nonfat milk.

No matter how severe your restrictions, you can eat almost anywhere, any time with a little advance planning. You may have to carry some or all of your own food if you are going to attend a catered table d'hôte meal, but even this is no great problem. Accept it as a challenge to eat as normally as possible, yet with respect to your diet. You can't expect hotel or restaurant or even a hostess having a meal catered to plan a special meal for you. Carry your own. Have a vacuum ice bucket (which you can buy for about six dollars) and let it work for you.

How to Use It: Prepare chicken or turkey parts (yes, you can buy them) or steak, cook a vegetable, and bake a potato in your own kitchen. Add a carton of homemade salad, low sodium or low fat roll and unsalted special margarine or Corn Oil Spread, and salt substitute, if allowed. You now have a good start on a well-rounded meal. Add an individual fruit pie or turnover — and it's a meal fit for the finest.

You and the ice bucket can arrive at your destination with

the ice bucket making a quick delivery to hostess or steward. When dinner is served, few if any guests, and sometimes not even the dieter, will remember that his meal was specially prepared and so different in some details from the other dinners. A word of caution: the unsalted margarine or Corn Oil Spread won't carry well in the bucket with hot dishes. You had better pack it separately to slip in pocket or purse for those meals away from home.

Picnics or outdoor meals in your own garden or patio are good beginning experiences in preparation for the more formalized ones of restaurant eating. If your dieter is a man and if you can get that man interested in outdoor cookery, you can make even restricted meals seem attractive to him.

There is something about the anticipation of a meal in its preparation and actual cooking out-of-doors that makes good food taste better. Barbecued corn or potatoes with flavorsome meats seem to rate high with most men. Perhaps it's the informality of the setting; perhaps it's the open air; perhaps it is the flavor of the food, specially prepared. At any rate, such service lends variety and pleasure to home meals.

If you don't have a barbecue or don't particularly like to eat in your garden, why not plan an occasional informal meal around casserole cookery? With an earthenware casserole seasoned with garlic and vegetable oil, it is easy to duplicate the distinctive European cookery. A fish or vegetable chowder, a wonderful Italian minestrone; whole broiling chickens with fresh mushrooms; veal with wine, vegetable oil, and herbal seasonings — or even a thick vegetable stew with fresh garden vegetables redolent with pungent spices — could form the basis of such a meal.

Work out at least one casserole dish that is uniquely your own. Build it around a starch, perhaps — such as one of the noodle or spaghetti pastas or rice, brown or white.

It is but an additional step to move from these special occasion meals at home and restaurant meals to an overnight trip. Your physician may not encourage this at the beginning, until you have been on the low sodium or fat program for some months. It takes a lot of know-how to get away from your own kitchen — when the health of a person is so dependent upon the products of that kitchen. But travel-minded we Americans certainly are, and you can be right in that throng whenever your physician gives you the green light. Now every major transportation system, whether it be train, plane, or ship can take care of your special diet needs if you specify them in advance to your travel agent or reservation clerk.

It is much more satisfactory to *list individual requirements in writing.* These may include nonfat or low sodium nonfat milk, unsalted special margarine, low sodium bread, vegetable oil other than olive, fresh vegetables cooked without salt, or special canned dietetic low sodium ones (specify string beans, peas, et cetera). Major hotels are also set up to serve you. Here too, an advance letter with your requirements will bring you quite often some special goody. The Parker House in Boston has been known to make Parker House rolls low in sodium, New York hotels have bought delicious little low sodium dietetic muffins for their dieting guests, and the maître d' will always see that your food is specially prepared (particularly so if you pass one of those green bills over his palm).

Your task will be simpler when you elect to travel by automobile. You can take some of your diet items with you or have them shipped to your principal stopover points.

Don't start out expecting to find all the items that line your grocer's shelves. If you cannot find an essential diet item in a local market, contact the local or state Heart Association for product information.

How can you transport food items, if you travel by automobile? Simply store diet items in a shallow carton in the trunk compartment where you can get to them easily. For hotel or roadside eating, try a wicker basket, a carrying kit, a covered can, such as a fruitcake tin or a large substitute milk powder tin, for the daily basics.

For summer travel, some kind of refrigeration for perishables is a must. Portable coolers and iceboxes are available in stores carrying camping equipment. Be sure to watch those casserole and egg dishes when the mercury soars. For the bacteria that cause food poisoning, life begins at 40 and ceases at 140 degrees Fahrenheit. Keep hot foods hot and cold foods cold when you are on the road.

For snacks or roadside picnics, shop for the junior-size carrying containers that are just right for two. One smart container we saw in a plaid tartan covering includes two Thermos bottles — a regular one for beverages and a wide-necked one for soups and casserole dishes. A large center section with a plastic box and cover is ample for sandwiches, fruit or salad. And there is space to tuck in eating utensils.

There is one more thing for the traveler with a low sodium diet to consider. It is the public water supply.* The sodium content of the water supply of most cities is low enough to be ignored; but in some areas certain supplies are entirely unsuited to severely sodium-restricted diets. Under certain circumstances the doctor may specify that diet meals are to be cooked with distilled water. Count about 500 milligrams sodium if the local water supply contains 220 milligrams per quart.

Here is a final admonition about travel and restricted diets for the heart patient. *If you have to be on a restricted food program, stick to it wherever you are.*

Diet is not the only consideration in planning a trip. Before the heart patient leaves the doctor's supervision, he should know enough about his ailment to function effectively while traveling.

Uncertainties should be cleared up, and time should be taken

* See "Sodium-Restricted Diets" — Food and Nutrition Board, the National Research Council. Publication 325, July 1954, pp. 27–29, 59–70. Or check with local Heart Association or local purveyor of water.

to review the "Don't" list. Discuss these with your doctor when you go in for a travel checkup.

Often the doctor wants the patient to travel with a medical report, in case medical care is needed away from home. Such a report is ease-of-mind insurance, and provides any doctor with important information for evaluating the emergency situation. This report usually includes the latest electrocardiogram. If you are departing on a long trip and your doctor does not offer you a medical report, ask him to prepare one for you.

There is the matter of medicine. Some of the new drugs are hard to get. Your doctor may decide it is wise for you to travel with enough of the precious pills to last your stay. Also, carry a copy of all prescriptions in case of change of travel plans or loss of baggage.

"The biggest block to travel," one San Francisco cardiologist told us, "is the patient's concern about getting a doctor away from home." Today medical care is as near you as the nearest telephone in any of the cities and communities stretching from Maine to California. Sponsored by the Council on Medical Services of the American Medical Association in 1948, county medical societies have developed this medical plan, known as the Emergency Call Plan.

If you're away from home and need a doctor, all you have to do is to pick up a telephone and ask the operator to get you a doctor. Give her a statement about your illness and whether you prefer a general practitioner or specialist. In many cases, it will hasten medical care if you have a number to call, such as the local medical society or hospital. Turn to the classified section of the telephone directory and see if an emergency call service is included with the listing of physicians and surgeons.

In large cities the operator will refer your call to a special switchboard operated by or in cooperation with one of the local health societies. Increasingly, this is on a round-the-clock basis seven days a week. In smaller communities, a shut-in may fill the role of the PBX operator of the large city, and the call may be referred to the local hospital, police or other public agency ready to contact and speed medical assistance when needed.

Your doctor may give you the names of a few doctors he knows along your route. He may suggest a person-to-person call to him by the emergency physician, if he thinks it is important.

What does this all add up to, if you have had some form of heart or blood vessel disease and want to travel?

1.   In the first place, the doctor is the core of any travel plan. He alone can tell you the when, where, and how long.

2.   Advance planning is essential for both safe and pleasurable traveling.

3.   A checkup is a must.

4.   In this checkup, do the following:

. . . clear up any uncertainties about your ailment

. . . know what orders you must follow and how they are to be carried out

. . . carry a copy of all prescriptions in case luggage is lost, and plan for enough medicines to last the trip

. . . ask for a medical report, including the last electrocardiogram

. . . understand your diet program and whether you must consider the sodium content of public water supplies in making your plans

. . . know how to get emergency medical care away from home and whether your doctor is to be notified.

5.   If you must be on a restricted diet, stick to it. And for greater flexibility in eating, carry some diet items with you when you are to be away from home, if you have severe sodium restrictions. Remember, that the more severe your restrictions, the better advance planning you must do.

6.   Call your local Heart Association to see if it has Dining Out information for your reference.

18

UNFINISHED BUSINESS

You know that "woman's work is never done" if you want to be an alert and competent homemaker. So many labor-saving devices and foods wearing new faces appear on the market these days that it is hard to keep up with them all.

We find ourselves confronted with exactly the same problem in completing this book. It is amazing how much has been made available to improve variety and flavor in restricted diets during the time we have been working on this project.

So we have decided to add this chapter — to include some new products, a few late discoveries, and to share recipes which were insufficient in number to warrant a chapter by themselves.

EGGS

We just can't leave them out, even if they must be used so sparingly. If you are permitted the whole egg, your physician will have specified your allowance, and what part of the egg is best for your particular diet needs. As was pointed out earlier, you will have to choose, on the planning end of things, how that egg allowance is to be used. If you use it in cooking, of course you will have to forgo serving it otherwise on the same day.

So special is the egg allowance in these diets that it deserves special care and preparation. Unfortunately, the egg is carelessly handled all too often in many kitchens — it may not be kept fresh to yield its best flavor; it may be improperly cooked with too high heat and toughened; it may be poorly seasoned, and often is; it may be used without imagination, poor thing, and lose its wonderful versatility. Let's try to get maximum goodness from it when it is such a precious commodity in restricted cookery. Store it properly in the refrigerator with large end up, and for best flavor and cooking quality, use within a week.

Cholesterol-Free Egg Substitutes

New in this edition are two excellent cholesterol-free egg substitutes — Fleischmann's Egg Beaters and Second Nature — that will be special bonuses to those of you with saturated fat restrictions. We have experimented with them in preparing scrambled eggs and omelets, egg salad, baked specialties, and in casseroles. We can't say enough in their favor for those of you who must limit the use of egg yolk or the whole egg. You will find their producers listed in Appendix 3 (B).

How to Flavor the Egg or Its Substitute

1. Line egg cup with a sprinkling of thyme or sweet basil for a completely new savor.

2. Be imaginative in your flavoring of eggs. Try:

Minced parsley, with sweet basil and chives

Thyme and a few grains of cayenne

Marjoram and minced garlic

Low sodium dietetic cheese sprinkled over top of omelet and lightly browned under broiler for those without saturated fat restrictions (low fat cheese for fat-controlled diets)

Port wine jelly (1 tablespoon for each serving) spread on puffy omelet, before folding; if jelly is very stiff, set in pan of hot water or heat slightly to encourage easy spreading

Vegetable of choice, or combination of vegetables for omelet filler

Divide omelet in 2 sections and spread with herb-flavored tomato sauce canned without added sodium; top with other half of omelet

The addition of a little sherry or dry white wine to scrambled eggs or omelet in place of some of the other liquid — with or without herbs, a wonderful delicacy (but whatever you do, don't overdo this)

A *sprinkling* of Bakon Yeast for a bacon flavor that is bound to earn you the gratitude of your dieter

How to Use Eggs in Low Sodium Cookery

Batter: Combine with flour, low sodium baking powder, and low sodium or nonfat milk

Cake: Combine with flour, low sodium baking powder, low sodium or nonfat milk, sugar, and seasonings

Custard: Boil, steam, or bake with low sodium or nonfat milk

Dessert: Combine with other food ingredients

Macaroons: Egg white(s) combined with sugar, flavoring, coconut or nuts

Meringue: Egg white(s) combined with sugar and lemon juice

Mayonnaise: Beat with oil and vinegar — seasonings added to taste

Pancakes: Beat with flour, low sodium or nonfat milk, low sodium baking powder, and cook on special grill

Sandwiches: Scrambled, fried, or hard boiled make good fillers

Sauces: Combined with flour, liquid, and seasonings for special use

Sherbet: Beat whites raw with fruit juice or combine with puréed fruit and freeze

Soufflé: Beat, mix with low sodium or nonfat milk sauce, low sodium cheese, and seasonings, and bake

Rarebit: Combine with low sodium cheese, beer, or low sodium white sauce, and seasonings — for a rich rarebit

Torte: Beat whole and combine with other ingredients, the base of which will be sugar, nuts, and flavoring(s)

Waffle: Special low sodium batter cooked on special irons

HOW TO USE EGGS IN SATURATED FAT RESTRICTED COOKERY

If egg yolk is restricted, use two egg whites for each whole egg in our recipes and in adapting your own favorites.

Do not use regular butter or margarine; instead spray skillet with coating to prevent sticking. Or use ¼ to ½ teaspoon special margarine if diet allows.

If you use an egg in cooking, remember that you must count it in your daily or weekly allowance.

For egg in your meal of choice, use one of the following methods of cooking:

bake	soft boil
coddle	hard boil
poach	scramble

BASIC OMELET
3 Servings

½ cup nonfat milk
1 tablespoon flour
2 tablespoons nonfat milk powder
½ teaspoon sweet basil
½ teaspoon minced parsley
⅛ teaspoon white pepper
Yellow food coloring
4 fresh egg whites
¼ cup chopped fresh mushrooms
1 teaspoon vegetable oil

Put milk into a jar with flour, nonfat milk powder, seasonings, and food coloring. Cover and shake to blend. Pour into a saucepan and heat over slow heat, stirring constantly until thickened. Put egg whites into large bowl, beat until they stand in rounded peaks. Fold in the thickened sauce (the substitute egg yolk). Add mushrooms sautéed in skillet prepared with a vegetable spray-on coating or lightly greased with ¼ teaspoon unsalted special margarine. Lightly oil sides and bottom of medium-sized skillet. Pour the egg white mixture into the skillet and cook over moderate heat until mixture is puffy and a golden brown on the underside. Then place in broiler to lightly brown the top. Add ½ teaspoon salt if sodium is not restricted.

ONE SERVING	TOTAL RECIPE	
	Without salt	
104	311	milligrams sodium
trace	1	gram total fat
trace	trace	gram saturated fat
6	18	grams carbohydrate
62	185	calories

One serving: ⅓ teaspoon vegetable oil.

VARIATIONS

Use low sodium liquid nonfat milk or milk powder for a lower sodium count.

Parsley (about 2 teaspoonfuls), or a few drops of Angostura Aromatic Bitters, or 1 teaspoon white dinner wine may be substituted for the mushrooms in this and scrambled egg recipes.

Instant potato (about 2 teaspoonfuls) may be added to white sauce blend if sodium is not restricted, for added body to egg dishes.

SCRAMBLED YELLOW EGG WHITES
3 Servings

The yellow coloring is very important in egg white recipes as it makes your dishes look like the real thing, and taste more like it, too.

½ cup nonfat milk
1 tablespoon nonfat dry milk powder
Dash marjoram

Dash thyme
5 egg whites
⅛ teaspoon freshly ground black pepper
1 drop yellow coloring
1 teaspoon chopped chives
1 teaspoon chopped parsley
Parsley sprigs

Combine and mix all ingredients except egg whites. Add the egg whites. Beat lightly with a fork. Lightly coat the sides and the bottom of the skillet with a vegetable spray-on or use a Teflon pan. Pour in egg white mixture. Cook over low heat, stirring constantly with fork. Serve onto warm plates and garnish with parsley sprigs. Portion very carefully if your dieter is on strict sodium restriction. Add salt for those without sodium restriction as you serve.

ONE SERVING	TOTAL RECIPE	
109	327	milligrams sodium
trace	trace	gram total fat
3	8	grams carbohydrate
43	130	calories

VARIATION

Low-sodium, nonfat dry milk and powder may be used if sodium restriction requires. See the variations for Basic Omelet (page 404).

CHOLESTEROL-FREE EGG SUBSTITUTE SCRAMBLED EGGS
1 Serving

Use amount of egg substitute that equals 1 large egg.
¼ teaspoon unsalted special margarine or vegetable oil

¼ cup egg substitute
1 teaspoon sherry
⅛ teaspoon thyme

Heat special margarine or oil in small skillet over low heat. Combine all ingredients and pour into skillet. Begin to stir when edges begin to set. Stir only occasionally for a soft, delicious treat. Serve at once with garnishing of choice. Sprinkle with salt if no sodium restriction.

ONE SERVING	
109	milligrams sodium
9	grams total fat
1	gram saturated fat
2	grams carbohydrate
149	calories

DIETETIC CHEESES AND WAYS TO USE THEM

FOR SODIUM RESTRICTION:

Now that several companies manufacture low sodium cheese you can adapt some of your favorite recipes to restricted dishes by substituting dietetic low sodium cheese for regular, omitting the addition of salt, and using the kind of milk specified on your diet list. Tillamook Low Sodium Cheddar Cheese* is sharp and as easy to use as regular cheddar cheese. Similarly with Cellu Low Sodium Cheese†. This cheese, of medium texture, has approximately 1 milligram sodium in 1 tablespoon cheese, grated. It is sold in various sizes and is usually to be

* Tillamook County Creamery Company, Tillamook, Oregon 97141.
† The Chicago Dietetic Supply House, Inc. P.O. Box 40, La Grange, Illinois 60525.

found only in health food stores. Foreign cheeses, as Ricotta, Danish Export, and Dorset are among imported cheeses that are lower in sodium than many of our domestic ones, and are sometimes allowed on your diet. The Danish Cheese Company* also manufactures a diet cheese known as a "Gouda Type."

FOR LOW SATURATED FAT RESTRICTION:

Two relatively new products in the field of fat-controlled cheese spreads are the Fisher Company's† Count Down and Cheez-ola. Count Down is 99 percent fat-free, and is a pasteurized skim milk cheese spread similar in flavor to the well-known Velveeta (which is not for dieters). Cheez-ola is a pasteurized process-filled cheese made with corn oil. Other recommended cheeses for the cholesterol- and fat-controlled diets are those made from skimmed or partially skimmed milk, such as low fat, partially-creamed cottage cheese (wash it through a colander to reduce the creaming), dry cottage cheese, Farmer's, Baker's, Hoop cheese, Mozzarella and Sapsago cheese. The Italian Ricotta (in dry form) and the German-made Harzkäse,‡ soft and jelly-like in texture, brown in color with a moldy rind, may be found in ethnic delicatessens. Baker's cheese, a fresh cheese used in making cheese cake, looks like cream cheese and may be used as such. Made from skim or low fat milk, Baker's cheese may be combined with a softened vegetable fat, as a special margarine, for a cheese spread for bread, celery sticks or dips. Sapsago, Geska brand,§ is a Swiss green cheese and contains only about 1 percent fat. It is a grating-type cheese and can be used on this diet for flavor additions. For easy grating, put cone through meat grinder. Store in covered jar in refrigerator. Its fat content is approxi-

* Nisqually, Washington 98504.
† Fisher Cheese Company, Wapakoneta, Ohio 46895.
‡ *Cheese Varieties and Descriptions*, USDA Handbook, No. 54, 1953.
§ May be found in local food specialty store or mail order food store, or write to the distributor, Otto Roth & Co., Inc., 14 Empire Building, Moonachie, New Jersey 07074

mately 0.3 grams per ounce. The only fat-free cheese easily available is the uncreamed curds of cottage cheese, which may be obtained from your local dairy, creamed and seasoned to taste.

FOR FAT-CARBOHYDRATE RESTRICTION:

See the suggestions given under Low Saturated Fat Restriction and use only the amounts specified on your diet list.

CHEESE TOAST
1 Serving

Spread one piece of low sodium bread with a slice of dietetic low sodium cheese (1 ounce). Sprinkle with paprika. Place under broiler and cook until cheese bubbles and begins to brown. Serve at once.

ONE SLICE
(with cheese slice)

9	milligrams sodium
10	grams total fat
5	grams saturated fat
22	grams carbohydrate
215	calories

LOW SATURATED FAT VARIATION

If not restricted in sodium, and diet allows low fat cheese, use low fat bread and 1½ tablespoons Count Down Spread (page 407). Omit broiling. Or cover bread with ½ slices Count Down. Sprinkle with paprika and broil until cheese bubbles. Serve at once.

SAVORY MACARONI-CHEESE
4 Servings

2 cups cooked macaroni
1 cup grated low sodium dietetic cheese
1 cup low sodium dietetic tomato juice
Pinch sweet basil
White pepper

Lightly oil a 1½ quart casserole; arrange macaroni to layer bottom. Top with grated cheese. Repeat layer of macaroni and cheese. Measure tomato juice and add seasonings; blend. Pour over macaroni mixture. Cover and bake in a preheated 350° (moderate) oven, 25 to 30 minutes. Uncover for last 10 minutes of baking for golden, crunchy top.

ONE SERVING	TOTAL RECIPE	
6	24	milligrams sodium
9	35	grams total fat
5	19	grams saturated fat
20	78	grams carbohydrate
197	789	calories

VARIATIONS

Low sodium or regular nonfat milk (thickened or not with 2 tablespoons flour) may be substituted for tomato juice in equal amount. One tablespoon white dinner wine may be added to milk to heighten flavor and for a piquant flavor use ¼ teaspoon dill weed. Sprinkle paprika over top before baking.

For extra richness, simmer ½ cup sliced fresh mushrooms in ¼ cup white dinner wine and blend with each layer.

LOW SATURATED FAT VARIATION

If not restricted in sodium, substitute a low fat cheese, such as Count Down, for the low sodium dietetic cheese and use regular tomato juice or nonfat milk. Add ½ teaspoon salt.

WELSH RAREBIT WITH BEER

2 Servings

¾ cup grated low sodium dietetic cheese
1 tablespoon vegetable oil
1 teaspoon cornstarch
1 teaspoon dry mustard
Few grains cayenne
Dash sweet basil
¾ cup beer (about)
Paprika

Blend all ingredients together except beer and paprika and put into heavy-duty skillet or in top of double boiler. Melt cheese slowly over very low heat, stirring constantly to avoid scorching or lumping. Add beer and continue to stir until first bubbles appear at rim of pan. Serve at once on slices of low sodium toast. Sprinkle paprika over each serving.

ONE SERVING
Without toast

11	milligrams sodium
20	grams total fat
8	grams saturated fat
6	grams carbohydrate
272	calories

One serving: 1½ teaspoons vegetable oil.

VARIATIONS

Brick cheese (low sodium, of course) may be cut into small cubes and melted over slow heat.

LOW SATURATED FAT VARIATION

Substitute Count Down for the low sodium dietetic cheese. Use this recipe only if beer is allowed on your menu plan.

CASSEROLE DE LUXE
8 Servings

Now here's a dish to carry you back to some of the specialties you used to make before taking over restricted cookery.
The extra special thing about this casserole is that it is better
each time you reheat it — and, as if that were not enough, it
freezes beautifully. Be careful to package in small container
for freezing, because cheese dries out quickly, once it has
thawed.

4 cups cooked elbow macaroni
2 tablespoons vegetable oil
½ cup chopped onion
1 tablespoon minced parsley
¼ cup sliced fresh mushrooms
1 pound *lean* ground beef
Dash allspice
¼ teaspoon thyme
½ teaspoon freshly ground pepper
¾ cup low sodium dietetic tomato juice
¼ cup white table wine
1 can Number Two low sodium dietetic cream-style corn
1 cup low sodium dietetic grated cheese
Paprika

Measure macaroni and set aside. Put oil into heavy-duty skillet
and sauté onions, parsley, and mushrooms until light golden
brown. Crumble meat into small pieces and add to onion mixture. Sprinkle with seasonings. Stir to blend, and cook over
low heat until meat is lightly browned on all sides. Add tomato
juice, macaroni, wine, and corn; stir to blend. Stir in ¾ cup
low sodium cheese. Remove from heat and pour into lightly
oiled 2-quart casserole. Sprinkle remaining cheese over top and

garnish with paprika. Cover and bake in a preheated 350° (moderate) oven 30 minutes, or until mixture bubbles. Uncover for last 10 minutes of baking for a colorful, crunchy top. Add salt for those without sodium restrictions.

ONE SERVING
(1½ oz. meat, cooked weight)

44	milligrams sodium
14	grams total fat
5	grams saturated fat
33	grams carbohydrate
338	calories

VARIATIONS

With this Basic Recipe, you may alter flavors and seasonings to suit.

LOW SATURATED FAT VARIATION

If total fat is not limited, sauté onions, parsley, and mushrooms as in Basic Recipe. Brown meat under broiler until lightly browned. Add to onion mixture and follow Basic Recipe, but being sure to use ground top round steak or chuck (trimmed of all visible fat) for the meat; omit cheese or use low fat cheese, if no sodium restriction.

One serving: 2 grams saturated fat; ¾ teaspoon vegetable oil.

CHILI CON CARNE
8 Servings

½ pound red kidney beans
Water
2 tablespoons vegetable oil
¼ cup chopped onions
1 pound *lean* ground meat

1 crushed clove of garlic
½ teaspoon freshly ground pepper
2 cups fresh tomatoes, cut in small pieces
1 teaspoon curry powder
4 dried red peppers
Dash cayenne
1 tablespoon wine vinegar
Dash sugar
2 tablespoons grated low sodium dietetic cheese

Soak beans overnight. In the morning cook in same water until skins split and beans are tender. Meanwhile, put into a heavy-duty skillet 2 tablespoons vegetable oil. Heat and add onions. Sauté 5 minutes. Add crumbled ground meat and garlic. Brown lightly; add to beans. Add remaining ingredients except cheese, breaking peppers into small bits if desired. Cook over low heat about 1 to 1½ hours. Watch for scorching last half hour and add water if necessary. About 10 minutes before serving, add 2 tablespoons grated cheese. Stir to blend and to avoid scorching. Add salt for those without sodium restrictions at time of serving.

ONE SERVING
(1½ oz. meat, cooked weight)

43	milligrams sodium
10	grams total fat
3	grams saturated fat
22	grams carbohydrate
260	calories

LOW SATURATED FAT VARIATION

Brown meat (using top round or chuck, trimmed of all visible fat) under broiler heat and proceed as in Basic Recipe. If no sodium restrictions, substitute Count Down, cubed in small pieces, or other similar type cheese spread for low sodium dietetic cheese in Basic Recipe. Lightly salt for the regulars. Chill dieter's portion in refrigerator and remove any solid fat; reheat.

One serving: 3 grams saturated fat; ¾ teaspoon vegetable oil.

YOGURT

Yogurt has been a connoisseur's food through the centuries, although it has only rather recently become popular in this country. With such a historical background as it enjoys, you may be sure it has passed the taste-test and is a fit delicacy for your table. It has a subtle, tangy flavor, a custard-like texture, and a fragrance uniquely its own. However, it is a cultured milk product, so will have to be used with discretion because of its sodium content of approximately 63 milligrams per ½ cup. And it is not for you with saturated fat restrictions, unless your dairy has yogurt made with nonfat milk.

Many people enjoy eating it plain, but it does combine pleasantly with many foods. Combining it with other foods, you get the yogurt flavor without running up the sodium content too high.

Here are a few suggestions as a starting point:

Use as topping for puddings or desserts

Use as topping for fruits or blended with cheese

Combine with low sodium salad dressing for flavor change

Beat and combine with fruit juices for refreshing and unusual beverages

Spread lightly over fish before baking

SPECIAL NEWS

Protein Supplements

If your physician believes that you should have a protein supplement, he will specify it by brand and the amount necessary to ensure your dietary adequacy. Don't buy over-the-counter supplements in this or any category unless you have first checked with your physician or dietitian.

Sugar Substitutes

You will have to get professional guidance if you must control calories or for other reasons use a sugar substitute, for as we go to press there is still some uncertainty about allowables in this field.

SUGGESTED MENUS FOR SPECIAL OCCASIONS

There are always those special occasions in family living which in their very nature invite special foods. You don't have to give up all of your pleasures in good eating just because you are on a highly restricted diet. A few special menus, worked out with respect to the count and palate, can simplify company dinners and special-occasion meals and enhance your reputation as a cook, restrictions or not.

Here are some of the things you will have to consider:

1. Do your planning so that you stay within the prescribed limitations.

2. Strive for at least *one* unusual flavor or dish in every

special meal. *Let it be the center of interest. Keep other dishes simple.*

3. Work out some combinations which do not require too much last-minute kitchen work. No one wants to be in the kitchen any more than necessary after the guests have arrived. *Plan ahead and work ahead (preferably the day before you are to entertain).*

4. If you are responsible for your own service — and most of us are these days — combine courses or otherwise simplify your meals so that you are not eternally serving the meal. After all, it is not the number of courses or the variety (in numbers) that spells the meal a success or failure. It is rather the appropriateness of the foods selected — the blending qualities, and the skillful food preparation which will win you your laurels.

MENUS

Sunday-Night Suppers

I. Welsh Rarebit* (*Made the day before and reheated in double boiler*)

Lettuce wedges

Low sodium Bread Sticks* (*Made on weekly baking day and stored in refrigerator or freezer*)

Apple Torte* (*Made the day before and reheated while assembling meal*)

Beverage

LOW SATURATED FAT VARIATIONS

Use this meal only if low fat cheese appears on your diet list.

* See Index for recipe.

II. Casserole de Luxe* (*Made at least one day before use; better with each reheating*)
Tossed green salad
100 percent Whole Wheat Rolls* (*Made on baking day and brought from freezer in time to let rise*)
Orange-Prune-Walnut Whip*
Beverage

LOW SATURATED FAT VARIATION

Use the variation suggested for the Casserole de Luxe (page 412).

Birthday Dinners

I. Basic Tossed Salad* (*Made at table and served with meal*)
Sirloin of Beef* (*As directed in recipe in this book*)
Baked Stuffed Potatoes*
Broccoli* (*Prepared just before serving*)
Homemade Standard Rolls* (*Prepared on baking day and thawed and cooked as directed*)
Blackberry Velva* (*Made about 6 hours before use*)
Basic Low Sodium Two-Egg Birthday Cake* (*Made in morning or day before use or taken from a home freezer*)
Beverage

LOW SATURATED FAT VARIATION

Use baked potato for dieter.
Substitute Basic Low Saturated Fat Cake* for the Basic Low Sodium Two-Egg Cake.

II. Outdoor Celebration, Western Style
Tossed green salad (*Made in a large wooden bowl and tossed for all to see*)

* See Index for recipe.

Chicken Pilau* (*Of course, you have some slices of chicken stored in the home freezer. Prepare this dish early in the day, or take from freezer*)

Corn on the cob (*Barbecued or boiled before serving — used in place of bread for a change*)

Watermelon compote (*Scooped out watermelon filled with fresh fruit of choice — elegant with fresh peaches aged a half-day in a sweet dinner wine, or assorted melon balls — fresh and appetizing on a scorching day*)

Basic Low Sodium Two-Egg Birthday Cake* (*Made ahead; perhaps frozen until day of use*)

Beverage

LOW SATURATED FAT VARIATION

Substitute Basic Low Saturated Fat Cake*

THANKSGIVING DINNER

Take a look at the sodium content of turkey and do your planning so the dieter may have a little extra portion for this special eating occasion. It is the day of days for good food, for it has held first place throughout our Nation's history on the family dinner table.

Apple Cider Ring* (*Made the day before*)

Turkey stuffed with Low Sodium Dressing* (*Made at least the day before the big day if you have a freezer or refrigerator; but do not stuff the bird until time to roast. Garnish platter with boiled "buttered" with special margarine (unsalted) pearl onions — enough for*

* See Index for recipe.

*individual servings, of course; gravy if you omit the
giblets for the dieter and include the count*)

Sweet Potatoes (or yams)* mashed with orange juice
(*Try adding ¼ cup crushed pineapple for each person
to be served — all done the day before, of course, and
stored in your refrigerator*)

Fresh or Frozen String Beans*

Uncooked Cranberry-Orange Relish* (*If you want a
change*)

Parker House Rolls* (*Made ahead of time, of course*)

Pumpkin Ice Cream* (*Substitute 1 cup pumpkin for fruit.
This dessert is a particularly good choice if the young
generation is to be present — eliminates the necessity of
making 2 desserts; pumpkin pie may be substituted if
you feel you must have your holiday pie. Let the
youngsters have the "filling" for their portions*)

LOW SATURATED FAT VARIATIONS
Refer to Low Saturated Fat Variations of various recipes.

Christmas Dinner

The automobile has brought with it many changes in the
ways of family celebrations so that there are apt to be several
family dinners during Christmas week. Why not show a little
originality in your menus and get away from too many turkey dinners all at once? If there is to be a big family gathering
Christmas Eve, why not have cold chicken or some specialty
for family billing Christmas day? You could even plan to serve
buffet style, if the gathering is large, and have a casserole
dish as an accompaniment. To keep you out of the kitchen,
here's a suggestion or two:

I. Stuffed cabbage salad with apples, walnut meats,
shredded cabbage (*Outer side of cabbage may be*

* See Index for recipe.

decorated with toyon berries by piercing berries with pins. Fill cabbage with unpeeled apple cubes, sprinkled with lemon juice, shredded cabbage, and 1 cup broken walnut meats for 8 servings. Blend and dress with your favorite salad dressing. Beautiful to look at and so-o good)

Cold roast chicken (*Cooked at least the day before; a week before if you have a home freezer*)

Spanish Rice with Wine*

Cranberry jelly, pure fruit

Peas (*Do not use frozen for those with sodium restrictions: peas canned without added sodium may be used for them*)

Clover-leaf Rolls*

Cranberry Pie* (*The beauty of a gelatin dessert is that it can be made ahead of use*)

Beverage

II. A change for the Day of Days

A tray of raw vegetables — radishes, cauliflower flowerets, tomato wedges

Homemade chicken soup (*Without salt for those with sodium restrictions*)

Tamale Pie* (*Made ahead of time and stored in freezer*)

White pearl onions with unsalted special margarine

Toasted Herb Bread* "buttered" with unsalted special margarine

Green Tomato Mince Meat Pie*

Beverage

* See Index for recipe.

LOW SATURATED FAT VARIATIONS

One tablespoon vegetable oil may be substituted for margarine if diet requires, or sprinkle lightly with a few grains of nutmeg. Refer to Low Saturated Fat Variations for individual recipes.

19

A PRIMER OF QUANTITY RECIPES

For MANY YEARS requests have come to us to develop quantity dietary-restricted recipes. Now dietitians tell us that an introduction to quantity planning and a few recipes would be a great help not only to hospitals, but particularly to smaller institutions concerned with convalescent and long-term care of patients on restricted diets. Food dollars are hard to come by, especially in times of rising costs, and high prices make it impossible to buy many prepared convenience foods for patient use.

We can't hope to meet all of these needs in this book. Nor can we cover all food categories. It is relatively easy to increase cake, cooky, and pie recipes to amounts needed. Suggestions for salads and vegetables may be found in most general cookbooks. So we will just give a few special recipes that can be managed for a large number of people, are considerate of restricted-sodium, -fat, or -carbohydrate needs, and are not too expensive to prepare. We hope they will add variety and pleasure to institutional meals.

SOUPS

RED BEAN SOUP SUPREME
24 Servings (¾ cup = 1 serving)

1 pound, 4 oz. red beans
1 ¼ quarts water
4 oz. low sodium margarine
1 cup chopped onion
¼ cup chopped carrot
⅓ cup chopped celery
3 quarts low sodium meat stock
8 whole cloves
3 crumbled bay leaves
1 tablespoon dry mustard
½ teaspoon thyme
1 cup dry sherry
Parsley

Soak beans in water in refrigerator overnight. The next day cook vegetables lightly in margarine. Add to beans. Add stock, cloves, bay leaves, mustard, and thyme. Bring to a gentle boil, then simmer about 2 to 3 hours, until beans are well done. Pour soup through a food mill to purée beans or strain if diet requires. Add sherry. Keep hot, but not boiling, until served. Garnish with chopped parsley or float a sprig on the top of each serving.

ONE SERVING	TOTAL RECIPE	
With sherry		
12	287	milligrams sodium
4	101	grams total fat
1	17	grams saturated fat
17	413	grams carbohydrate
138	3323	calories

CHILLED TOMATO "CREAM" SOUP
24 Servings (½ cup = 1 serving)

2 qts. unsalted tomato juice
1 qt. nonfat milk
6 fresh, ripe tomatoes
⅓ cup minced parsley
1½ tablespoons sweet basil
½ cup sherry
24 slices lemon

Blend tomato juice very briefly with milk. Peel and seed tomatoes; cut into small pieces. Add with seasonings to blended mix. Blend briefly. Chill. Garnish each serving with a slice of lemon. Serve with low sodium bread sticks. Add salt for "regulars." Substitute low sodium milk for nonfat milk when a lower sodium content is required.

ONE SERVING	
Without bread sticks	
26	milligrams sodium
trace	gram total fat
trace	gram saturated fat
7	grams carbohydrate
46	calories

VARIATIONS

Vary seasonings to taste, such as thyme or dill weed.

Substitute 2 cups uncooked, cubed zucchini for fresh tomatoes for a flavor change.

ENTRÉES

BRAISED BEEF

24 Servings (½ cup = 1 serving)

5 pounds *lean* beef stew
3 tablespoons vegetable oil
¾ cup flour
1 tablespoon sugar
2 cups water
3 tablespoons vegetable oil
½ pound green pepper, chopped
½ pound onions, chopped
1 pound fresh mushrooms, sliced
1 quart canned tomatoes, low sodium dietetic
¾ cup catsup, low sodium dietetic

Put meat into a large casserole or baking pan; brown in 3 tablespoons oil for 30 minutes in a preheated 400° (hot) oven. Meanwhile blend flour, sugar, and water to a smooth paste; set aside.

In a large skillet, add 3 tablespoons oil; warm. Add peppers, onions, and mushrooms, and cook over low heat for about 10 minutes until onions are clear but not brown, adding 1 tablespoon water if needed to prevent scorching. Combine the flour and vegetable mixtures with tomatoes and catsup. Pour over browned meat. Cover, and bake for 2 hours in preheated 350°

(moderate) oven. Remove cover; bake 45 minutes longer until meat is tender and brown. Serve at once over low sodium baking powder biscuits or rice.

ONE SERVING (2½ oz. meat, cooked weight) *Without biscuits or rice*	TOTAL RECIPE	
67	1677	milligrams sodium
8	196	grams total fat
2	60	grams saturated fat
8	209	grams carbohydrate
191	4787	calories

CHICKEN POLENTA

24 Servings (¾ cup = 1 serving)

1⅓ cups cornmeal

1⅓ cups cold water

1 quart boiling water

¼ pound grated cheese, low sodium dietetic (optional)

2½ pounds *lean* ground, skinned chicken

½ pound onions, thinly sliced

2 garlic cloves, minced

3 cups low sodium dietetic canned tomatoes, cut up

2 cups tomato purée, low sodium dietetic

1½ cups California Burgundy wine

¼ cup cornmeal

3 bay leaves

1 teaspoon oregano

2 tablespoons sugar

¼ teaspoon pepper

6 ounces grated low sodium dietetic cheese for topping (optional)

Mix cornmeal with cold water; pour into boiling water, stirring until smooth. Cover; cook over low heat until thick (about 30 to 40 minutes). Remove from heat and stir in cheese. Set aside for lining baking pan.

Bake chicken or use leftover chicken. Add onion and garlic and cook until onion is transparent. Add tomatoes, tomato purée, wine, cornmeal and seasonings. Bring to a boil and then simmer for 30 minutes.

Spread half of cornmeal mixture in bottom of baking pan. Top with half of meat-vegetable sauce. Repeat layers. Bake in a preheated 350° (moderate) oven until thoroughly heated (about 45 minutes). Top with grated cheese and bake 5 minutes longer. Cut through both layers of cornmeal when serving.

ONE SERVING	TOTAL RECIPE	
(1¼ oz. meat,		
cooked weight)		
Without cheese		
35	831	milligrams sodium
5	121	grams total fat
2	55	grams saturated fat
12	276	grams carbohydrate
148	3542	calories

CHILI CON CARNE

24 Servings (½ cup = 1 serving)

1 pound 3 ounces dry kidney or pinto beans (1½ quarts cooked beans)

2½ pounds *lean* ground beef

¼ pound chopped onions

1 quart tomato purée, low sodium dietetic

2 cups bean liquid and water

¼ cup flour

¼ cup water
1⅓ tablespoons chili con carne seasoning powder

Soak beans overnight; drain and cover with fresh water. Cook beans until tender (but not mushy). Drain and save cooking water. Brown beef lightly. Add onions and cook until onions are clear but not brown; drain. Add tomato paste and 2 cups bean liquid and water. Simmer until beef is tender.

Make a paste of flour and the ¼ cup water; add to beef mixture, stirring constantly. Add beans and chili seasoning powder. Cover and cook 1 to 1½ hours to blend flavors and thicken mixture. Stir occasionally to prevent sticking.

ONE SERVING (1¼ oz. meat, cooked weight)	TOTAL RECIPE	
35	867	milligrams sodium
5	122	grams total fat
2	55	grams saturated fat
19	465	grams carbohydrate
178	4452	calories

BAKED COD FILLETS IN SPANISH SAUCE

24 Servings

5 pounds cod fillets
¼ pound onions, chopped
¼ cup green pepper, chopped
¼ cup vegetable oil
6 tablespoons flour
3 cups canned tomatoes, low sodium dietetic
2 teaspoons sugar
¼ teaspoon pepper

1 bay leaf, crushed
Dash ground cloves

Place fish fillets, about 3 ounces each, in a single layer on oiled baking pan. In a skillet, cook onions and green pepper in oil until onions are transparent but not brown. Blend in flour. Add tomatoes and seasonings. Cook until thickened, stirring occasionally. Cover fish with sauce. Bake in a preheated 350° (moderate) oven for 30 to 40 minutes until fish flakes easily when tested with a fork.

ONE SERVING
(2½ oz. cod, cooked weight)

62	milligrams sodium
2	grams total fat
trace	gram saturated fat
3	grams carbohydrate
102	calories

VARIATION

Halibut, haddock, and sole fillets may be substituted for the cod.

LASAGNE, AMERICAN STYLE
24 Servings

1 pound *lean* ground beef chuck
1 cup finely chopped onion
¼ teaspoon ground cloves
½ cup vegetable oil
1 can (No. 5) low sodium dietetic tomatoes or purée
2 cans (No. 1) low sodium dietetic tomato paste
Water
1½ cups finely chopped parsley

1½ tablespoons oregano
¾ teaspoon white pepper
1 tablespoon sugar
3 packages (3 pounds) lasagne
3 pounds low fat cottage cheese

In a large heavy Dutch oven, sauté ground chuck, onion, and cloves in oil until lightly browned. Drain off excess fat. Add the tomatoes, tomato paste, water, parsley, oregano, pepper, and sugar.

Simmer covered for about 30 minutes, stirring occasionally.

Meanwhile, bring 6 quarts of water (for each pound of lasagne) to a boil in a large pot, then gradually add lasagne so that water continues to boil. Cook according to package directions for 10 to 12 minutes.

Drain and separate noodles into a single layer placed on waxed paper. Or for long holding, drain and return lasagne to the cooking pot, adding just a little lukewarm water to facilitate handling.

Cover the bottom of two greased 3-quart oblong baking pans (13 × 9 × 2 inches) with sauce, then layer as follows: lasagne noodles, cheese, sauce, lasagne, cheese, lasagne noodles and remaining sauce. (At this point, the dish may be set in the refrigerator until ready to bake.)

Bake in a preheated 350° (moderate) oven for 45 minutes to 1 hour or until lightly browned and bubbly. Remove from oven and let stand 10 to 15 minutes before cutting into 24 3-inch servings.

ONE SERVING (½ oz. meat, cooked weight)	TOTAL RECIPE	
32	764	milligrams sodium
8	185	grams total fat
2	44	grams saturated fat
23	542	grams carbohydrate
232	5566	calories

BASIC MEAT LOAF

24 Servings

3 eggs
1 ⅓ cups red dinner wine
2 ¼ cups nonfat milk
4 ½ oz. (3 cups) low sodium bread crumbs
¾ cup chopped onion
¼ teaspoon pepper
1 tablespoon dry mustard
1 ½ teaspoons dill weed (dry)
6 lbs. *lean* ground beef
1 ½ cups low sodium catsup
⅓ cup light brown sugar
3 tablespoons red table wine
24 sprigs parsley (optional)

Beat eggs lightly in mixing bowl. Mix in table wine, milk, bread crumbs, seasonings, then add meat. Blend well but do not overmix. Pack into loaf pans or form into 3 loaves and put into baking pans. Bake in preheated 350° (moderate) oven about 1 hour, or until loaves are almost done. Drain off juice to use for gravy, if desired.

Blend catsup, sugar, and remaining table wine. Spread half of glaze over loaves. Bake 10 to 15 minutes. Spread remaining glaze over loaves and cook another 10 minutes. Cut into slices. Garnish with parsley, if desired.

ONE SERVING (3 oz. meat, cooked weight)	TOTAL RECIPE	
without gravy		
106	2551	milligrams sodium
13	304	grams total fat
6	140	grams saturated fat
17	417	grams carbohydrate
338	8110	calories

Low sodium nonfat milk may replace regular nonfat if lower sodium content is required.

Seasonings may be varied, using oregano or sweet basil for the dill weed.

SALISBURY STEAK

24 Servings (Two 2½-inch patties = 1 serving)

2½ cups nonfat milk
1 cup low sodium bread crumbs
¼ cup onion, finely chopped
¼ teaspoon pepper (optional)
5 lbs. *lean* ground beef
⅔ cup vegetable oil
1 cup fresh sliced mushrooms
⅔ cup flour
2½ cups unsalted beef stock
2½ cups red dinner wine
⅔ cup chopped parsley

Mix milk, bread crumbs, onion, and pepper. Add meat and mix gently. Shape into 48 patties. Pour oil in large skillet or braising pan. Use only part of oil in beginning if pans are small, adding remaining oil as needed to prevent scorching. *Brown patties on both sides, but do not cook until done.* Remove "steaks" to a large casserole or baking dish, place them neatly in rows. Cover with mushroom sauce.

MUSHROOM SAUCE

1 cup fresh, sliced mushrooms
⅔ cup flour
2 cups red table wine
2½ cups unsalted beef stock
⅔ cup chopped parsley

Sauté mushrooms in oil left in pan from the braising of meat. After 2 minutes, stir in flour, blending carefully. Stir as this cooks over low heat for 2 minutes. Pour in wine and beef stock, blending thoroughly. Stir and cook until sauce becomes thickened and glossy. Add parsley, stirring to blend. Pour sauce over steaks. Bake in a preheated 350° (moderate) oven 30 to 45 minutes, until sauce is bubbling hot and steaks done. Skim excess fat before serving.

ONE SERVING (2½ oz. meat, cooked weight)	TOTAL RECIPE	
With mushroom sauce		
83	1985	milligrams sodium
16	382	grams total fat
5	126	grams saturated fat
9	207	grams carbohydrate
298	7155	calories

SWEDISH MEATBALLS
24 Servings (Two 1-inch meatballs = 1 serving)

5 lbs. *lean* ground beef
1 tablespoon fresh grated lemon peel
½ cup fresh lemon juice
1½ teaspoons nutmeg
½ teaspoon pepper

Mix ingredients together, blending thoroughly. Form into 1-inch balls. Place on 2-part broiler pan designed to allow fat to drain away. Bake in preheated 375° oven for 25 to 35 minutes until nicely brown. Makes 96 meat balls. If desired, serve over cooked noodles with Mushroom Sauce (page 433).

ONE SERVING
(2⅓ oz. meat, cooked weight)

40	milligrams sodium
5	grams total fat
2	grams saturated fat
trace	gram carbohydrate
135	calories

CREAMY TUNA RICE

Adapted from a Wine Institute recipe shared with us, this tuna dish is bound to please many dieters.

2 lbs. 4 oz. (2 qts.) unsalted cooked rice
8 oz. fresh sliced mushrooms
8 oz. (1 cup) onion, chopped fine
6 oz. unsalted special margarine
4 oz. (1 cup) flour
¼ teaspoon white pepper
1 lb. 8 oz. tuna, flaked, canned low sodium
1½ qts. nonfat milk
8 oz. low sodium cheese, grated (optional)
2½ cups California white table wine
1½ cups low sodium bread crumbs
⅓ cup melted special margarine

Cook mushrooms and onion in margarine until onion is light brown and clear. Add flour and pepper. Cook over low heat

5 to 10 minutes. Drain liquid from tuna. Heat milk almost to boiling. Add flour mixture; stir until smooth. Cook until thickened.

Fold in cheese (optional), wine and tuna. Stir in previously cooked rice. Spread in baking pan. Top with "buttered" low sodium crumbs. Bake in preheated 350° (moderate) oven until lightly browned and thoroughly heated, about 30 minutes.

For a lower sodium count, make with low sodium nonfat milk.

ONE SERVING (1 oz., scant, tuna) *Without cheese*	TOTAL RECIPE	
51	1219	milligrams sodium
9	214	grams total fat
2	39	grams saturated fat
23	550	grams carbohydrate
246	5904	calories

TURKEY SUPPER SANDWICHES

24 Sandwiches

6 oz. unsalted special margarine
12 oz. mushrooms, sliced
4 oz. (1 cup) flour
4½ cups hot nonfat milk
¼ teaspoon white pepper
1 teaspoon dry mustard
1½ cups white dinner wine
24 slices low sodium toast
3 pounds unsalted turkey, sliced thinly
⅛ teaspoon paprika
½ cup low sodium cheese (optional)

Melt margarine. Add mushrooms and cook 5 minutes. Blend in flour, stirring to prevent scorching. Cook over low heat 5 minutes. Stir in a little hot milk to blend; when smooth, stir in the white pepper and mustard. Add the rest of the hot milk to this mixture, stirring carefully to thoroughly blend. Cook over medium heat until thick and smooth, stirring often to prevent burning. Stir in wine and cook 2 minutes. Remove from heat.

Place toast slices in rows on baking pan or trays. Place slices of turkey on each piece of toast (2 ounces per sandwich). Spoon ¼ cup sauce over each sandwich. Sprinkle with paprika. Sprinkle with low sodium cheese (optional). Bake in a preheated 400° (hot) oven until hot and lightly browned, about 10 to 15 minutes. Serve immediately.

ONE SERVING
(2 oz. meat, cooked weight)
Without cheese

81	milligrams sodium
9	grams total fat
2	grams saturated fat
19	grams carbohydrate
261	calories

VARIATIONS

For lower sodium count, use low sodium, nonfat milk.
For added flavor, add ½ teaspoon savory to milk-flour mix.

TURKEY VEGETABLE STEW

24 Servings (¾ cup = 1 serving)

8 oz. unsalted special margarine
6 oz. (1½ cups) flour
¼ teaspoon white pepper

½ teaspoon nutmeg
1 qt. nonfat milk
1 ¼ qts. turkey or chicken stock
1 ½ cups white dinner wine
2 lbs. (2 qts.) unsalted cooked turkey meat, diced into
    ¾ -inch pieces
1 lb. 2 oz. (1 qt.) unsalted diced carrots
1 lb. 4 oz. (1 qt.) unsalted cooked peas
⅛ teaspoon paprika
24 sprigs parsley

Melt margarine. Blend in flour, pepper, and nutmeg, stirring carefully. Cook over low heat 5 minutes. Heat milk in double boiler over low heat. Add to flour mixture; stir until smooth. Cook until thick and glossy. Stir in the stock and wine, and blend. Then add turkey pieces and cooked vegetables. Keep hot until ready to serve. May be served over low sodium Baking Powder Biscuits (page 264), shortcake, or low sodium toast. Sprinkle with paprika and garnish each serving with parsley sprig.

For a lower sodium count per serving, substitute low sodium nonfat milk for regular nonfat milk.

Sprinkle salt over servings for those not limited in sodium.

ONE SERVING
(2 oz. meat, cooked weight)
Without biscuits

79	milligrams sodium
10	grams total fat
2	grams saturated fat
13	grams carbohydrate
253	calories

SALADS

CHICKEN-WINE ASPIC
24 Servings

An excellent salad for a Sunday night supper or any lunch or dinner, courtesy of the Wine Institute.

4 tablespoons gelatin
1 cup white dinner wine
2 cups hot unsalted chicken stock
3 cups cold unsalted chicken stock
2 teaspoons dry mustard
½ teaspoon curry powder
1 cup unsalted mayonnaise
1 lb. 8 oz. (1½ qts.) unsalted chicken meat, diced fine
8 hard cooked eggs, diced
¼ cup green onion, chopped fine
6 oz. (1½ cups), celery, chopped fine
¼ cup parsley, minced
24 lettuce leaves
24 parsley sprigs

Soften gelatin in wine. Add to hot chicken stock and stir until gelatin dissolves. Add cold chicken stock. Stir in mustard and curry powder. Chill until thick but not set.

Stir mayonnaise into thickened gelatin. Gently stir in chicken, eggs, and vegetables. Pour into flat pans or individual molds. Chill until set. Serve each portion on a lettuce leaf. Garnish with parsley sprig.

ONE SERVING
(1 oz. chicken, cooked weight)

58	milligrams sodium
11	grams total fat
2	grams saturated fat
2	grams carbohydrate
153	calories

JELLIED FRUIT SALAD ROSÉ

24 Servings

1½ cups (9 oz.) low sodium dietetic strawberry gelatin
3 cups boiling water
2 cups California rosé wine
¾ cup pineapple juice
⅓ cup low sodium mayonnaise
3 cups fruit cocktail (light sirup), drained

Dissolve gelatin in boiling water. Stir in wine and pineapple juice. Add mayonnaise and stir with whip until mayonnaise dissolves completely. Pour into a flat pan. Stir in fruit cocktail. Chill until set. This salad forms two layers, with lighter layer containing mayonnaise on top. Do not stir during setting.

ONE SERVING	TOTAL RECIPE	
12	277	milligrams sodium
3	65	grams total fat
trace	11	grams saturated fat
16	384	grams carbohydrate
101	2422	calories

VARIATIONS

If no sodium restrictions, use regular gelatin dessert powder and mayonnaise.

For a lower carbohydrate and calorie count, use artificially sweetened gelatin dessert powder and water-pack fruit or artificially sweetened fruit.

Other fruits may be substituted for the fruit cocktail. Cut into ½-inch pieces before stirring into gelatin mixture.

NAMASU

24 Servings

A special treat from the Sunkist Growers Test Kitchen for those who can digest cucumbers.

6 cucumbers, peeled
6 California-Arizona oranges
1½ cups thinly sliced fresh mushrooms
6 tablespoons sugar
1½ teaspoons fresh grated lemon peel
¾ cup fresh squeezed lemon juice
¾ cup white vinegar

Cut cucumbers in half lengthwise, then slice crosswise into thin half-moon slices. Peel oranges; cut in half lengthwise. In each, make shallow V-shaped cut, removing white center core, then place halves cut-side down and cut lengthwise and crosswise into bite-size pieces. Add orange pieces and mushrooms to cucumbers. In small bowl, combine remaining ingredients, mixing well. Add to fruit and vegetable mixture. Toss, coating thoroughly. Cover and refrigerate until ready to serve.

ONE SERVING	
8	milligrams sodium
trace	gram total fat
trace	gram saturated fat
8	grams carbohydrate
30	calories

POTATO SHRIMP SALAD
24 Servings

8 pounds potatoes
2 cups zucchini, diced in cubes
1 cup onion, chopped
⅔ cup cider vinegar
3 tablespoons dry mustard
1 teaspoon white pepper
1 teaspoon dill weed
3 cups Special Never-Fail Mayonnaise (page 239)
4 cans low sodium dietetic shrimp, drained and washed
Lettuce

Cook unpeeled potatoes in boiling water until fork tender, then peel and slice thinly while still warm.

Combine zucchini, onion, vinegar, mustard, pepper, and dill weed. Pour over warm potatoes. Cool thoroughly. Add mayonnaise and shrimp. Mix lightly. Chill until serving time. Spoon onto lettuce cups.

ONE SERVING (¾ oz. fish, cooked weight)	TOTAL RECIPE	
27	641	milligrams sodium
25	666	grams total fat
3	66	grams saturated fat
23	553	grams carbohydrate
361	8656	calories

VARIATIONS
Red wine vinegar may be substituted for cider vinegar.

Shrimps may be omitted, and 2 cups tomatoes, peeled and chopped, added to the basic mixture.

BASIC SALAD DRESSING
24 Servings — 1½ Cups

Once you have this basic dressing recipe you can modify it in many ways for variety. We have allowed 1 tablespoon per serving but many dieters may require a lesser amount.

½ cup wine vinegar
½ teaspoon paprika
1 teaspoon oregano, crushed
1 cup vegetable oil

Combine vinegar, paprika, and oregano in a jar. Pour in oil. Cover jar and shake well. Chill. Shake again before serving. Add salt for regulars.

ONE SERVING
1 *Tablespoon*

1	milligram sodium
9	milligrams total fat
1	gram saturated fat
trace	gram carbohydrate
82	calories

VARIATIONS

Add ¼ cup low sodium Chili Sauce and grate egg yolk, if allowed, over top. Substitute 1 teaspoon sweet basil, finely crushed for oregano.

LOW SATURATED FAT VARIATION

Use Count Down cubes in place of grated egg yolk in above variation.

OTHER DRESSINGS

In your basic recipes calling for sour cream, substitute an equal amount of low fat cottage cheese.

For a Mock Blue Cheese Dressing, put cottage cheese in a colander and let water dribble through it; drain. Put in blender, add the juice of 1 large lemon. Set at medium speed to smooth it. Then combine with low sodium mayonnaise and a dash of low sodium Worcestershire sauce.

For a Thousand Island Dressing to serve approximately 24, simply combine 1 cup low sodium mayonnaise, ⅓ cup low sodium Chili Sauce, 1 egg yolk, and 1 *small* fresh horseradish, grated (if you can find it at your supply outlet). For fat-control dieters, use ¼ cup scrambled, cholesterol-free egg substitute, diced in very small pieces.

DESSERTS

SHERRY BREAD PUDDING
24 Servings

6 slices low sodium toast
7 eggs
1¼ cups sugar
¾ cups California sherry
1½ qts. nonfat hot milk
⅛ teaspoon nutmeg

Cut toast into ¾-inch pieces. Spread in baking pan. Beat eggs and sugar until well mixed. Add sherry and milk. Mix until well blended. Pour milk mixture over bread. Sprinkle with nutmeg.

Place pan on tray with ¼ inch water. Bake in a preheated 350° (moderate) oven until lightly puffed and until knife inserted near center comes out almost clean. For a lower sodium count, use low sodium nonfat milk.

ONE SERVING	TOTAL RECIPE	
52	1253	milligrams sodium
2	48	grams total fat
1	14	grams saturated fat
17	407	grams carbohydrate
111	2670	calories

VARIATION

If no sodium restrictions, use regular bread and add 1 teaspoon salt.

For a lower carbohydrate and calorie count, substitute an approved sugar substitute for the sugar.

ORANGE WHIP

24 Servings (2 × 2 inches)

3 tablespoons (1 ounce) gelatin
⅞ cup sugar
1 quart boiling water
1 ¾ cups frozen orange juice concentrate, thawed

Blend gelatin and sugar. Stir into boiling water until gelatin is dissolved. Blend in orange concentrate. Chill until slightly thicker than unbeaten egg white. Whip until double in volume. Chill until set. Serve with Port Sundae Sauce, following.

ONE SERVING	TOTAL RECIPE	
Without Sauce		
1	23	milligrams sodium
trace	trace	gram total fat
15	356	grams carbohydrate
65	1549	calories

PORT SUNDAE SAUCE

24 Servings

Another Wine Institute special recipe sent to us for our inclusion here.

¼ cup cornstarch
1 cup sugar
1½ cups California port
½ cup water
1 cup grape or currant jelly
¼ teaspoon cinnamon
⅛ teaspoon nutmeg
Unsalted special margarine
Lemon juice

Mix cornstarch and sugar in saucepan. Add port wine, water, jelly, and seasonings. Stir until all of cornstarch is suspended without lumps. Bring to a boil over medium heat, stirring often to prevent lumping. Cook until mixture is thick and clear, about 1 minute of boiling. Remove from heat. Stir in margarine and lemon juice. Serve warm or at room temperature over low sodium ice cream, pudding, cake, or apple pie.

ONE SERVING	TOTAL RECIPE	
3	67	milligrams sodium
1	22	grams total fat
trace	4	grams saturated fat
19	464	grams carbohydrate
100	2394	calories

VARIATION

If no sodium restrictions, add ⅛ teaspoon salt. For a lower carbohydrate and calorie count, substitute approved sugar substitute and artificially sweetened jelly for sugar and regular jelly.

TROPICAL APPLES

24 Servings (½ cup)

1 quart peeled, sliced apples (approximately 1½ pounds apples, unpared)
1¼ pounds sugar
¾ cup flour
½ pound unsalted special margarine, melted
¾ cup orange juice
¼ cup lemon juice
¾ cup pineapple juice
2 teaspoons lemon rind
Dash yellow food coloring (⅛ teaspoon)

Place apples in baking pan. Mix sugar and flour; blend into melted margarine. Add juices and lemon rind; cook until clear. Add food coloring. Pour over apples. Bake for 30 minutes in preheated 350° (moderate oven). Serve with Whipped Cream Topping (page 320), allowing 1 tablespoon per serving.

ONE SERVING	TOTAL RECIPE	
Without Topping		
3	63	milligrams sodium
8	193	grams total fat
1	34	grams saturated fat
44	1066	grams carbohydrate
242	5810	calories

APPENDICES

Here are all the working tools you will need to plan the sodium- or fat-restricted diet, including the metric conversion table, and the all-important table for the mathematics-minded reader who must count those special milligrams of sodium — or grams of total fat or saturated fat — or carbohydrate — and/ or calories — every day. Here, too, is a list of some of the available low sodium products with the names of the concerns manufacturing or handling them — to lighten your task in the kitchen and to make for more pleasurable eating in the dining room. Sections on foods low and high in saturated fats, fatty acid content of foods, and other pertinent matters.

Appendix 1. Metric Conversion Table
Appendix 2. Sodium, Potassium, Carbohydrate, Fat and Calorie Content of Common Foods and Miscellany
Appendix 3.
   A Sodium, Carbohydrate, Fat and Calorie Content of some Commercial Products Restricted in Sodium and/or Fat Content
   B Some Commercial Firms Supplying Analyses Data for Dietary Products
Appendix 4. Average Sodium Content of Alcoholic Beverages and Cocktails
Appendix 5. A. Common Foods Low in Saturated Fats
             B. Common Foods High in Saturated Fats
Appendix 6. Carbohydrate Content of Common Foods
   A Foods with Negligible Carbohydrate Content
   B Foods with 10 Grams or Less Carbohydrate in Amounts Specified
   C Foods with 10 to 15 Grams Carbohydrate in Amounts Specified
   D Foods Usually Considered High in Carbohydrate

Appendix 7. Fat, Fatty Acid, Cholesterol, Carbohydrate and
Calorie Content of Common Foods
General Index
Recipe Index

1. METRIC CONVERSION TABLE*

APPROXIMATE CONVERSIONS *To* METRIC MEASURES

WHEN YOU KNOW	MULTIPLY BY	TO FIND
Weight		
ounces (oz.)	28	grams (g.)
pounds (lb.)	0.45	kilograms (kg.)
Volume		
teaspoons (tsp.)	5	milliliters (ml.)
tablespoons (tbsp.)	15	milliliters (ml.)
fluid ounces (fl.oz.)	30	milliliters (ml.)
cups (c.)	0.24	liters (l.)
pints (pt.)	0.47	liters (l.)
quarts (qt.)	0.95	liters (l.)
gallons (gal.)	3.8	liters (l.)

APPROXIMATE CONVERSIONS *From* METRIC MEASURES

WHEN YOU KNOW	MULTIPLY BY	TO FIND
Weight		
grams (g.)	0.035	ounces (oz.)
kilograms (kg.)	2.2	pounds (lb.)
Volume		
milliliters (ml.)	0.03	fluid ounces (fl.oz.)
liters (l.)	2.1	pints (pt.)
liters (l.)	1.06	quarts (qt.)
liters (l.)	0.26	gallons (gal.)

* Adapted from the November, 1972, Revision of the Metric Conversion
Card published by the National Bureau of Standards, United States Department of Commerce.

2. SODIUM, POTASSIUM, CARBOHYDRATE, FAT, AND CALORIE CONTENT OF COMMON FOODS AND MISCELLANY*

ITEM	MEASURE	MILLIGRAMS SODIUM	MILLIGRAMS POTASSIUM	GRAMS CARBOHYDRATE	GRAMS FAT	CALORIES
Ala, Fisher's (bulgur)	1 cup, dry	5	353	117	2	545
Anchovy paste	1 tsp.	686	unknown	trace	1	14
Apples, raw	1 medium	1	152	18	trace	70
Frozen, sweetened	½ cup, sliced	14	68	24	trace	93
Juice	½ cup	1	126	15	trace	60
Sauce, with sugar	½ cup, canned	3	83	30	trace	115
Without sugar	½ cup, canned	3	99	13	trace	50
Apricots, raw	3 medium	1	301	14	trace	55
Canned, heavy sirup	4 halves	1	285	27	trace	105
Without sugar	4 halves	1	300	12	trace	46
Dried, uncooked	5 small halves	5	186	12	trace	49
Frozen, sweetened	4 halves	5	279	31	trace	120
Nectar	½ cup	trace	189	18	trace	70
Arrowroot	1 tbsp.	trace	unknown	trace	none	29
Artichoke, globe	1 large	41	413	10	trace	45
Asparagus, raw	6 stalks	2	278	5	trace	26
Canned	6 stalks	227	159	3	trace	20
Cooked, cut	½ cup	1	161	3	trace	18
Frozen, uncooked	6 stalks	2	239	4	trace	23
Avocado	½ small	4	652	6	18	185
Bacon, raw, cured	1 long strip	136	26	trace	14	133
Fried crisp	2 short slices	163	38	1	8	90
Baking powder	1 tsp., regular	408	64	1	trace	4

* Sources for the calculations are given in the Acknowledgments, pages ix, xiv.

bananas	1 medium	1	377	23	trace	85
Barley, pearled, dry	1 cup	6	325	158	2	700
Beans, baked, with pork and tomato sauce	1 cup, canned	1208	548	49	7	310
Beans, dry (navy, pea, etc.)	½ cup, scant	19	1196	61	2	340
Beans, Lima, raw	½ cup, cooked	9	532	27	1	151
Canned	½ cup, scant	2	650	22	1	123
Cooked	½ cup	189	178	15	trace	77
Dry	½ cup	1	338	16	1	90
Dry	1 cup	7	2798	117	3	631
Frozen, uncooked	½ cup	196	583	31	trace	162
Beans, snap, green and yellow wax, raw	½ cup	4	122	4	trace	16
Canned	½ cup	149	60	3	trace	15
Cooked	½ cup	3	95	4	trace	15
Frozen, uncooked	½ cup	1	84	3	trace	14
Beef, raw, lean	1 oz.	18	99	none	4	63
Cooked, lean	1 oz.	17	104	none	2	58
Corned, canned	1 oz.	487	42	none	3	62
Dried	1 oz.	1204	56	none	2	58
Koshered, raw, lean	1 oz.	454	unknown	none	4	63
Tongue, raw, medium fat, unsmoked	1 oz.	20	55	none	4	58
Beets, raw	½ cup, diced	40	224	7	trace	29
Canned	½ cup, diced	196	139	7	trace	31
Cooked	½ cup, diced	36	173	6	trace	25
Beet, greens, raw	½ cup	130	570	5	trace	24
Beverages (average)						
Beer	1 cup	17	60	9	none	100
Brandy	1 jigger	1	unknown	trace	none	110
Carbonated waters						
Sweetened (quinine)	1 cup	unknown	unknown	19	none	74

ITEM	MEASURE	MILLI-GRAMS SODIUM	MILLI-GRAMS POTASSIUM	GRAMS CARBO-HYDRATE	GRAMS FAT	CALORIES
Beverages (*cont.*)						
Unsweetened (club)	1 cup	unknown	unknown	none	none	none
Gin, rum, vodka, and whiskey	1 jigger	trace	1	trace	none	110
Soft drinks (Cola drinks, fruit sodas, ginger ale, root beer, etc.)	1 cup	16	unknown	24	none	95
Wine, dessert,	1 cup	10	180	18	none	329
table	1 cup	12	221	10	none	204
Biscuit, baking powder, mix	1 biscuit, 2" diam.	272	32	15	3	90
Blackberries, raw	½ cup	1	122	10	1	43
Canned, heavy sirup	½ cup	1	136	28	1	114
Without sugar	½ cup	1	144	11	1	50
Frozen, sweetened	½ cup, scant	1	105	24	trace	96
Blueberries, raw	½ cup	1	57	11	1	43
Canned, heavy sirup	½ cup	1	69	33	trace	126
Without sugar	½ cup	1	75	12	trace	49
Frozen, sweetened	½ cup, scant	1	66	27	trace	105
Bouillon cube	1 cube	960	4	trace	trace	5
Boysenberries, canned without sugar	½ cup	1	106	11	trace	45
Frozen, sweetened	½ cup, scant	1	105	24	trace	96
Brains, all kinds	1 oz.	35	61	trace	2	35
Bread						
Boston brown	1 slice, 3" diam.	120	140	22	1	100
Cracked wheat	1 slice	122	31	13	1	65
French	1 loaf (1 lb.)	2633	409	251	14	1315
Italian	1 loaf (1 lb.)	2656	336	256	4	1250

White	1 slice	117	24	13	1	70
Whole wheat	1 slice	121	63	11	1	60
Broccoli, raw	1 stalk, 5½" long	15	382	6	trace	32
Cooked	½ cup	8	200	4	trace	20
Frozen, uncooked	1 stalk, 5½" long	17	241	5	trace	29
Brussel sprouts, raw	9 medium	14	390	8	trace	45
Cooked	½ cup	7	177	4	trace	23
Frozen, uncooked	9 medium	16	328	7	trace	36
Butter, salted	1 tsp.	49	1	trace	4	33
Cabbage, raw	½ cup	10	117	3	trace	13
Cooked	½ cup	12	139	4	trace	18
Chinese, raw	1 cup	23	253	3	trace	15
Cake, plain, uniced	1 piece, 3 x 2 x 1½"	165	43	31	8	200
Candy						
Caramels	1 oz.	63	54	22	3	115
Chocolate, milk, plain	1 oz.	26	108	16	9	145
Fudge, plain	1 oz.	53	41	21	3	115
Hard candy	1 oz.	9	1	28	trace	110
Marshmallows	1 oz.	11	2	23	trace	90
Cantaloupe	½ medium	22	454	14	trace	60
Carrots, raw	½ cup, grated	26	188	6	trace	23
	1 large	24	171	5	trace	20
Canned	½ cup, diced	177	90	5	trace	23
Cooked	½ cup, diced	24	162	5	trace	23
Catsup	1 tbsp.	177	62	4	trace	15
Cauliflower, raw	½ cup	7	148	3	trace	14
Cooked	½ cup	5	124	3	trace	13

ITEM	MEASURE	MILLIGRAMS SODIUM	MILLIGRAMS POTASSIUM	GRAMS CARBOHYDRATE	GRAMS FAT	CALORIES
Cauliflower (*cont.*)						
Frozen, uncooked	½ cup	6	113	2	trace	11
Caviar, sturgeon	1 rounded tsp.	220	18	trace	2	26
Celery	1 large outer	50	136	2	trace	5
Cereals						
Bran flakes, 40%	¾ cup	259	unknown	23	1	85
Corn, rice, and wheat flakes, mixed	1 oz.	266	unknown	24	trace	110
Corn flakes, plain	1 oz.	281	34	24	trace	110
Sugar-coated	1 oz.	217	unknown	26	trace	110
Corn, puffed, presweetened	1 oz.	84	unknown	26	trace	110
Corn, shredded	1 oz.	277	unknown	25	trace	110
Farina, regular	1 cup, cooked	1	21	21	trace	99
Quick-cooking	1 cup, cooked	95	24	21	trace	101
Instant, dry	1 oz.	2	23	21	trace	101
Oats, puffed	1 oz.	355	unknown	19	1	100
Oatmeal, regular	1 cup, cooked	1	141	23	2	130
	1 cup, dry	2	282	55	6	312
Rice, puffed	1 cup	trace	14	13	trace	55
Rice, flakes	1 cup	296	54	26	trace	115
Wheat, puffed	1 oz.	1	95	22	trace	105
With sugar and honey	1 oz.	45	28	25	1	105
Wheat, rolled	1 cup, cooked	1	198	40	1	175
Wheat, shredded	1 oz.	1	97	23	1	100
Wheat and malted barley flakes	1 oz.	218	unknown	24	trace	110
Wheat flakes	1 oz.	289	unknown	23	trace	100
Wheat germ, cereal	1 tbsp.	trace	38	2	trace	16

Cheese						
Cheddar	1 oz.	196	23	1	9	115
Cottage, creamed	1 cup	515	191	7	10	260
Uncreamed	1 cup	653	162	5	1	170
Cream	1 tbsp.	38	11	trace	6	60
Process	1 oz.	318	22	1	9	105
Parmesan	1 oz.	206	42	1	9	130
Pasteurized spreads	1 oz.	455	67	2	6	80
Swiss	1 oz.	199	29	1	8	105
Cherries, raw, sweet	1 cup	2	218	20	trace	80
Canned, sour, water pack	1 cup, pitted	5	338	28	1	112
Sweet, heavy sirup	1 cup	3	328	53	1	211
Frozen, sweetened	1 cup, pitted	5	338	72	1	291
Chicken, raw, light	1 oz.	14	90	none	1	33
Cooked, light	1 oz.	18	115	none	1	46
Raw, dark	1 oz.	19	70	none	1	36
Cooked, dark	1 oz.	24	90	none	2	49
Chili sauce	1 tbsp.	227	63	4	trace	20
Chives	1 tbsp., chopped	1	25	1	trace	3
Chocolate, bitter	1 square (1 oz.)	1	232	8	15	145
Semi-sweet bits	1 oz.	1	91	16	10	143
Sweet	1 oz.	9	75	16	10	150
Citron, candied	1 piece, 1" square	81	34	22	trace	88
Clams, raw, meat only	1 oz.	34	51	1	trace	22
Cocoa, Dutch process	1 tbsp.	50	46	4	1	15
Plain	1 tbsp.	trace	107	4	1	15
Coconut, fresh, shredded	1 cup	7	1705	60	14	246
	1 cup	30	333	17	46	450

ITEM	MEASURE	MILLI-GRAMS SODIUM	MILLI-GRAMS POTASSIUM	GRAMS CARBO-HYDRATE	GRAMS FAT	CALORIES
Coconut (*cont.*)						
Dry shredded, sweet	1 tbsp.	1	14	2	2	22
	1 cup	11	219	33	24	340
Water	½ cup	30	176	6	trace	26
Coffee						
Instant, dry powder	1 tsp.	trace	33	trace	trace	1
Roasted, dry	1 tbsp.	trace	unknown	none	none	none
Sanka	1 tbsp.	trace	unknown	none	none	none
Collard greens, raw	½ cup	43	401	7	1	40
Cooked	½ cup	24	222	5	1	28
Frozen, uncooked	½ cup	17	246	6	trace	30
Cookies, plain and assorted	1 cooky, 3" diam.	91	17	18	5	120
Corn, popcorn, popped, unsalted	1 cup	trace	unknown	5	trace	25
Popcorn, popped with salt and oil	1 cup	272	unknown	5	2	40
Sweet, raw	½ cup	trace	280	22	1	96
	1 medium ear	trace	216	16	1	74
Cooked	½ cup	trace	196	21	1	91
Canned, niblets	½ cup	196	81	11	1	70
Cream-style	½ cup	290	119	25	1	101
Frozen, uncooked	½ cup	1	202	20	1	82
Cornmeal, unbolted	1 cup, dry	1	335	90	5	435
Cornstarch	1 tbsp.	trace	trace	7	trace	30
	1 cup	trace	trace	112	trace	465
Cowpeas, fresh, uncooked	½ cup	1	362	15	1	85
Cooked	½ cup	1	303	15	1	88

Plain	1 piece	trace	unknown	17	trace	78
Oyster	10 crackers	110	12	7	1	44
Rye	2 crackers	115	78	10	trace	45
Saltines	2 crackers	88	10	4	1	25
Soda	2 crackers	121	13	8	1	50
Whole wheat	5 small	49	unknown	6	1	36
Cracker meal	1 tbsp.	110	12	7	1	44
Cranberries, raw	1 cup	2	93	12	1	52
Sauce, canned	1 tbsp.	trace	5	7	trace	25
Cranberry juice cocktail	½ cup	1	13	21	trace	80
Cream, fluid						
Half-and-half	1 tbsp.	7	19	1	2	20
Light, table or coffee	1 tbsp.	6	18	1	3	30
Light whipping	1 tbsp.	5	15	1	5	45
Heavy whipping	1 tbsp.	5	13	trace	6	55
Cream substitutes	1 oz.	161	unknown	17	7	142
Cucumber, raw	½ medium	6	166	4	trace	15
Currants, raw, red	1 cup	2	283	13	trace	55
Dried	½ cup	20	unknown	71	1	268
Dandelion greens, fresh, cooked	½ cup	40	209	6	1	30
Dates, pitted	4 dates	trace	194	22	trace	82
	1 cup	2	1153	130	1	490
Dextrose	1 tbsp.	trace	unknown	11	none	45
Doughnuts, cake type	1 doughnut	160	29	16	6	125
Duck, raw	1 oz.	21	80	none	2	46
Egg, whole	1 large	61	65	trace	6	80
White only	1 large	48	46	trace	trace	15
Yolk, only	1 large	9	51	trace	5	60
Eggplants, raw	½ cup	2	214	6	trace	25
Endive greens	4 long leaves	3	59	1	trace	3
Figs, raw	3 small	2	221	23	trace	90

ITEM	MEASURE	MILLI-GRAMS SODIUM	MILLI-GRAMS POTASSIUM	GRAMS CARBO-HYDRATE	GRAMS FAT	CALORIES
Figs (*cont.*)						
Canned, heavy sirup	3 figs	2	170	25	trace	96
Without sugar	3 figs	2	177	14	trace	55
Dried	1 large	7	134	15	trace	60
Fish						
Albacore, raw	1 oz.	11	82	none	2	50
Bass, raw	1 oz.	19	unknown	none	trace	26
Bluefish, raw	1 oz.	21	72	none	1	33
Buffalo fish, raw	1 oz.	15	82	none	1	32
Carp, raw	1 oz.	14	80	none	1	32
Catfish, raw	1 oz.	17	92	none	1	29
Codfish, raw	1 oz.	20	107	none	trace	22
Frozen, raw	1 oz.	71	107	none	trace	22
Dehydrated, salted	1 oz.	2268	45	none	1	105
Crab, boiled	⅝ cup	370	unknown	1	2	93
Canned	⅝ cup	1000	110	1	3	101
Croaker, raw	1 oz.	24	66	none	1	27
Drum, fresh water	1 oz.	20	80	none	1	34
Red, raw	1 oz.	15	76	none	trace	22
Flatfish (sole, flounder, sanddab)	1 oz.	22	96	none	trace	22
Haddock, raw	1 oz.	17	85	none	trace	22
Hake, raw	1 oz.	21	102	none	trace	21
Halibut, raw	1 oz.	15	126	none	trace	28
Frozen, raw	1 oz.	101	126	none	trace	28
Herring, Pacific, raw	1 oz.	21	118	none	1	27
Smoked	1 oz.	1745	44	none	4	84

Mackerel, Atlantic, raw	1 oz.	14	unknown	none	3	53
Mackerel, Pacific, (Spanish), raw	1 oz.	25	unknown	none	2	45
Mullet, striped, raw	1 oz.	23	82	none	2	41
Mussels, Atlantic and Pacific, raw	1 oz. (meat only)	81	88	1	1	27
Ocean perch, Atlantic, raw	1 oz.	22	75	none	trace	**25**
Ocean perch, Pacific, raw	1 oz.	18	109	none	trace	27
Oysters, Eastern, raw	1 oz.	20	34	1	1	20
Frozen, uncooked	1 oz. (solids and liquids)	106	59	unknown	unknown	unknown
Perch, yellow, raw	1 oz.	19	64	none	trace	25
Pike, walleye, raw	1 oz.	14	89	none	trace	26
Pollack, raw	1 oz.	13	98	none	trace	27
Porgy and scup, raw	1 oz.	18	80	none	1	31
Red and gray snapper, raw	1 oz.	19	90	none	trace	26
Rockfish, raw	1 oz.	17	109	none	1	27
Sablefish, raw	1 oz.	16	100	none	4	**53**
Salmon, Chinook, raw	1 oz.	13	112	none	4	62
Pink, raw	1 oz.	18	86	none	1	33
Canned	1 oz.	108	101	none	2	40
Sardines, Atlantic	1 oz. (canned)	230	165	trace	3	57
Scallops, raw	1 oz.	unknown	unknown	1	trace	23
Frozen	1 oz.	71	71	1	trace	23
Shad, raw	1 oz.	15	92	none	3	48
Sheepshead, Atlantic, raw	1 oz.	28	66	none	1	32
Shrimp, raw	1 oz.	39	62	trace	trace	25
Suckers, raw	1 oz.	16	94	none	1	29
Swordfish, raw	1 oz.	22	unknown	none	1	33

ITEM	MEASURE	MILLI-GRAMS SODIUM	MILLI-GRAMS POTASSIUM	GRAMS CARBO-HYDRATE	GRAMS FAT	CALORIES
Fish (*cont.*)						
Trout, lake, raw	1 oz.	15	unknown	none	3	55
Trout, sea, raw	1 oz.	17	unknown	none	unknown	unknown
Tuna, yellow fin, raw	1 oz.	10	unknown	none	1	37
Canned in water	1 oz.	245	77	none	trace	36
Weakfish, raw	1 oz.	21	89	none	2	34
Whale meat, raw	1 oz.	22	6	none	2	44
White fish, raw	1 oz.	15	84	none	2	43
Whiting, raw	1 oz.	23	70	none	1	29
Flour						
All-purpose or family	1 tbsp.	trace	7	5	trace	25
	1 cup	2	105	88	1	420
Bread	1 cup	2	106	84	1	409
Cake or pastry	1 cup	2	95	79	1	365
Rye, light	1 cup	1	125	62	1	286
Self-rising	1 cup	1187	99	93	1	440
Whole wheat	1 cup	4	444	85	2	400
Fruit cocktail, canned						
heavy sirup	½ cup	6	206	25	trace	98
Without sugar	½ cup	6	215	12	trace	47
Garlic	1 clove	trace	11	1	trace	3
Gelatin, plain	1 tbsp.	3	unknown	none	trace	35
Dessert flavored, dry	1 pkg. (½ cup)	270	unknown	75	none	315
Ginger, preserved	1 oz.	trace	unknown	24	trace	95
Goose, raw	1 oz.	24	118	none	2	45
Gooseberries, raw	½ cup	1	116	7	trace	29
Canned, heavy sirup	½ cup		88	23		90

Grapefruit, raw	½ medium	1	193	15	trace	58
Canned, with sugar	½ cup	1	169	22	trace	88
Without sugar	½ cup	4	173	9	trace	35
Frozen	½ cup	6	unknown	unknown	trace	unknown
Juice						
Canned, sweetened	½ cup	1	203	16	trace	65
Unsweetened	½ cup	1	203	12	trace	50
Frozen, sweetened	½ cup, diluted	1	213	14	trace	58
Grapes, raw						
American type (slip skin)	½ cup	1	77	8	1	33
European type (adherent skin)	½ cup	2	123	13	trace	48
Gravy flavoring (Kitchen Bouquet)	1 tsp.	4	unknown	none	none	none
Gum, chewing, spearmint	1 stick	4	unknown	3	trace	10
Ham, cured, medium fat, cooked	1 oz.	260	91	none	6	82
Hash, corned beef	3 oz. (canned)	459	170	9	10	155
Heart, beef, lean, raw	1 oz.	24	54	trace	1	30
Calf, raw	1 oz.	26	58	1	2	35
Chicken, raw	1 oz.	22	45	trace	2	38
Pork, raw	1 oz.	15	30	trace	1	32
Turkey, raw	1 oz.	19	67	trace	3	48
Hominy, canned	1 cup	605	unknown	26	trace	122
Honey	1 tbsp.	1	11	17	none	65
Honeydew melon	¼ small	12	251	8	trace	33
Horseradish, prepared	1 tsp.	5	15	trace	trace	2
Ice cream and frozen custard, without added salt						
10% fat	⅛ quart	45	129	14	7	128
12% fat	⅛ quart	28	80	14	9	147
16% fat	⅛ quart	23	67	14	12	165
Ice milk, without added salt	1 cup	127	365	29	7	200

ITEM	MEASURE	MILLIGRAMS SODIUM	MILLIGRAMS POTASSIUM	GRAMS CARBO-HYDRATE	GRAMS FAT	CALORIES
Ices, water, lime	½ cup	trace	4	45	trace	55
Jams and preserves	1 tbsp.	2	18	14	trace	55
Jellies	1 tbsp.	3	15	14	trace	55
Kale, fresh, cooked	½ cup	24	122	2	1	15
Frozen	½ cup, scant	26	241	6	1	32
Kidneys, beef, raw	1 oz.	49	63	trace	2	36
Lamb, raw	1 oz.	56	64	trace	1	29
Pork, raw	1 oz.	32	50	trace	1	30
Kumquat	6 medium	7	236	17	trace	65
Lamb, lean, raw	1 oz.	21	83	none	5	69
Cooked, lean	1 oz.	20	81	none	2	52
Leeks	1 leek, 5" long	1	87	3	trace	13
Lemon, peel, fresh	1 tsp., grated	trace	6	1	trace	unknown
Juice, fresh	1 tbsp.	trace	21	1	trace	5
Canned or bottled	½ cup	1	173	10	trace	30
Frozen, single strength	½ cup	1	173	10	trace	28
Lemonade, frozen	½ cup	1	173	9	trace	27
Lentils, dry	1 cup, diluted	trace	40	28	trace	110
Lettuce	½ cup, scant	30	790	60	1	340
Butterhead, as Boston types	1 head, 4" diam.	15	430	6	trace	30
Crisphead, as Iceberg	1 head, 4¾" diam.	39	754	13	trace	60
Looseleaf, or bunching varieties	2 large leaves	5	88	2	trace	7
	2 large leaves	5	132	2	trace	10
Limes, raw	1 medium	1	53	5	trace	15

Calf, raw	1 oz.	20	79	1	1	38
Chicken, raw	1 oz.	20	48	1	1	38
Goose, raw	1 oz.	39	64	2	3	51
Lamb, raw	1 oz.	15	57	1	1	38
Pork, raw	1 oz.	20	73	1	1	38
Turkey, raw	1 oz.	18	45	1	1	38
Loganberries, raw	½ cup	1	116	9	trace	42
Canned, heavy sirup	½ cup, scant	1	109	22	trace	89
Without sugar	½ cup, scant	1	115	9	trace	40
Macaroni, plain	½ cup, cooked	1	55	16	1	78
	1 cup, dry	2	217	83	1	406
Mangos, raw	1 medium	9	249	22	1	87
Margarine, salted	1 tsp.	49	1	trace	4	33
Margarine, soft, unsalted	1 tsp.	5	5	trace	4	33
Marmalade, citrus	1 tbsp.	3	7	14	trace	51
Mayonnaise	1 tbsp.	90	5	trace	11	100
Meat extract, flavored	1 tsp.	550	unknown	unknown	unknown	unknown
Milk						
Cow's						
Buttermilk	1 cup	320	344	12	trace	90
Condensed	1 tbsp.	21	60	10	2	61
Evaporated	1 cup, undiluted	297	764	24	20	345
Skim, fresh	1 cup	128	357	12	trace	90
Dry, whole	1 cup	417	1370	39	28	515
Dry, nonfat, instant	1 cup	368	1208	35	trace	245
Whole, fresh	1 cup	122	351	12	9	160
Goat's	1 cup	83	439	11	10	165
Malted, dry	1 tbsp.	40	65	6	1	37
Milk beverages						
Cocoa	1 cup	123	351	27	12	245

ITEM	MEASURE	MILLIGRAMS SODIUM	MILLIGRAMS POTASSIUM	GRAMS CARBOHYDRATE	GRAMS FAT	CALORIES
Milk (cont.)						
Chocolate milk, made with						
skim milk	1 cup	115	355	27	6	190
Malted milk	1 cup	246	540	28	10	245
Milk desserts						
Cornstarch pudding	1 cup	161	342	41	10	285
Custard	1 cup	196	362	29	15	305
Mixed vegetables, frozen	½ cup, scant	59	208	14	trace	65
Molasses, light	1 tbsp.	3	183	13	none	50
Blackstrap	1 tbsp.	19	585	11	none	45
Muffin, variety, average	1 muffin	240	97	17	4	120
Mulberries	½ cup	1	unknown	10	1	42
Mushrooms, raw	½ cup	18	497	5	trace	34
Canned	½ cup	488	240	3	trace	21
Mustard greens, fresh, cooked	½ cup	13	154	3	1	18
Frozen	½ cup	8	137	2	trace	14
Mustard, prepared, yellow	1 tbsp.	188	20	1	1	11
Nectarines	2 medium	6	294	17	trace	64
Noodles, egg	1 cup, cooked	3	70	37	2	200
Nuts						
Almonds, raw	1 cup	6	1098	28	77	850
Roasted, salted	14 nuts	30	116	3	9	94
Brazil nuts	1 cup	1	1001	15	94	915
Cashew, roasted	1 cup	20	626	41	64	785
Chestnuts	2 large	1	68	6	2	29
Filberts	11 medium	trace	106	3	9	95
Litchi, dried	6 nuts	trace	165	11	trace	42

Roasted, salted	1 cup					
Pecans, raw	1 cup	trace	651	16	77	740
Walnuts, black	1 cup	4	580	19	75	790
English	1 cup	2	450	16	64	650
Oils (all kinds)	1 tbsp.	none	none	none	14	125
	1 cup	none	none	none	220	1945
Okra, raw	8 pods	3	249	8	trace	36
Cooked	8 pods	2	148	5	trace	25
Frozen, uncooked	8 pods	2	219	9	trace	39
Olives, green, pickled	4 medium	384	9	trace	2	15
Ripe, pickled	3 small	75	3	trace	2	15
Onions, raw	1 tbsp., chopped	1	16	1	trace	4
	1 cup	16	251	14	trace	61
	1 onion, 2½" diam.	11	173	10	trace	40
Cooked	½ cup	7	116	7	trace	30
Orange-grapefruit juice Canned, sweetened	½ cup	trace	228	15	trace	62
Frozen	½ cup, diluted	trace	219	13	trace	55
Oranges, raw, navel	1 medium	1	237	16	trace	60
Florida	1 medium	1	319	19	trace	75
Juice, fresh	½ cup	1	248	13	trace	55
Canned, sweetened	½ cup	1	247	15	trace	64
Unsweetened	½ cup	1	249	14	trace	60
Frozen	½ cup, diluted	1	231	14	trace	55
Peel, raw	1 tsp., grated	trace	8	1	trace	unknown
Temple	1 orange	2	unknown	22	trace	93
Pancreas, beef, lean, raw	1 oz.	19	77	none	2	39
Pork, raw	1 oz.	12	61	none	1	68
Papayas, raw	½ cup	3	213	9	trace	35
Parsley, raw	1 sprig	trace	7	trace	trace	trace

465

ITEM	MEASURE	MILLIGRAMS SODIUM	MILLIGRAMS POTASSIUM	GRAMS CARBOHYDRATE	GRAMS FAT	CALORIES
Parsley (cont.)						
	1 tbsp., chopped	2	29	trace	trace	2
Parsnip, raw	½ large	12	541	18	1	76
Cooked	½ cup	6	296	12	1	50
Peaches, raw	1 medium	1	200	10	trace	35
Canned, heavy sirup	2 halves	2	152	24	trace	90
Without sugar	½ cup	2	169	10	trace	38
Dried, uncooked	½ cup	13	760	55	1	210
Frozen, sweetened	½ cup, scant	2	124	23	trace	88
Nectar	½ cup	1	98	16	trace	60
Peanut butter	1 tbsp.	97	107	3	8	95
Pears, raw	1 medium	3	196	25	1	100
Canned, heavy sirup	2 halves	1	98	23	trace	90
Without sugar	½ cup	1	108	10	trace	40
Dried, uncooked	2 halves	2	201	24	1	94
Nectar	½ cup	1	49	17	trace	65
Peas, raw	½ cup	1	212	10	trace	56
Canned	½ cup	189	77	13	trace	70
Cooked	½ cup	1	157	10	trace	58
Frozen, uncooked	½ cup	86	101	9	trace	49
Split	½ cup	40	895	63	1	348
Peppers, green, raw	1 tbsp. chopped	1	21	trace	trace	2
	1 shell	8	132	3	trace	15
Red, raw	1 shell	15	338	4	trace	20
Persimmon, raw	1 persimmon	1	375	20	trace	75
Pickle, dill	1 large	1928	270	3	trace	15
Pineapple, raw	½ cup, diced	1	102	10	trace	38

½ cup, crushed		1			trace	
Without sugar	2 small slices	1	121	12	trace	48
Frozen	½ cup, scant	2	100	22	trace	85
Juice, canned	½ cup	1	186	17	trace	68
Frozen	½ cup, diluted	1	170	16	trace	65
Pineapple-grapefruit drink	½ cup	trace	74	16	trace	65
Pineapple-orange drink	½ cup	trace	84	16	trace	65
Plums, raw	1 plum, 2" diam.	1	164	7	trace	25
Canned in sirup	2 medium	1	142	22	trace	83
Without sugar	2 medium	2	148	12	trace	46
Pomegranate	1 medium	3	259	16	trace	63
Pork, lean, raw	1 oz.	20	80	none	6	77
Cooked, lean	1 oz.	18	109	none	4	71
Salt	1 oz.	339	12	none	24	219
Postum, cereal beverage	1 tbsp., dry	2	unknown	unknown	trace	unknown
Instant dry	1 tsp.	1	unknown	unknown	trace	4
Potatoes, chips	10 pieces	200	226	10	8	115
Sweet, raw	1 small	10	243	26	trace	114
Cooked, baked	1 medium	13	330	36	1	155
Canned	½ cup	52	218	27	trace	118
White, raw	1 potato, 2¼" diam.	3	407	17	trace	76
	½ cup, diced	3	407	17	trace	76
Dehydrated Flakes, dry	1 oz.	25	448	24	trace	102
Granules, dry	1 oz.	24	448	23	trace	99
Frozen, without salt	½ cup, diced	8	170	17	trace	73
French fried	10 pieces	2	288	19	5	125
Frozen, mashed with milk and butter	½ cup	352	211	12	4	93
Pretzels	5 sticks	168	7	4	trace	20
Prunes, raw	2 medium	1	170	20	trace	75
Dried	4 medium	3	222	18	trace	70

ITEM	MEASURE	MILLIGRAMS SODIUM	MILLIGRAMS POTASSIUM	GRAMS CARBOHYDRATE	GRAMS FAT	CALORIES
Prunes (*cont.*)						
Juice	½ cup	2	301	25	trace	100
Pumpkin, fresh, cooked	½ cup	1	340	7	trace	26
Canned without salt	½ cup	2	274	9	1	38
Quail, raw	1 oz.	11	49	none	2	48
Rabbit, raw	1 oz.	12	108	none	2	45
Radish	4 small	7	129	1	trace	5
Raisins	1 tbsp.	3	76	8	trace	30
Raspberries, raw	1 cup	43	1221	124	trace	460
Canned without sugar	½ cup	1	104	9	trace	35
Frozen	½ cup	1	114	9	trace	35
Rennet tablet (Junket)	½ cup, scant	1	100	25	trace	98
	1 tablet	22	unknown	trace	trace	trace
Dessert mixes, dry	1 pkg., chocolate	74	unknown	96	4	406
	1 pkg., other	6	unknown	104	trace	402
Rhubarb, raw	1 cup	2	306	5	trace	20
Frozen, sweetened	½ cup	4	211	19	trace	75
Rice, brown	½ cup, cooked	2	59	15	trace	68
	1 cup, raw	19	445	161	4	749
Minute	½ cup, cooked	trace	trace	16	trace	71
	1 cup, raw	2	unknown	158	trace	714
White	½ cup, cooked	1	24	22	trace	93
	1 cup, raw	10	176	154	1	693
Wild	½ cup, cooked	1	46	16	trace	74
	1 cup, raw	11	359	123	1	575
Rolls, commercial Plain						

Hard	1 roll					
Sweet	1 roll	167	53	21	4	135
Rutabaga, raw	½ cup, cubed	5	239	11	trace	46
Cooked	½ cup	3	130	6	trace	27
Salad dressing, French	1 tbsp.	219	13	3	6	65
Sauerkraut, canned	1 cup	1755	329	9	trace	45
Sausage type meats						
Bologna, 4" diam.	2 slices	741	131	1	16	173
Frankfurters	1 frankfurter	561	112	1	8	85
Luncheon meat	1 oz.	346	62	trace	7	82
Pork links, cooked	4 oz.	1083	304	trace	50	540
Seasonings						
All spice, ground	1 tsp.	2				
All spice, whole	4	trace				
Almond extract	1 tsp.	trace				
Anise seed	1 tsp.	trace				
Banana extract	1 tsp.	trace				
Basil	1 tsp.	trace				
Bay leaf	1 leaf	trace				
Bouquet Garni for beef	1 tsp.	1				
Bouquet Garni for soup	5	5				
Caraway seed	1 tsp.	1				
Cardamom, ground	1 tsp.	trace				
Cardamom, seed	1 tsp.	trace				
Cassia, cracked	1 tsp.	1				
Celery flakes	1 tsp.	115				
Celery salt	1 tsp.	840				
Celery seed, ground	1 tsp.	2				
Celery seed, whole	1 tsp.	4				
Chervil	1 tsp.	1				
Chili con carne seasoning powder	1 tsp.	1				
Chili pequins	1 pod	trace				

All extracts, herbs and spices used in small quantities may be considered negligible in carbohydrate, fat and calories. Potassium content is unknown.

ITEM	MEASURE	MILLI-GRAMS SODIUM	MILLI-GRAMS POTASSIUM	GRAMS CARBO-HYDRATE	GRAMS FAT	CALORIES
Seasonings (*cont.*)						
Chili powder	1 tsp.	57	All extracts, herbs and spices used in small quantities may be considered negligible in carbohydrate, fat and calories. Potassium content is unknown.			
Cinnamon, ground	1 tsp.	trace				
Cinnamon, whole	¼" stick	trace				
Cloves, ground	1 tsp.	1				
Cloves, whole	1 clove	trace				
Coriander, ground	1 tsp.	1				
Coriander seed	1 tsp.	1				
Cream of tartar	1 tsp.	8				
Cumin, ground	1 tsp.	trace				
Cumin seed	1 tsp.	trace				
Curry powder	1 tsp.	1				
Dill seed	1 tsp.	trace				
Dill weed	1 tsp.	trace				
Fennel seed	1 tsp.	1				
Fenugreek seed	1 tsp.	1				
Fines herbes	1 tsp.	1				
Garlic	1 clove	trace				
Garlic chips	1 tsp.	1				
Garlic powder	1 tsp.	1				
Ginger, ground	1 tsp.	1				
Ginger, whole	1 piece	1				
Gumbo file	1 tsp.	1				
Horseradish	1 tsp.	1				
Juniper berries	1 berry	trace				
Lemon peel	1 tsp.	1				
Mace, ground	1 tsp.	2				
Mace, whole	1 tsp.	2				
Marjoram	1 tsp.					

Mushroom, powdered	1 tsp.	1
Mustard, ground	1 tsp.	trace
Mustard, prepared	1 tsp.	65
Mustard seed	1 tsp.	trace
Nutmeg, ground	1 tsp.	1
Nutmeg, whole	1 tsp.	1
Onion, instant minced	1 tsp.	2
Onion powder	1 tsp.	2
Onion, shredded green	1 tsp.	11
Orange peel	1 tsp.	1
Oregano leaf	1 tsp.	trace
Paprika	1 tsp.	2
Parsley, fresh	1 tbsp.	1
	1 sprig	trace
Parsley flakes	1 tsp.	29
Pepper, black	1 tsp.	trace
Pepper, Nepal	1 tsp.	1
Pepper, red	1 tsp.	1
Pepper, white	1 tsp.	trace
Peppercorns	4	trace
Peppermint extract	1 tsp.	trace
Peppermint (spice)	1 tsp.	3
Pickling spice	1 tsp.	1
Poppy seed	1 tsp.	trace
Poultry seasoning	1 tsp.	1
Pumpkin pie spice	1 tsp.	trace
Rosemary leaves	1 tsp.	trace
Saffron, Spanish	1 tsp.	1
Sage	1 tsp.	trace
Salad herbs	1 tsp.	trace
Salt	1 tsp.	2361
Savory, powdered	1 tsp.	trace

ITEM	MEASURE	MILLIGRAMS SODIUM	MILLIGRAMS POTASSIUM	GRAMS CARBOHYDRATE	GRAMS FAT	CALORIES
Seasonings (*cont.*)						
Sesame seed	1 tsp.	2	All extracts, herbs and spices used in small quantities may be considered negligible in carbohydrate, fat and calories. Potassium content is unknown.			
Spearmint	1 tsp.	2				
Spice Parisienne	1 tsp.	1				
Tarragon	1 tsp.	trace				
Thyme	1 tsp.	1				
Turmeric	1 tsp.	1				
Vanilla extract	1 tsp.	trace				
Vinegar, cider	1 tbsp.	trace	15	1	trace	2
	1 cup	2	240	15	trace	34
Vinegar, wine, red	1 tbsp.	4	unknown	1	trace	2
	1 cup	70	unknown	15	trace	34
Vinegar, wine, white	1 tbsp.	5	unknown	1	trace	2
	1 cup	84	unknown	15	trace	34
Worcestershire sauce	1 tbsp.	315	unknown	unknown	unknown	unknown
Semolina	½ cup, cooked	trace	unknown	unknown	unknown	unknown
Shortenings						
Lard	1 tbsp.	none	none	none	13	115
	1 tbsp.	none	none	none	205	1850
Vegetable fats	1 cup	none	none	none	13	110
	1 tbsp.	none	none	none	200	1770
Sherbet, orange	1 cup	19	42	59	2	260
Sirup, chocolate, thin	1 cup	10	56	13	trace	50
Fudge type	1 tbsp.	18	57	11	3	66
Maple	1 tbsp.	2	35	13	none	50
Table blends, corn	1 tbsp.	14	1	15	none	60
Cane and maple	1 tbsp.	trace	5	13	none	50
Soft drinks — See Beverages						

Beef noodle	1 cup	955	80	7	5	90
Tomato	1 cup	970	230	16	3	80
Vegetable with beef broth	1 cup	863	245	14	2	403
Soy beans, dry	½ cup, scant	5	1677	34	18	329
Flour, defatted	1 cup	1	1838	38	1	78
Spaghetti, plain	½ cup, cooked	2	43	16	1	347
Spices — See Seasonings						
Spinach, raw	1 cup, raw	71	185	4	1	26
Canned	½ cup	212	470	3	trace	23
Cooked	½ cup	45	225	3	1	20
Frozen, uncooked	½ cup, scant	57	292	4	1	24
Sprouts, Mung bean, raw	1 cup	5	354	6	trace	30
Squab, raw	1 oz.	59	201	none	trace	40
Squash, summer, raw	½ cup, scant	1	unknown	4	2	19
Cooked	½ cup	1	202	4	trace	15
Frozen, uncooked	½ cup, scant	3	148	5	trace	21
Winter, raw	½ cup	1	167	12	trace	50
Cooked, baked	½ cup	1	369	16	trace	65
Frozen, uncooked	½ cup, scant	1	475	9	1	38
Strawberries, raw	1 cup	1	207	13	trace	55
Canned, without sugar	½ cup, scant	1	244	6	1	22
Frozen, sweetened	½ cup, scant	1	111	28	trace	109
Succotash, frozen, uncooked	½ cup, scant	45	112	22	trace	97
Suet, beef, raw	1 oz.	14	273	none	26	239
Sugar, brown	1 tbsp.	4	48	13	none	50
	1 cup	66	757	212	none	820
Granulated	1 tbsp.	trace	trace	12	none	45
	1 cup	2	6	199	none	770
Powdered	1 tbsp.	trace	trace	8	none	30
	1 cup	1	4	127	none	495
Sweetbreads, beef, raw	1 oz.	27	101	none	4	58

ITEM	MEASURE	MILLI-GRAMS SODIUM	MILLI-GRAMS POTASSIUM	GRAMS CARBO-HYDRATE	GRAMS FAT	CALORIES
Tangerine, raw	1 medium	2	106	10	trace	40
Juice, unsweetened	½ cup, canned	1	221	13	trace	53
Frozen	½ cup, diluted	1	216	14	trace	58
Tapioca, dry	1 tbsp.	trace	2	9	trace	35
	1 cup	5	27	131	trace	535
Tartar sauce	1 tbsp.	106	12	1	9	80
Tea, blend, dry	1 tsp.	trace	unknown	trace	trace	trace
Tomatoes, raw	1 medium	5	366	7	trace	35
Canned	½ cup	157	263	5	trace	25
Catsup	1 tbsp.	177	62	4	trace	15
Juice, canned	½ cup	242	275	5	trace	23
Purée	1 cup	994	1061	22	trace	97
Toothpastes						
Amm-i-dent	1 gram	2	unknown	unknown	unknown	unknown
Pepsodent	1 gram	65	unknown	unknown	unknown	unknown
Squibb	1 gram	2	unknown	unknown	unknown	unknown
Tooth powders						
Colgate	1 gram	5	unknown	unknown	unknown	unknown
Dentrix	1 gram	8	unknown	unknown	unknown	unknown
Tripe, commercial, raw	1 oz.	20	3	none	1	28
Pickled	1 oz.	13	5	none	trace	17
Turkey						
Light meat, raw	1 oz.	14	90	none	trace	32
Cooked	1 oz.	23	115	none	1	49
Dark meat, raw	1 oz.	23	87	none	1	36
Cooked	1 oz.	28	111	none	2	57
Turnip, greens, fresh, cooked	½ cup	10	unknown	3	trace	15
Frozen, uncooked	½ cup	17	137	2		

Cooked	½ cup	27	147	4	trace	18
Veal, raw, lean	1 oz.	25	90	none	2	44
Vinegar — See Seasonings						
Water, distilled	1 cup	none	none	none	none	none
Watermelon, raw	½ cup, scant	1	100	6	trace	26
Wheat germ — See Cereals						
Whiskey — See Beverages						
Wine — See Beverages						
Yeast						
Baker's, compressed	1 oz.	4	171	3	trace	25
Dry, active	1 oz.	15	559	11	trace	80
Brewer's, debittered	1 tbsp., dry	10	152	3	trace	25
Yogurt, partially skim milk	1 cup	125	352	13	4	125

COMPARATIVE FAT VALUES OF
MEAT CUTS

ITEM	GRAMS FAT[*]	ITEM	GRAMS FAT[*]
Beef		Lamb (*Continued*)	
Chuck, choice grade	7	Shoulder, choice grade	8
Flank steak, choice grade	2	Good grade	7
Good grade	2	Pork, medium fat class	
Porterhouse, choice		Fresh	
grade	12	Ham, picnic	9
Good grade	11	Loin, Boston butt	8
Rib, choice grade	11	Cured	
Round, choice grade	4	Ham	6
Rump, choice grade	8	Boston butt, picnic	7
Good grade	7	Veal, medium fat class,	
Sirloin, double-bone		untrimmed	
steak, choice grade	10	Chuck	4
Good grade	8	Flank	9
Lamb		Foreshank	3
Leg, choice grade	5	Loin	4
Good grade	5	Plate	6
Loin, choice grade	8	Rib	5
Good grade	8	Round with rump	3
Rib, choice grade	10		
Good grade	9		

* All fat values are based on one ounce meat, cooked weight, edible portion, trimmed to retail level. Veal is untrimmed. Source of values: COMPOSITION OF FOODS – RAW, PROCESSED, PREPARED, AGRICULTURE HANDBOOK NO. 8, 1963 Revision, and Errata Sheet for 1968 Printing.

3 A. SODIUM, CARBOHYDRATE, FAT, AND CALORIE CONTENT OF SOME COMMERCIAL PRODUCTS RESTRICTED IN SODIUM AND/OR FAT CONTENT*

Effective January 1, 1975, federal regulations required that any product making a nutritional claim or designated for dietary use must have nutrition information on the label including serving size and analysis. Be sure to read the label on your brand selection for the analysis relative to your diet restrictions.

Food	Brand	Measure	Milli-grams Sodium	Grams Carbo-hydrate	Grams Fat	Calo-ries
Asparagus	Average	6 stalks	3	3	trace	19
Purée	Cellu	½ cup	4	4	trace	24
Baking powder						
Commercial	Average	1 tsp.	trace	2	trace	7
Non commer-cial formula	Average	1 tsp.	none	1	trace	4
Beans, Lima	Average	½ cup	3	14	trace	76
Beans, snap, green & yellow						
wax	Average	½ cup	1	3	trace	14
Purée	Cellu	½ cup	2	8	trace	46
Beets	Average	½ cup	38	7	trace	31
Purée	Cellu	½ cup	57	9	trace	43
Biscuit mix	Bernard	1 serving (1 oz.)	4	18	3	85
Bouillon cube						
Beef	Cellu	1 cube	10	2	trace	11
Chicken	Cellu	1 cube	2	2	trace	11
Bread, fresh, white, whole wheat, rye	Average	½ in. slice	7	12	1	60
Bread Italian, sticks	Stella D'Oro	1 stick	1	7	1	43
Bread, Melba toast	Cellu	3 pieces	1	9	1	46
Butter, unsalted	Average	1 tsp.	trace	trace	4	33
		1 tbsp.	1	trace	12	100
		1 cup	23	2	184	1620

* Values for food items listed as average were calculated from *Agriculture Handbook No. 8, Composition of Foods — Raw, Processed, Prepared*, and from *Publication 325, Sodium Restricted Diets, The Rationale, Complications, and Practical Aspects of Their Use.*

Food	Brand	Measure	Milligrams Sodium	Grams Carbohydrate	Grams Fat	Calories
Cake, canned	Cellu	1 slice (1 oz.)	3	14	8	144
Cake mix	Bernard	1 slice (1 oz.)	19	17	2	93
Candy*	Cellu	1 pkg. (10 oz. dry)	34	179	58	1312
Chocolate bars Almond	Estee	1 bar (¾ oz.)	33	4	8	123
Bittersweet	Estee	1 bar (¾ oz.)	22	2	9	125
Coconut	Estee	1 bar (¾ oz.)	30	3	9	124
Milk	Estee	1 bar (¾ oz.)	31	3	9	126
Peppermint	Estee	1 bar (¾ oz.)	31	3	9	126
Chocolates, boxed, assorted	Estee	1 piece	1 to 12	1	1 to 3	5 to 50
Gum drops, assorted	Estee	1 piece	trace	none	trace	3
Hard candies (assorted)	Estee	1 piece	trace	none	trace	12
Carrots	Average	½ cup	29	4	trace	19
Cheese, cheddar	Cellu	1 tbsp. grated	1	trace	2	27
		1 cup grated	11	4	34	431
		1 oz.	3	1	8	116
	Clearfield Di-et	1 oz.	386	2	2	67
	Tillamook	1 oz.	10	1	9	110
Cheese, Colby	Cellu	1 oz.	3	1	9	115
Cheese, Cottage	Average	½ cup	23	3	1	98
Cheese spread Count Down	Fisher	1 oz.	439	3	trace	42
Cookies† Almond wafers	Estee	1 cooky	2	1	2	27
Angel Puffs	Stella D'Oro	8 pieces	25	12	8	140
Apple pastry	Stella D'Oro	2 pieces	25	28	9	210

* Carbohydrate content of candy does not include sorbitol and mannitol.
† Carbohydrate in Estee products does not include sorbitol or manitol content.

Food	Brand	Measure	Milli-grams Sodium	Grams Carbo-hydrate	Grams Fat	Calo-ries
Cookies (*cont.*)						
Assorted filled wafers	Estee	1 cooky	3	2	1	25
Chocolate Chip	Estee	1 cooky	7	3	1	32
Sandwich	Estee	1 cooky	3	3	2	42
Coconut	Stella D'Oro	3 pieces	6	20	6	140
Egg biscuits	Stella D'Oro	2 pieces	8	14	1	77
Fig pastry	Stella D'Oro	2 pieces	6	30	7	200
Fruit wafers	Estee	1 cooky	1	1	1	22
Holland filled, plain & chocolate	Estee	1 cooky	1	1	2	31
Kichel	Stella D'Oro	20 pieces	20	15	9	160
Love	Stella D'Oro	2 pieces	6	26	11	220
Oatmeal raisin	Estee	1 cooky	2	3	1	36
Peach-apricot pastry	Stella D'Oro	2 pieces	6	27	11	220
Prune pastry	Stella D'Oro	2 pieces	10	27	11	220
Rice	Cellu	3 cookies	2	8	1	43
Royal nuggets	Stella D'Oro	75 pieces	35	11	7	120
Sandwich wafer	Estee	1 cooky	3	3	2	42
Sesame	Stella D'Oro	3 pieces	3	16	6	130
Corn						
Cream style	Average	½ cup	2	23	1	101
Whole kernel	Average	½ cup	2	15	1	63
Crackers						
All rye	Cellu	1 wafer	1	5	trace	22
Plain	Cellu	4 crackers	trace	11	2	63
Rice	Cellu	4 wafers	trace	8	trace	37
Egg substitutes						
Bud Diet-Lite scrambled egg mix	Anheuser-Busch (whole-sale product)	¼ cup	103	1	trace	38

Food	Brand	Measure	Milli-grams Sodium	Grams Carbo-hydrate	Grams Fat	Calo-ries
Egg substitutes (*cont.*)						
Eggbeaters	Fleisch-mann's	¼ cup	109	2	8	100
Eggstra	Tillie Lewis	¼ cup	80	2	1	43
Second Nature	Avoset Foods Corp.	3 tbsp.	79	1	2	35
Fish, canned						
Salmon						
Coho	Average	1 oz.	15	none	2	43
Pink	Average	1 oz.	18	none	2	39
Sockeye (Red)	Average	1 oz.	13	none	3	48
Shrimp	Feather-weight	1 oz.	22	trace	trace	19
Tuna	Average	1 oz.	11	none	trace	36
Gelatin, flavored assorted	Bernard	1 serving	5	none	trace	6
	Cellu	1 serving	3	1	trace	12
Margarine unsalted	Average	1 tsp.	trace	trace	4	33
		1 tbsp.	1	trace	11	100
		1 cup	23	1	184	1635
Meat analogs						
Dinner cuts						
NSA	Loma Linda	1 cut	5	2	1	41
Regular	Loma Linda	1 cut (1½ oz.)	229	2	1	41
Vegeburger						
NSA	Loma Linda	3 tbsp.	6	1	1	43
Regular	Loma Linda	3 tbsp.	130	1	1	43
Meat purées						
Beef	Cellu	1 oz.	16	none	1	25
Chicken	Cellu	1 oz.	37	none	2	31
Lamb	Cellu	1 oz.	17	none	1	30
Meats and Main Dishes						
Beans, rich brown	Loma Linda	½ cup	754	24	1	131
Beans, soy, Boston style	Loma Linda	½ cup	838	16	5	151

Food	Brand	Measure	Milligrams Sodium	Grams Carbohydrate	Grams Fat	Calories
Meats and Main Dishes (*cont.*)						
Beef stew	Feather-weight	1 can (8 oz.)	68	16	7	182
Chicken, boned	Feather-weight	1 oz.	9	none	2	39
Chicken stew	Feather-weight	1 can (8 oz.)	58	15	2	118
Chili with beans	Loma Linda	½ cup	426	19	3	134
Ham	Cellu	1 oz.	23	none	1	39
Lamb stew	Feather-weight	1 can (8 oz.)	56	14	20	292
Spanish rice	Feather-weight	1 can (8 oz.)	28	34	2	164
Milk						
Nonfat milk	Feather-weight	1 tbsp.	2	4	trace	29
dry		1 cup, dry	36	64	1	436
		1 cup, liquified	7	12	trace	79
Partly skimmed	One-Eleven	1 cup, liquid	12	14	2	117
Whole milk, dry	Lonalac	1 tbsp., dry	2	3	2	40
		1 cup, liquified	6	12	8	160.
Milk beverages		1 can				
Chocolate	Cellu	(8 oz.)	12	24	6	195
Vanilla	Cellu	1 can (8 oz.)	12	19	6	175
Mixed vegetables	Cellu	½ cup	28	7	trace	36
Mushrooms	Feather-weight	½ cup	2	3	trace	28
Peanut butter	Cellu	1 tbsp.	1	2	9	98
	Peter Pan	1 tbsp.	none	2	8	96
Peas						
Alaska (Early or June)	Average	½ cup	2	11	trace	62
Sweet (sugar peas)	Average	½ cup	2	10	trace	58
Peas and carrots	Tillie Lewis	½ cup	7	12	trace	42
Peas, purée	Cellu	½ cup	8	11	trace	71
Potatoes						
Sweet	Average	½ cup	13	27	trace	118
White	Average	3 very small	1	10	trace	44

Food	Brand	Measure	Milli-grams Sodium	Grams Carbo-hydrate	Grams Fat	Calo-ries
Puddings						
Butterscotch	Bernard	½ cup	24	32	2	156
Chocolate	Bernard	½ cup	32	32	2	156
Coconut	Bernard	½ cup	24	32	2	156
Vanilla	Bernard	½ cup	32	32	2	156
Relishes, sauces and flavorings						
Catsup	Average	1 tbsp.	6	4	trace	15
Chili sauce	Average	1 tbsp.	6	4	trace	20
Cucumber relish	Feather-weight	1 oz.	1	1	trace	7
Mustard	Feather-weight	1 tsp.	trace	none	none	none
Salad dressings, fat-control						
Blue and Roquefort cheese	Average	1 tbsp.	170	trace	trace	3
French	Average	1 tbsp.	118	trace	trace	2
Italian	Average	1 tbsp.	118	trace	1	8
Mayonnaise type	Average	1 tbsp.	18	1	2	20
Thousand Island	Average	1 tbsp.	105	2	2	27
Salad dressings, sodium-control						
All purpose	Bernard	1 tbsp.	1	trace	trace	trace
French style	Bernard	1 tbsp.	1	trace	trace	trace
	Cellu	1 tbsp.	trace	1	11	88
Mayonnaise	Average	1 tbsp.	8	trace	12	110
Soyamaise	Cellu	1 tbsp.	2	trace	12	106
Soups (Diluted with water)						
Bouillon powder diluted						
Beef	Bernard	1 cup	7	4	negli-gible	16
Chicken	Bernard	1 cup	3	4	negli-gible	16
Vegetable	Bernard	1 cup	5	4	negli-gible	16
Celery, cream of	Bernard	1 cup	16	4	2	33
Chicken broth	Feather-weight	1 cup	96	none	1	26

Food	Brand	Measure	Milli-grams Sodium	Grams Carbo-hydrate	Grams Fat	Calo-ries
Soups						
(cont.)						
Chicken,						
cream of	Bernard	1 cup	16	4	2	33
Chicken noodle	Feather-					
	weight	1 cup	18	6	1	48
	Tillie					
	Lewis	1 cup	40	5	5	54
Mushroom,	Bernard	1 cup	16	4	2	33
cream of	Campbell	1 cup				
		(scant)	20	10	9	130
	Feather-					
	weight	1 cup	30	10	2	64
Pea, condensed	Campbell	1 cup				
		(scant)	40	22	3	140
	Feather-					
	weight	1 cup	25	18	1	111
Pea, split	Tillie					
	Lewis	1 cup	25	27	1	162
Tomato	Bernard	1 cup	8	37	5	56
	Campbell	1 cup				
		(scant)	30	18	2	100
	Feather-					
	weight	1 cup	22	20	1	88
	Tillie					
	Lewis	1 cup	35	13	1	73
Tomato with	Feather-					
rice	weight	1 cup	13	15	trace	72
Turkey noodle	Campbell	1 cup				
		(scant)	40	7	2	60
Vegetable	Campbell	1 cup				
		(scant)	40	14	2	80
	Tillie					
	Lewis	1 cup	60	13	1	68
Vegetable-beef	Campbell	1 cup				
		(scant)	45	8	3	80
	Feather-					
	weight	1 cup	21	8	1	58
Spinach	Average	½ cup	29	3	1	23
Squash	Cellu	½ cup	1	8	trace	44
Sugar substitutes	Adolph's	1 tsp.	1	trace	none	1
	Bernard	1 tsp.	trace	none	none	none
	Tillie					
	Lewis	6 drops	1	none	none	none
Tomato juice	Average	½ cup	4	5	trace	23

Food	Brand	Measure	Milli-grams Sodium	Grams Carbo-hydrate	Grams Fat	Calo-ries
Tomato paste	Cellu	1 can (6 oz.)	69	27	1	144
Tomato purée	Average	1 cup	15	22	trace	97
Tomatoes	Average	½ cup	4	5	trace	25
Yams	Feather-weight	½ cup	37	12	trace	60

3 B. SOME COMMERCIAL FIRMS SUPPLYING ANALYSIS DATA FOR DIETARY PRODUCTS

BRAND	ADDRESS
Adolph's Low Sodium	Jeannette Frank, Adolph's Ltd., Box 828, Burbank, CA 91503
Andersen's Dietetic	Andersen Foods, Division of Tillie Lewis Foods, Inc., General Offices, Drawer J, Stockton, CA 95201
Bernard Special Diet	Bernard Food Industries, Inc., 1125 Hartrey Ave., P.O. Box 1497, Evanston, IL 60204
Bud Diet-Lite	Anheuser-Busch, Inc., Executive Offices, St. Louis, MO 63118
Campbell's Low Sodium	Food Service Products Division, Campbell Sales Co., Camden, NJ 08101
Cellu	Chicago Dietetic Supply, Inc., P.O. Box 40, La Grange, IL 60525
Chicken of the Sea Dietetic	Van Camp Sea Food Co., Division of Ralston Purina Co., 772 Tuna St., Terminal Island, CA 90731
Clearfield Di-Et	Clearfield Cheese Co., Inc., Curwensville, PA 16833
Count Down and Cheez-ola	Fisher Cheese Co., Inc., P.O. Box 12, Wapakoneta, OH 45895
Eggbeaters	Standard Brands Foods, 625 Madison Ave., New York, NY 10022
Eggstra	See Tillie Lewis Foods
Estee Dietetic	Estee Candy Co., Inc., 169 Lackawanna Ave., Parsippanny, NJ 07054
Featherweight	See Cellu
Fleischmann's	See Eggbeaters
Loma Linda	Loma Linda Foods, 11503 Pierce St., Riverside, CA 92505
Nutradiet	S and W Fine Foods, San Mateo, CA 94402
One-Eleven	LSM Lo-Sodium Dairy Products Co., 346 Rose Ave., Venice, CA 90291
Stella D'Oro Dietetic	Stella D'Oro Biscuit Co., Inc., 184 West 237th St., Bronx, N.Y. 10463
Second Nature	Avoset Corporation, 80 Grand Ave., Oakland, CA 94610
Tasti-Diet	See Tillie Lewis Foods
Tillamook	Tillamook County Creamery Assn., P.O. Box 313, Tillamook, OR 97141
Tillie Lewis Dietetic	Tillie Lewis Foods, Inc., General Offices, Drawer J, Stockton, CA 95201

4. AVERAGE SODIUM CONTENT OF ALCOHOLIC BEVERAGES AND COCKTAILS*

BEVERAGE	MEASURE	MILLIGRAMS SODIUM
Beer, lager	1 cup	17
Wine, red	1 cup	20†
Wine, rosé	1 cup	38†
Wine, dry white	1 cup	28†
Wine, sweet white	1 cup	24†
Wine, champagne	1 cup	16†
Wine, dessert		
Muscatel	1 cup	52†
Port	1 cup	20†
Sherry	1 cup	20†
Vermouth	3 ounces	10
Brandy	1 jigger	1
Gin	1 jigger	0
Rum	1 jigger	unknown
Whiskey, bourbon	1 jigger	trace
Whiskey, Scotch	1 jigger	unknown
Vodka	1 jigger	0

* Analyses supplied by the Home Advisory Service of the Wine Institute through the courtesy of Leake, Chauncey D., and Silverman, Milton, *Alcoholic Beverages in Clinical Medicine,* Year Book Medical Publishers, Chicago, 1965.

† Some wines, both European and American, may contain as much as 50 milligrams sodium per 100 cc, or 120 milligrams in one cup. In severely restricted sodium diets, it may be necessary to have a special analysis made on the wine used.

5 A. COMMON FOODS LOW IN SATURATED FATS

Beverages
Alcoholic (ale, beer, brandy, whiskey, wine)
Carbonated (Coca-Cola, ginger ale, root beer, etc.)
Cider
Cocoa Powder
Coffee, black
Fruit juices
Lemonade
Milk, buttermilk
Milk, nonfat
Postum
Tea

Bread and Bread Products
Commercial except biscuits, muffins, and quick breads
Homemade (with vegetable oil; without butter, egg yolk, regular margarine, whole milk)

Cereals and Cereal Products
Barley
Bran
Bran flakes
Corn flakes
Cornmeal
Cream of wheat
Grape-Nuts
Macaroni
Maltex
Muffets
Oats
Pettijohns
Popcorn (without butter or margarine)
Ralston
Rice
Spaghetti
Tapioca
Wheat (flakes and puffed)
Wheat, shredded

Crackers
Bread sticks
Matzoth
Melba toast
Pretzels
Rye wafers

Dairy Products
Cheese, cottage, uncreamed, dry
Cheese, low fat
Egg substitutes
Egg white
Milk, buttermilk
Milk, nonfat (powder or fluid)

Desserts
Angel cake
Cakes and cookies, homemade with vegetable oil; without whole milk, egg yolk, chocolate, coconut
Gelatin
Ices, plain
Pies, homemade with vegetable oil; without cream, egg yolk, whole milk
Puddings, homemade without whole eggs, whole milk

Fats and Oils
Vegetable oils (corn, cottonseed, peanut, safflower, soybean, sunflower)
Special margarines (in limited amounts)

Fish (canned, fresh, or frozen)
Bass
Bluefish
Butterfish
Cod
Flounder
Haddock
Halibut
Herring

Mackerel
Perch
Porgy
Salmon
Sardines
Shellfish
Swordfish
Tuna
Whiting

Flours and Flour Products
Barley
Cake (not mixes)
Cornstarch
Gluten
Graham
Rice
Rye
Wheat
Whole wheat

Fruit (canned, fresh, or frozen)
Apples
Apricots
Avocado
Bananas
Berries
Cherries
Cranberries
Dates
Figs
Grapefruit
Grapes
Lemons
Limes
Melon
Oranges
Peaches
Pears
Pineapple
Plums
Prunes
Rhubarb
Tangerines

Miscellaneous
Catsup
Cocoa powder
Mustard
Relishes

Seasonings
Vinegar

Nuts (plain or with vegetable oil)
Almonds
Brazil nuts
Butternuts
Cashew nuts
Peanut butter (nonhydroge-
nated)
Peanuts
Pecans
Walnuts

Sauces
Homemade with vegetable oil,
special margarine, nonfat milk,
egg white

Sirups and Sugars
Corn sirup
Honey
Maple sirup
Molasses
Sugar (brown, powdered, gran-
ulated)
Table sirup

Soups
Bouillon
Chowders (homemade with nonfat milk, vegetable oil, special
margarine; without butter, regular margarine, meat)
Consommé
Cream soups (homemade with
vegetable oil, special margarine, nonfat milk)

Sweets
Candy (homemade without but-
ter, regular margarine, whole
milk)
Gum drops
Jams
Jelly beans
Jellies
Marmalades
Marshmallow

Mints, cream
Necco wafers

Vegetables (canned, fresh, or
    frozen)
  Artichoke
  Asparagus
  Bean sprouts
  Beans (dried, green, Lima, snap)
  Beets
  Broccoli
  Cabbage
  Cauliflower
  Celery
  Corn
  Cucumber
  Eggplant

Garlic
Greens (chicory, dandelion, es-
    carole, kale, spinach, et cetera)
Leeks
Lettuce
Mushrooms
Onions
Peppers
Potatoes
Pumpkin
Radish
Rutabaga
Squash (all types)
Sweet potatoes
Tomatoes
Turnip
Yams

5 B. COMMON FOODS HIGH IN SATURATED FATS

Beverages
  Chocolate milk
  Cocoa (with whole milk)
  Eggnog
  Milk shakes
  Milk, whole
  Soda, ice cream

Bread and Bread Products
  Commercial (with butter, hy-drogenated shortening, lard, whole egg, whole milk)
  Coffee cake
  Corn bread
  Danish pastry
  Doughnuts
  Homemade (with butter, hy-drogenated shortening, lard, regular margarine, whole egg, whole milk)
  Muffins (all kinds)

Cereal Products
  Macaroni and cheese
  Spaghetti with meat sauce

Crackers (with lard or hydroge-nated shortenings)
  Cheese
  Graham
  Saltines
  Soda
  Wheat

Dairy Products
  Butter
  Cheese (made from cream or whole milk)
  Cream
  Eggs (whole and yolk)
  Ice cream
  Milk, chocolate
  Milk, condensed
  Milk, dried whole

Milk, evaporated
Milk, goat's
Milk, malted
Milk, whole
Yogurt, from whole milk

Desserts (except homemade with special margarine, vegetable oils; without whole egg, whole milk, coconut, or chocolate)
  Brownies
  Cakes (all kinds except angel)
  Cookies
  Custards
  Eclairs
  Ice cream
  Pies
  Puddings (bread, tapioca, rice, with whole milk, whole eggs)
  Sherbets, milk

Fats and Oils
  Bacon
  Butter
  Chicken fat
  Coconut oil
  Cooking fats (hydrogenated)
  Lard
  Margarine (except special mar-garine in limited amounts)
  Mayonnaise or salad dressing with coconut oil
  Meat fat

Fish
  Creamed with whole milk, but-ter, regular margarine
  Fried in saturated fats
  Soups and chowders with whole milk, salt pork, butter, regular margarine

Flours and Flour Products
  Bisquick

Cake mixes
Cookie mixes
Muffin mixes
Pancake mixes
Pie crust mixes

Meats
Bacon
Beef
Chicken*
Cold cuts
Duck
Frankfurter
Goose
Ham
Heart
Kidney
Lamb
Liver
Pork
Rabbit
Sausage
Tongue
Turkey*
Veal*

Nuts
Chocolate coated nuts

Coconut
Peanut butter (hydrogenated)

Sauces
Commercial and homemade with whole milk, whole egg, butter, regular margarine
Gravies

Soups
Commercial or homemade with whole milk, meats, salt pork, lard, hydrogenated shortenings, butter, regular margarine

Sweets (candies)
Commercial or homemade with chocolate, coconut, whole egg, whole milk, butter, regular margarine

Vegetables
Canned, fresh, or frozen prepared with added butter, regular margarine, salt pork, whole egg, whole milk such as fried or creamed
Potato chips

* Chicken and turkey (without skin) and veal are lower in saturated fat content than other meats.

6. CARBOHYDRATE CONTENT OF COMMON FOODS

Carbohydrate foods (sugars and starches) may be restricted on your diet to attain and maintain your "ideal" body weight, and to reduce the cholesterol and triglyceride content of your blood.

Carbohydrates occur naturally in many foods such as fruits, vegetables, and cereals or other grain products. Carbohydrate also is added to many processed foods, mainly in some form of sugar. In controlling carbohydrate intake, concentrated or refined sources (such as sugar, honey, molasses, or sirup) are considered to be the worst offenders. This means that most sweets and desserts must be restricted or eliminated. Instead, your dietary allowance of carbohydrate will favor vegetables, unsweetened fruits, and limited amounts of breads and cereals.

This Appendix lists common foods in four carbohydrate groupings: negligible; 10 grams or less; 10 to 15 grams; and foods usually considered high in carbohydrate. Even with foods negligible in carbohydrate content, you will need to follow your diet specifications strictly. Many foods low in carbohydrate are high in sodium, cholesterol, and/or fat content.

A.   FOODS WITH NEGLIGIBLE CARBOHYDRATE CONTENT

Beverages
Alcoholic (brandy, gin, rum, vodka, whiskey)
Carbonated (sugar-free cola, ginger ale, root beer, et cetera)
Coffee, black
Lemonade (with sugar substitute)
Tea, black

Dairy Products
Cheese
Eggs

Desserts
Gelatins and ices (with sugar substitute)

Fats and Oils
All kinds

Fish (canned, fresh, or frozen)
All kinds (except mixtures containing milk, flour, bread, or other high carbohydrate food)

Fruits (unsweetened or with sugar substitute)
Cranberries
Lemon
Rhubarb (up to 1 cup cooked)

Meats
All kinds (except mixtures containing milk, flour, bread, or other high carbohydrate food)

Miscellaneous
Catsup (1 tablespoon limit)
Cocoa powder (no sugar)
Herbs
Jams and jellies (artificially sweetened)
Mustard
Pickles (unsweetened)
Salt and pepper (as allowed)
Soy sauce
Vinegar
Worcestershire sauce

Soups
  Bouillon
  Consommé

Vegetables (unlimited raw; up to
  1 cup cooked)
  Asparagus
  Beet greens
  Broccoli
  Cabbage
  Cauliflower
  Celery
  Chard
  Chicory
  Collards
  Cucumber
  Dandelion
  Escarole

Eggplant
Kale
Lettuce
Mushrooms
Mustard greens
Okra
Parsley
Pepper, green
Radish
Romaine
Sauerkraut
Spinach
String beans
Summer squash
Tomatoes (limit 1 medium)
Turnip greens
Watercress

B.   FOODS WITH 10 GRAMS OR LESS CARBOHYDRATE
IN AMOUNTS SPECIFIED

Beverages
  Beer, 1 cup
  Wine, ½ cup

Fruits (unsweetened or with sugar
  substitute)
  Apple, 1 small
  Apple juice, ⅓ cup
  Applesauce, ½ cup
  Apricot juice, ⅓ cup
  Apricots, fresh, 2 medium
  Apricots, dry, 4 halves
  Banana, ½ small
  Berries (blackberries, raspberries,
    and strawberries), 1 cup
  Blueberries, ⅔ cup
  Cantaloupe, ¼ of 6″ diam.
  Cherries, 10 large
  Dates, 2
  Figs, dried, 1 small
  Figs, fresh, 2 large
  Grapefruit, ½ small
  Grapefruit juice, ½ cup
  Grapes, 12
  Grape juice, ¼ cup
  Honeydew melon, ⅛ of 7″ diam.
  Mango, ½ small

Nectarines, 1 medium
Orange, 1 small
Orange juice, ½ cup
Papaya, ⅓ medium
Peach, 1 medium
Pear, 1 small
Pineapple, ½ cup, cubed
Pineapple juice, ⅓ cup
Plums, 2 medium
Prune juice, ¼ cup
Prunes, dried, 2 medium
Raisins, 2 level tablespoons
Tangerine, 1 large
Watermelon, 1 cup diced

Nuts
  Almonds, ⅓ cup
  Cashew, ¼ cup
  Coconut, shredded, 1 cup loosely
    packed
  Peanut butter, 3 tablespoons
  Peanuts, ⅓ cup
  Pecans, ½ cup
  Walnuts, ½ cup

Vegetables (½ cup cooked)
  Beets
  Carrots

Onions   Rutabaga
Peas, green   Squash, winter
Pumpkin   Turnip

C.   FOODS WITH 10 TO 15 GRAMS CARBOHYDRATE
IN AMOUNTS SPECIFIED

Beverages
    Cider, ½ cup
    Milk (all kinds), 1 cup

Bread and Bread Products
    Bread, bakery, 1 slice
    Biscuit, 2″ diam.
    Cornbread, 1½″ cube
    Muffin, 2″ diam.
    Roll, 2″ diam.

Cereals and Cereal Products
    Cereals (cooked), ½ cup
    Cereals (dry, flakes, puffed) unsweetened, ¾ cup scant
    Rice, macaroni, noodles, spaghetti, ½ cup cooked

Crackers
    Graham, 2 (2½ x 2¾″)
    Oyster, 20 (½ cup)
    Saltines, 5 (2″ square)
    Soda, 3 (2½ x 2¾″)
    Round, thin varieties, 6–8 (1½″ diam.)

Dairy Products
    Milk (all kinds), 1 cup

Desserts (no icings)
    Angel cake, 1½″ cube
    Fruit ice, ¼ cup
    Gelatin dessert, ⅓ cup
    Pudding, plain, ½ cup
    Sherbet, ½ cup

Flours and Flour Products
    Cornstarch, 2 tablespoons
    Flour, 3 tablespoons

Sugars and Sweets
    Candy (jelly beans, gum drops, hard candies, marshmallow, mints), ½ ounce
    Jams and jellies, 1 tablespoon
    Sugar, honey, molasses, sirup, 1 tablespoon

Vegetables
    Beans and peas, dried, cooked, ½ cup scant
    Corn, ⅓ cup or ½ ear
    Corn, popped, 1 cup
    Parsnips, ½ cup
    Potatoes, white, 1 small or ½ cup
    Potatoes, sweet, ¼ cup

D.   FOODS USUALLY CONSIDERED HIGH IN CARBOHYDRATE

Beverages
    Carbonated (cola, ginger ale, root beer, etc.)
    Fruit drinks, sweetened
    Milk drinks, sweetened
    Soda fountain items (frappes, milk shakes, sodas, et cetera)

Bread and Bread Products
    All items (except in amounts allowed on diet list)

Cereal and Cereal Products
    All kinds, particularly presweetened (except in amounts allowed on diet list)

Desserts
    All items containing flour, cornstarch, milk, or sugar (including honey, molasses, and sirup)

Fish
Creamed or in milk chowders; or combined with other high carbohydrate foods

Flour and Flour Products
All items (except in amounts allowed on diet list)

Fruits
All kinds sweetened with sugar, honey, or sirup. Dried fruits contain more carbohydrate than unsweetened fresh fruits.

Meats
All items combined with other high carbohydrate foods such as macaroni, rice, or spaghetti

Nuts
All kinds (except in amounts allowed on diet list)

Sauces and Soups
Commercial or homemade including high carbohydrate foods such as milk, rice, pastas (except in amounts allowed on diet list)

Sweets (including candies)
All kinds (except in amounts allowed on diet list)

Vegetables
All kinds with added sugar, bread, flour, or milk

7. FAT, FATTY ACID, CHOLESTEROL, CARBOHYDRATE AND CALORIE CONTENT OF COMMON FOODS*

Item	Measure	Grams Total Fat	Grams Saturated Fatty Acids	Grams Unsaturated Fatty Acids Oleic	Linoleic	Milligrams Cholesterol	Grams Carbohydrate	Calories
Avocado, California	½ small	18	4	8	2	none	6	185
Florida	½ small	14	3	6	2	none	6	160
Bacon, raw, cured	1 long strip	14	4	7	1	14	trace	133
Fried, crisp	2 short slices	8	3	4	1	unknown	1	90
Bacon, Canadian	1 oz.	4	1	2	trace	17	trace	60
Barley, pearl	1 cup, dry	2	trace	1	1	none	158	700
Beans, baked with pork and tomato sauce	1 cup, canned	7	2	3	1	unknown	49	310
Beef, raw, lean	1 oz.	4	2	2	trace	18	none	63
Cooked, lean	1 oz.	2	1	1	trace	25	none	58
Corned, canned	1 oz.	3	2	1	trace	unknown	none	62
Dried	1 oz.	2	1	1	trace	unknown	none	58

* Sources of calculations are *Agriculture Handbook No. 8, Composition of Foods — Raw, Processed, Prepared* and *Home and Garden Bulletin No. 72, Nutritive Value of Foods*, United States Department of Agriculture; Cholesterol Content of Foods, R. Feeley et al, *Journal of the American Dietetic Association*, 61:2, August, 1972, and "The Fatty Acid Composition of Milk and Eggs" — Provisional Tables — by L. P. Posati, J. E. Kinsella, and B. K. Watt, Nutrient Data Research Center.

Because of the variances in ingredients, the cholesterol content of most recipes such as breads, crackers, cakes, cookies, sauces, et cetera, has been designated as "unknown." If these recipes are made with vegetable shortenings or oils,

Biscuit, baking powder, from mix	1 biscuit, 2" diam.	3	1	1	1	unknown	15	90
Brains, all kinds	1 oz.	2	unknown	unknown	unknown	560	trace	35
Breads								
Cracked wheat	1 lb. loaf	10	2	5	2	unknown	236	1190
	1 slice	1	trace	trace	trace	unknown	13	65
French or Vienna	1 lb. loaf	14	3	8	2	unknown	251	1315
Italian	1 lb. loaf	4	trace	1	2	unknown	256	1250
Raisin	1 lb. loaf	13	3	8	2	unknown	243	1190
	1 slice	1	trace	trace	trace	unknown	13	65
White	1 lb. loaf	15	3	8	2	unknown	229	1225
	1 slice	1	trace	trace	trace	unknown	13	70
Whole Wheat	1 lb. loaf	14	3	6	3	unknown	216	1110
	1 slice	1	trace	trace	trace	unknown	11	60
Bread crumbs, dry	1 cup, grated	5	1	2	1	unknown	65	390
Butter, regular	1 tsp.	4	2	1	trace	12	trace	33
	1 tbsp.	12	6	4	trace	35	trace	100
	1 cup	184	102	60	6	564	2	1620
Whipped	1 tbsp.	8	4	3	trace	22	trace	65
Cakes								
Angel food	1/12 of 10" diam. cake	trace	trace	trace	trace	none	32	135
Chocolate, iced	1/16 of 9" diam. cake	9	3	4	1	33	40	235
Gingerbread	1/9 of 8" square cake	4	1	2	1	trace	32	175
Poundcake	1 slice, 2¾ x 3 x ⅝"	9	2	4	1	unknown	14	140
Sponge cake	1 sector, 2"	4	1	2	trace	98	36	195
White cake, uniced	1/16 of 9" diam. cake	8	3	3	1	1	45	250
Yellow, chocolate icing	1/16 of 9" diam. cake	10	3	4	1	36	45	275
Candy								
Butterscotch	1 oz.	1	1	trace	trace	unknown	27	111
Caramels	1 oz.	3	2	1	trace	unknown	22	115
Chocolate, milk plain	1 oz.	9	5	3	trace	unknown	16	145
Chocolate coated Almonds	1 oz.	12	2	8	2	unknown	11	159

Item	Measure	Grams Total Fat	Grams Saturated Fatty Acids	Grams Unsaturated Fatty Acids		Milligrams Cholesterol	Grams Carbohydrate	Calories
				Oleic	Linoleic			
Candy (*cont.*)								
Coconut	1 oz.	5	3	2	trace	unknown	20	123
Fudge, caramel, and peanuts	1 oz.	6	2	3	1	unknown	18	121
Peanuts	1 oz.	12	3	6	2	unknown	11	160
Raisins	1 oz.	5	3	2	trace	unknown	20	119
Fudge, plain	1 oz.	4	2	1	trace	unknown	21	115
Hard candy	1 oz.	trace	trace	trace	trace	none	28	110
Marshmallows	1 oz.	trace	trace	trace	trace	none	23	90
Peanut bars	1 oz.	9	2	4	3	unknown	13	144
Peanut brittle	1 oz.	3	1	1	1	unknown	23	118
Sugar-coated almonds	1 oz.	5	trace	3	1	unknown	20	128
Caviar, sturgeon	1 rounded tsp.	2	unknown	unknown	unknown	30	trace	26
Cereals								
Oats, puffed	1 oz.	1	trace	1	1	none	19	100
Oats, rolled	1 cup, cooked	2	trace	trace	1	none	23	130
Wheat germ, cereal	1 cup, dry	6	1	2	2	none	55	312
Crude	1 tbsp.	trace	trace	trace	trace	none	2	16
	1 tbsp.	trace	trace	trace	trace	none	3	15
	1 cup	7	1	2	4	none	56	245
Cheese								
Blue or Roquefort	1 oz.	9	5	3	trace	24	1	105
Cheddar	1 oz.	9	5	3	trace	28	1	115
	1 tbsp., grated	2	1	1	trace	7	trace	30
	1 cup, grated	36	20	12	1	112	2	445
Cheese foods, cheddar	1 oz.	7	4	2	trace	21	2	90
Cottage, creamed	1 cup, 4% fat	10	6	3	trace	48	7	260

Cream	1 tbsp.	6	3	2	trace	16	trace	60
Process	1 oz.	9	5	3	trace	25	1	105
Parmesan	1 oz.	9	5	3	trace	27	1	130
Pasteurized spreads	1 oz.	6	3	2	trace	18	2	80
Swiss	1 oz.	8	4	3	trace	26	1	105
Chicken, raw, light	1 oz.	1	trace	trace	trace	19	none	33
Cooked, light & dark	3 oz.	3	1	1	1	72	none	115
Chocolate, bitter	1 square (1 oz.)	15	8	6	trace	none	8	145
Semisweet bits	1 oz.	10	6	4	trace	unknown	16	143
Sweet	1 oz.	10	6	4	trace	unknown	16	150
Cocoa, plain	1 tbsp.	1	1	trace	trace	unknown	4	15
Coconut, fresh, shredded	1 cup	14	8	6	trace	unknown	60	246
Dry, sweetened	1 cup	46	39	3	trace	none	17	450
	1 cup, shredded	24	21	2	trace	none	33	340
Cookies (made with vegetable shortening)								
Brownies with pecans	1 piece, 2 x 2 x ¾"	9	2	5	1	25	15	146
Chocolate chips	1 cooky, 3" diam.	3	1	1	1	unknown	6	50
Fig bars	1 small	1	trace	trace	trace	unknown	11	50
Macaroons	2 small	6	4	1	trace	unknown	17	119
Sugar	1 cooky, 3" diam.	3	1	2	trace	unknown	14	89
Corn, popped with salt and oil	1 cup	2	1	trace	trace	none	5	40
Cornmeal, degermed	1 cup, dry	2	trace	trace	trace	none	108	500
Whole ground, unbolted	1 cup, dry	5	1	2	2	none	90	435
Crackers								
Cheese	2 crackers	2	1	1	trace	unknown	4	34
Graham, chocolate coated	2 crackers	4	1	2	trace	unknown	10	71
Oyster	10 crackers	1	trace	1	trace	unknown	7	45
Saltines	4 crackers	1	trace	1	trace	unknown	8	50
Soda	2 crackers	1	trace	1	trace	unknown	8	50
Cracker meal	1 tbsp.	1	trace	1	trace	unknown	7	44

Item	Measure	Grams Total Fat	Grams Saturated Fatty Acids	Grams Unsaturated Fatty Acids		Milli-grams Cholesterol	Grams Carbohydrate	Calories
				Oleic	Linoleic			
Cream								
Half-and-half	1 tbsp.	2	1	1	trace	6	1	20
Light table, or coffee	1 tbsp.	3	2	1	trace	10	1	30
Whipped topping	1 tbsp.	1	trace	trace	trace	3	trace	10
Whipping, heavy	1 tbsp.	6	3	2	trace	20	1	55
Cream substitutes								
Liquid, frozen	1 tbsp.	2	1	trace	0	0	2	20
Powdered	1 tsp.	1	trace	trace	0	0	1	10
Doughnuts, cake type	1 doughnut	6	1	4	trace	unknown	16	125
Yeast-leavened	1 doughnut	8	2	5	1	unknown	11	124
Egg, whole	1 large	6	2	3	trace	252	trace	80
White only	1 large	trace	trace	trace	trace	none	trace	15
Yolk only	1 large	5	2	2	trace	252	trace	60
Egg substitutes								
Bud Diet-Lite	¼ cup	trace	trace	unknown	unknown	trace	1	38
Eggbeaters	¼ cup	8	1	unknown	unknown	trace	2	100
Eggstra	¼ cup	1	unknown	unknown	unknown	58	2	43
Second Nature	3 tbsp.	2	unknown	unknown	unknown	trace	1	35
Fish								
Albacore, raw	1 oz.	2	1	trace	trace	20	none	50
Clams, raw	1 oz.	trace	unknown	unknown	unknown	14	1	22
Cod, raw	1 oz.	trace	unknown	unknown	unknown	14	none	22
Crabmeat, canned	1 oz.	1	unknown	unknown	unknown	28	trace	24
Fish Sticks, breaded	1 stick (1 oz.)	3	1	1	1	unknown	2	50
Eel, raw	1 oz.	5	1	2	trace	unknown	none	65
Smoked	1 oz.	8	2	3	trace	unknown	none	65
Flounder, raw	1 oz.	trace	unknown	unknown	unknown	14	none	22
Haddock, raw	1 oz.	trace	unknown	unknown	unknown	17	none	33

Halibut	1 oz.	trace	unknown	unknown	unknown	14	none	28
Herring, Atlantic raw	1 oz.	3	1	trace	1	20	none	49
Pacific, raw	1 oz.	1	trace	trace	trace	20	none	27
Lobster, cooked	⅔ cup	2	unknown	unknown	unknown	82	trace	95
Mackerel, raw	1 oz.	2	unknown	unknown	unknown	27	none	49
Oysters, meat only	1 oz.	1	unknown	unknown	unknown	14	1	20
Salmon, chinook, raw	1 oz.	4	1	1	trace	10	none	62
Canned	1 oz.	4	1	1	trace	10	none	59
Pink, raw	1 oz.	1	trace	trace	trace	10	none	33
Canned	1 oz.	2	1	1	trace	10	none	40
Sardines, canned, drained	1 oz.	3	unknown	unknown	unknown	39	none	56
Scallops, raw	1 oz.	trace	unknown	unknown	unknown	10	none	23
Shrimp, raw	1 oz.	trace	unknown	unknown	unknown	42	trace	25
Trout, rainbow or steelhead, raw	1 oz.	3	1	1	trace	15	none	55
Canned	1 oz.	3	1	1	trace	20	none	59
Tuna, bluefin, raw	1 oz.	1	trace	trace	trace	20	none	41
Yellowfin, raw	1 oz.	1	trace	trace	trace	20	none	37
Canned in oil	1 oz. drained	2	1	trace	1	18	none	57
Flour, white, family	1 cup	1	trace	trace	trace	none	88	420
Whole wheat	1 cup	2	trace	1	1	none	85	400
Ham, light cure								
Boston butt, raw	1 oz. lean	3	1	1	trace	25	none	56
Picnic, raw	1 oz. lean	2	1	1	trace	25	none	47
Hash, corned beef	3 oz. canned	10	5	4	trace	unknown	9	155
Heart, beef and pork	1 oz., raw	1	unknown	unknown	unknown	42	trace	31
calf	1 oz., raw	2	unknown	unknown	unknown	42	1	37
chicken	1 oz., raw	2	unknown	unknown	unknown	48	trace	37
turkey	1 oz., raw	3	unknown	unknown	unknown	42	trace	48
Ice cream and frozen custard								
10% fat	⅛ quart	7	4	3	trace	27	14	128
16% fat	⅛ quart	12	7	4	1	43	14	165
Ice Milk	1 cup	7	4	2	trace	26	29	200

Item	Measure	Grams Total Fat	Grams Saturated Fatty Acids	Grams Unsaturated Fatty Acids		Milligrams Cholesterol	Grams Carbohydrate	Calories
				Oleic	Linoleic			
Kidneys, beef, raw	1 oz.	2	unknown	unknown	unknown	105	trace	36
Lamb or pork raw	1 oz.	1	unknown	unknown	unknown	105	trace	30
Lamb, raw, lean	1 oz.	5	3	2	trace	20	none	69
Cooked, lean	1 oz.	2	1	1	trace	28	none	52
Liver, raw, beef, calf, pig, and lamb	1 oz.	1	unknown	unknown	unknown	84	1	38
Chicken, raw	1 oz.	1	unknown	unknown	unknown	140	1	38
Goose, raw	1 oz.	3	unknown	unknown	unknown	84	2	51
Turkey, raw	1 oz.	1	unknown	unknown	unknown	122	1	38
Margarine, hydrogenated or hardened fat	1 tsp.	4	1	2	1	1) All vegetable fat has no cholesterol. 2) two-thirds animal fat and one-third vegetable fat. 1 tsp – 2 1 tbsp – 7	trace	33
	1 tbsp.	12	2	6	3		trace	100
	1 cup	184	34	92	50		1	1630
Liquid oil (soft)	1 tsp.	4	1	1	1		trace	33
	1 tbsp.	11	2	4	4		trace	100
	1 cup	184	34	68	68		1	1635

Mayonnaise	1 tbsp.	100	trace	10	6	2	2	11
Milk								
Cow's								
Buttermilk	1 cup	90	12	5	unknown	unknown	unknown	trace
Condensed	1 tbsp.	61	10	7	trace	7	1	2
Evaporated	1 cup, undiluted	345	24	79	unknown	unknown	11	20
Skim, fresh	1 cup	90	12	5	trace	2	unknown	trace
2% nonfat milk solids added	1 cup	145	15	22	1	9	3	5
Dry, whole	1 cup	515	39	112	unknown	unknown	16	28
Dry, nonfat	1 cup, instant	245	35	15	trace	3	unknown	trace
Whole, fresh	1 cup	160	12	34	trace	2	5	9
Goat's	1 cup	165	11	unknown	unknown	4	6	10
Milk beverages								
Cocoa	1 cup	245	27	35	trace	2	7	12
Chocolate milk, with skim milk	1 cup	190	27	20	trace	unknown	3	6
Malted milk	1 cup	245	28	unknown	unknown	3	unknown	10
Milk desserts								
Cornstarch pudding	1 cup	285	41	35	trace	5	5	10
Custard	1 cup	305	29	278	1	2	7	15
Muffin, corn	1 muffin	125	19	28	trace	2	2	4
Variety, average	1 muffin	120	17	21	1	1	1	4
Noodles, egg	1 cup, cooked	200	37	50	trace		1	2
Nuts								
Almonds, raw	1 cup	850	28	none	15	52	6	77
Roasted, salted	14 nuts	94	3	none	2	6	1	9
Beechnuts	1 oz.	159	15	none	4	8	1	14
Brazil	1 cup	915	15	none	24	45	19	94
Cashew	1 cup, roasted	785	41	none	4	45	11	64
Filberts	11 medium	95	3	none	2	5	trace	9

Item	Measure	Grams Total Fat	Grams Saturated Fatty Acids	Grams Unsaturated Fatty Acids		Milligrams Cholesterol	Grams Carbohydrate	Calories
				Oleic	Linoleic			
Nuts (*cont.*)								
Hickory	15 small	10	1	7	2	none	2	101
Peanuts, raw with skin	1 cup	68	14	29	20	none	27	812
Roasted, salted	1 cup	72	16	31	21	none	27	840
Pecans, raw	1 cup	77	5	48	15	none	16	740
Pistachios	30 nuts	8	1	5	2	none	3	89
Walnuts, black	1 cup	75	4	26	36	none	19	790
English	1 cup	64	4	10	40	none	16	650
Oils								
Corn	1 tbsp.	14	1	4	7	none	none	125
	1 cup	220	22	62	117	none	none	1945
Cottonseed	1 tbsp.	14	4	3	7	none	none	125
	1 cup	220	55	46	110	none	none	1945
Olive	1 cup	220	24	167	15	none	none	1945
Peanut	1 cup	220	40	103	64	none	none	1945
Safflower	1 cup	220	18	37	165	none	none	1945
Sesame	1 cup	220	31	84	92	none	none	1945
Soybean	1 cup	220	33	44	114	none	none	1945
Olives, green pickled	4 medium	2	trace	2	trace	none	trace	15
ripe, pickled	3 small	2	trace	2	trace	none	trace	15
Pancake, buckwheat	1 cake, 4" diam.	2	1	1	trace	20	6	55
Peanut butter	1 tbsp.	8	2	4	2	0	3	95
Pie crust, plain unbaked vegetable shortening	1 crust, 9" pie	60	16	28	12	none	79	900
Pies (1/7 of 9" pie)								
Apple	1 sector	15	4	7	3	none	51	350
Cherry	1 sector	15	4	7	3	none	52	350

Lemon meringue	1 sector	12	4	6	2	112	45	305
Mince	1 sector	16	4	8	3	unknown	56	365
Pecan	1 sector	27	4	16	5	unknown	60	490
Pumpkin	1 sector	15	5	6	2	79	32	275
Pizza, cheese, 14" pie	⅛ of pie	6	2	3	trace	unknown	27	185
Pork, lean, raw	1 oz.	6	2	3	1	17	none	77
Cooked, lean	1 oz.	4	1	2	trace	25	none	71
Salt Pork	1 oz.	24	9	11	1	20	none	219
Potatoes, chips	10 pieces	8	2	2	4	unknown	10	115
French, fried, frozen	10 pieces	5	1	1	2	unknown	19	125
Mashed, with milk and butter	½ cup	4	2	2	trace	unknown	12	93
Rabbit, raw	1 oz.	2	1	1	trace	18	none	45
Rolls, commercial								
plain	1 roll	2	trace	1	trace	unknown	15	85
hard	1 roll	2	trace	1	trace	unknown	31	160
sweet	1 roll	4	1	2	trace	unknown	21	135
Salad dressings								
Blue and Roquefort	1 tbsp., regular	8	2	2	4	unknown	1	75
	1 tbsp., low fat	trace	trace	trace	trace	unknown	trace	3
French	1 tbsp., regular	6	1	1	3	unknown	3	65
	1 tbsp., low fat	trace	trace	trace	trace	unknown	trace	trace
Mayonnaise type	1 tbsp., regular	6	1	1	3	10	2	65
	1 tbsp., dietary	2	trace	trace	1	unknown	1	20
Thousand Island	1 tbsp., regular	8	1	2	4	unknown	2	80
	1 tbsp., dietary	2	trace	trace	1	unknown	2	27
Sausage type meats								
Braunschweiger	1 oz.	8	3	3	1	unknown	trace	89
Capicola	1 oz.	13	4	5	1	unknown	none	140
Country-style sausage, pork	1 oz.	9	3	4	1	unknown	none	97
Deviled ham, canned	1 oz.	9	3	4	1	unknown	none	98

Item	Measure	Grams Total Fat	Grams Saturated Fatty Acids	Grams Unsaturated Fatty Acids		Milligrams Cholesterol	Grams Carbohydrate	Calories
				Oleic	Linoleic			
Sausage type meats (cont.)								
Frankfurter, cooked	1 oz.	8	unknown	unknown	unknown	17	1	85
Head cheese	1 oz.	6	2	3	1	unknown	trace	75
Ham, boiled	1 oz.	5	2	2	1	unknown	none	66
Luncheon meat	1 oz.	7	3	3	1	unknown	trace	82
Minced ham	1 oz.	5	2	2	1	unknown	1	64
Pork links, cooked	1 oz.	11	4	5	1	unknown	trace	125
Souse	1 oz.	4	1	2	trace	unknown	trace	51
Shortenings, lard	1 tbsp.	13	5	6	1	13	none	115
	1 cup	205	78	94	20	209	none	1850
Vegetable	1 tbsp.	13	3	6	3	none	none	110
	1 cup	200	50	100	44	none	none	1770
Sirup, chocolate, thin	1 tbsp.	trace	trace	trace	trace	unknown	13	50
Fudge type	1 tbsp.	3	1	1	trace	unknown	11	66
Soups, canned, diluted with water								
Bean with pork	1 cup	6	1	2	2	unknown	22	170
Beef noodle	1 cup	3	1	1	1	unknown	7	70
Beef bouillon, broth, consommé	1 cup	none	none	none	none	none	3	30
Chicken, cream of	1 cup	6	1	2	3	unknown	8	95
Chicken noodle	1 cup	2	trace	1	1	unknown	8	65
Mushroom, cream of	1 cup	10	1	3	5	unknown	10	135
Pea, green split	1 cup	3	1	2	trace	unknown	21	145
Tomato	1 cup	3	trace	1	1	unknown	16	90
Soups, dehydrated	1 oz. dry	2	1	1	trace	unknown	17	108
Soups, frozen, cream of								

in tomato sauce	1 cup, canned	10	2	3	4	39	28	260
Suet beef	1 oz.	26	13	12	1	21	none	239
Sweetbreads, beef, raw	1 oz.	4	unknown	unknown	unknown	70	none	58
Turkey, raw	1 oz.	2	1	1	trace	19	none	34
Veal, raw, lean	1 oz.	2	1	1	trace	20	none	44
Waffle	1 waffle, ½ x 4½ x 5½"	7	2	4	1	45	28	210
Yogurt, partially skim milk	1 cup	4	2	1	trace	17	13	125

GENERAL INDEX

RECIPE INDEX